Harbans Singh was born in Samba, in the Jammu region of Jammu and Kashmir. He began his career as a college professor before moving on to journalism and occasional writing. Over the years, he has worked as a reporter for the *Observer of Business and Politics*; been a book critic and reviewer for *The Tribune*; and was a regular columnist for *Dainik Bhaskar*.

Singh has authored books in both Hindi and English. His primary area of interest is Jammu and Kashmir. He is the author of *Sufi Satta aur Samaj*, written in Hindi, which examines the impact of Sufism on Jammu and Kashmir and the overall Indian society. His books in English include a trilogy on the history of Jammu and Kashmir from 1925 to contemporary times.

A MODERN HISTORY OF JAMMU AND KASHMIR

VOLUME ONE

The Troubled Years of
Maharaja Hari Singh (1925-1949)

HARBANS SINGH

SPEAKING
TIGER

SPEAKING TIGER BOOKS LLP
125A, Ground Floor, Shahpur Jat, near Asiad Village,
New Delhi 110049

First published as *Maharaja Hari Singh: The Troubled Years* in 2011
This revised edition published by Speaking Tiger Books in 2023

ISBN: 978-93-5447-491-0
eISBN: 978-93-5447-497-2

10 9 8 7 6 5 4 3 2 1

Typeset in Minion Pro by SÜRYA, New Delhi
Printed at Shree Maitrey Printech Pvt. Ltd., Noida

Dedicated to the memory of the soldiers of the State Forces who laid down their lives in the making and defence of the State of Jammu and Kashmir.

Contents

Foreword

Harbans Singh has emerged as a significant re-interpreter of Dogra history, specifically dealing with the period that begins with the reign of Maharaja Hari Singh. This volume is the first part of a trilogy—*Modern History of Jammu and Kashmir*—about the contemporary political history of Jammu and Kashmir.

Volume One, *The Troubled Years of Maharaja Hari Singh (1925-1949)*, deals with the events during my father's reign. The author holds that it is unfortunate that Maharaja Hari Singh is remembered only for the accession of the State, which had come under very severe pressure due to the tribal invasion from Pakistan. He points out that from when my father ascended the *Gaddi* in 1925, all the way to 1946, he undertook a series of far-reaching and progressive measures, including throwing all temples open to the Harijans (Dalits); abolishing the obnoxious Forced Labour System of *begar*; paying attention to girls' education, which was far ahead of the situation in most of the rest of India; setting up first class hospitals and colleges both in Srinagar and Jammu; beautifying the Dal Lake by constructing a boulevard; and so on. His first statement, after assuming the high office in 1925, was 'justice is my religion'. In a memorable speech at the Round Table Conference on Indian Constitutional Reforms held in London in 1930-1931 he had stated, 'As Indians and loyal to the land of our birth, we stand as solidly as the rest of our countrymen for our enjoyment of a position of honour and equality in the British Commonwealth.' All these seem to have been forgotten and his rule has been overshadowed by the accession imbroglio, which is grossly unfair. Sheikh Abdullah, who was bitterly anti-Dogra, had launched a protracted movement against the Maharaja way back in 1931, which fructified in the crisis of 1947. Abdullah had seized the opportunity during Partition and had come to oust Maharaja Hari Singh and assumed power himself with the blessings of Pandit Nehru. All of this led to my father virtually going into exile in Bombay (Mumbai) in 1949. It was only his ashes that I brought back to Jammu after he passed away in April 1971.

From the vantage point of hindsight, it may be easy to say that the Maharaja could have handled the entire crisis better. But, in my *Autobiography*, I have recounted in some detail the events that took place during those tumultuous times, the difficulties my father faced during the political crises of Partition and also my ideological divergence from his views. Regretfully, he has received a lot of negative press and, therefore, I am glad that this first volume not only puts the Maharaja in the right focus but also highlights the valiant role of the Jammu and Kashmir State Forces that historians have generally ignored. Readers will, no doubt, judge my father more fairly than the contemporary historians have done.

The next volume in this series covers the events of the eighteen years that I was the Head of State under three different appellations—first as Regent, then as Sadar-i-Riyasat and finally as the Governor. This period also saw the ten-year rule of Bakshi Ghulam Mohammad and also the advent of G.M. Sadiq, who drastically moved towards further integrating the State into the Indian Union. The Presidential Order was welcomed in 1964 and the nomenclature of Sardar-i-Riyasat and Prime Minister was changed to Governor and Chief Minister respectively, in line with the other States of the Union. Harbans Singh brings out the fact that right from the beginning, in my correspondence with Pandit Jawaharlal Nehru, I constantly put forward the importance of Jammu and Ladakh, which were generally neglected due to New Delhi's Kashmiri-centrism. This period also covers the arrest and prolonged exile of Sheikh Abdullah for over ten years, until he finally returned as Chief Minister in 1965 following an accord with Indira Gandhi. The second volume takes the story up to March 1967 when I resigned as Governor and joined Indira Gandhi's Cabinet as Minister for Tourism and Civil Aviation.

The third and final volume in this trilogy traverses the period of the history of the State from 1975 to contemporary times. This covers the beginning of aggressive militancy in 1988, which resulted, among other disasters, in the mass exodus of the highly talented Kashmiri-Pandit community from the Valley. The volume also studies the drastic and dramatic events of 5th August 2019 whereby the State was bifurcated for the second time, with Ladakh and Jammu and Kashmir regions becoming Union Territories. Harbans Singh has evidently studied this whole period closely and his trilogy will surely become essential for all those interested in the history of Jammu and Kashmir. The series is a welcome opportunity to understand the Dogra point of view and set right the blatant anti-Dogra distortions by some historians.

I commend Harbans Singh for performing such a valuable service and congratulate him for his detailed research, which, I am sure, will be widely read and appreciated.

KARAN SINGH

March 2023

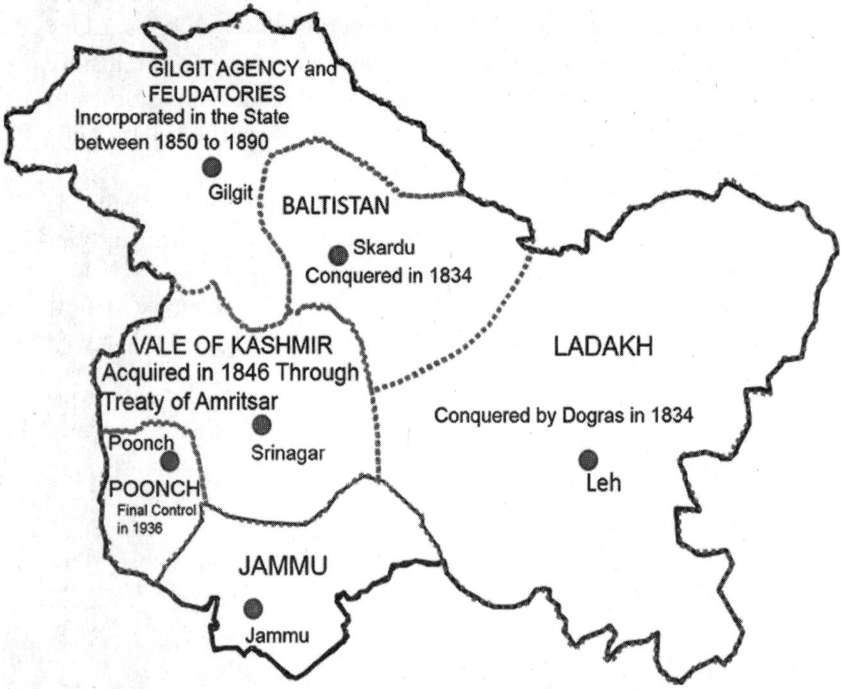

The Princely State of Jammu and Kashmir during Dogra rule.

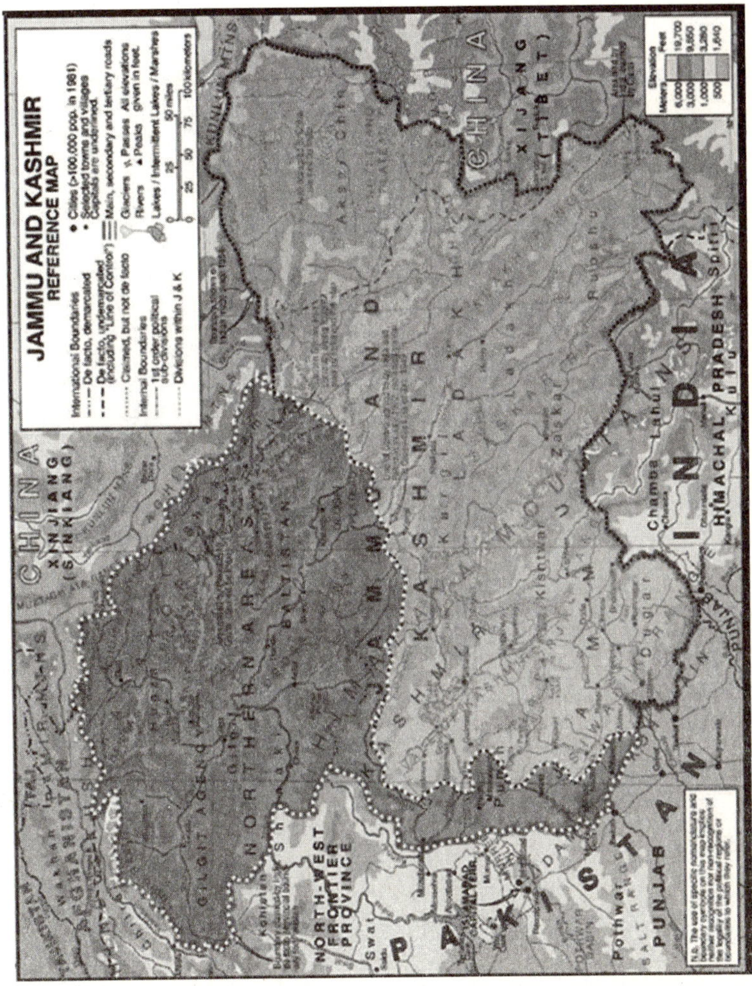

The map of Jammu and Kashmir after the Indo-Pak War of 1947-48 and the Ceasefire Agreement

Introduction

Historians in general write about the modern history of Jammu and Kashmir focusing on the politics that led to Partition and India's independence as a reference point. And the Kashmir Valley is at the centre of that narrative. Alastair Lamb acknowledges that, 'People who write about the history of Kashmir generally have in mind the Vale of Kashmir only, and forget the other regions which today go to make up the bulk of the State of Jammu and Kashmir.'[1] Lamb then immediately goes on to justify this emphasis on the Kashmir Valley by arguing that even though the Valley constituted only 10 per cent of the area of the erstwhile Princely State of Jammu and Kashmir under the Dogras, yet it had almost half of the total population and most of its wealth. In doing so he applies the logic and standards of modern political discourse to the past. The period he talks about—and which is the subject of this book—was not a period of democracy of numbers anywhere in the world. So he ignores other factors that went into the idea of a state, and claims to power in a state. Lamb ignores the fact that the raw material for the wealth of the Kashmir Valley was *pashm*—through the *pashm*-based shawl industry, which also laid the foundation of other handicrafts, including carpet-weaving and silk—and this *pashm* came from western Tibet and eastern Ladakh, and to ensure its uninterrupted supply, the Dogras of Jammu had shed the blood of thousands of their soldiers in the first half of the nineteenth century. It was the Dogras under Gulab Singh who thwarted the machinations of the East India Company in diverting the *pashm* trade from Tibet to Almora and Bashahar, both in British-controlled areas. This is borne out by Bawa Satinder Singh, who noted that the East India

Company was interested in acquiring a share of the pashmina traffic, but Dogra intervention in Ladakh prevented it.[2] And so the Dogras, even before they came to rule Kashmir, claimed a preeminent position in the region. Of course, after the creation of the unlikely Princely State—with the Dogras bringing together Jammu, Kashmir, Ladakh and other regions as a political unit—this claim was, by the standards of the time, incontestable and legitimate. Therefore, even when in a minority, the Dogras were entirely dominant and felt they deserved the dominance. After 1947, in a democratic set-up, this claim and position was, naturally, not tenable. The resulting shift in the balance of power has been a major reason for the internal conflict—while the Dogras were unable to accept their displacement, the vengeful power-wielding by Kashmiri politicians made things worse.

Any study of the modern history of Jammu and Kashmir cannot focus entirely on the aspirations of the Kashmir Valley and ignore the events that led to the making of the Indian state of Jammu and Kashmir and the concentration of all power in the hands of the Kashmiri leadership after 1947. But this is precisely what almost every mainstream contemporary historian has done. Because of this skewed and faulty approach to history, Maharaja Hari Singh, the fourth and last ruler of the Princely State, and the events leading up to his decision to accede to India have been placed at the centre of every narrative, without taking into consideration other factors, like the events of the nineteenth century, and the role of the Muslim League, the Indian National Congress and the political formations in Britain.

Till the recent past, most historians have written books with a heavy bias in favour of Kashmir and Pakistan. This book is an attempt to view the State's history in general and the role of Maharaja Hari Singh in particular, during the decades leading to the independence of India and the issue of accession of the State and, in particular, the events that followed. This is important since it was during these decades and the post-accession years that the historical fault lines between the three main regions of the State, Jammu, Kashmir and Ladakh, got accentuated.

Most studies of the region suffer from some basic flaws. The main one being that they fail to realize their approach has been heavily influenced by the narrative about the State and the Dogra dynasty that they have received from colonial records. If only they had paused and studied that period with fair objectivity, they would have found that some of the phrases that they frequently use have been borrowed directly from colonial sources.

For example, it is routinely mentioned that the acquisition of Kashmir by Maharaja Gulab Singh was through a 'sale deed'. But this phrase is misleading, and deliberately so. The phrase was coined by the British who wanted to erase or mask the fact that they had willingly given up Kashmir to Gulab Singh, the founder of the Dogra dynasty, and recognized him as the Maharaja of Jammu and Kashmir. The facts of the case are as follows: The First Anglo-Sikh War between the East India Company and the Sikh Empire ended in 1846 with the defeat of the Sikh forces. As part of the Treaty signed between the victors and the losers in Lahore (the capital of the Sikh Empire), the Sikhs had to surrender to the East India Company the areas that lay between the Beas and Sutlej rivers, and were also required to pay a war indemnity of 15 million rupees. The Sikh empire could not raise the money and in return, ceded Kashmir and other hill regions to the Company. The British then offered these territories to Gulab Singh, the Raja of Jammu, a vassal state of the Sikh empire, if he paid the indemnity that the Lahore Durbar could not. The British were not confident about defending these areas from the Afghans and other aggressors, but they knew that Gulab Singh with his long years of experience of successful battles in these challenging terrains would be able to do so, thus ensuring a buffer between the British territories in India and hostile powers across the mountains. So it made sense for them to work out an arrangement with Gulab Singh. The latter agreed to pay the indemnity and thus not only retain Jammu but also add to his kingdom Kashmir and other areas ceded by the Sikhs to the British. This was recorded in the Treaty of Amritsar, signed by the East India Company with Gulab Singh on 16th March 1846[3]—a week after the Treaty of Lahore, signed on 9th March 1846 between the Company and the Lahore Durbar[4]. The Princely State of Jammu and Kashmir, one of the largest in India, was thus created, with Gulab Singh as Maharaja.

So Kashmir did not come to the Dogras through a 'sale deed'. There *was* no sale deed; there was a *treaty*. Why did the British spread the canard, then? The main reason is that a contrary view had begun to emerge in British power circles soon after 1846 that a mistake had been made and not only Kashmir but the entire region governed by the Dogras—who owed allegiance to the Sikh Durbar—should have been annexed. This view had its seeds in the stillborn Treaty that William Moorcroft, the English veterinarian and explorer in the service of the East India Company, had negotiated with the Ladakhis during his stay in Leh between 1820 and 1822. The treaty envisaged bringing Ladakh in the sphere of influence of the British as a bulwark against the Sikhs and the Russians. However, that was rejected by the Company, to the regret of English expansionists.[5] And in 1834 the Dogras under Gulab Singh conquered Ladakh. The British, thus, lived with this regret. And throughout the 100 years of Dogra rule in Jammu and Kashmir this feeling of regret ebbed and flowed with the internal politics of Westminster which, in turn, depended on which lobby was dominant in the British Parliament—whether the advocates of aggressive forward policy in the Frontier region, or those who preferred to safeguard their core Indian territories and were content to have a strong and friendly Princely State as an ally to contain any move by the Russians towards Afghanistan and into India.

In the twentieth century, when the Soviet Union emerged as a superpower, these fears of the British were again aroused, and thus their obsession with Jammu and Kashmir, especially the Gilgit-Baltistan region, and their prjudiced view of Dogra rule of the State. When this factor is not adequately understood, there is every possibility of a historian getting swayed in favour of an anti-Dogra and anti-Hari Singh narrative. Not surprisingly, these historians and commentators have painted the Dogra dynasty in black. Ironically, in the post-Independence period, this campaign was led by the first Prime Minister of India, Jawaharlal Nehru, although for different reasons, and by the officers of the Indian army who visited the State and participated in the 1947-1948 Indo-Pak war. In the process, Hari Singh was portrayed not only as an irresponsible ruler, but also an indecisive and bigoted Hindu. This was far from the truth, as any objective study of that period will reveal. In fact, in the process, the Jammu and Kashmir State Armed Forces, which remained a loyal pillar of support to all British campaigns in the Frontier region and Afghanistan, too were vilified. This was not only uncalled for but far from the truth as the events of 1955 proved when, because of the bravery, tenacity and strategic acumen of the men and officers of the State Forces, an attempt by Pakistani Forces to capture Indian territory in the Hussainiwala sector in Ferozepur was repelled.[6] It was then that the Indian Army and the Government of India felt compelled to absorb all the men and officers of the State Forces into the Indian Army without screening. They were deemed to be equally well trained and qualified as the manpower of the Indian Army. The Jammu and Kashmir State Forces became the only state force to have been absorbed into the Indian Army without any screening.

Any student of the history of Jammu and Kashmir must be first acquainted with the making of the princely State of Jammu and Kashmir and the role played by the armed forces that created a State during the first half of the nineteenth century, when all other regional powers were falling in the face of the assault of the British on the Indian kingdoms. Much of the eighteenth century was marked by the falling apart of the Mughal empire and the race by the regional forces and the colonial powers to fill the vacuum by carving out portions of the subcontinent for themselves. The Sikhs, in the north, were vying to establish their superiority over many warring Sikh *misls* and replacing the Afghans in north-west India, who had emerged as a prominent power after the decline of Mughals and attacks by Ahmed Shah Abdali. In the north-east, the Gurkhas of Nepal had begun to make ambitious forays into the Himalayan states and had, after annexing the Kumaon and Garhwal hills, crossed the Sutlej and the Beas rivers to lay siege on Kangra. Closer to Delhi, the Jats had emerged as a threat to the remaining vestiges of the splendour of Delhi, and in the west, it appeared that the Marathas would succeed in throwing the British out of the subcontinent. Among the colonial powers, the British, the French and the Portuguese had been struggling to create their colonies but it soon became clear that the French and the Portuguese would only have a nominal presence in the coastal regions, and that the British would be the dominant colonial power of the subcontinent.

Before the end of the first half of the nineteenth century, the Nepalese, after losing to the Sikhs in Kangra, had been further forced to surrender their conquests of the Garhwal hills and retreat to their own land; the Marathas had been defeated and only those of their penny states remained that accepted British suzerainty; the Jats too had been confined to a limited area around Delhi. The Sikhs, who under Maharaja Ranjit Singh had consolidated themselves into a power to reckon with, and had even re-conquered Peshawar and Attock from the Afghans, had finally auto-destructed because of the incompetent, corrupt, decadent and short-sighted successors who followed Ranjit Singh, the Lion of Punjab. But improbably, the Dogras of Jammu had emerged during this time as the rising power, not of the plains of Punjab but the Himalayan States of the region. How and why this happened, in fact, explains the major events of the twentieth century in the subcontinent, and has a bearing on the characters who played a pivotal role during the tumultuous days leading to Indian independence.

After Maharaja Ranjit Singh had made Raja Sansar Chand of Kangra his vassal in 1809 and forced other hill states of the Shiwaliks of the present-day Himachal Pradesh to accept his suzerainty, he had turned his attention to Kashmir, which had once been part of the Mughal Empire. But his first campaign in 1813 failed because one of the Dogra hill states, Rajouri, had turned against him and attacked his army from the rear, forcing it to hurriedly retreat. This failure necessitated the taming of the hill states of Jammu region. This was important in Ranjit Singh's scheme of things since the Dogra-land was traditionally thought to have contained twenty-two states, of whom Jammu was the preeminent. Of these twenty-two, eight were Muslim states between the Jhelum and Chenab rivers. Since Maharaja Ranjit Singh had his eyes focused on the conquest of Kashmir, which was still ruled by the Afghans, the conquest of all these Dogra states that led to the Pir Panjal range and the Valley across it, was essential.[7] Thus, with an eye on Kashmir, the Sikh ruler set about conquering Jammu, whose ruling dynasty had fallen on bad days with a much weakened ruler after the hey-days of Ranjit Deo. Though the Jammu ruler presented himself before Maharaja Ranjit Singh and accepted his suzerainty, there were numerous individual Dogra leaders, including the most enterprising, Mian Dedo, who refused to accept an alien rule. This led Maharaja Ranjit Singh to look towards a young Gulab Singh of Jammu's royalty to quell the rebellion in the hills.

Gulab Singh, whose family had fallen on bad days and who had been forced to take up employment in the Sikh Army, had risen very fast to play crucial roles in almost all the campaigns of the Sikh army and was, therefore, chosen to bring some order in Jammu. Having succeeded, he soon became the most trusted general of the Khalsa army. By now Maharaja Ranjit Singh had recognized the fact that instead of trying to rule Jammu through a Sikh Governor it was much better to give that responsibility to Gulab Singh who was a Dogra himself. The Sikh ruler was also confident of the loyalty of Gulab Singh and, therefore, he made the young general the Raja of Jammu in 1822.

After consolidating the Jammu hill states under his leadership, Gulab Singh was drawn to the affairs of Ladakh, which lay to the east of his kingdom. It had a direct access from Kishtwar and Gulab Singh's best general, Zorawar Singh, was tasked with the responsibility of settling the affairs of Ladakh, as the East India Company had begun to make forays into western Tibet from Almora and Bashahar to purchase *pashm* directly by bypassing the Treaty of Tingmosgang, 1684, by which all *pashm* trade was to take place via traders designated by the Ladakh ruler. There are records available showing the British machinations for obvious financial gains. Had the British succeeded, the lucrative *pashm* trade would have fallen into their hands and severely affected the economy of Kashmir and also the revenue receipts of Punjab, as Kashmir was under the rule of the Lahore Durbar. Intriguingly, during all those years, between 1834 and 1842, when Ladakh was finally annexed into the Jammu kingdom, Maharaja Ranjit Singh seems to have ignored what was going on in Ladakh with Zorawar Singh's campaigns, except the time when the Sikh Governor complained to him regarding these incursions and the diverting of the *pashm* trade from Ladakh to Jammu.[8] The Maharaja did not seem to have paid any attention to the complaint as any revenue generated in Jammu ultimately meant that the total revenue of the Sikh empire was not impacted. It is also possible that the Ladakh campaigns had the tacit and not overt blessing of Maharaja Ranjit Singh because he might have suspected that any interference in the affairs of Ladakh, and therefore Tibet, might have been construed as an unfriendly act by the British as that could have brought a strong reaction from the Chinese under whom Tibet had been for many centuries. This was the period when China and the British had strained relations due to trade disputes. However, the fact in the present case was that the first intrusion into Tibet had been made by the British by way of subverting the Tibet-Ladakh Treaty of 1684 governing the *pashm* trade. Maharaja Ranjit Singh's use of Gulab Singh was a tactical and prudent move. If the British had protested too strongly, even then he might have absolved himself of any blame by reprimanding the Dogra ruler. But eventually, Raja Gulab Singh was able to secure his interests as well as those of Ladakh, Kashmir and the Lahore Durbar.

The Ladakh and Baltistan campaign of Raja Gulab Singh's Dogra army had demonstrated their indomitable courage and ambition, but the successes had been achieved at an enormous human cost. In the process, Gulab Singh's prowess and loyalty to Maharaja Ranjit Singh had stood out, and it earned him riches and honour, though also many enemies in the Lahore Durbar. Remarkably, he continued to enjoy the complete trust and loyalty of the soldiers of the Khalsa army. This fact was obvious when the suicidal struggle among the successors of Maharaja Ranjit Singh brought into the open the opposition of the Sikh Sardars in Lahore to Gulab Singh. Even at this time the Khalsa army stood steadfastly behind him and ensured that no physical harm came to him, even when both his brothers, two sons and a nephew had been killed during that period. The modern narrative emanating from Punjab-based historians about the State that this same man, Gulab Singh, founded, has to be judged in the light of these facts.

But coming back to the British interests, even though their ambition to corner the *pashm* trade had been thwarted, their interest in the region had not diminished, because of the proximity to Afghanistan and separation from the Russian border by a narrow strip of land. If earlier its interests were purely commercial, then soon they had become geostrategic, on which, they were convinced, depended the security of the British Jewel in the Crown. From then onwards, they remained focused on somehow reducing the Dogra-ruled Jammu and Kashmir State to a status similar to that of other princely states, appoint a Political Resident and gain policy and military access to the Frontier areas. In this they failed as long as Maharaja Gulab Singh was alive and only partially succeeded during the reign of Maharaja Ranbir Singh, when an Officer-on-Special Duty was appointed, ostensibly to look after the interests of foreigners visiting the Valley. But by the time of the coronation of Maharaja Pratap Singh in 1885, the British had succeeded in gaining considerably more control in the State. For the first time a Political Resident was appointed. This was the period when the British had become hypersensitive to the affairs of Afghanistan and beyond, due to what they called 'the Great Game'. In view of the perceived threats from Russia, the necessity of controlling the affairs of Jammu and Kashmir increased manifold. In this, the cause of the State was not served by the tragic famine of 1877-78, which saw the shattering of the economy, migration of a large number of people and the exposure of the State's old agricultural policies not only as outdated but also oppressive. This gave enough reason to the British to interfere in the internal administration of the State, too. Soon thereafter, the British discovered that Maharaja Pratap Singh neither had the guile nor the determination of his two illustrious predecessors, and the State and its Forces were increasingly used in the service of British geostrategic interests in the Frontier regions like Chitral and other Pakhtoon areas.

A new page in the relationship between the British and the State was turned when it became clear that Maharaja Pratap Singh would not have any progeny of his own and a successor had to be found. The Maharaja's younger brother Raja Amar Singh had a son who was immediately taken by the British under their wing. Thus, Prince Hari Singh had the most modern education of the time and was also taught western etiquettes and manners. The Prince, upon being designated the Yuvraj, or heir, had the distinction of becoming the first of the Dogra dynasty to visit the West and was thought to have imbibed British culture so thoroughly that it was believed that he would serve British interests well.

It was under Hari Singh's influence as the Yuvraj that education was radically transformed in Jammu and Kashmir by implementing the policy of *jabran taleem* (compulsory education) in municipal areas. More social and economic reforms followed when Yuvraj Hari Singh became the Maharaja in 1925. As a ruler, he also guarded the space of his State from the British efforts to gain more control, since the rise of the Bolsheviks in Russia, the replacement of the monarchy by the proletariat and the march of communism in Central Asia had become threatening. Because of his independent streak, the British did not trust Hari Singh for the affairs of the Gilgit region, in case the Russians (Soviets) chose to march towards Afghanistan or even further. It is this period of the State's history, along with the rise of other forces in the region, including the democratic and the communal, which is the subject of this book.

The issue of the Accession of the State has been dealt with in detail, though the focus of attention is the bigger picture rather than only one aspect of the State's history. It is in this context that it is important to keep in mind the peculiar history of this State, along with the fact of the diversity of the constituent regions that once formed this unlikely State. In fact, the issue of Accession and the 'Kashmir problem' has to be always seen in this context as that alone helps in understanding and appreciating the reverberations that occupy so much of our mind in contemporary times. Moreover, it is important to remember the facts of the history of Ladakh's assimilation into Jammu and Kashmir State, into the Indian political map, and then into in the Indian Republic. It is this fact, much more than the acquisition of Kashmir, that the Dogras have always taken particular pride in and therefore have felt special and deserving, rightly or wrongly, of special treatment within Jammu and Kashmir. But it is a status that the Kashmiris are loathe to give them, and this causes much resentment among the Dogras.

All of the issues mentioned above—which rarely, if ever, receive the objective attention of mainstream contemporary historians and commentators—make the modern history and politics of Jammu and Kashmir extremely complex. The rule of the last Dogra ruler, Maharaja Hari Singh, was a continuous struggle among these complexities and the contrary pulls and pressures of the State, and these are what this book attempts to analyse and understand.

1

Seeds of Flowers and Weeds

Born in 1895, Prince Hari Singh, son of Raja Amar Singh, the younger brother of the ruler of the Princely State of Jammu and Kashmir, Maharaja Pratap Singh, had spent his childhood in the Amar Mahal built on the right bank of the river Tawi in Jammu. Since the ruling monarch did not have any progeny of his own it was known that his nephew would be the next king of the State, and therefore, great care was taken about his upbringing and education not only by his family but also the British who knew that at some point in time they would be dealing with him. The events of the past two decades had made this investment in the grooming of the future monarch important for both the State and the British because of the threat they both perceived from Tsarist Russia. Prisoners of Geography, the British could never really bury the ghosts of the 1807 Treaty of Tilsit between Napoleon Bonaparte of France and Tsar Alexander I, which had crudely planned a Russo-Franco land attack in Central Asia to reach the Indian empire of the British. Though the plan had been stillborn, the British would suffer nightmares about such a threat, and hence, looked at any move beyond the Himalayas with suspicion. One of the strategies that they had devised was to attempt to take control of the affairs of the State of Jammu and Kashmir, which lay between Russia and their Indian empire.

So it is not surprising that though during the nineteenth century, devastating famines had struck many of the southern and western Indian states under British administration, claiming, according to modern estimates, about eight million lives, the famine of 1877-78 in Kashmir under the Dogras became a ruse for the British to portray the Dogra dynasty as being autocratic, insensitive and corrupt, so that greater interference could be made in the affairs the State. The aggressive imperialists and expansionists among the British policy-makers had been inimical to the Dogra rulers of Kashmir from the beginning. This group of policy makers in England, and even some influential members of the East India Company, had always resented the handing over in perpetuity of the State, particularly Kashmir and Ladakh, to the Dogra Raja Gulab Singh. Having failed in their efforts to grab Jammu, Kashmir and Ladakh after the collapse of the Sikh Kingdom which had controlled these areas, these imperialists had lost no opportunity to point out the 'oppression' and autocratic administration of the Dogras while conveniently ignoring the fact that at about the same time, in 1859 to be precise, the peasantry of Bengal had risen in rebellion against the inhuman and profit-driven English *zamindars* who had forced them to cultivate only Indigo. But since, for the English, only strategic and imperial necessities mattered rather than ideals of conduct, therefore, even at great human cost, only profits and self-interest were given importance. Thus focused, British imperialists lost no opportunity to denigrate the Dogra kings. British missionaries were particularly active in this project, presumably because the religiously tolerant policy of the State did not suit the divisive and proselytising goals of these men of god.

In such a political environment, the famine of 1877-78, came as a heaven-sent opportunity for British interference. The ruler of the State was aware that in the face of the catastrophe, there was neither any excuse nor defence with the State government. Even though the famine was the outcome of prolonged rains from September 1877 to January 1878, there was no denying the fact that it could have been averted as there was ample time to import food grains from Punjab, if needed. But indifference, inefficiency and corruption among the officials had led to a situation where the city of Srinagar lost nearly half of its population.[9] This had happened during the reign of Gulab Singh's son, Maharaja Ranbir Singh, at a time when he was battling ill-health and was misled about the situation by his senior advisers. The brunt of this failure had then been borne by his son and successor Maharaja Pratap Singh who had to agree to the appointment of a British Political Resident in the State in 1885. This meant that no major decision could be taken by the ruler without the Resident's consent and he was also to follow any advice that was rendered by the Resident. A new chapter was thus added to the history of the State. And this happened because the imprialist lobby had finally succeeded and the British had gone back on the provision of the Treaty of Amritsar, by which the Dogra Gulab Singh had legally acquired Jammu and Kashmir after the British defeated the Sikhs and the Khalsa kingdom, of which Jammu and Kashmir had been a part, collapsed. (For details of the Treaty of Amritsar, see the Introduction.)

While the other princely states remained as autocratic as ever, the British, for their geostrategic goals, got an opportunity to particularly interfere in the affairs of Jammu and Kashmir. But, ironically, it bore some positive results as the first steps towards modernization were now taken in the State. Maharaja Pratap Singh realized that even though the Kashmiris, particularly the Muslims, had been suffering the excesses of their rulers since the 14th century, beginning with the Shah Mir dynasty, and then the Mughals, Afghans and the Sikhs—and had been quietly enduring oppression, to the extent that they had come to be known as were routinely *zulm-parast*, worshippers of atrocities—only the Dogras were blamed for the hardship faced by the Kashmiri populace, even though both Maharaja Gulab Singh and Maharaja Ranbir Singh were, by all accounts, sympathetic to the poor while being hard on the feudal lords and leaders. Nevertheless, the tragedy of the famine did happen, and it pointed to serious gaps in the State's administration. Pratap Singh now worked to bring about a radical change in the approach to administration. But not before the British policy makers had made one last effort to wrest control of the State by implicating Maharaja Pratap Singh in a nonexistent conspiracy against the British Crown in 1888. It was alleged that he was conspiring with the Tsar of Russia and was stripped of all powers and would have been tried for 'treason' and deposed. However, this conspiracy was exposed by the *Amrita Bazar Patrika* of Calcutta as a ruse to grab Gilgit and there the direct efforts of the British against the Dogra rulers ended. After that episode, while the British did little in their territories to ameliorate the lot of the common people, particularly the peasants, as the numerous peasant agitations show, the Dogra State of Jammu and Kashmir entered an era of reforms that had few equals in the subcontinent.

Between 1889 and 1895, Walter Lawrence, whose services had been requisitioned by Maharaja Pratap Singh as the Settlement Commissioner, produced six reports, which after implementation changed the status and attitudes of the peasantry in Jammu and Kashmir. For the first time education for the general people also received serious attention and before the reign of Maharaja Pratap Singh came to an end, Sri Pratap College, Srinagar had become the second largest college affiliated to the Punjab University, Lahore in terms of the number of students.

It was during this period of change that Hari Singh was born and the British decided to take a keen interest in his upbringing and education. He was chosen as a Page of Honour during the 1903 Delhi Durbar of Lord Curzon held to celebrate the coronation of the new British monarch, Edward VII. Unfortunately, Hari Singh lost his father, Amar Singh, when he was only fourteen years of age and then the British began to take even keener interest in him. Major A.K. Barr was made young Hari Singh's guardian and the person responsible for taking decisions in the matter of his education. Hari Singh was sent to Mayo College in Ajmer and after completing his schooling, to the British-run Imperial Cadet Corps in Dehradun for military training. After completion of his training, in 1915, being the Yuvraj, or Crown Prince, he was appointed the commander-in-chief of the State Forces. Under the watchful eyes of his uncle, the Maharaja, he began to take keen interest in the affairs of the State and gave greater impetus to the reforms in education. The preceding decades had proved that even if the Muslim subjects had become accustomed to suffering and oppression over centuries, things were changing. Of late, periodic outbursts of the people had given a glimpse of the intensity of resentment and anger against their rulers, most of whom had been oppressive and exploitative for many centuries and the volcano could burst if not addressed in time. Fortunately, the reforms recommended by Walter Lawrence had been accepted and implemented by Maharaja Pratap Singh with the result that there was now reason to believe that the condition of the Kashmiri peasantry would change for the better after almost seven hundred years.

The change was already visible even before Walter Lawrence had taken up the assignment of the Settlement Commissioner in 1889. But it was accelerated by the implementation of reforms. Commenting on this situation, Lawrence noted, 'Before 1887 the peasants rarely tasted their beloved food, rice. Now all eat rice, and enjoy salt, and the luxury of tea. Little shops are springing up in the villages, and whereas I never saw a metal vessel in any peasant's house three years ago, now a brass cooking-pot is by no means rare.'[10] He continued, the oppression and exploitation of centuries, the peasantry had developed a defence mechanism by becoming cunning and distrustful of the State even as they submitted to the oppression—*zulm*—of the State. Many foreign visitors had commented on this aspect of the life of Kashmiris without fully appreciating the evolution of their character in the face of their consistent degradation at the hands of those foreigners who were, in fact, guilty of being 'grasping and corrupt' and 'unsympathetic'. The considered opinion of Lawrence was that historically 'Mughal Subahs, Pathan Sirdars, Sikh and Dogra Governors dismissed all difficulties of administration, and all humane suggestions emanating from their masters, with the remark that the Kashmiris were dishonest, treacherous and *zulm parast*.' But Maharaja Pratap Singh's administration, on the recommendations of the Settlement Commissioner, had implemented policies that began the process of transformation of the society. Commenting on the change, Lawrence further remarked: 'Security of tenure has a magical effect, but I think that immunity from forced labour has been as efficacious in promoting confidence among the villages. The construction of the Gilgit road, and the organization of the transport service have done much to abolish the worst incidents of the *corvée*...[11] but if the Maharaja himself had not set the example of limiting the demands made by the camp-followers, "Purveyance"...[12] would have lingered for years.'[13]

But there was also a note of caution and warning by Lawrence. He added: 'It is well to remember that people so broken and degraded as the Kashmiris do not in a few years harden into a resolute and self-respecting community...There is not a single middleman left in the villages at the present time, but if the State withdrew its vigilant watch, some 40 percent of the peasants might again become serfs of middlemen and officials.'[14] Having seen the change, and aware of the fact that any misstep would give the British a chance to further encroach upon the sovereign authority of the State, Maharaja Pratap Singh scrupulously followed the advice but the same could not be said of his officials, as subsequent decades demonstrated.

Meanwhile, the Maharaja and Yuvraj Hari Singh continued their efforts to uplift the Kashmiris from their state of hopelessness and resignation by encouraging them to acquire new skills and modern education. By now, the exposure of the young Yuvraj to the British way of life and the qualities that had made them better than the Indians, had been complete and he was convinced that education, health facilities and social reforms needed a greater push from the State if it was to transform the tradition and convention bound society. With his active participation, the wings of transformation had grown stronger and he was ready to play a proactive role in a world that was changing at a fast pace when his coronation as the new king took place in 1926 upon the death of Maharaja Pratap Singh in 1925.

Colonel Bhagwan Singh, who functioned as Hari Singh's Aide-de-camp, records in his book, *Political Conspiracies of Kashmir*, that upon his *Raj Tilak*—coronation—he conferred upon the villagers the right to possess additional land, up to 100 percent of *shamlat deh*, or village commons, out of the Government Khalsa land available in their villages. He also commented that this 'mostly benefitted the villagers of the Kashmir valley, as no such land was available in Jammu villages.' In an unheard of step among dynastic rulers, Hari Singh also 'assimilated his private property yielding an annual income of Rs 24 lacs into the State.'[15] In brief, he embarked upon a policy of social and economic welfare of his people and most of his steps could be measured by comparison with the standards set in those states that were directly ruled by the British.

While completely devoted to his State and the wellbeing of his people, it is hard to explain the antipathy Hari Singh had developed for the British authority, even though he knew well that there was no escaping British control and interference. This is more intriguing in view of the fact he had been trained by the British and had been exposed to the British influence since his childhood. Even the palace that his father had built, and where he had been raised, was in the style of a chateau rather than the Rajput-Mughal style with a shade of European influence. It is in this context that his resistance to British authority in the State affairs is perplexing.

As has been noted earlier, the British had begun to regret the clauses of the Treaty of Amritsar, 1846, as soon as it had been signed. While they had made desperate efforts to have a Political Resident appointed in the State, Maharaja Gulab Singh had always successfully outmanoeuvred them. Even Maharaja Ranbir Singh had warded off this threat for a long time, till he had to finally succumb to British influence and appoint a British officer in Gilgit, though not a Political Resident. However, Maharaja Pratap Singh was forced to agree to such an appointment. This practice was resented by all self-respecting rulers as the British Political Resident was not only a symbol of the real centre of power but his condescending attitude was also galling for such rulers. However, many other rulers were happy with the arrangement, as their role was limited only to keeping the Resident pleased, and once this was done, they had unbridled freedom in their private affairs. In such cases, it was a mutually beneficial arrangement, where the responsibility for good governance lay with the Resident and the ruler was then free to pursue his idle but profligate hobbies. Al Carthill commented in his book, *The Lost Dominion* that the 'British Army was always on hand to give succour to each imperilled tyrant and stamp out any attempts by the people to express their discontent. As one staunch imperialist boasted, the princes had been "mostly rescued from imminent destruction by British protection."'[16] 'Even the illiberal Lord Curzon had been appalled by the standard of the princely behaviour during the viceroyalty…He had written to Queen Victoria that, "for all these failures, we are responsible. We have allowed the chiefs when young to fall into bad hands. We have condoned their extravagances, we have worked at their vices."'[17]

The *Private Journals of Marquis of Hastings of 1st February 1814*, recorded: 'In our treaties with them [Indian Princes] we recognize them as Indian sovereigns, then we send a Resident to their courts. Instead of acting in the manner of Ambassador, he assumes the functions of a dictator, interferes in all their concerns, countenances refractory subjects against them and makes the most ostentatious exhibition of this exercise of authority.'[18] In fact, famous historian, diplomat and administrator, K.M. Pannikar observed in *The Evolution of British Policy towards Indian States* that in general the Residents conducted themselves in an obnoxious manner, and he quoted Colonel Macaulay's letter to the Raja of Cochin: 'The Resident will be glad to learn that on his arrival near Cochin, the Raja will find it convenient to wait upon him.' Exploited because of their own failings, subservience to the British Agent by the princes had become the norm if they desired to continue their frivolous and profligate ways.

Maharaja Hari Singh was determined not to allow such liberty to the Resident and to restore the independence and self-respect that the ruler of the State enjoyed during Maharaja Gulab Singh and Maharaja Ranbir Singh's times. As a first step, he asked the Resident in Srinagar to remove the Union Jack from the Residency Buildings and when he failed to comply, he had it removed by a detachment of State Forces. This was a very daring step and invited serious correspondence with the Political Department and consequently after some parleys, the Resident was allowed to fly the Union Jack at Srinagar, though 'he was prohibited from moving down to Jammu during winter as he had been previously doing. During winter, therefore, he shifted to Sialkot in British India instead of Jammu.'[19] Colonel Bhagwan Singh also recalls that 'once in 1925...the British Resident in Srinagar was to fly from Srinagar to Gilgit for the first time for the inauguration of a fair weather airfield constructed five miles from Gilgit town...The British political agent [posted at Gilgit] was to receive him at the aerodrome but the Deputy Commissioner Thakur Chattar Singh Charak was directed by Maharaja Hari Singh to receive the Resident at the point three and a half miles from the town and no further.'[20] This symbolic assertion notwithstanding, the State had surrendered considerable internal sovereignty and it had no jurisdiction over the British and Indian subjects within its own borders. So in all earnestness, Maharaja Hari Singh took up this matter with the British and finally succeeded in securing full criminal jurisdiction of all British-Indians for the State's law court and full civil jurisdiction over everybody regardless of the nationality.

The new King was acutely aware of the complex challenges that the construct of his State faced. He was also conscious of the fact that there were no easy solutions. The most formidable challenge was the demography where a great majority of the subjects were Muslims. In a modern democracy, with a fair election process, this would not have been a challenge, but the State was a monarchy, like almost every other in the rest of the subcontinent, and indeed in most of the world at that time. So the dynastic Dogra ruler had to devise a balancing strategy, keeping in mind the Hindu minorities who, especially the Dogras, had made great sacrifices to help his ancestors expand their territories to Tibet in the east, China in the north and Afghanistan in the west. Even though the history of the subcontinent boasted of many very brave and tenacious warriors, it was the Dogras of Maharaja Gulab Singh and Maharaja Ranbir Singh who had fought battles beyond the borders of the Indian subcontinent and in the process expanded them. It was an unheard of achievement in the annals of sub-continental history. This was remembered by the Dogras all the time and, in a way, they nursed the feeling of owning the State even if it was inhabited by a vast majority of Muslims. This posed a challenge in administering the State and required the ruler to be wise, sagacious and also pragmatic. It was obvious that even though all the ancestors of Maharaja Hari Singh were devout and practising Hindus, religious bigotry in administration would be resented and cause for trouble. It was in this light that upon his coronation, Hari Singh declared that 'Justice' was his religion and merit the deciding factor in all types of employment. While giving shape to his concept of justice and policy, he tried to make sure that caste or creed received no consideration. However, to keep the Dogras satisfied, he did give them some extra powers, disproportionate to their numbers. He also did not change the system of recruitment for the army and followed the traditional and British criteria that recruited only those castes and community groups that were listed as martial. Thus, the State Forces were drawn mainly from among the Dogras of Jammu and Kangra, and also from among Sikhs and Gorkhas. The Muslims who were recruited from the Jammu region.

The construct of the State of Jammu and Kashmir was such that the people of all the regions had their own distinctive characteristics and aspirations. Jammu region was dominated by the warrior and the trading class with the rest dependent upon agriculture, Gilgit-Baltistan too provided muscle to the State, but it was Kashmir that had most of the population and provided wealth; it had weavers, craftsmen and agriculturists. Therefore, while the nobility, soldiers and civil and police bureaucracy came from Jammu and from among the Kashmiri Pandits, most of the reforms of Maharaja Hari Singh were for giving relief to the farmers, tillers, weavers and artisans of Kashmir. His educational reforms, stipends and scholarships too were meant for the uplift of the Kashmiris so as to draw them out of their traditional professions and encourage them to opt for newer career opportunities.

In a reform of far reaching consequences, Mahataja Pratap Singh had declared Urdu as the official language of Jammu and Kashmir in 1889, replacing Persian after three centuries. Persian by then had become the language of the scholars and the elite and could no longer be the instrument of governance. But soon it was realized that this change was not enough to govern satisfactorily since people capable of reading and writing Urdu were also scarce in the State. Consequently, most of the government jobs were manned by outsiders, mostly Punjabis. In view of this, the Kashmiri Pandits, who with their knowledge of Persian had traditionally held most jobs in the administration under different regimes, took the initiative and demanded that the jobs should be given to the local people. The new Maharaja responded favourably by passing a 'Hereditary State Subject Order, 1927' that specified who would be considered State Subjects, and that jobs were reserved only for them. (The term Hereditary State Subject later came to be defined to mean all persons born and residing within the State before the commencement of the reign of Maharaja Gulab Singh, as well as those who settled there before the commencement of the Samvat year 1984 (1927 A.D.) and have been residing in Jammu and Kashmir permanently since then.) Maharaja Hari Singh also introduced free and compulsory primary education in all Municipal Towns and increased the number of educational institutions from 706 in 1925 to 2,0728 by 1945. Recognizing the backwardness of the Muslims, he raised the special grants for encouragement of scholars of backward communities and Muslims to more than double what they were before his time. He also sanctioned special scholarships for Sikh students. Hospitals, with latest equipment and maternity wards with separate blocks, were constructed in Jammu and Srinagar. Several dispensaries, leper asylums and centres for anti-rabies treatment too were established. On the front of social reforms, smoking by children below fourteen years of age was prevented by law; widow marriage was legalized, child marriages banned, and minimum age limit for marriages fixed as eighteen years for boys and fourteen years for girls. For the benefit of agricultural growth, cooperative societies and agricultural credit societies were introduced and the consolidation of land holdings was accelerated. Since the old, subhuman system of forced labour, or *begar*, had crept into the society again, this time it was abolished by law, and grain control was introduced to help the poorer sections of the society. The famine of 1877-1878 had also affected the cottage industries of Kashmir since a large number of craftsmen had migrated from the valley to Punjab. Along with British machinations that had disrupted the *pashm* trade via Ladakh to Kashmir, the sector was in doldrums. These migrated craftsmen had settled in the British administered cities and towns like Amritsar, Nurpur and Bashahar. To reinvigorate the industry, the State constituted an Industrial Board. In other words, Maharaja Hari Singh did all that the situation demanded to put the State on the road to prosperity.

In this way, the new regime began its tenure on a note of optimism for a better and brighter future. On the face of it, almost every move of the Maharaja had been in the right direction but the British had noticed an independent streak in his temperament with the episode of the ordering of the lowering of Union Jack from the buildings of the Resident in Srinagar. Soon thereafter, the First Round Table Conference had been held in London in 1930. The Conference had been called to discuss the future of India and the constitutional reforms that needed to be affected so that the discontent among the Indians demanding *Poorna Swaraj*—Total Self Rule—could be contained. By then, opinion had been veering towards giving a dominion status to India. That had necessitated discussions about the required constitutional reforms. Since the princely states too were stakeholders in the future dispensation, the representatives of the Princes had also been chosen to express their opinions. Maharaja Hari Singh was one among them. During his address he said:

> "Allied by treaty with the British Crown, and within our territories independent rulers, we have come with a full sense of the responsibility to our states and all India. As allies of Britain we stand solidly by the British connection. As Indians and loyal to the land of our birth, we stand as solidly as the rest of our countrymen for our lands the enjoyment [*sic*] of a position of honour and equality in the British Commonwealth. Our desire to cooperate to the best of our ability with all sections of the Conference is genuine as also is our determination to base our cooperation upon the realities of the present situation…We must exercise patience, tact and forbearance and be inspired by mutual understanding and goodwill. We must give and take. If we succeed, England no less than India, gains. If we fail India no less than England loses.[21]

It is hard to find fault with the speech, but the British concluded that the speech was evidence that Hari Singh was defiant of the British and was supportive of the peoples' movement demanding independence. They also recalled that upon his coronation too he had demonstrated defiance and belligerence when he had ordered the Union Jack to be pulled down from the Residency building in Srinagar. Their distrust of Hari Singh was exacerbated by the fact that the geostrategic interests in Central Asia had radically changed with the consolidation of the Soviet Union under Stalin.

Once again, the British had begun to hallucinate about the invader coming down from the north-west of India to disrupt their empire in Asia and were convinced that in such an eventuality, the ruler of Jammu and Kashmir could not be trusted and a way had to be found for the British to take direct control of the region. From there on, the troubles of Maharaja Hari Singh began, and with this began a chain of events resulting in never-ending conflict and tension which continues to this day.

The British bided their time and soon found opportunities that were, ironically, the outcome of the progressive policies implemented by the State in general and Maharaja Hari Singh in particular.

2

The British Web

O, what a tangled web we weave when we first practice to deceive.
—Walter Scott

The British attempt to dethrone Maharaja Pratap Singh and take direct control of the affairs of the State in 1888, were thwarted because it was clumsily planned and executed, and was exposed by a newspaper—*Amrit Bazaar Patrika* of Calcutta. After that, both the sides had learnt their lessons well. The Maharaja realized that he could not turn down a British request without repercussions, and the British realized that the State needed to be managed in a subtle manner, and only when the circumstances were favourable for this.

By 1930, much had changed in the State, as in fact, it had changed in the country. Modern education had not only made the people aware about the idea of liberty, equality and fraternity but also ignited a desire for self-governance and the confidence to stand up for human dignity and equality. In Jammu and Kashmir, the spread of education had thrown up an additional challenge. The number of educated graduates and college going students had risen manifold, both in the Jammu and Kashmir regions. However, the opportunities that could accommodate them according to their qualifications had not grown. The result, particularly in Kashmir, was that as the number of unemployed grew and they spent their time idling. Consequently, on the one hand, frustration and resentment began to grow, and on the other hand, the poor people felt a sense of hopelessness and despair.[22] The unemployed graduates would often be subjected to ridicule and taunts and their parents were reminded of the futility of education in their society. By now, the communal divide too had become visible and as the Indian National Congress demanded self-governance in India, the Muslims began to grow nervous because of the fear of being swamped by the vast majority of Hindus. Though this fear was not significant or apparent in Jammu and Kashmir, those Kashmiri Muslims who had returned after completing their education in Aligarh Muslim University, had become acutely aware of the Muslim identity in a Hindu-ruled State.

This was disappointing for Maharaja Hari Singh, for most of the economic reforms, particularly regarding land, introduced after he became ruler were particularly targeted towards the welfare of the rural peasantry that constituted the bulk of the society and were overwhelmingly Muslim. This was both enlightened policy and pragmatic policy. Outside the State, the movement for Indian Independence was changing society. The winds of change that were blowing in the country were primarily due to the frail-looking Mahatma Gandhi who had breathed vigour, fearlessness and steel into the souls of the Indian people. Even the despairing and the resigned were no longer prepared to submit to the never-changing lifestyle that had been the lot of the people for centuries. They had begun to shed their diffidence and fear and their courage grew with each *lathi* blow during demonstrations against the British. The Champaran, Kheda and Bardoli peasant movements had demonstrated that even the underfed, oppressed and hungry Indian peasant had begun to realize that he or she could not continue to live in fear and indignity. As a Yuvraj, Hari Singh had felt the winds of change crossing the Pir Panjal and had made efforts to pre-empt the consequences of the impoverishment of and sense of abandonment among the majority population, who had not received due attention for centuries. Therefore, he had encouraged his majority Muslim subjects to pursue modern education, acquire new skills and break away from the shackles of tradition-bound professions. He had made education free and compulsory in municipal limits and gave liberal scholarship to those who wanted to continue higher eduction in Indian Universities.[23] Could he have imagined that his largesse and liberality would be the cradle of the coming storm? The educated young now expected immediate and radical change in their situation upon completion of education, and not finding jobs that satisfied their aspirations, they turned to the Muslim Readers' Club[24] that instead of becoming the agent for transition turned into a hotbed of communal sentiments and destructive emotions instead of constructive ideas for change. Being educated and well-travelled, and therefore, aware of what was happening in the rest of the country and the world, these members of the Readers' Club were listened to carefully by the ordinary people. Thus, they used their strength to subvert the State.

The summer of 1931 proved to be the turning point. A man called Abdul Qadir appeared mysteriously in Srinagar. This fiery and openly bigoted man would set the State ablaze. The Maharaja's intelligence service completely failed in finding out who Abdul Qadir[25] was or what he was doing in Srinagar. No one knew for sure from where he had come to Srinagar, as a cook to a European tourist, and where he went after igniting a fire. But, during his stay he had succeeded in fomenting trouble in Srinagar. Even today no one knows who he was. Was he an Ahmadiya,[26] as the All Jammu and Kashmir Muslim Conference[27] suggested? Was he an agent provocateur from Rawalpindi in the service of the secret service of the British? There were no answers then and there are no definitive answers even today.

The events of 1931 left no one in doubt that the Maharaja and his administration had failed to match the British in cunning, stratagem or resources and had, therefore, also failed to keep the passions of Kashmiri Muslims in check. The storm brewed with patently inflammatory rumours doing the rounds, and such was the intensity of the passions that all the goodwill that the Maharaja had earned had fallen short. It was alleged that with the approval of the Maharaja's Government a mosque in Reasi had been demolished by Hindus, that the Jammu Muslims were prevented from offering their prayers, and that the Imam of a mosque in Jammu had been stopped from saying his customary *khutba* during prayers on a Friday. The worst of the rumours was that pages of the Holy Koran had been found discarded in a public facility! Many of the educated Kashmiri activists who should have countered this openly communal rhetoric used it to their advantage instead. It was an unfortunate, cynical strategy. It brought religion into the political discourse by encouraging emotive slogans, rumours and speeches which declared that Islam was in danger.

The agitation culminated on 21st June 1931 when the mysterious Abdul Qadir made an inflammatory and dangerously communal speech after the Friday prayers in the precincts of Khanqah of Shah Hamadan.[28] He repeated the rumours regarding the persecution of Muslims in Jammu and this incited passions. He was appropriately arrested. But if the intelligence agencies had failed to find out about the credentials of that agent provocateur in the first place, they compounded this by failing to assess the magnitude of the passions that had been aroused by Qadir's propaganda and other allied activities of the disgruntled educated Kashmiri Muslim activists. To its utter shock, the Maharaja's government realized that it was impossible to hold Qadir's trial in the Sessions Court and after ceaseless demonstrations it was decided to shift it to the Central Jail. It was then that the unimaginable happened when on 13th July—the day the trial was to be held—about 5,000 people stormed the jail. While the gates of the jail were being battered, the prisoners inside had become restive and a riot-like situation had been created. With the telephone line cut, the administration was on the verge of losing all control when the forces opened fire killing twenty-one people on the spot.[29] It was a black day, indeed. A blot on Hari Singh's reign; for he had endeared himself to the common Kashmiris both as the Yuvraj and as a member of the State Council of Maharaja Pratap Singh. He had made a successful attempt to understand and address their problems and difficulties in 1921.

That was the year when scarcity of food grains could have led to as ghastly a famine as the one that had struck in 1877–79.[30] The stains of that famine were still there, for the received memory of Kashmiris had kept it alive and, therefore, many remembered the havoc that it had caused to life and human relations. As Yuvraj and future Maharaja, Hari Singh was determined not to have that kind of stain as long as he was responsible for the wellbeing of his uncle's subjects. His compassionate but firm handling of the situation had averted a severe famine in the valley in 1921. The people of the valley too had acknowledged his successful efforts, for the grains released by the administration reached the people across the State on time and in sufficient quantities. Thus, by the time his coronation took place, he had evolved as a Prince and had formed definite ideas about his State and its people and what he wanted to do for them. Upon his coronation he had demonstrated his responsive and reformist views of administration and he genuinely believed that he was doing all that a modern king should be doing.

During those heady early years that inaugurated his reign, he had joined the congregation of his Muslim subjects for the *namaz* of Id in Srinagar.[31] Though not versed in the ritual, he had only made a symbolic gesture to his subjects by joining them. There was consternation and furore among his Hindu subjects. The fanatics among them had begun to whisper that the day was not far when he would recite the *kalma*! Some even said that he had actually converted but had not disclosed this for fear of revolt among his Hindu subjects.[32] The Maharaja had laughed when told of this. Personally he did not care much about religion or even about the existence of God. Indifferent to the insinuations and rumours, he had found the best of Muslims for appointment at the court, in administration and the army. The army, indeed, was a fine blend of the brave Dogras, Rajputs, Gorkhas, Pathans and Muslims from the region of Poonch, Mirpur and adjoining Punjab. Poonch and Mirpur were in fact a happy hunting ground for recruitment by the British Indian Army as well. These soldiers had proved their mettle earlier during the campaigns in the north-west region and later, during the Great War and could be relied upon to sacrifice their lives in obeying the commands.

Hari Singh believed that he was more enlightened than many other princes as he was far ahead of many of them in the subcontinent in matters of responsive administration. His father, Raja Amar Singh had long ago realized the importance of western education and had wisely invested in his son's education. He had thus discerned very early in his life that if the Princes were to escape the fate of the Tsar and the Ottoman Turks then they had to change and be more liberal and responsive to their people. The people of his State too were aware of his commitment and trusted his word.

In fact there was not a single example of any person being jailed or punished without following the due process of law. He did not even exercise the absolute power of being the final arbiter of justice and had constituted a Judicial Board of Advisors, whose decisions he never overturned.[33] He was genuinely respected for his fairness and principles, and importantly, loved. He could not have wanted more from his subjects. But then the First Round Table Conference of 1930 happened. His speech there made him a suspect in the eyes of the British. Then on, he was a marked man. Abdul Qadir and the tragic killing of twenty-one Kashmiris was just the beginning.

With those bloody events of the summer of 1931, all of a sudden for the media in Punjab, Kashmir became the only issue of consequence. Suddenly Kashmir's dominant Muslim character and the fact that it was being ruled by a Hindu dynasty became the only reality of the State. It was the only State in the subcontinent where such a situation existed. Modern democratic principles cannot be applied to the past; almost every ruler and dynasty was a product of its times. Hindu Dogra rule in Kashmir was far from perfect, but then so was a quarter century of Sikh rule and certainly the centuries of Muslim rule when oppression of the Kashmiris was common and almost constant. But all this was forgotten and a communal colour was given to grievances. Inexplicably, the refrain of the Punjab media was taken up by the rest and a concerted effort began to question Hari Singh's administration and his ability to be just and fair to his Muslim subjects. Though he had lost no time in appointing an official committee presided over by the Chief Justice of the State High Court to enquire into the firing and the unfortunate deaths, yet the Muslims were swayed by some hidden power to boycott it and claimed that it was not independent. It was a galling accusation for the Maharaja and he was deeply offended.

Even as the events of 1931 were unfolding, the fact of the British taking too keen an interest in the whole affair became clear when the Resident came with a message from the Viceroy himself. There was concern over the events and the fear that the consequences of the events might spill over to British India. He, therefore, suggested that the circumstance warranted an independent, outside assistance for a commission of enquiry. The least that he could do, according to the alternative given by the Viceroy, was to appoint a Muslim High Court Judge as its chairman. This was clearly not acceptable to the Maharaja as it would have destroyed the very basics of his administration, which he was trying hard to run with the principles of fairness and secularism.

The message to his subjects would have been that the State High Court was incapable of delivering justice with an even hand. It would have been tantamount to admitting that the State High Court was prejudiced against the majority community of the State. Such a step would certainly have detracted from the prestige of the State High Court and, therefore, he had no choice but to reject the suggestion. However, the British were relentless in their pursuit and began to apply overt and covert pressure by allowing *jathas*—groups—of the Muslims from Punjab to enter the State in support of the local agitators. It was now obvious that communalism had raised its head with the blessing of the British who, by the Treaty of Amritsar, were bound to protect him from outside enemies and certainly these Muslims from Punjab were outside elements, and were no friends of his or his people. It was then that he realized that the British wanted something else from him and were therefore playing the game that colonial powers were adept at playing. He needed to act fast if he was to escape from the web that the British had woven. He invited the Muslim leaders for talks on 26th August and assured them that when presented with all their grievances he would deal with them fairly and that not only would all prisoners be released but all the cases would be withdrawn as well. In return the agitation was to be immediately suspended.[34]

Little had he realized that he was assuring only the puppets and that their strings were in the hands of the All India Kashmir Committee, as the Kashmir Muslim Conference of Lahore had designated itself. The unlikely combination of Sir Muhammad Iqbal[35], of Kashmiri descent, and Mirza Bashir Ahmad[36], the head of the Ahamadiya sect with headquarters at Qadian (Punjab), led the demand for intervention on behalf of the Muslims. It was in these circumstances that Sheikh Abdullah, one of those new breed of Muslims who had got an education at the prestigious Aligarh Muslim University and probably thought that he deserved a better appointment in life than that of a school teacher, emerged. A fiery orator, he reignited the agitation, violating the truce.

Lending him support was the Mirwaiz Moulvi Mohammed Yusuf Shah[37] with his religious prestige. Maharaja Hari Singh realized that a formidable, but unholy, nexus had been formed when it became clear that his senior minister G.E.C. Wakefield was acting as the agent of the British government in Delhi. On that fateful day when the Governor of Kashmir, Raizada Tarlokchand, rang him up to inform him of the grave situation that was emerging, Wakefield was already in touch with the British Resident.[38] The Kashmiri Muslims were back on the roads, this time not sparing the property of the Hindus. Riots broke out, and unwisely, the Maharaja notified the draconian ordinance that allowed for summary punishment, public flogging and shooting. Later, he knew that it was difficult to justify this Burma Law or the Notification 19–L, but he was angry and frustrated, for he had made up his mind to concede all the just demands of his subjects but somewhere the lines of communication had failed. Somewhere his ministers had failed him again by not conveying to the agitators what the ruler was about to do. Everyone knew that he was not a man who was demonstrative of his emotions or communicative, for that matter. It should logically have fallen upon the ministers to assume this role but most of them continued to live in the past era and, therefore, they brooked none who displayed defiance or demanded reform and change. Riding on the high horses of their egos and the achievements of the preceding generations, they had let him down.

He paid a heavy price not only in prestige but in power too. In the face of mounting British pressure and oblique threats he finally withdrew the ordinance and declared general amnesty. That, however, did not bring an end to his problems. Trouble broke out when British authorities in Punjab allowed Punjabi-Muslim *jathas*—delegations—to enter the State from Mirpur, to express their solidarity with the agitating Kashmiri Muslims. A dejected Hari Singh was forced to seek the help of the British troops to quell the violence. The troops arrived on 3rd November 1931. But before that he had to agree to constitute an enquiry commission headed by B.J. Glancy of the Political Department to go through the grievances of the Muslims. No sooner had he done this than on the 7th of November, the British government issued an ordinance prohibiting sending of the *jathas* of the Muslims from Punjab to the State. There was no room for speculation as to who had orchestrated the sending of the *jathas* in the first place!

The Maharaja knew that steps had to be taken to contain the communal virus that was shaking the foundation of the State. The immediate challenge was that the Muslims of Jammu, so indifferent to the fate of Kashmiri Muslims, were geographically and culturally closer to the Muslims of Punjab. As a consequence, they were getting swayed by the politics of that province. Unfortunately, the politics in Punjab had become more and more communal and this had begun to put strains on the traditional amity of the general population in the Dogra region. The more he tried to pacify the Muslims, the more the Hindu Dogras got annoyed. They believed that only strong tactics could keep the Muslims in control. In any case, the majority among them nursed a historically ingrained bias and belief that the Muslims were not to be trusted. The bolder and brasher among the Dogras had begun to openly say that they could never be loyal to the Maharaja and a few had begun to surreptitiously question his ability to keep the kingdom together if he continued to trust the Muslims.

Even at that stage, the Maharaja, despite his disappointment, was sensitive to and understood some of the grievances—those that related to economic factors. The carpet industry and the weavers needed urgent attention. The *begar* system needed to be genuinely eradicated.[39] It was, indeed, time to look forward and implement reforms. He knew what needed to be done but what troubled him was the charge that his rule was discriminatory towards the Muslims. He believed his credentials were impeccable but did not want to be seen to be taking decisions under pressure. It was he who, as the Yuvraj, had influenced his uncle to see the writing on the wall and change. Therefore the new education policy had begun to be shaped during his uncle's time. He had only shown more determination and energy in implementing the education policy and encouraging his Muslim subjects to acquire the requisite qualifications and abilities to avail of the equal opportunities that he was determined to give them. It was up to them to grab the opportunities in the face of stiff competition. Of course now and then there would be cases where, because of the competition and the limited jobs, an equally qualified and competent person might find himself out of the pale of government service or in a job that might not be befitting the qualification. But then there were examples of not only Kashmiri Pandits but also Dogras who suffered the same fate. However many such Pandits and Dogras had not hesitated to travel beyond the borders of the State in search of better opportunities. A large number among those who dared to walk the untrodden path had distinguished themselves in various walks of life in British India.

But Sheikh Abdullah and his ilk had were convinced that the fewer numbers of Muslims in government offices was because of religious prejudice. Sheikh Abdullah asked why 'Muslims were being singled out for such treatment. We constituted the majority and contributed the most towards the State's revenues, still we were continually oppressed…Was it because a majority of Government servants were non-religious?…I concluded that the ill-treatment of Muslims was an outcome of religious prejudice.'[40] Unfortunately, the Muslim leaders of the Valley had been completely excised from their collective memory, not only the brutal rule of the Afghans but also the fact that earlier too when Persian was the court language, the Kashmiri Muslims had been left out of important positions because they did not have the incentives to improve their qualifications. The *zulm-parast* tag was not given to them under Sikh or Dogra rule; the rather demeaning tag had been given much earlier because it was believed that they suffered quietly during the long centuries of Muslim rule. Now, under a Hindu dynasty they had developed the habit of transferring all the misfortunes of the past on to Dogra rule. As a consequence, this set of Muslims, as diverse as the son of a *pashm* dealer, Sheikh Mohammad Abdullah and Mirza Afzal Beg and Khwaja Ghulam Mohammad Sadiq, were not inclined to test themselves in alien conditions. They had taken up the mission of ridding the Valley of Dogra rule, which they saw as 'foreign' rule.

A post graduate in physics, Sheikh Mohammad Abdullah had preferred to work on a monthly salary of sixty rupees as a school teacher rather than go to India and search for a better career. But having chosen to stay, he was not happy with his situation and spent much of his time agitating. Like the Pandits who had created a special niche for themselves all over the Indian subcontinent, he too could have found better employment that gave expression to the abundant talent that he undoubtedly possessed. But this was a choice he did not make.

In 1931, it had barely been a decade since education had begun to spread and the Maharaja was certain that in the not too distant future his Muslim subjects would see their children competing with the best in greater numbers. One needed to just look at the enrolment figures of the students of Sri Pratap College, Srinagar to realize the gains made by the Muslims. During the academic session of 1920–21, there were twenty-two Muslim and 192 non-Muslim students, and this figure barely reached twenty-eight for Muslims in the year 1923–24 while that of non-Muslims had jumped to 270. However, after the coronation of Maharaja Hari Singh this figure began to steadily rise for Muslims from fifty-one in 1924–25 to ninety-three in 1929–30. During this period, the number of non-Muslim students too had dramatically increased as his message of change and progress reached to the people. Their number had increased from 304 in 1924–25 to 453 in 1929–30.

Thus even though the number of Muslim students rose in the Sri Pratap College, Srinagar, the number of other communities too rose and so the disbalance continued, and this must have made gaining entry into the administrative service difficult and more competitive. With the limited number of jobs on offer, the situation was not easy. Hari Singh had done all that could be done to encourage the Muslims to avail of the facilities they were being provided. An amount of Rs 3,000 in the form of annual grant for the students of Srinagar College was being spent. In addition, they could also avail the scholarships that were on offer. There were five scholarships of Rs 15 per month each for the students from the frontier region and 30 per cent free scholarships. The Maharaja was sure that the facts would not hold him guilty of neglecting his Muslim subjects.

The justification for some of the regrets and incriminations notwithstanding, the fact was that the Maharaja had been caught in the pincer of a clearly communalized agitation and British complicity, and to buy time and get out of it, he decided to appoint a British as his prime minister. The moment he appointed Lt Col E.J.D. Colvin of the Foreign and Political department as the Prime Minister along with three other officers of the Indian Civil Service as the Home, Revenue and Police Ministers of the State, the communal violence and agitation vanished. There will continue to be debates, but it would be hard for any objective study of the period to conclude that the 1931 agitation and violence were not planned and motivated; that the British hadn't played mischief, and the educated Muslim activists had not aligned with the colonial project, just as they had aligned with communal Muslim elements from outside the State. However, even though the Maharaja had been forced to appoint a British man as the PM, and ICS men in key posts, he had now allowed the effective administrative control to pass on to the representatives of the British.

It was Prime Minister Colvin who was instrumental in delivering the cruellest cut of all when he persuaded Hari Singh to lease out Gilgit to the British. Situated in some of the densest and lofty mountain ranges of the world, cradled by the mighty Himalaya's and Karakoram ranges, it has fascinating valleys and majestic mountains. It happens to be locked between the frontiers of some of the great and ancient empires—India, Afghanistan, Russia and China. Because of its strategic location Gilgit has always remained at the centre of affairs between these countries and has been influencing their strategic calculations. Gilgit has, from times immemorial, remained a part and parcel of the Indian subcontinent and has been within the ambit of its political and cultural influence. This reality was put into sharp focus with the discovery of the now internationally famous Gilgit manuscripts, which were discovered in 1931 and which are an authentic source of Buddhist influences and lore in these far-flung territories.

Gilgit has been a part of the territories of Kashmir State from early times. But towards the second half of the nineteenth century, things began to hot up in the turbulent region as the Czarist Russia began to evince rather abnormal interest in the region, and British rulers of India became apprehensive of a possible southward thrust by Czarist expansionists. Taking no chances, they decided to put up a watch tower in Gilgit. They placed a British Officer there in 1868 to monitor intelligence reports and other related moves. In 1889 a full-fledged Gilgit agency was established which included areas of Yasin, Punial, Kuh-Ghizar, Ishkman, Chilas etc. But the civil and administrative control continued to vest in the Government of Maharaja. It continued to be administered by the Maharaja's Government. Most of its garrison consisted of Dogra soldiers and the Dogra and Kashmiri official drawn from the State Government cadre, often belonging to Jammu and Kashmir, continued to be posted in Gilgit.

But with the creation of the Soviet Union and the fear of communism running over monarchies, the British had more overt designs for Gilgit. In spite of having had to agree to the leasing out of Gilgit, the Maharaja was very particular to assert his State's sovereignty on the region and insisted that only the State flag should fly over the frontier territory. Although the British had agreed for a while, they had become apprehensive about the intentions of the Bolshevik regime in what was re-christened as the Soviet Union. They used the influence of Hari Singh's own Prime Minister to put pressure on him to agree to lease out the Agency of Gilgit. While the Maharaja resisted hard, he knew that unless he agreed there would be serious repercussions, particularly with the communal atmosphere getting more and more toxic in the Punjab. It would not take long to foment trouble in the valley by spreading rumours, and then putting the pressure of the Muslims from Punjab on those of Jammu.

Maharaja Hari Singh remembered the day when he had asked his courtiers for their opinion about his intention of leasing out Gilgit. Since it was known that the decision was almost taken already, all of them, especially those of the Dogra-Rajput *biradari*, had vociferously supported the deal. Some even argued that the move would save the State considerable amount of money in maintaining the troops and official machinery. The Maharaja had finally turned to Sardar Abdul Rehman Effendi—Bhai Jaan—a relative of the Afghanistan King Amanullah, and a migrant. He had been the lone dissenting voice. The court had remained stunned for a while. Bhai Jaan had pointed out that the decision was not in keeping with the prestige of an independent State. The Maharaja had then gently told him and the court of the compulsions and the inability to stand up to the British any longer!

The web had successfully ensnared the prey.

3

The Dream of Naya Kashmir

The worst form of inequality is to try to make unequal things equal.
—Aristotle

The events of 1931 had resulted in the appointment of a Commission of Inquiry to go into all the grievances of the Muslims of the State. It was chaired by B.J. Glancy of the Political Department, and included P.N. Bazaz, G.A. Ashai and Ghulam Abbas as members. The sole nominee from Jammu was Lok Nath, but he did not remain for long and resigned since 'the Commission found itself unable to exclude from the scope of enquiry, questions relating to Hindu Law of Inheritance.'[41]

The sittings of the Commission had begun before the end of November and after going through the complaints and grievances of all the communities, it submitted its report to the Maharaja on 22nd March 1932. Its recommendations, in brief were: There should be no interference with religious observance. The officers of the State should take severe notice of any action of insult to religion, and those desiring to change their religion should not be harassed or discouraged. The report, however, did not say if the original rumours that led to the bloody events of 13th July 1931 were the result of any dereliction of duty on the part of the Maharaja's Government or if any of the officials was actually involved in them. It also did not mention any acts of omission or commission on the part of the Maharaja or his administration in this regard.

The more substantial recommendations related to education and employment. It was recommended that the expansion of primary education should be accelerated, though the fact was that this was already in the process. A Muslim specific demand was that for the benefit of the Jammu Muslims, the proposal to have an Islamia High School in Gandoo Di Chawani deserved favourable consideration. It was said that care should be taken to encourage the Muslims so that they get educated, but it did not mention the significant stride that had already taken place in the preceding period. The Commission also recommended that Muslims be given fair share in orphanage scholarships and that a Muslim inspector should be appointed for monitoring the progress of education among Muslims. As regarding employment, the Commission opined that 'While there need not be different standards for different communities, the standard should not be more exacting than efficiency demanded and those who possessed qualifications in excess of that standard should not be held to deserve appointment as a matter of right.' It further added that 'policy of His Highness's Government in the matter of reserving State appointments should be adhered to as far as possible.'[42] As regards to the demand of the Muslims—that since they constituted 78 percent of the State's population, they should be given government jobs in that proportion—the Commission observed that it rested with the Muslims to increase their numbers in State services by availing the educational opportunities that were available and get the jobs on merit. It also observed that the hereditary occupation of the vast number of Muslims in the State was agriculture and it was reasonable to suppose that the great majority of agriculturists would continue to prefer that occupation in the near future.[43]

Most of the recommendations of the Commission were accepted by the Maharaja and a notification was issued to that effect on 10th April 1932. The follow up to these recommendations was swift and the Maharaja also lifted restrictions on the freedom of press and the platform to express views. The Press Laws too were brought in line with those that existed within British India. But even more significant was the desire expressed by Maharaja Hari Singh to associate his people with the administration of the State and to achieve that goal; Glancy was given the responsibility to give shape to the process. Consequently, a Constitutional Reforms Commission was convened in the middle of March 1932, which finished drawing up the road map in April. 'The Conference recommended that a Legislative Assembly should be established as soon as possible and made suggestions regarding its composition, powers and functions. At the same time the Conference suggested the appointment of a Committee to collect the necessary data on which further action should be based.'[44] In May 1932, a Franchise Committee under the Presidency of Sir Barjor Dalal was appointed and in March 1933; Sir Ivo Elliot, I.C.S. (Retired) was appointed Franchise Officer. Following this, 'Lieutenant Colonel Colvin, the Prime Minister of Kashmir, states that in order to assure a favourable atmosphere for the work of the Franchise Inquiry Committee [appointed by the Maharaja], orders have been issued that prisoners of all communities, both those convicted and those on trial under the temporary regulation and notifications shall be released on giving an undertaking to refrain in future from all forms of agitation.'[45]

With this began the first attempt by Maharaja Hari Singh to identify the people with the administration by deciding to set up a Council that would pass legislation, ask questions, discuss budget and pass resolutions. On 22nd April 1934, the Maharaja enacted and issued a Constitutional Act (Regulation No. 1 of Samvat 1991 i.e. 1934 A.D.) thereby establishing Legislative Assembly and laying down his own Legislative, Executive and Judicial Powers. Regulation No. 1 consisted of forty-six Sections and declared the Maharaja's intent for associating his subjects in matters of legislation and administration of the State. The Legislative Assembly of the State was to be called the 'Praja Sabha'. It was to consist of seventy-five members, sixty of whom were non-officials, including thirty-three elected members, twenty-one Muslims, ten Hindus and two Sikhs. A modern reader will obviously conclude that it was a deeply flawed attempt at coopting the people in representative democracy but this step needs to be judged in comparison with what was the condition prior to this, and in other States, including those directly administered by the British. In fact, it was only a decade or so ago, that full democracy, that also gave women the right to vote, was introduced in England—the mother of all parliamentary democracies where the democratic process had begun in 1215, when the Magna Carta was agreed upon by the King of England. In this context, what Maharaja Hari Singh had done was a significant step forward.

It must be accepted that there was no revolutionary change, for after all, we are not talking of a modern democracy. Not surprisingly, then, the franchise was limited, and barely 3 per cent of the population participated in it. Moreover, though the Maharaja intended to give up many of his absolute powers, yet 'under Section 3 of the Regulation, he fully reserved for himself all of his pre-existing legislative, executive and judicial powers. Under Section 30 also it had been laid down that no measure should be deemed to have been passed by the Praja Sabha until and unless His Highness signified his assent thereto. A vote of the Sabha was not binding on the Council of Ministers and the Council had power to reject any Bill or resolution...The Council of Ministers was responsible to His Highness and not to the Sabha...Any Bill effecting public revenues, maintenance and discipline of His Highness's troops and Privy Purse could not be introduced in the Sabha, as all these matters were "reserved subjects".'[46]

Women too were altogether excluded. But again, this limited democracy was not peculiar to the State as it was a rule rather than an exception in that period. In British India, the qualification to become an eligible voter was extremely restrictive and even the constitutional reforms of 1935 led to creating a system where popular democracy and government was a far cry. Elsewhere in the world, it was only in 1928 that women were given the same voting rights as men in England, and in USA too women got their voting rights in 1920 while many other groups, including Afro-Americans, Native Americans and non-Anglo-Saxon immigrants, were granted this right even later. Thus, the history of democracy everywhere has been chequered and it is futile to judge the past with contemporary standards that have evolved over a long period of time. The importance of Regulation No.1 should, therefore, be seen and judged as part of that historical process.

With the publicly stated grievances addressed after the constitution of the Glancy Commission, there was little for the

Muslims to agitate for in the State, except to continue to put pressure on the Maharaja's Government by way of sending *jathas* from adjoining Punjab. But this limited success had galvanized them into organizing themselves as a political party.

The All Jammu and Kashmir Muslim Conference was born in 1932 by the joint efforts of Sheikh Mohammad Abdullah, Mirwaiz Yusuf Shah and Chaudhary Ghulam Abbas—the first two from Kashmir and the third from the Poonch region of Jammu. Sheikh Abdullah had started his college education in the State but was uncomfortable studying either at Sri Pratap College, Srinagar or Prince of Wales College, Jammu. He had therefore migrated to the Islamia College, Lahore to finally earn his postgraduate degree in M.Sc. Physics. On the other hand Chaudhary Ghulam Abbass had graduated from Prince of Wales College, Jammu. Having completed his law degree from Lahore, he had been a practicing lawyer in Jammu. A staunch champion of Muslim causes, he had reorganized the Young Men's Muslim Association, a socio-political organization that had been established in 1909, but had gone defunct thereafter. He had gradually earned himself a reputation as champion of Muslim causes and had soon become an undisputed leader of Muslims in Jammu. Sheikh Abdullah had been employed as a teacher for a while but had opted out of it to devote to the causes of the Muslims of Kashmir. Joined by other educated Kashmiris like Ghulam Mohammad Sadiq and Mirza Afzal Beg, a Readers' Club had been established in Srinagar. However, by 1932 they knew exactly what they wanted and had organized their political outfit. In the meantime, the British had continued to use the Muslims of Punjab to pressurize the Maharaja and force him into a corner from where he could escape only after yielding to the British by giving them Gilgit on lease. This was achieved in 1935, after which the pressure was eased and the Jammu and Kashmir Muslim Conference was left high and dry till some need arose in the future. It was obvious, the British and the Muslims had by then realized that the massive majority of the Muslims could be manipulated and wielded as a very potent weapon against the Hindu Maharaja, who, like any dynastic monarch, would be vulnerable to both legitimate and unfair criticism.

During these manoeuvres it had dawned upon Sheikh Abdullah that he and the Muslims were being used as tools by the British to serve their interests. He came to the conclusion that the best course of action for them was to align with another rising power in the country—that which was clamouring for democracy and transfer of power to Indians. The Indian National Congress was fighting its battles on three fronts. It was in a struggle for attaining independence from the British and wanted them to handover all powers of governance; it also lent support to all those organizations in the princely states that wanted transfer of executive and legislative powers to people for their greater participation in governance; but, even more importantly it was competing with the Muslim League of Mohammad Ali Jinnah for influencing Muslims of India so that the composite culture of India continued to prevail. This ambition brought the focus on the Jammu and Kashmir State being one of its kind, where the Muslims had a majority but also had an influential minority of Pandits of Kashmiri origin, which was an integral part of its culture and composition. Therefore it had the potential to confront Muslim separatism with the idea of secularism and co-existence.

This suited both the Congress as well as Sheikh Abdullah, who found the additional virtue of retaining the Pandits in the Kashmiri fold, flaunting its secular credentials and, in return, getting the support of the Congress. He had felt the need of taking the Pandits on board in his struggle to dislodge the Hindu Dogra rule from Jammu and Kashmir because of the influence they had all over the country. According to the 1941 census, there were 78,800 Kashmiri Pandits in the Kashmir Valley and they were mainly distributed in two districts of Valley—the Baramulla district, where Hindus constituted 2.1 percent of the population(12,919 Hindus out of 6,12,428 total) and the Anantnag district, where they were 7.84 percent of the population. A comparative study of demography at various times would suggest that roughly the Pandit population had been six percent of the total population in the valley.[47] During the course of his political activities, Sheikh Abdullah came in close contact of national leaders like Mahatma Gandhi, Jawaharlal Nehru, Abdul Ghaffar Khan, Mohammad Ali Jinnah,[48] and others. In the process, he and many others in the Muslim Conference, either realized on their own, or had been persuaded by the national leaders to become a part of the greater movement for the socio-economic equality and political freedom that had already taken root in the country. Therefore, Sheikh Abdullah mooted the proposal to adopt secularism as one of its principles and moved a resolution during the general meeting of the All Jammu and Kashmir Conference in 1939 to rename the party as All Jammu and Kashmir National Conference. The proposal was passed with a massive majority. Since Chaudhary Ghulam Abbas was vehemently opposed to the change, he soon thereafter parted company with Sheikh Abdullah to revive the Muslim Conference. With the two comrades-in-arms parting, the fault line between Kashmir and Jammu regions also got exposed as Sheikh Abdullah had negligible influence in Jammu and the same was true of Chaudhary Ghulam Abbas in relation to Kashmir.

However, this period was overtaken by the threat that had emerged to the world from Nazi Germany, and later, Japan. Soon the British colonies too were drawn into the war efforts of the Empire but, adopting a contrarian view, the Congress chose to stay out of it. Mahatma Gandhi and the Congress remembered that the Empire had not rewarded India for its efforts, contributions and sacrifices during the First World War. Ironically, as the Congress stayed away from the war effort and, in fact, in 1942, launched the Quit India movement to force the British to free India; the National Conference chose to suspend all its over ground political activities. It was only when the war was drawing to a close that the National Conference came into action and presented its charter of demands to Maharaja Hari Singh, who had returned home after attending a meeting of the Imperial War Cabinet of Great Britain followed by a tour of the war zones of Europe and the Middle East in 1944. The manner in which the demands were presented was dramatic. On his return, the citizens of Kashmir had lined the roads to welcome him and as his cavalcade (consisting of a flotilla of boats on the river Jhelum) approached Mujahid Manzil, the headquarters of the National Conference, Sheikh Mohammad Abdullah, along with his party members, garlanded him with flowers and bouquets were presented to him. Then Sheikh Abdullah submitted a memorandum containing far reaching democratic reforms that would lead to the establishment of the Jammu and Kashmir State as a constitutional, democratic and welfare State with the Maharaja as its nominal constitutional head.

This forty-four pages long memorandum was written in response to an initiative by the Maharaja to consult different parties about political and constitutional reforms. It became famous as the Naya Kashmir document. Attached with this document was an economic plan projecting a humanistic view of development which all progressive people endorsed and lauded as being far ahead of the times. It was a hugely ambitious document and was actually a draft constitution and combined economic program and party manifesto. 'It proposed constitutional monarchy with universal suffrage for those aged eighteen and over; equal rights, irrespective of race, religion or nationality; freedom of speech, press and assembly; free and compulsory education in the mother tongue; state ownership and management of all key industries; and the abolition of feudalism through an agrarian programme of which the key points were "abolition of landlordism" and "land to the tiller."'[49]

The radicalism of the memorandum was not surprising since the making of the document was a collaborative effort of avowed communists, primarily based in Lahore, with strong links to Kashmir. At that time, its authorship was opaque but Sheikh Abdullah in his autobiography clarified that the job of drafting Naya Kashmir was given to his friend B.P.L. Bedi. He wrote, 'to compile the manifesto we requisitioned the services of a famous progressive friend from Punjab [*sic*], B.P.L. Bedi…Bedi's sharp minded, elegant wife Freda typed the manuscript.'[50] But Bedi had worked with a small group of friends who were avowedly leftists and from outside the State—K.M. Ashraf, Mohammed Din Taseer[51], Danyal Lateefi, and the poet Ihsan Danish assisted in its drafting. Mohammad Din Taseer, a Punjabi, had been appointed, first as the Principal of Sri Pratap College, Srinagar and then of Amar College, Srinagar. Since he was an appointee of the Maharaja, it was inconceivable that his communist credential were not known to the State government or even the Maharaja. He was a name among the progressives of his time and yet the fact that he was allowed to carry on his activities in a State whose Maharaja had been routinely accused of autocracy, speaks volumes of the considerations of merit, tolerance and freedom that existed in the State. Other sources mention the names of Pandit Jia Lal Kilam and the celebrated poet Hafeez Jullundhri, although Sheikh Abdullah does not acknowledge their role. All those involved had communist leanings and Naya Kashmir had the support of all progressive elements and leading communists of the region. It was claimed to be a 100 percent communist document though a closer examination of it will reveal that it was hardly an original document. P.N. Jalali, a veteran activist, told BBC's Andrew Whitehead that it was, in fact, a carbon copy of a Soviet document. The ideas for other provisions too had been borrowed from many *kisan sabha* documents. The foreword was written by Sheikh Abdullah and was communist in tone and tenor.

The fact of the matter was that once again, as in 1931, Lahore, including Punjabis of Kashmiri descent, had begun to set the agenda for Kashmir. Bedi and his English wife Freda had become close friends with Sheikh Abdullah and they, along with many like-minded friends from Punjab, came up to Kashmir for a long sojourn during summers. Jalali is of the firm opinion that Bedi had been deputed by the Punjab communist party to look after the affairs of Jammu and Kashmir. It was easy for Bedi to work through his association with Sheikh Abdullah and his National Conference as there was the risk of his getting thrown out for spreading communist propaganda. With the National Conference working for the diminishing of the monarchy, there were a number of leaders and activists within that party who were sympathetic to communism, and this made Bedi's work easier. G.M. Sadiq and G.M. Karra were notable leftists in the National Conference and both played important roles in spreading the philosophy among the youth. It is believed that it was Bedi who manoeuvred Sheikh Abdullah in a manner that he kept the National Conference away from the Quit India movement launched by the Congress during the War, since the communists had aligned with the western powers against the Nazis. This also suited the British plans.

Whatever the influence of communism and the Soviet Union upon Bedi was, the document was an outline of a plan to convert the Jammu and Kashmir State from an absolute monarchy to a constitutional democracy, with the Maharaja remaining as the Head of the State, just as the Monarch was in Britain. The economic plan of the memorandum was subsequently adopted by the National Conference as its manifesto and translated into Urdu so that the majority of the people of the State could understand it. It also envisaged all aspects that affected the life of a citizen and defined citizenship, their basic rights and obligation in the following words:

> A single State Citizenship is hereby established for all citizens of Jammu, Kashmir, Ladakh and the Frontier Regions, including the Poonch and Chinani illaqas. The equality of the rights of all citizens, irrespective of their nationality, religion, race, or birth, in all spheres of national life—economic, political, cultural, and social shall...be an irrevocable law. Any direct or indirect restriction of these rights, or conversely, the establishment of direct or indirect privileges for any citizens or class of citizens on account of nationality, religion, race or birth, as well as the propagation of national, racial or religious exceptionalism or hatred and contempt shall be punished by law.[52]

On the subject of the defence of the State, the document was unequivocal in stating, 'The defence of the Motherland is the supreme and sacred duty of all citizens. Treason to the Motherland, violation of oath, desertion to the enemies of the Motherland, impairing the military power of the State, [or] espionage shall be punishable with the full severity of the Law as the gravest crime. In pursuance of this sacred task, every citizen is obliged to arm himself to use and shall be ensured the right to bear arms.'[53] In retrospect, it is hard to say if this Section had motives but it could also have been directed at the Maharaja to assure him that the National Conference was not antagonistic to the army of the State and that it was prepared to put all its weight behind it. The Dogras, particularly the Rajputs, famously possessed firearms and other conventional weapons, and this clause could have been added to appease them. But it is also likely that, like the Second Amendment of the American Constitution, this was meant for the Kashmiri populace who had hitherto been thought of as lacking martial attributes.

Significantly, Naya Kashmir was one of the earliest documents to speak of the right to work, food and security in old age through social insurance. In an early warning of things to come, it also said: 'The right of personal property of citizens, as well as the right of inheritance of personal property of citizens, is protected by law within the limits of the planned economy of the State.'

The subject and the need of a planned economy was inspired by the Soviet model that was also to be adopted by India after it gained independence. Nevertheless, it was a very progressive document. On the subject of constituting the National Assembly of the State, it read: 'The highest legislature of the State, the National Assembly, is elected by the citizens of the State by electoral districts on the basis of one deputy per 40,000 populations for a period of five years.' It also categorically stated that 'subject to the general control of H.H. the Maharaja Bahadur, the jurisdiction of the National Assembly shall include: representation of the State in exterior relations, conclusion and ratification of treaties with other States; approval of alterations of the boundaries of the States; organization of the defence of the State and the direction of its armed forces; foreign trade upon the basis of State monopoly; protection of State security; establishment of the National Economic Plan of the State; approval of the State Budget; administration of banks, industrial and agricultural establishments…'[54]

It also contained a clause on the role of the Maharaja of the State and said that the ruler of Jammu and Kashmir shall:

> Convene sessions of the National Assembly twice a year; shall convene extraordinary sessions of the Assembly at his own wish or at the request of the speaker of the Assembly; and dissolve the National Assembly and fix new elections; conduct a referendum upon his own initiative or upon the demand of the majority of the legislators; declare general or partial mobilization; ratify international treaties after they have been approved by the National Assembly. Summon the leader of the largest single party in the National Assembly to form the Ministry.[55]

In the matter of the electoral process, it had some unusual points to make, saying:

> Deputies to the National Assembly as well as to the People's Panchayats are selected by the electors upon the basis of universal, equal, direct, suffrage by secret ballot. Franchise shall be universal: all citizens of the State who have reached the age of eighteen years, irrespective of race and sex, nationality or religion, educational qualifications, residential qualifications, social origin, property, status, or past activity shall have the right to participate in the elections of deputies and to be elected with the exception of insane persons and those deprived of electoral rights by court sentence. Franchise shall be equal: every citizen takes part in elections upon an equal basis. Every citizen shall have one vote, provided that, during the transitional period, Sikhs, Kashmiri Pandits and Harijans shall be provided with two reserved seats each, and for this purpose they shall exercise the right of a second vote. Women shall have the right to elect and to be elected upon equal terms with men in all institutions of the State.
>
> Citizens serving in the armed forces shall have the right to elect and be elected on equal terms with all citizens.
>
> Candidates shall be put forward for election according to electoral districts. Any one hundred electors residing in an electoral district may sponsor a candidate. No other precondition, whether money security or otherwise, shall be required of a candidate.[56]

This document, that was to assume the form of a manifesto, long before India amended its law, had made eighteen years old eligible for voting. It also visualized dual vote for the minority communities of Sikhs, Kashmiri Pandits and Harijans, and allowed even the serving personnel of the State Forces the right to contest election while making the support of 100 voters essential for the nomination as a candidate for the election.

On the subject of the judiciary, Naya Kashmir had an extremely radical take and is justifiably accused of blindly following the communist model of the Soviet system that makes all institutions subservient to the Party. 'Justice is administered by the High Court of Jammu and Kashmir, and by the District and Tehsil People's Courts. In all courts, cases shall be tried with the participation of the people's Judges with the exception of cases specially provided for by law...The High Court of Jammu and Kashmir is elected by the National Assembly for a period of five years. The lower courts are appointed by the High Court for a period of five years, with the exception of the People's Courts, which are elected by the People's Panchayats for a period of five years.'[57]

Naya Kashmir was extremely articulate on the subject of local administration, the level where the reputation of a government is made and unmade. It said:

> The organs of State power in District of the Tehsils, Cities and Villages, shall be the People's Panchayats. The People's Panchayats direct the activities of the organs of administration subordinate to them, ensure the maintenance of State order observance of laws and the protection of the rights of citizens, direct local, economic and cultural development in fulfillment of the National Plan, organize civil defence, and draw up the local budget. The People's Panchayats adopt decisions and issue orders within the limits of the powers vested in them by law. The executive and administrative organs of the People's Panchayats are the Executive Committees elected by them, composed of a Chairman, Vice Chairman, Secretary and Members.
>
> The Executive Committee of the People's Panchayats are directly responsible to the People's Panchayats which elected them and are also subject to the Council of Ministers of the States. The People's Panchayats are elected by the people of their area of jurisdiction for a period of five years. The ratio of representation in the People's Panchayats shall be determined by law.[58]

This again was a model adopted from the communist mode of governance that was followed in USSR. However, the success of this model had been questioned even at that point of time. Additionally, it also depended heavily on the widespread presence of the cadre of workers at the village and local level. It can be conceded that the National Conference had the presence of sufficient numbers in the valley, but the same was far from true in the Jammu, Ladakh, Poonch and Gilgit-Baltistan region. This situation carried the seeds of resentment in the majority who did not support the National Conference, and was undemocratic and blatantly unjust. But if the provisions regarding the functioning of the local administration as well as the judiciary and the role of the elected nominees were to be selectively implemented, then it had the seeds of debilitating corruption and oppression.

On the important subject of economy, it did have a separate clause, but confined itself to saying: 'The economic life of the State shall be determined and directed by the National Economic Plan for the purpose of increasing public wealth, of ensuring a steady rise in the material and cultural level of working men and women, and consolidating the defence capacity of the State.'[59] It must be clarified that the word 'National' in the context of the State only meant Jammu and Kashmir State and not India.

The Naya Kashmir plan, as the document was titled, despite its flaws, was a document of change and proved to be immensely popular in Kashmir. It was a blueprint for a welfare state and was far in advance of its times. But it would have been unrealistic to expect Maharaja Hari Singh to accept these demands though he was favourably inclined on a number of them. He, by his own admission, was willing to assume the role of a constitutional head but to expect him to concede certain other demands, particularly regarding the judiciary and local administration, was expecting too much of any dynastic monarch. In fact, even the sympathizers of the National Conference in India were not too keen to go to the extent that Naya Kashmir had gone. As for the land reforms, the Maharaja had already initiated the process of radical reforms on becoming the ruler of the State. Apart from bestowing proprietary rights upon the tenants and distributing the village lands, he had freed the peasantry from the clutches of usury. He could be expected to accept some reasonable reforms, but certainly not the kind of sweeping reforms that the National Conference envisaged.

On the face of it, the Naya Kashmir vision was a significant improvement in the stance towards the State. Historically, the anti-Dogra movement, of first the Muslim Conference and then the National Conference, had consistently claimed that the Dogra rule in Kashmir was a product of a document that was nothing more than a 'sale deed', and as such, did not have the authority to subjugate the people of one region to another. The implied meaning of the National Conference movement had been that it did not recognize the 'State of Jammu and Kashmir', as created by the Dogras. Having thus argued in the past and without retracting the stated philosophy, and the fact that the demands presented to the Maharaja in 1944 bore the title of Naya Kashmir, it was obvious that the manifesto thus created was only for the people of Kashmir, and other regions of the State were only in the peripheral vision of the movement. The unstated purpose was of pushing these other regions into subordinate roles. Interestingly, the most influential persons in the life of Sheikh Abdullah during that period—Mahatma Gandhi and Nehru, along with other stalwarts of the Congress—were behind bars, and this gave Bedi and his English wife Freda the opportunity to push their ideology in Kashmir through Abdullah. From the available writings of Freda Bedi and her husband, it is clear that their primary interest was Kashmir, which they had come to like and know. Whether they also knew of the conditions that prevailed in Jammu, Ladakh and Baltistan, is not known since these regions hardly find any mention in their writings. Protestations regarding the separate identity of the Kashmiri people apart, in reality, neither Sheikh Abdullah nor the National Conference were willing to accept that the reforms, as suggested, did not take into account the realities of the regions and cultures of Ladakh and the tribal moorings of the Northern regions of Gilgit, Baltistan, Punial, Hunza, Rondu and other smaller feudatories.

It is also ironical that the commitment of Sheikh Abdullah to the leftist ideology was limited and partial and probably it was no more than a tool to destroy the monarchy and the Dogras. Once he had visited Lake Success to address the Security Council, he was a changed man and had, from then onwards, come closer to the Americans and the western world.

4

The Politics of Quit Kashmir Movement

It is very difficult to say if the State administration failed to suspect the activities of the outsiders, particularly those coming from Punjab, or the British involvement was so strong and obvious that the Maharaja and his administration could not ward off the ever increasing danger from these elements. This had begun in the summer of 1931 and had only accelerated as the years passed. In fact, every summer, people from Punjab camped in Kashmir for long and relaxing sojourns in which, under the mask of leisure, political activity took centre stage among the educated communists. With the configuration of nations in the wake of the Nazi threat in Europe and the England-Soviet Union friendship, the Indian communists too had developed very cordial relations with their fellow ideologues internationally. In Kashmir, the communist visitors from India had discovered a willing partner in Sheikh Abdullah and his political party, the National Conference. Among the regular visitors were Mulk Raj Anand, Balraj Sahni and K.A. Abbas. With Mohammad Din Taseer already present in Srinagar, they made a powerful team to influence young minds.

In the meantime, Congress had launched the 'Quit India' movement against the British but the national party found itself in a very difficult situation as the British, because of the ongoing war efforts, were not prepared to tolerate any jarring note, and promptly put all its leadership in jail. It had happened at a critical stage in the progress towards independence, and as later developments showed, Jinnah and his Muslim League took full advantage of the absence of the top Congress leadership by cooperating in the war effort and getting full support from the British in return.

Quit India had been launched in August of 1942 and it so happened that Bedi was in Srinagar. In his later life he was to record in an interview that he had persuaded the National Conference leadership to stay away from it. But in all probability, Bedi had exaggerated his role in the whole affair as it was widely believed that most of the actions of the Muslim leaders and National Conference had happened with the approval of the British, though Bedi claimed otherwise. 'Sheikh Abdullah, Sadiq and Bakshi all three were lunching with me that day. So instead of arriving at 12 o'clock for lunch, they arrived at 10.30 a.m. "Ah," they came laughing and joking and said, "now goodbye Bedi Saheb, instead of lunching we will be behind bars by the time lunch comes, because this is the situation which has come about." So, we immediately went into consultations and realized that the ruthless administration of the Maharaja was looking for an opportunity to smash the national movement in Kashmir...We said, "Leave alone anti-fascism and anti-imperialism, who is there if the National Conference is removed at the moment to stand between the Maharaja's ways and the people and stem the tide of destruction and suffering." With this argument we completely assessed the situation and came to the conclusion that no 1942 movement could be launched in Kashmir.'[60]

The claim of Bedi notwithstanding, the hard reality was that the movement would not have gone down well with the Maharaja since he was not only completely immersed in the war effort but the 4 Jammu and Kashmir Battalion (Shibji) was in the thick of war in Burma (Myanmar) and was being much lauded by the British commanders. So there was no doubt that no quarter would have been given by the Maharaja who would have, in the circumstances, got all the support from the British as well. Thus the wisest course for the National Conference was to lie low during that period. Understandably, because of the British and Soviet alliance, the communists too had suspended all their anti-government activities. By the time the war ended the National Conference leaders had begun to fret. But with the war having ended, it was clear as daylight to the British that the victory notwithstanding, they were set to lose their empire since it was no longer feasible to hold on to the colonies. Being exhausted by the war effort and the destruction of the economy and society as it existed before the war, they would have been less inclined to support the Maharaja to eliminate the communist threat from within.

It was then, after the Naya Kashmir memorandum had been presented to the Maharaja in 1944 and without waiting to see if any of the demands were conceded by him, that Sheikh Abdullah launched the 'Quit Kashmir' movement in May 1946 just as Mahatma Gandhi had launched the 'Quit India' movement against the foreign rule of the British in 1942. However, there was a fundamental difference between the two movements. The one launched by Mahatma Gandhi was against a foreign power that had enslaved India. But who was Abdullah asking to quit and from where? He was asking the Dogra ruler of the State of Jammu and Kashmir to quit the State so that Sheikh Abdullah or his chosen Kashmiris could govern not only the valley of Kashmir but the whole State of Jammu and Kashmir. If the Dogras were 'foreigners' in the valley, as Abdullah claimed, then by the same yardstick the Kashmiris too were 'foreigners' in Jammu and Ladakh and the Gilgit-Baltistan regions. In this context, it needs to be recalled that before deciding to launch the 'Quit Kashmir' movement, Sheikh Abdullah had telegraphically approached the British Cabinet Mission—with Lord Pethick-Lawrence (Secretary of State for India), Sir Stafford Cripps (President of the Board of Trade), and A.V. Alexander (First Lord of the Admiralty) as its members—and petitioned for the abrogation of the Treaty of Amritsar, 1846, which he called 'Sale Deed of 1846'. It is not known if he realized the full implication of the demand since it would have meant that Jammu, Kashmir, Ladakh and Gilgit-Baltistan region along with the feudatory States would become separate and independent entities as they were before the Treaty of Amritsar. But certainly, after assuming power, he completely forgot his demand and ruled over areas other than Kashmir as if they were the enslaved colonies of Kashmir. Ironically, he still continued to harp on the theme of the said Treaty being a 'sale deed'.

If Abdullah claimed that his Quit Kashmir was against the autocratic monarchy and not against the Dogra community as a whole, then this movement should have had support from outside the valley as well. But the fact was that there was no such demand in Jammu, Ladakh or the Gilgit-Baltistan region. In fact, the demand of Abdullah did not even have the support of all the Muslims of the whole State. Support from the Hindus was out of the question; and Chaudhary Ghulam Abbas, the undisputed leader of the Muslims of Jammu, had publicly opposed Abdullah's 'Quit Kashmir' call. Consequently, the movement met its deserved fate and failed. Abdullah was arrested but his deputy, Bakshi Ghulam Mohammad, and Ghulam Mohammad Sadiq had escaped to Punjab. They briefed Pandit Jawaharlal Nehru in such a manner that he made a most damaging statement that profoundly affected his relationship with Maharaja Hari Singh. Probably he did that in the heat of the moment and because he could not believe that a movement launched with so much fanfare and support had turned out to be such a flop.

Nehru, a staunch democrat, had an inherent dislike for kings and believed that being relics of the past, they could not have popular support and in the case of Jammu and Kashmir, therefore, popular support for the Maharaja could not possibly be the reason why the movement there had failed. He probably argued that the failure was a result of some sinister design leading to the king's survival, and that the failure of a movement that he thought had popular support was simply not possible. Thus, out of that deep-seated distrust he must have made the statement that was to create so much bitterness and affect the affairs of the State. He said, 'Dead bodies are not handed to the relations for burial according to religious rites but are soaked in petrol and burnt. The mosques, including their inner shrines, have been occupied by the military. A wall of the Juma Masjid of Srinagar has been knocked down to allow passage for military lorries.' He also announced his decision to visit Kashmir to see for himself and express solidarity. Shocking as it was, it also pre-empted the need to see, enquire and then pass judgement, the reason for which Nehru wanted to come to the State. On the other hand, the decision and the statement of Nehru was not appreciated by the Maharaja and he was convinced that partisan and prejudiced minds would bring nothing but trouble in their wake and that such people should not be permitted entry in the State in those contentious times.

When Mohammad Ali Jinnah visited the State in 1943, it had ended on a sour note. Not surprisingly, he bore a grudge against Kashmiris and, later, had been the reason for the forcible attempt of Pakistan to annex Kashmir. There was little doubt that during his visit he had first approached Abdullah in order to enlist him as his commander in the State, little knowing that just as he believed in his destiny of being the messianic leader of the Indian Muslims, similarly Sheikh Mohammad Abdullah believed that he alone was preordained to lead the Kashmiris towards a New Kashmir. Therefore, Jinnah had failed in his primary mission and failed with Abdullah, and consequently, bared his communal fangs and cast his support for Chaudhary Ghulam Abbas as the leader of the Jammu Muslims and a rival of Sheikh Abdullah. On his way back to Rawalpindi he addressed a public meeting at Baramulla, exhorting the people of Kashmir to rally behind the Muslim Conference led by Chaudhary Ghulam Abbas. He was stunned when the Kashmiri Muslims hooted him and he had to make good his escape from the venue. He had again sought permission to visit Kashmir during those tumultuous years when the State was visited not only by Mahatma Gandhi but also by the then President of the Congress, Acharya J.B. Kripalani. While Mahatma Gandhi had announced that he had not come to secure the release of Sheikh Abdullah, Kripalani had confined his visit to holding meetings with the Maharaja. Great as they both were in their own right, they had demonstrated exemplary restraint in respecting the Princely State's policy of not permitting any outside interference in the internal affairs of the State. Jinnah had clearly lost the confidence of the Government of His Highness and was therefore refused permission to enter the State. Now there was Jawaharlal Nehru who not only wanted to enter the State with the explicit purpose of securing the release of Abdullah but had also made unsubstantiated and wild allegations, which the State administration believed were designed to incite the people against the Maharaja.[61]

Thus, Jawaharlal Nehru too was refused permission to enter the State. Contrary to what the partisan reporters accompanying him claimed, Nehru had tried to force his entry by pushing the guard, at which point the ADC of Maharaja Hari Singh, Colonel Bhagwan

Singh, had tactfully allowed him to enter. Later Bhagwan Singh recalled[62] that Nehru had been accompanied not only by some political activists but also by a large contingent of journalists. It was obvious that the purpose of his visit was not just to enquire what had happened in the State following the arrest of Sheikh Abdullah but to also create a spectacle. To diffuse the situation, Bhagwan Singh had escorted Nehru to the Domel Dak Bungalow where he was provided with all facilities, including a car of the State to return to India. It was only after three days of his stay there, and after the Congress Working Committee passed a resolution, supported by the combined might of the Congress President Kripalani, Sardar Patel and Viceroy Lord Mountbatten, that he finally agreed to return without securing the release of Sheikh Abdullah. He was sullen all the while and returned to Delhi after promising that he would return soon. He, of course, did return as one of the defence team for Abdullah, which was headed by Asaf Ali, lived in a house boat and made discreet enquiries about the happenings following Abdullah's arrest. The court finally found Abdullah guilty and he was sentenced to three years of imprisonment.

But in thc process the Maharaja had antagonized a person who was becoming the sole voice and representative of the aspirations of the people of the subcontinent, and for whom Sheikh Abdullah was the key to exposing the fallacy of the two nation theory and then establishing the secular credentials of free India. British India's press too was quick to pounce upon the developments to present the whole episode as another example of an Indian Prince acting arbitrarily and autocratically to satisfy his personal whims. It claimed that Jawaharlal Nehru had made a friendly overture to His Highness' Government that had been reciprocated with a display of grave discourtesy and arrogance. These reports completely ignored the fact that when Sheikh Mohammad Abdullah was arrested on 20th May 1946 in the wake of the ill-advised 'Quit Kashmir' movement, his followers had instigated disturbances not only in Srinagar but also other places. It was in these circumstances, when the State police and military had been patrolling the disturbed areas, that Nehru expressed his desire to visit Kashmir to study the situation. It was a sensitive time, and not the best time for such a visit, yet the Prime Minister Ram Chandra Kak had clearly answered to a query of the press that Nehru would be welcome to come for such a study on 26th May 1946.

But inexplicably, Jawaharlal Nehru, instead of coming to study the situation had chosen to make those wild allegations about dead Muslim bodies not being handed over to relatives for burial and being burnt and the mosque being damaged to make a passage for the military lorries, even before his visit. Mercifully, he later regretted that the issue of the Ruler continuing or not was raised, but in Kashmir serious damage had been done, even though correspondents of the Associated Press, *The Statesman* and *The Hindustan Times* denied that what was alleged to have happened, really took place. They had written this on the basis of the information gathered from their sources within the National Conference. Earlier, on 30th May 1946, the Maharaja's Government had also denied all the charges in an official communiqué.

Unfortunately, Nehru had been taken in by the communist propaganda launched by Lahore-based friends of Sheikh Abdullah and the National Conference. It is also interesting to note that even though the English press portrayed Maharaja Hari Singh as another example of a typical Indian autocratic prince of wayward ways, during that crucial period, Freda Bedi remained in Srinagar without being forcibly deported, and actively rendered help to the underground workers of the Quit Kashmir movement. While she was in Kashmir, with her newborn son Kabir Bedi, and when the movement started, 'the Police wanted me to leave Kashmir as they knew Papa [B.P.L. Bedi] and I were friends of the rebels. So they issued a notice to me to leave. I wrote on the back of the notice that I didn't accept it, as I didn't recognize the people who issued it.'[63] She was also served a deportation order, which also was ignored by her.[64]But no coercive methods were used by the State. Not once did she accuse the Maharaja's government of any harsh treatment except that she was continuously followed by the Intelligence people. She had continued to do what she had wanted to do till, according to another letter written by her, she was sent a message by Sheikh Abdullah to leave the State.[65] By no stretch of imagination could such a kid-glove treatment be attributed to a 'wayward autocrat' that the Maharaja was accused of being.

Clearly, Nehru was visiting Kashmir on a mission to denigrate Maharaja Hari Singh and called upon the All States Peoples' Conference, consisting of the Praja Mandals, the Lok Parishads, the State Congresses and other like-minded parties of the princely states to hold a meeting on 2nd June 1946 to express solidarity with the 'suffering' people of Kashmir. Not everyone agreed with him and there were many who believed that the movement against the Maharaja was a tactical blunder and were critical of the many inflammatory speeches of Sheikh Abdullah. It was then that Nehru was constrained to withdraw his irresponsible allegations and express regret.[66]

The All States Peoples' Conference was clearly not happy with the direction their struggle had taken in Kashmir and the consequent intervention of Nehru. By the summer of 1946 it was obvious that the exhausted British had no longer the will to hold on to the colonies and were willing to leave and hand over power to the Indians. With the victory so close, the parties in the princely states did not desire to have the bogey of communism raised against them as that could lead to repression. But in Kashmir, the communists had found a willing partner. Unmindful of the hatred that Sheikh Abdullah bore for the Dogras, they therefore did not pay heed to its long term consequence. They were pleased with what they had done, and more so since Nehru too had been drawn into that struggle.

With the turn of events at the All States Peoples' Conference, Nehru partially recognized his error. On 12th June 1946 he publicly contradicted his earlier statement by confessing that 'I have no present information which can substantiate them [the allegations] and regret that I gave publicity to these two incidents without sufficient proof…as regards to the allegation about the wall of Juma Masjid, it appears that there is a wooden gate and a military lorry passing through accidentally dislodged some bricks of a column. This may have given rise to the story. Anyhow I am sorry that I stated something which was not correct.' Amazingly, the regret notwithstanding, he did not let the matter rest there and added that this did not alter anything as the allegations were in themselves really not important. To him what was more important was the 'wholly uncalled for and unwise' act of arresting Sheikh Abdullah and the subsequent action taken by the authorities. He went on to reiterate his demand that Sheikh Abdullah be immediately released and that there could be no peace till he had been released.

One did not need to be on the same page as Prime Minister Kak to see that Nehru was partisan as far as Kashmir was concerned, and that no useful purpose would be served by his visit to Kashmir. On the other hand there was a possibility that the situation might deteriorate. Nehru though was adamant and he sent a telegram to the Maharaja on 17th June 1946 that he was coming to Kashmir to help put an end to the complicated situation. He also suggested that he be extended a welcome and all facilities. The Maharaja's response was immediate and categorical. He was determined to avert all unfortunate consequences that might arise because of the visit. In response, Nehru did send a reply but it reached the palace on 19th June, and before an answer could be given he had tried to force his entry into the State with a large number of supporters from British India, including a press party.

It was not the first time that the Maharaja had to face trouble because of the unfettered support to miscreants coming from British India. The British had earlier used the Punjab border to encourage Punjabi Muslims to create trouble so that the Maharaja could be coerced to part not only with the sovereign control over the whole of the Gilgit agency but also the administrative matters of the State. Once again, he had to face the same situation, though at the hands of his countryman for whom he had high regard. Not surprisingly, he suspected that what happened at Domel was a classic case of an overenthusiastic republican, that is, Nehru, who had gone overboard with his statements. If he had been coming to the State to help resolve the complicated situation, as he claimed, then where was the need to bring along the press and a crowd of supporters? He did not have an open mind when it came to Kashmir and the Dogras, and his tirades against the Maharaja were usually borne out of deep seated prejudice against the old order in general and Maharaja Hari Singh in particular.

The tirades coming from Nehru were disappointing for the Maharaja as they came from a person who had such an incisive and critical intellect for understanding the various stages of progression of historical forces. Nehru must have read the account of Kashmiris given by Sir Walter Lawrence in his book *The Valley of Kashmir*. He had not treated the accounts of many foreigners who had come visiting Kashmir in the past as truthful and objective. In his opinion, they had only known the Kashmiris superficially and hence their opinions could not be taken seriously. And indeed, looking at some such opinions, he was right in thinking so. For example, Doctor Arthur Neve, who was among the first foreigners who entered Kashmir, who worked as a missionary for years, and was considered a great well-wisher of Kashmiris, described them thus: 'They are as treacherous as the Pathan, [but] without his valour; more false than the Bengali but equally intelligent; cringing when in subjugation, they are impudent when free.'[67] These are not the words of an objective person but of an ignorant racist.

But not all accounts of travellers could be dismissed. Moorcraft's description of Kashmir five years after Maharaja Ranjit Singh had annexed it to his kingdom was not biased or ignorant opinion, it was reportage, and it was gloomy. It was in 1824 that Moorcroft had thus described the situation in Kashmir: 'Everywhere the people were in the most abject condition, exorbitantly taxed by the Sikh government, and subjected to every kind of extortion and oppression by its officers—not one six-tenth of the cultivable surface is in cultivation, and the inhabitants, starving at home, are driven in great numbers to the plains of Hindustan.' Even more revealing was the observation that 'The Sikhs seemed to look upon the Kashmirians as little better than cattle—the murder of a native by a Sikh is punished by a fine to the Government from sixteen to twenty rupees of which four rupees are paid to the family of the deceased if a Hindu and two rupees if a Mohammadan.' It was in the context of such assessments of Kashmir and its people that Lawrence had explained the reason behind outsiders' view of the Kashmiri massses as 'untruthful, treacherous and roguish'; that they did not trust anyone, because they had no reason to, and therefore their attitudes were a defence mechanism. They had been oppressed and degraded. Moorcroft reasoned that it was the Dogra rule that had restored some dignity among them. The reforms of Maharaja Pratap Singh and Maharaja Hari Singh had instilled in them not only faith in the governments but in society in general. No ruler prior to Maharaja Hari Singh had done so much for the Kashmiris. In fact, one of the non-Muslim deponents before the Glancy Commission had cribbed that with each new reform, it was the Kashmiri Muslim who stood to gain.

It was the Kashmir described thus by the early foreigners that was brought under the rule of law during Pratap Singh's and Hari Singh's reigns, and laws were sought to be applied even-handedly. Yet Nehru was adamant about the evil character of the Dogra rulers and judged them as he and others judged some of the notoriously despotic rulers among the princes in the rest of the Subcontinent. But probably because of the rise of Jinnah as the undisputed leader of the Muslims and the demand for a separate Muslim homeland, Nehru was constrained to throw his weight behind Sheikh Abdullah, and therefore, had to be an opponent of the Maharaja. Little had he realized that by doing so, he had unwittingly driven a wedge between the Hindus and the Muslims in Jammu and Kashmir. The new politics that had taken roots was inadvertently widening the fault lines that existed in the composition of the State.

5

Under the Shadows of Partition

No sooner had Winston Churchill successfully led the Allies to victory, ending the World War II in 1945, than he was defeated in the general elections in Britain. With the war over and the Congress leaders freed, the approach of the new Labour government led by Prime Minister Clement Attlee, changed towards the Indian leaders. The reality of the end of Britain as a great power had dawned upon them. It had also become clear that the halcyon days of Mohammad Ali Jinnah, when he was humoured so that the Muslim support to British war effort was not affected, had come to an end. He *had* rendered invaluable service to the British Empire during that period of crisis when the Congress had opposed it. Rallying maximum support from India had won him gratitude of virtually every Conservative leader, including Churchill. 'However, that phase was over and the Labour government was looking for an opportunity to withdraw quickly and make it appear a triumph of British policy to transfer power in a negotiated manner, *while ensuring that their strategic interests were properly safeguarded. On that issue, the Conservatives, Liberals and Labour members shared a consensus*' (emphasis added).[68]The new government also realized that as representatives of the vast majority of people, the Congress leaders could no longer be ignored. They were the largest stakeholders in India.

It also needs to be remembered that Jinnah and Dr Bhimrao Ambedkar had taken full advantage of the absence of the Congress during that crucial period when the British had needed all the support that could be mustered. As a consequence, both had efficiently and effectively presented their case to the British. But of the two, it was the Muslim League leader who was to play a defining role in history. With Jinnah's politics, the process, the seeds of which had been sown in the nineteenth century, culminated in the Partition of India, creation of a new State, Independence, and a trail of bloodshed and dark memories that continue to haunt both India and Pakistan to this day.

The first murmurs about the Hindus and Muslims being two nations had found articulation in an editorial dated 19th May 1888 in the weekly magazine *Rafique-i-Hind* by Muharram Ali Chishti of Lahore. Like Sir Syed, Chishti too had opposed the participation of Muslims in the activities of Indian National Congress.[69] The Muslims had, in fact, been going through a period of churning ever since the 1857 War of Independence had brought down the curtain on Mughal rule, or whatever remained of it, in India. Since they were seen to be the main force that had challenged the British authority in India, they also bore the brunt of the brutal British retribution that was unleashed. After 1857, therefore, the social, cultural and educational conditions of the Muslims of India, especially northern India, went into decline. The Hindus, who had also suffered during British retaliation after 1857, but not to the extent that the Muslims had, were quick to recover. They had immediately realized that for much too long they had been the victims of a social order and a system of their own making that discouraged genuine learning and inquisitiveness. The Hindu middle-class found in the end of the Mughal era and the beginning of the British, an opportunity and incentive to break free of the shackles of superstitions, irrational conventions and beliefs. In this they found western education a handy tool and embraced it with enthusiasm and vigour. This new education also gave the Hindus an opportunity to gain employment in the new system of governance and curry favour with the British regime. Thus while the Hindus were turning a leaf, the Muslims' fortunes were ebbing away.

The Muslim middle and upper classes had been worried about their future with the establishment of British rule in India. In fact, ever since the East India Company replaced Persian with

Urdu as the official language among the lower echelons of United Provinces in 1837, they had begun to feel insecure. The awareness among Hindus and Muslims about their respective identities also began with it simultaneously. While the Muslims felt the first signs of uncertainty about their future, the Hindus began to entertain thoughts of assertion and reawakening, along with the simultaneous weakening of the Muslim community. Thus, there were two mutually antagonistic strains running through Indian society, pulling both the communities in opposite directions.

In the twentieth century, these divisions became sharper with a number of Hindu and Muslim ideologues coming to the forefront and presenting their respective religions as not only superior but also exclusive. Among the Muslims, Allama Dr Mohammad Iqbal emerged as the leading light. In literary history, a partisan can argue that he was a superior poet to Mir Taqi 'Mir'[70] as well as Mirza Ghalib[71]. He began his poetic career as a proponent of Indian nationalism and went to the extent of calling Lord Ram as 'Imam-i-Hind'. But after his return from England and Europe, he began to champion exclusively Muslim causes, proclaiming the superiority of Islam. By the time the Allahabad session of the All India Muslim League took place in 1930, Iqbal had concluded that the Muslims could not achieve the glory that they were destined for unless a separate Muslim State was created. This demand, titled 'Iqbal's Call', has been debated and analyzed by historians to no end but till date there is no definitive answer to the contours of Iqbal's 'State'. He had contested the interpretation that had been lent to it by the media and had clarified that by 'State' he never meant a separate country for Muslims. However, notwithstanding his protestations, the 'call' had caught the imagination of Muslims.

Iqbal's call was picked up by another Punjabi, Chaudhary Rahmat Ali. In 1933, as a student at Cambridge University, along with some other students, Ali produced a pamphlet, 'Now or Never', in which the idea of a separate Muslim State was presented. It was in that pamphlet that the name Pakistan first appeared. 'It was an acronym derived from the five Muslim-majority regions of north-western India—Punjab, Afghania [North-West Frontier Province], Kashmir, Sind and Baluchistan [where *tan* stood for Baluchistan]...

[Ali] began to lobby conservative British politicians to support his political schemes.'[72]He argued that 'We have as a nation, nothing in common with them [Hindus], nor they with us. Individual habits, as in national life, we differ from them as fundamentally as from any other civilized nation in the world...We do not inter-dine, we do not intermarry. Our national customs and calendars, even our diet and dress are different.'[73]

Among the Hindus too, there had been hard and exclusivist opinions for decades since the crushing of the 1857 uprising and the end of Mughal rule after that. Now, these opinions and voices became stronger in the early 20th century and galvanized a section of the Hindus into organizing themselves into a semi-militant organization in 1925 in Nagpur. With the rise of Nazis and their apparent invincibility by 1939, this brand of Hindus felt that their philosophy of being superior had been validated with the assertion of the superiority of the Aryan race in Germany. The rise of this fundamentalist strain among the Hindus had raised alarm bells among the Muslims and they gradually began to set a new agenda in which the need for a separate Muslim state was emphasized. Actually, this was at odds with the concept of Islam since Islam did not recognize territorial criteria for a Muslim homeland. However, now that the politics and the challenges of the day had redefined the principles of a State, they pushed for a separate homeland.

In this, they received considerable support from the British since as early as 1906, when the Muslim League was established. Theodore Beck[74] and Theodore Morison[75] were among the earliest English voices that advocated the cause of the Muslims, just as there were some English voices in India espousing the cause of Indian nationalists. No sooner had the Muslims begun to organize themselves as a political force, than the British voices had begun to encourage and support them into establishing themselves as a separate identity, in order to prevent the coming together of both the communities under the banner of the Indian National Congress.

As noted earlier, after the end of the Second World War, the goal of the Labour government of Clement Attlee was to transfer power to Indians in a manner that it appeared like a victory of the British policy of negotiated transfer of power while also safeguarding the British geostrategic interests in the region. Clearly, for the British, their own interests were as important as the need to transfer power to the Indians who yearned to live as free, independent and sovereign people. These contradictory considerations of the British—which is, their realization of the impossibility of sustaining their Indian colonial enterprise after World War II and therefore an urgency to shed the colony soon; and their desire to still safeguard their geostrategic interests in South Asia—must be understood and borne in mind when thinking of modern Indian history. This is as important as Partition and the Independence of India. It is particularly of great significance since it had a direct bearing on the State of Jammu and Kashmir and turned it into a land of never ending conflict.

No sooner had the British intention of transferring power to Indians been made known than the British military minds were redrawing their plans for the future from the military's point of view. Sir Claude Auchinleck, the Commander-in-Chief of the British Indian Forces wrote a top secret memorandum on 11th May 1946 about the 'Strategic Implications of the inclusion of "Pakistan" in the British Commonwealth' either as one unit in the north-west of the subcontinent, or as two with the second part in the north-east zone. He opposed it on the ground that in such a scenario it would not serve British interests in the Indian Ocean because it would be a weak state in military and economic terms. He argued that on the other hand, India would not only be stronger but also estranged from Britain and in that case it would drift closer to the Soviet Union. Therefore, he argued that the unity of India should be maintained and India should be kept in the British Commonwealth so that Britain had the freedom of the seas in the Indian Ocean. By doing so, India would, in time of need, be ready to share Britain's defence to the limit of her resources. Even at this stage, the interests of India were not a concern for the British and the only thing Auchinleck was worried about was how to contain the Soviet Union, stop it from increasing its influence and keeping the sea lanes under the control of Britain.

The Indian scholar K.M. Pannikar wrote in 1943: 'The victory of the Allies will see the Soviet Union established as the mightiest power on the Eurasian continent. With her enemy in Europe crushed beyond recovery for a generation and Japan with her international ambitions foiled for a time, Russia will find it easy to resume her southward march, which was interrupted in the nineties of the last century. The Indian Ocean gives her not merely the outlet to the sea for which she has been working for two centuries, but a commanding position on one of the oceanic areas...Russia no doubt has no desire to annex the territories of other nations; but integral alliances with other nations organized on the basis of Soviet republics, is her policy in Asia as well as in Europe...If India passes into the orbit of the Soviet Union and finds a stable position in that alliance, the latter, already dominant in the Balkans and Central Europe, will become a world organization, such as Lenin could not have dreamed of: irresistible in its power, unequalled in its economic resources and manpower, and having a territorial basis spread over practically the whole of Asia and Europe. The eclipse of the British Empire would be the natural and inevitable outcome.'[76] Coming at the time as it did, when the War was still in progress, it was a scary thought for the British.

The note of Auchinleck needs to be read in the light of Pannikar's comment for appreciating the British desperation. However, this was one voice among many and there were peers of the commander-in-chief who held a contrary view. Among the dissenters was General Officer Commanding-in-Chief of the Eastern Command, Lieutenant General Sir Francis Tuker, who was convinced that Hinduism was a superstitious religion and because of the prevalent caste system, development of national solidarity was almost impossible. He argued that in its absence the oppressed Indian masses would drift towards communist ideology and, therefore, closer to the Soviet Union. In fact, Lieutenant General Tuker had a grand fantasy about creating a Muslim power in alliance with Britain to halt the Soviet Union's march towards the Persian Gulf. He had this quixotic vision of creating a Muslim strip from North Africa through Islamia Desertia (Arab land), Persia and Afghanistan to the Himalayas to serve British interests.

Interestingly, even General Auchinleck had a second thought about India soon after and he expressed his doubts about India's dependability. But even before that there was considerable support for the idea of Pakistan among the British officers and politicians. Alex von Tunzelmann, a modern day historian and journalist who wrote *Indian Summer: The Secret History of the End of an Empire* in 2007, asserted that a secret pact between Churchill and Jinnah existed as far back as 1940 in which the former pledged Pakistan as a reward for the Muslim help during the Second World War. This pact did not come to light since its exposure would have presented Jinnah as a British agent. Moreover, even Churchill would have been accused of treason since division of India was not the official policy of Britain at that point in time.[77] Tunzelmann goes on to confidently claim that documentary evidence existing in 1943 revealed that Churchill was convinced that Pakistan needed to be created. It was not only Churchill who was rooting for Pakistan in England as, according to Tunzelmann, even Emperor George VI, and his Queen, were '100% [for] Pakistan'.

As far as Jinnah's relationship with Churchill was concerned, he had met him at his country house on 7th December 1946 and, subsequently, invited him to a luncheon party at Claridge's on 12th December. However, Churchill warmly wrote to Jinnah a day before the invitation to excuse himself from being publicly associated 'at this juncture'. He instead directed him to correspond at a different address and that he would always sign as 'Gilliat' in future correspondence! He also enquired about the pseudonym that Jinnah would be using.[78] Even Wavell had mentioned in his diary dated 29th March 1944 that when he met Churchill in 1944, 'the PM…launched a long jeremiad about India which lasted for about forty minutes. He seems to favour partition into Pakistan, Hindustan, Princestan etc.'[79] The truth was that the message to Wavell was to 'Keep a bit of India'. Thus for the English, Indians were dispensable in the interest of English geo-strategy, just as they had been during the War when Churchill had ordered hoarding of food grains to augment the war effort even if Bengal suffered the worst of human misery in the form of famine that resulted in the death of millions of people. It is no coincidence that this famine too had occurred in 1943 when Churchill had already committed himself to delivering Pakistan to Jinnah.

It is very obvious that the British had no doubts about their objectives. The fact that the Conservatives, Labour and Liberals were one in their mind regarding what the British geostrategic interests in the region were, makes it hard to believe that they did everything to avert the tragedy, horror and trauma that was to be the fate of the subcontinent. A colonial power that could deliberately allow millions from their colony to die of hunger to serve their interests—and whose prime minister, when informed of the millions who were dying and needed extra food by the Viceroy Lord Wavell would respond by asking 'why Gandhi hadn't died yet!'—[80] such a power could go to any extent to serve its geostrategic interests, too. Therefore, the events that happened before the departure of the British need to be critically examined.

Soon after it was made known that the plans of transferring power in India were at an advanced stage, the country was plagued by communal violence. This began a full year before the British actually handed over power and the person who lighted the first matchstick was Mohammad Ali Jinnah. He gave a call for 'Direct Action'[81] on 16th August 1946 to get his demands fulfilled. It was, in effect, a call for violence and more than 4,000 lives were lost in Calcutta. The violence soon spread to other places, notably Noakhali, Bihar, United Provinces (modern Uttar Pradesh), Punjab, and the North-West Frontier Province. In most of these places there were Congress governments in power and the British conveniently passed the responsibility of the orgy of violence on to them.

The violence that had followed the call for Direct Action had cast a shadow on the future of India as a united country. By December 1946, communal violence had reached the Hazara district of the North-West Frontier Province (NWFP) on the border of northern Punjab, not far from the boundary of Jammu and Kashmir. Hundreds of Hindus and Sikhs were murdered. They were a prosperous but small minority in the predominantly Muslim district and had been living with traditional amity and dominating the entire wholesale and retail trade.[82] In addition they were also moneylenders to whom the majority of rural Muslims were heavily indebted. These killings were followed by violence in other places in Punjab on 24th January 1947. By March, the rioting, loot, plunder, rape and murder became rampant all over Punjab. On 2nd March, 1947, the Unionist Chief Minister of Punjab, Khizr Hayat, had thrown in the towel and resigned. Jinnah welcomed the news with glee and hoped that Khan Abdul Jabbar Khan, better known as 'Khan Saheb', Chief Minister of NWFP, would follow suit. Punjab had literally begun to burn and the heat and flames had triggered passions in Mirpur, Poonch, Jammu and the Kathua districts of Jammu and Kashmir.

Maharaja Hari Singh had begun to worry as the communal passions could affect his State too and took stock of what was needed to meet any emergency. State Forces had participated in the Second World War and had been recognized for their gallant contribution. As the war came to an end, the 9th Battalion was the first to return home on 30th September 1945 while the 2nd Battalion was the last to reach home on 30th January 1946.The remaining three, including two Mountain Batteries and the 7th Battalion, never returned since the mountain batteries had been taken over by the British Indian Army and the 7th Battalion disbanded. Thus, when the State was about to enter a very challenging time in its history, it had a diminished capacity to face the situation that was about to arise. The War effort in the State, like elsewhere, had adversely affected the economy, making it difficult for the Maharaja to immediately replenish the trained manpower. Those of the Forces that had comeback and those who hoped to have a period of quiet and rest after long years in the battlefield had hardly settled in, when they were again called for domestic duties. In fact, the 'shadows of coming events had perhaps started appearing even as the last shots of war were being fired and the State Government, in anticipation of the troubled times ahead, requested the Government of India to release the State Forces serving under the Crown as early after the War as possible.'[83]

The communal cauldron had been simmering in the State too and there was danger of violence breaking out. The most serious challenge was in the Mirpur and Poonch regions, which were adjacent to Punjab where communal passions had reached boiling point. This region was predominantly Muslim and since it also had better connectivity with Punjab than with the rest of the State, it had been influenced by the Muslim League propaganda. But even more important was that this region had strong ties with British India through the Indian Army with their youth getting recruited in large numbers. Almost every able-bodied youth, particularly from the Sudhan-Muslim-Rajput community, was a soldier in the Indian army. With the end of the War, the soldiers began to come back home, many among them being part of the demobilization exercise of the British. The fact that a large number of these demobilized soldiers in Punjab had been participating in the loot and plunder that accompanied communal rioting clearly showed that the British had not learnt any lessons from the events that followed the end of the First World War. They cared little for the mental health of their soldiers who had remained in alien lands during their participation in war, without any respite or proper rehabilitation. In India it had culminated in the massacre in Kissa Khwani Bazar of Peshawar in April 1930, following the sustained expression of disapproval of colonial rule. Most soldiers came from areas with poor agricultural facilities and output. Hence when these soldiers suddenly found themselves unemployed and unwanted, they were tempted to take what they could by means fair and foul. The British had done little to find gainful employment for such demobilized soldiers from the princely states which, in turn, had few resources of their own to create jobs for them. With the call for a Muslim homeland reaching a crescendo, they found a calling in addition to the hope of loot from plunder.

The Mirpur-Poonch region had been restive since the 1930s when Chaudhary Ghulam Abbas and Sheikh Abdullah had worked for the unity of the Muslims under the banner of the Muslim Conference. After Sheikh Abdullah parted ways, Chaudhary Ghulam Abbas had carried the Muslim flag with unflinching dedication and had built bridges with the Muslim League. On the basis of a few genuine and many imaginary grievances, low key trouble had been engineered. Accordingly, the 9th Battalion of the State Forces was sent in October 1945 to maintain law and order. The Battalion conducted flag marches and visited almost all the villages of Mirpur and Poonch. Maj. K. Brahma Singh notes, 'These visits served the dual purpose of flag marches and of making contact with the people to listen to their grievances.'[84] It was noted that one of the main grievances was the lack of roads and connectivity. The State government was aware of this but its efforts to construct roads had been stalled by the onset of the Second World War. On their part, the only effort of the British government for helping the princely states that contributed with manpower to the war effort was to give some funds for the development of those recruiting centres. This allocation depended upon the number of recruits that a region had contributed and when the heads were being counted for this purpose, the ex-servicemen got the impression that they were to receive their share individually. When there was no sign of this happening the miscreants took advantage of the situation and spread the propaganda that the Hindu Maharaja had taken their share of money. Later many historians and commentators fell into the same trap and the communal violence was presented as a general rebellion of Poonch against the Maharaja for assimilating the Poonch *Jagir* in 1936. It had hitherto enjoyed a separate special status and was also allowed to raise a small Force of its own. This 'rebellion' would also soon be used by Pakistan as the reason for its armed intervention on behalf of its co-religionists.

Communal violence broke out in the State in March 1946 when the Muslims of Kotli alleged that the Hindu Headmaster of a local school had hurt their feelings by making derogatory remarks. The Government responded by ordering an investigation. The verdict held the Headmaster guilty and dismissed him from service. This turned out to be a provocation to the Hindus who came out in protest. This was countered by the Muslims by taking out a counter procession to welcome the decision. The situation was finally brought under control by the end of the month with the arrest of some militant leaders from both the communities.[85]

Even as the State struggled to remain calm, the Muslim League call for the Direct Action on 16th August 1946 once again threw the State off balance, as by then, even the British had begun to sow the seeds of dissension. When violence broke out again in December in the north and north-western region of Muzaffarabad in Punjab, refugees started pouring into Jammu and Kashmir with about 1,500 of them having come to Muzaffarabad who were then taken care of by the 8th Battalion of the Jammu & Kashmir Rifles.[86] This was followed by more violence across Kohala in Punjab in January 1947 and more refugees took shelter in the safety of Muzaffarabad. Now there were approximately 3,000 refugees that were being looked after by the State Force. By then more violence had broken out in Punjab, making the Poonch-Mirpur border so tense that it required regular patrolling. This meant that the long border with Punjab from Lachaman Pattan in Palandri Tehsil through Owen, Saligram, Hil and Chechian right through Sukhchainpur, Alibeg south of Mirpur and up to Bhimber and Manawar had to be patrolled, to prevent gangs of rioters coming into the State was real.

Even as they tried to ensure peace within the State, the help of the forces was sought by the British when three Sikh villages across the west of Kohala in British India were attacked by a mob of Muslims. By the time the forces reached, many houses had been burnt. However, their arrival had saved the main Gurdwara and about 150 residents were escorted to the safety of Jammu and Kashmir State. According to the notes of Brigadier Krishana Singh, as reproduced by Major K. Brahma Singh, the Chief Secretary of Punjab expressed his appreciation by writing a letter to the British Resident in Kashmir.[87] A portion of the letter read: 'The grateful thanks of the Punjab Government may please be conveyed to the Kashmir Government for the assistance rendered by their troops and police in the British district on the Kashmir State border during the present communal disturbances in Punjab.' Barring the burning of a temple in Palandri, a Gurdwara at Hil and some Hindu shops in Rajouri Tehsil, the month of April was relatively quiet and the army carried out many search operations in the region to recover girls in the region who had been abducted from Punjab and brought to the State by miscreants. Maharaja Hari Singh also made a whirlwind tour of Bhimber, Mirpur, Jhangar, Pander, Kotli, Hajira, Rawalakot and Nowshera. The soldiers were greatly enthused by his presence. He met groups of ex-servicemen in each of these places, and at Rawalakot, an impressive gathering of 600 former soldiers was paraded by retired Captain Khan Mohammad Khan of Palandri, who individually assured the Maharaja of their loyalty.[88]

In the meantime, after much deliberation and exploration of

possibilities, on 20th February 1947, Prime Minister Clement Attlee declared the intention of His Majesty's Government to transfer power to Indians and withdraw from India altogether by June 1948. Among other things he also said:

> His Majesty's Government wish to make it clear that it is their definite intention to take the necessary steps to effect the transfer of power into responsible Indian hands by a date not later than June 1948...His Majesty's Government will have to consider to whom the powers of Central Government in British India should be handed over on the due date, whether as a whole to some form of Central Government for British India, or in some areas to the existing Provincial Governments, or in such other way as may seem reasonable and in the best interest of the Indian people... In regard to Indian States, as was explicitly stated by the Cabinet Mission, His Majesty's Government do not intend to handover their powers and obligations under the paramountcy to any Government of British India...[89]

In hindsight it is apparent that the only goal of the British was to get out of India with hardly any care, either for the country that they had ruled and exploited to the hilt or the princely states which were left to make their own plans for their future. Suddenly, the reality of their economic bankruptcy had dawned upon the British. As Alex von Tunzelmann notes, 'An economic aspiration had started the British Empire. An economic reality would end it.'[90]

The English had arrived in India when it was the most prosperous country of the world with almost a quarter of the world's wealth as its share. When they were ready to withdraw, they had impoverished it to the extent that it had barely 4 percent of the world's wealth. India was wallowing in poverty and squalor and by the end of the war 'Britain [too] was broke. The gap in the balance of payments at the end of war had widened to $8 billion, roughly the cost of administering the Empire for two years. Keynes had told Attlee frankly that he was facing a "financial Dunkirk", and the only option was to seek an aid of around $5 billion from the United States.'[91] Now that the war had ended, the United States felt it opportune to let Britain know that it was not comfortable with its continued colonial history as it reminded it of its own past and the consequent Civil War. The Indian leaders, particularly from the Indian National Congress, had many sympathetic ears in the US and they supported India's freedom. The US, in fact, was in a position to set the agenda for the new world that was emerging from the ruins of the old and looked forward to a role of leadership in the new world. Meanwhile Britain for the first time experienced how a dependent power is treated by the more powerful, and showed all signs of being in a hurry to finish the unpleasant task of packing up.

The British did not even know if they were transferring power to a single authority or more than one or worse, even many. As far as the princely states were concerned, with the lapse of suzerainty of the Crown, all treaties, agreements and functions exercisable by the British would lapse when the British left and the Princes would have the choice of joining either India or Pakistan, failing which they would be independent rulers of their states. But before that there was the challenge of transferring power and dealing with the allied problem.

At that point in time, when Lord Wavell, a quietly efficient man but with little charisma, was the Viceroy of India, Prime Minister Attlee suddenly called Lord Mountbatten and offered him the viceroyalty on 18th December 1946. Mountbatten was reluctant to take up the assignment and put up many excuses, including the need for change of protocol so that he and Edwina could move around and meet Indians unencumbered by the staff. As a final excuse he wanted His Majesty's Government to fix an exact date for the termination of the British Raj. Accordingly, Attlee had fixed the date as 'no later than June 1948'. In his memoirs, Attlee recalled that Mountbatten had concluded that the only course was to set a time-limit and say: 'Whatever happens, our rule is ending on that day.'[92] Thus, a firm date was set for ending the Raj though Attlee was put under intense pressure by the British administrators in India, particularly Bengal, Punjab and United Provinces. He was warned of large-scale violence, civil war and massacres, including the assassination of Mahatma Gandhi and the possibility of famine. But the British Cabinet was of the opinion that the setting of a deadline would force the Congress and Muslim League to cooperate, and that, in the absence of a deadline, the British would be suspected of making communal difference as an excuse to continue the Raj.

The die had been cast and on 19th March 1947, Lord and Lady Mountbatten boarded a plane for India. After a couple of breaks in journey, they landed at Palam airport in New Delhi, where the twin challenges of the transfer of power to Indian leaders and the question of the future of the princely states awaited them. In the end, both the challenges ended in an ongoing tragedy that has kept the successors of Great Britain locked in a state of constant strife.

6

The Maharaja Vacillates?

What went before the accession of Jammu and Kashmir has been subjected to sustained falsehoods for such a long time that historians have routinely accepted those assertions as facts. As a matter of scholarly training, historians often go to the primary sources to test the veracity of any claim. Unfortunately, for long there was little documentary evidence regarding the actual events before the accession. Therefore, opinions were formed on the basis of perceptions and prejudices which became fixed over a period of time as they were never challenged by anyone. But in the light of new evidence in the form of a memorandum[93] written by the Maharaja in 1952 to Dr Rajendra Prasad, President of India, the dominant narrative about accession has to be revisited. An objective appreciation of the Maharaja's contention will also help us in understanding not only the India-Pakistan conflict but also the compulsions of the geography of the region.

Maharaja Hari Singh has been routinely accused of procrastinating the accession to India. Because of this supposed 'delay' it is believed that India nearly lost the State, and is still without large areas of the State that are under the occupation of Pakistan. The Indian army had reached just in time after the so-called 'tribal invasion' to rescue Srinagar and the valley. There is little doubt that had the armed intervention taken place earlier, it would have averted the ongoing war with Pakistan, though even this assumption can be challenged since a Muslim-majority State was, and would have been, and continues to be, central to Pakistan's ideology. But to fully understand the events before the Instrument of Accession was signed, we need to go back to the events that were unfolding and the role played by different characters, including Maharaja Hari Singh. We have seen that when Prime Minister Attlee announced the British decision of drawing the curtain on the Raj, neither he nor his Cabinet had any idea as to who they would be handing over power to. Even as that statement was made on 20th February 1947, Jinnah had been working hard, arousing passions, inciting religious hate and fear among Muslims and literally putting Punjab and Bengal to flames to press his demand for a separate Muslim homeland.

The fate of India and its people, in any case, had been sealed much before Lord Mountbatten arrived in India to oversee the transfer of power. The partition of India became inevitable after the disagreements between the Congress and the Muslim League over the Cabinet Mission Plan.[94] Gandhi was also not prepared to concede that only the Muslim League could nominate candidates from the Muslim quota while the Congress could only nominate from other communities. This would have meant admission that the Congress did not represent the Muslims, which Gandhi would not accept. After that suspicion of Muslims became so deep that partition appeared to be the only course left if civil war was to be averted. Initially, Jinnah had supported the Cabinet Mission's proposal and even Patel and Nehru were willing to accept it, even in the face of pressure being built by Gandhi. This had aggravated the Muslim mistrust of Gandhi.[95] Finally, when Nehru informed Lord Wavell of his willingness to form a government under the plan on 10th August 1946, Jinnah not only backed out but also gave a call for Direct Action to press the demand for the creation of Pakistan. This was the signal that triggered communal violence across the fault lines. However, the final declaration of the British decision to quit India came the following year as in the meantime efforts were being made to reach some kind of agreement on who would be the recipient of power, and whether India could, and should be kept united or partitioned.

The champions of imperialism did their best to delay the exit on various grounds, failing which they advocated partition of the country, not really to avoid civil war and bloodshed but because they still believed that Britain should have a pivotal role in the region. Mountbatten has routinely been blamed for the partition and the bloodshed that followed. But as Prof. Kenneth Galbraith wrote in his review of Philip Zeigler's book, *Mountbatten*, there was little that he could have averted, neither partition nor its aftermath. 'I've never been persuaded that facts speak for themselves; in my observation they can be very reticent as to the real truth. ...By the time the Mountbattens arrived in India, there had ceased to be any alternative to partition. Positions, especially, that of Jinnah, were fixed, irrevocable. Perhaps delay would only have meant months of mounting anger and more deaths when partition and independence finally came,' he wrote.

The Mounbattens arrived in New Delhi on 22nd March 1947 and soon Lord Mountbatten realized that there was really no plan with the British to make an orderly exit and to avoid civil strife. The best that Lord Wavell, his predecessor, had planned was a gradual transfer of power to the democratic provinces and the Indian Princes, effectively Balkanizing the country, which suited neither the military plans of the British army nor was it acceptable to Nehru. The Congress had been demanding the British exit for long and believed that the Indians were capable of sorting out their problems and differences without British interference. The Americans too had been pressurizing the British to grant undiluted democracy to the Indians as soon as possible. On the other hand, the British argued that the aftermath of their exit would create an incendiary situation that would reflect badly upon them. It goes to his credit that Lord Mountbatten began his stint as Viceroy with sincerity and honesty as at that point in time Britain had only the limited objective of guarding its geostrategic interests. Therefore, in his first address he candidly confessed, 'I am under no illusion about the difficulty of my task. I shall need the greatest goodwill of the greatest possible number and I am asking India today for that goodwill.'[96] He had in his own style announced his policy for a 'regime [that] was to be frank, inclusive and open-minded. It was now full steam ahead to the transfer of power, and the old guard could come on board or stay on shore as they pleased.'[97] But it soon became clear that his words had failed to impress the people. The economic inequality between the prosperous Hindus and Sikhs and the impoverished vast majority of Muslims in Punjab had triggered violence and Sikhs and Hindus were killed in Rawalpindi and Multan. In Delhi, even as Mountbatten arrived in the capital, a gathering in a mosque in old Delhi was attacked and Muslims were killed.

The challenge of transfer of power had manifested in all its ugliness for the new Viceroy. He had civil war on his hands and he was in no position to handle it. Mahatma Gandhi offered a solution that could only be called utopian. He suggested to the Congress to make Jinnah the Prime Minister. Everyone but Gandhi acknowledged that with inflamed communal passions the offer to make a Muslim Prime Minister and expecting the 75 percent population of Hindus and Sikhs to accept, was an impossible ask. By now even the most devoted followers of Gandhi, like Patel and Nehru, had become weary of this impractical proposal that he had tried to make acceptable a number of times in the past. In the meantime, April had really proved to be a cruel month, with violence breaking out in Delhi, Calcutta, Bombay, Peshawar and Kanpur and the Sikh leaders, Master Tara Singh, Kartar Singh and Baldev Singh demanding a partition of Punjab and creation of a Sikhistan or Khalistan that included Lahore and Shimla, failing which they warned of an armed struggle.

Before the month of April ended the communal environment had worsened. As Fredrick Burrows, Governor of Bengal, commented, he was no longer sitting on a barrel of gunpowder since he had got off it to sit on a whole magazine of gunpowder that was ready to go off any moment.[98] On 30th April, Jinnah reiterated his demand for Pakistan that consisted of Muslim-majority provinces of Sindh, Punjab, the North-West Frontier Province and Baluchistan in the west, and Bengal and Assam in the east, which also included the city of Calcutta, even though the population of the city was mainly Hindu. Anything less, particularly any sub-partition of Bengal or Punjab, would result in a 'truncated or mutilated, moth-eaten Pakistan',[99] he added. But the fact was that the only practical answer to the problem was to partition Bengal and Punjab on the grounds that if the country could be partitioned then so could the States. Jinnah vigorously argued against the partition of the two

States while demanding partition of India. He disputed that in both Bengal and Punjab the Hindus identified themselves as Bengalis and Punjabis respectively and less as Congress supporters and that the integrity of the provinces needed to be preserved. But Mountbatten replied that this could be argued for the country as well and if this was accepted then there would be no Pakistan.[100]

By May, it had become exceedingly clear to Mountbatten that the transfer of power to a united India was impossible. However, he also felt that partitioning the country was madness since it would 'reduce the economic efficiency of the whole country'. But the communal frenzy among Muslims, Hindus and Sikhs that had seized the country left him with no other option. He, therefore, concluded that the 'most we can hope to do…is to put the responsibility for any of these mad decisions fairly and squarely on the Indian shoulders in the eyes of the world, for one day they will bitterly regret the decision they are about to make.'[101] Meanwhile, as the drift of Mountbatten's thought was caught by the Congress too, Gandhi laid all the blame of communal violence on the presence of the British on Indian soil. He told Reuters, 'If the British were not here, we would still go through the fire no doubt, but the fire would purify us.'[102]By now Mountbatten was fairly clear about what he wanted to do and by the middle of May 1947 he had devised a plan and presented it to His Majesty's Government in London. But when the contours of the plans were accidentally and unofficially revealed to Nehru by the Viceroy, he was livid with white rage. It was clear that if the plan were made public now, Nehru would openly and summarily reject it, and that would cause huge embarrassment for London too, besides irreparably damaging the credibility of Mountbatten.

To begin with, the plan which shocked and angered Nehru was inappropriately called 'Plan Balkan'. It entailed the partition of India in which there would be two dominions, India and Pakistan, and each of the provinces could choose which one to join. It also envisaged the division of Bengal and Punjab, if they so desired, or, if they so wanted, they could become independent nations. The North-West Frontier Province was also given the choice of becoming independent if it did not wish to join either India or Pakistan. Extending the same principle of self-determination to the 565 princely states, each one of them, big or small, could join the dominion of its choice which, in Nehru's opinion, meant becoming feudatories or Allies of Great Britain. Nehru clearly saw the nightmarish scenario of the 'Balkanization' of India and creation of numerous small but mutually antagonistic nation-states, and being too small and weak to survive, serving the interests of neighbouring giants as well as Britain, USA, Russia, China and Afghanistan. 'It would stir up civil conflict, undermine the central authority, and split the army, police and services.'[103]

When Mountbatten informed Whitehall that the transfer of power plan was not acceptable, the British government was naturally upset with him for it believed that he had led the Government up the proverbial garden path and was called to London and reprimanded. This was not taken kindly by him and he threatened to resign. It took Lady Mountbatten and V.P. Menon a while to calm him down.[104] Thereafter, a repeat exercise of intense confabulations took place before Nehru could be made to accept dominion status in return for an early transfer of power. This satisfied the powers in London. Mountbatten again went to London, presumably to finalize the details of the transfer of power and also met Churchill and other Conservative leaders of the opposition. Even the irascible imperialist, Churcill, seemed in agreement, for it satisfied his ego of remaining on top of the Empire and he informed Prime Minister Attlee that the Conservatives would support the proposal in parliament if India decided to accept dominion status and not full independence. Both, the aborted plan about transfer of power and the one that found approval of the opposition too, clearly demonstrated the British intention was more focused on its own interest rather than on Indian interests and preferences. After failing with the balkanization plan, the next desirable plan was for India to remain connected with the Empire in some form. While for Lord Mountbatten it had more to do with the brotherhood of the Commonwealth, world peace and understanding, for the Conservatives it was because the emphasis remained on British advantages.

Finally, after securing the broad consent of the main stakeholders in India and after internal debates in London, on 3rd June 1947 the partition plan for India was announced, under which the successor states were to be given dominion status and were to have autonomy as well as their own constitutions. As far as the princely states were concerned, they had the right to decide which of the two dominions they desired to join. It was known as the Mountbatten plan, since he had thought of it. He also had the responsibility of making the Congress and Muslim League agree to it and then had the burden of executing it. As far as the states administered by the British were concerned, there was not much debate and conflict barring the regret about the partition of Bengal and Punjab. The challenge was with the princely states that had come to enjoy their internal autonomy and many among them were arbitrarily ruled. In fact, the behaviour of some of the rulers was so appalling that even a staunch conservative like Lord Curzon had frankly written to Queen Victoria that 'for all these failures we are responsible...we have condoned their vices, we have worked at their vices.'[105] This last part of the comment was more telling since the British had left no incentive with the princes for improving their governance. Unless their excesses were too scandalous, the British were not inclined to interfere in their affairs and gradually a stage had come where they firmly believed that their interests lay with the British. Some of them did not want even the dominion status because it threatened change in the existing system where 'foreign invaders would be dealt with, domestic challenges neutered, and the ravening mob readily suppressed, all by the might of the British Indian Army.'[106] In case a prince was too bold or crazy as to raise the banner of rebellion, the British would only remove him from the throne and put some other family member on the throne. Nurtured thus over long years, the princes were the most worried lot with the announcement of the British exit plan.

On 4th July 1947, the Bill of Indian Independence was presented to the British parliament for discussion, which passed it after due deliberation for the King to sign on 18th July 1947. The Indian Independence Act read:

> Be it enacted by the King's most Excellent Majesty, by and with the advice and consent of the Lords Spiritual and Temporal, and Commons, in this present Parliament assembled, and by the authority of the same, as follows:-

1. (i) As from the fifteenth day of August, nineteen hundred and forty-seven, two independent Dominions shall be set up in India, to be known respectively as India and Pakistan...

2. (1) Subject to the provisions of subsections (3) and (4),territories of this section, the territories of India shall be the territories under the sovereignty of His Majesty which, immediately before the appointed day, were included in British India except the territories which, under subsection (2) of this section, are to be the territories of Pakistan.

(2) Subject to the provisions of subsections (3) and (4) of this section, the territories of Pakistan shall be:

(a) The territories which, on the appointed day, are included in the Provinces of East Bengal and West Punjab, as constituted under the two following sections;

(b) the territories which, at the date of the passing of this Act, are included in the Province of Sind and the Chief Commissioner's Province of British Baluchistan; and

(c) if, whether before or after the passing of this Act but before the appointed day, the Governor-General declares that the majority of the valid votes cast in the referendum which, at the date of the passing of this Act, is being or has recently been held in that behalf under his authority in the North West Frontier Province are in favour of representatives of that Province taking part in the Constituent Assembly of Pakistan, the territories which, at the date of the passing of this Act, are included in that Province...

7. (1) As from the appointed day:

(a) His Majesty's Government in the United Kingdom have no responsibility as respects the government of any of the territories which, immediately before that day, were included in British India;

(b) the suzerainty of His Majesty over the Indian States lapses, and with it, all treaties and agreements in force at the date of the passing of this Act between His Majesty and the rulers of Indian States, all functions exercisable by His Majesty at that date with respect to Indian States, all obligations of His Majesty existing at that date towards Indian States or the rulers thereof, and all powers, rights, authority or jurisdiction exercisable by His Majesty at that date in or in relation to Indian States by treaty, grant, usage, sufferance or otherwise; and

> (c) there lapse also any treaties or agreements in force at the date of the passing of this Act between His Majesty and any persons having authority in the tribal areas, any obligations of His Majesty existing at that date to any such persons or with respect to the tribal areas, and all powers, rights, authority or jurisdiction exercisable at that date by His Majesty in or in relation to the tribal areas by treaty, grant, usage, sufferance or otherwise.[107]

Notably, the Act had just allowed the paramountcy to lapse on the fifteenth day of August 1947, thereby making them technically independent. Now this was a situation that had made Nehru furiously reject the earlier 'Plan Balkan' of Mountbatten. But this time around, he was assured that the princely states would have to merge with either of the two dominions. For this purpose, Mountbatten had already set up a States Department since he had been convinced that they needed to be merged in either of the two countries. According to its plan, India asked them to give control of foreign affairs, defence and communications to the Government of India and in return, their privy purses and other domestic affairs would be their concern. One of the wisest steps during those crucial days was to make Vallabhbhai Patel in-charge of the States Department, who immediately realized that with his semi-royal status, Lord Mountbatten could be an asset in the gigantic task of merging the States. His personal friendship with many of the princes was an additional qualification. As far as London was concerned, it had left this task deliberately vague for Mountbatten to sort out with the only instruction that he should persuade the rulers to rapidly move towards democratic government.[108] Accordingly, he went about the task of persuading the princes to be more democratic, which in the circumstances meant that they should consult the majority in their kingdom before taking a decision regarding merger. This was never meant by the Act but interpreted thus by Mountbatten. It was to be the cause of further conflict in one of the States. He also pledged to Patel that he would deliver a 'full basket of apples'.

On 9th July 1947, representatives of the princely states met in Delhi where it became clear that a great majority among them were prepared to join India. Some, however, proved difficult but the combined onslaught of Mountbatten's charm, gentle knocks on their heads and the tough line adopted by Patel brought them to heel. Many at that time in Britain questioned the strong-armed tactics of Mountbatten but the truth was that he was only trying to bring in as many princes as possible within the democratic fold of India. Unlike those sitting in Britain, he was aware that all the princely states had people's organization that were working hard to gain democratic control of their states, and Nehru was the President of the All India States Peoples' Conference. If the princes could not be cajoled into merging with democratic India, no time would be lost for those organizations to turn rebellious and violent. With the British committed to withdraw on the appointed day, the recalcitrant princes would be devoid of the strength and support that they got from the British in times of emergency. To his critics, Mountbatten replied that he was ensuring that by helping India, he also ensured the goodwill and friendship of independent India. Patel, on the other hand, was blunt enough to tell the princes that only if they willingly signed the Instrument of Accession could they have their privy purses and the attendant baubles.

However, Hyderabad, Kashmir, Bhopal and Junagarh were reluctant. The Nizam of Hyderabad wanted to remain independent and it was rumoured that USA and France were willing to recognize his State as an independent country. The Nawab of Bhopal too wanted to be independent. In both these states, the rulers were Muslim but the majority population was Hindu. Junagarh too was a Hindu majority State with a Muslim ruler. Both Hyderabad and Bhopal were located in the middle of the country and their existence as independent countries could not have been acceptable to Nehru who absolutely loathed balkanization of the country. Both had no contiguity with Pakistan. Junagarh, on the other hand, asserted its discretion of 'joining any of the dominions' and chose to merge with Pakistan. It was argued that even if it did not have land contiguity with Pakistan, it shared the sea territory with Sindh which was to be merged in Pakistan.

The case of Jammu and Kashmir was a peculiar one and for long, challenged the legal minds of all the luminaries. It was the only State that was contiguous to both India and Pakistan. In addition, most of its connectivity was through the proposed nation of Pakistan. The only rail connectivity too was from Pakistan. Another factor in favour of Pakistan was that approximately 75 percent of the population was Muslim even though the ruler was Hindu. In fact, it was the only state in the subcontinent where the majority was Muslim and the ruler Hindu. Thus, on the face of it, everything appeared to be in favour of Pakistan. If Hyderabad, Bhopal and Junagarh were not to merge with Pakistan because the majority population was Hindu in those states then, by the same token, Jammu and Kashmir too could not have merged with India.

Soon, the ruler of Bhopal saw the hopelessness of his situation and finally gave assent for his State's merger with India. However, Hyderabad held out even after 15th August had come and gone. When the Nawab of Junagarh acted in a bizarre manner by signing the Instrument of Accession in favour of Pakistan on 16th September 1947 and then absconded to Karachi (Pakistan), along with his 800 dogs and their keepers but without his Begum, the Congress immediately cried foul and the principle of determination of the will of the people was applied to the State. The result of the plebiscite was lop-sided with 1,90,779 votes in favour of India and ninety-one for Pakistan. But the story of Junagarh had a bearing on the events of Jammu and Kashmir and it has been suggested by historians that there was more that met the eye in that episode. Alastair Lamb, no friend of India's cause, believes that 'there was certainly a close relationship between Jinnah and his advisors and the Dewan of Junagarh, Sir Shah Nawaz Bhutto, a prominent supporter of the Muslim League who had taken over charge of the State in May 1947.'[109] The same historian has also pointed out that H.V. Hodson in Chapter 24 of his book *The Great Divide: Britain-India-Pakistan* mentions that Jinnah and his government had seen Junagadh as a weapon in the struggle for Jammu and Kashmir. There were numerous possibilities because of Junagarh. There could be straight trade off with Junagarh for Jammu and Kashmir, with communalism rather than the will of the ruler becoming the deciding factor. The sending of military into Junagarh could also be a ruse to justify the intervention of Pakistan in Jammu and Kashmir and finally, the plebiscite of Junagarh could be an argument for holding the same in Jammu and Kashmir.[110]

While these four States did not accede to any of the dominions by the appointed day, there was the comical and quixotic case of Travancore, which had baulked before signing the accession papers on 30th July 1947. Rumours had been doing the rounds that Travancore had reached an agreement with the British government over the uranium deposits that had been found in the State and that it had also approached the US government to enquire if it was interested in its new found mineral wealth. But the Americans had no desire to put a spanner in the story of an emerging democracy in Asia. The US States Department had warned its Consulate in Madras of showing any interest in Travancore. 'Direct and formal correspondence should be avoided [with officials of Indian princely states] since it definitely encourages US government giving support to moves by certain Indian States to assert their independence from the rest of India…We do not wish to take any action that might interfere with the sound objective of avoiding further balkanization of India.'[111] This had gone a long way in dampening the spirits of the Prime Minister of the State, Sir C.P. Ramaswamy Iyer, who had already declared, during the 25th July 1947 meeting of the Chamber of Princes, that Tavancore would remain independent since it was socially and economically ahead of other merging states and the British administered states too. Merger with India would set the State back. But when he called upon Lord Mountbatten, the treatment that he was given exemplified the firm line that Mountbatten could adopt with those who were not amenable to reason. Mountbatten told Iyer that 'it was reported that Seth [R.K.] Dalmia [the richest industrialist in India at that time and a supporter of the Congress Party] had that morning paid Rs 5 lakh into [the] Travancore Congress Party funds in anticipation of starting internal trouble in the State after 15th August.' The Viceroy, further reported, 'Shortly after his return to his State [from Delhi] at the end of July he was assaulted with a bill-hook and very nearly killed. The State Peoples' Organization turned the heat full on and Travancore immediately gave in. The Maharaja telegraphed his acceptance of the Instrument of Accession to me personally and Sir C.P. Ramaswamy Iyer's friends asked Sardar Patel to call off the State Peoples' movement.'[112] Whatever the methods adopted by

Mountbatten and Patel, they were effective and after the Travancore incident, those who had still not made up their minds to join India, hurriedly sent in their signed documents.

However, these strong-arm tactics could not be applied to Maharaja Hari Singh, either by Lord Mountbatten or Sardar Patel. Jammu and Kashmir was uniquely placed in geography where the interests of various powers and countries converged and conflicted. It was not only contiguous to India and Pakistan, allowing both to stake their claims over it, but also Tibet and Afghanistan. Moreover, only a narrow strip of land separated it from Russia, the big bugbear of Britain. With such a background, it needed a tactful and foresighted handling of the situation.[113]

The only primary source that gave information about what was going through the mind of Maharaja Hari Singh during that time was a Memorandum that he wrote to President Dr Rajendra Prasad in 1952, which rejected the claim of the central government that during the crucial period of 1946-47, the Maharaja had not paid heed to advice being given to him by the Congress leaders. He pointed out that in '1946 when the leaders of the Indian National Congress formed the Viceroy's Cabinet for the Interim Government, I had occasion to meet Mahatma Gandhi and Shri J.B. Kripalani, the then President of the Indian National Congress, when they both visited the State. Mahatma Gandhi suggested that I should have the backing of the people in whatever I did, Shri J.B. Kripalani suggested the immediate release of Sheikh Abdullah because the nominees of the National Conference who were in the Government had resigned.'[114] The Maharaja pointed out that he had already inducted two nominees of the National Conference in the Government and that it was neither proper nor just to entrust the entire Government to only one group. He further said that he was prepared to make more concessions but in doing so he had to bear in mind the safety of the State and maintain balance between the divergent views of different parts of the State.

Meanwhile the proposed Pakistan had already laid claim on Jammu and Kashmir on the basis of its Muslim majority. But for the Maharaja, it was not such a simple case of numbers. In view of the fact that the Maharaja had not let the Viceroy's Cabinet know about his decision, Lord Mountbatten visited the State on 17th June 1947 and spent the next few days talking to the Maharaja, urging him to take a 'reasoned' decision, as he had done with many other rulers. Nehru did not approach the Maharaja because he might have feared that since there was already bad blood between the two because of the detention episode at Kohala in the wake of Sheikh Abdullah's arrest for the Quit Kashmir movement, he may not succeed in cutting any ice with the Maharaja. Therefore, ostensibly, Lord Mountbatten arrived in Kashmir in June 1947 on behalf of Nehru and, contrary to the claims of most historians who have written about the visit, had several rounds of talks. During the course of the talks Mountbatten urged the Maharaja and his Prime Minister, Ram Chandra Kak, not to make any declaration of Independence but to find out in some way the will of the people as soon as possible. He suggested that this be done before 14th August, and also advised them to send a representative to one Constituent Assembly or another. Lord Mountbatten told the Maharaja that the 'newly created States Department was prepared to give an assurance that if Kashmir went to Pakistan, it would not be regarded as an unfriendly act by the Government of India.'[115] The Viceroy went on to stress that Kashmir would find itself in a very dangerous situation if it was not part of one dominion or another. But what left the Maharaja wondering about the real motive of Lord Mountbatten's visit was that he had come prepared with a number of maps to impress upon Hari Singh the geographical reality of the State in relation to India and the proposed new country, Pakistan. In the Maharaja's opinion, by doing this, Mountbatten had subtly suggested that it would be practical and advisable for the State to accede to Pakistan.

Hari Singh suspected the Viceroy's intention because no one was more aware of the British intentions about his State than the Maharaja himself. Right from the time Kashmir came under Dogra rule by the Treaty of Amritsar, 1846, the Dogra rulers had come under pressure from the British to cede control over it. Suspecting the intention of the Viceroy, whose job, in his role as His Majesty's representative, was to protect British interests in the region at all cost, the Maharaja avoided any further conversation on the subject. Lord Mountbatten thus turned his attention to Prime Minister Kak.

(*Transfer of Power* papers, as cited by Alastair Lamb.[116]) He advised Kak that unless the State acceded to either India or Pakistan, it would have great difficulty in protecting itself. He added that 'it was not for him to suggest which Constituent Assembly they should join, but clearly Kashmir should work this out for themselves on the basis of the best advantage to the ruler and his people, and in consideration of the factors of geography and the probable attitude of the Congress and of the Muslim League respectively to Kashmir. If Kashmir joined the Pakistan Constituent Assembly, presumably Mr Jinnah would protect them against pressure from the Congress. If they joined [the] Hindustan Assembly it would be inevitable that they would be treated with consideration by Hindustan.'

Alastair Lamb also does not believe that Mountbatten's advice was even-handed. But unlike the Maharaja, his assessment is that the Viceroy was batting for India. He claims that in case of the Congress, Mountbatten's opinion about Congress' intention to protect the interests of the ruler and his people was unequivocal. However, in the case of Pakistan there was only a probability of doing so. Perhaps Mountbatten was making a subtle suggestion that in the case of Pakistan, there was the risk of a Hindu Raja being overthrown upon encouragement to the majority Muslim population, while the Congress would not allow such a thing to happen.

However, the Maharaja and later many Indian scholars smelt a different British design, which is that Mountbatten was trying to influence Hari Singh and his prime minister by suggesting the geographical option of joining Pakistan. There will always be contrary opinions about Mountabatten's intention and role, but in judging him it needs to be remembered that he was the representative of the British government and this government, headed by the Labour Party, had a newfound zeal for democratic values. Hence, even though there was no mention of the will of the majority in the India Independence Act, in accordance to the instruction of Prime Minister Attlee, Mountbatten had given his own interpretation to the Act and applied it to the princely states.[117] In most cases he appeared to favour India's case, but with Jammu and Kashmir, he may have been a conflict between his personal wish and the wish of his government in Britain.

Soon after Prime Minister Attlee had concluded that winding up the Empire was the only course to take Britain out of its difficult financial situation in a post-World War scene, the only challenge was to withdraw in a manner that would show that Britain was transferring power with the higher goal of democracy in mind, and yet at the same time secure the British geostrategic interests in the region. In this, Labour, Conservatives, the Liberals as well as the King were on the same page. Thus, what Mountbatten was trying to achieve from his visit to Kashmir may have been to secure British interests in the region, which lay in having a friendly power take control of that region. In the opinion of most British politicians, India appeared to be more inclined towards Russia, and hence they thought of the proposed Pakistan as a friendlier ally.

It was at this point that the Maharaja offered the Standstill Agreement to India and Pakistan. Some commentators have suggested that this offer was proof of his inability to take a decision.But more likely, the offer was meant to buy time till sanity had been restored in the subcontinent. During that period in history, India, on both sides of the proposed new border, was in the grip of communal frenzy which ruled out level-headed decisions in a multi-religious State like Jammu and Kashmir. And those who conclude that Hari Singh was vacillating, need to remember that Jammu and Kashmir was not the only State not to have signed the Instrument of Accession in favour of either India or the proposed Pakistan. As Karan Singh records, quoting his father: 'His difficulties [in his words] were as follows: "The People of the State were divided in several groups... The Border Feudatory Territories such as Hunza, Nagar and Chitral and the District of Gilgit where the British influence was supreme were definitely for accession to Pakistan and pressing me to accede to Pakistan without delay and threatening me with dire consequences... The Muslim population of the State was also divided...Mirpur, Poonch, Muzaffarabad, were for accession to Pakistan...Muslims of Kashmir and some Muslims of Jammu who were led by Sheikh Abdullah...did not want the question of accession decided at that stage but wanted me to part with power in their favour so that they could decide the question independently of me...Hindus of Jammu and all the people of Ladakh were for affiliation with or accession to India.'[118] It is obvious from this statement of facts that in the atmosphere then prevailing, any decision would have led to massive resentment and anger among those groups of the State who would have felt aggrieved. With the Standstill offer, this situation could be hopefully averted. Pakistan was quick to accept. Perhaps it was confident that the geographical location and the demography of the State left only one option for it. But soon as time passed, it became impatient with the Maharaja. India on the other hand dilly-dallied, which was probably interpreted by Pakistan as a sign of indifference on its part. In the opinion of the Maharaja, India dealt with the issue in a desultory and half-hearted manner, creating confusion in the minds about its motives.

Having lost patience, Pakistan violated the Standstill Agreement by blockading the supplies to the State. With all routes passing through Pakistan, except one dusty fair-weather cart route from Jammu-Samba-Kathua to Pathankot across the river Ravi, the State was in a precarious situation. Obviously, Pakistan wanted to blackmail the State into submitting to its will. The State soon felt the choke of the blockade unbearable and approached the Government of India for help. But instead of sending immediate help, Lord Mountbatten sent his chief of staff Lord Ismay to impress upon the Maharaja that it was imperative that he decide on the issue of accession. The Maharaja felt that the Viceroy was unable to appreciate the difficulty in taking an apparently straightforward decision about the choice. In fact, there was hardly any pragmatic choice that seemed possible because of the complex character of the State. According to him the people of the State were divided into several groups and each had its own ideas about accession.

There is no doubt that the State was heavily populated by Muslims but in reality they too were a divided lot. The spread of the population was complex. The northern regions, including the Feudatory States were almost completely Muslim in composition and almost 90 percent of Kashmir had a Muslim population. Ladakh was mostly Buddhist with Muslims being in a majority in Kargil. In Jammu region, the western districts of Poonch and Mirpur were heavily populated by Muslims and Hindus were the majority in Udhampur, Jammu and Kathua. The Maharaja also accused the National Conference of obstructing him in deciding the question of accession in favour of India. In this the Maharaja had a point because at that time when a deadline was looming, priority should have been given to taking a decision regarding the accession and leaving the issue of devolution of power to a later date, since that was an internal affair. But obviously, because of their inexperience in such matters, the National Conference had a skewed preference.

As far as the Hindus of Jammu and all the people of Ladakh were concerned, they wanted affiliation with or accession to India. Hari Singh also candidly admitted that a portion of the population in Kashmir wanted accession to Pakistan. Such sharp divisions of opinions were aggravated by the atmosphere created by the madness of Partition. He believed, rightly or wrongly, that in such a communally vitiated atmosphere the minds of the people had been unhinged and it was futile to consult them. He wanted time till these passions subsided and normalcy in human discourse was restored to its civil levels. In view of the cumulative effect of all these factors, namely, Gandhi's and Kripalani's advice to ascertain the will of the people, and the oblique suggestion—at least as it had seemed to the Maharaja—of Lord Mountbatten about accession to Pakistan, and the State's internal contradictions, the Maharaja had offered the Standstill agreements to India and Pakistan. In his opinion that would have bought him enough time to seek the reasoned opinion of the various groups of people and communities. This, however, was not to be because of the impatience of Pakistan.

Most of the blame for the delay in accession has been laid at the doors of the Maharaja, but to be fair to him the advice being given to him by the stalwarts of new India has to be weighed on a fair scale. Not only Mountbatten but also Mahatma Gandhi and Kripalani had given almost identical advice of determining the opinion of the majority. Campbell Johnson is of the opinion that even Sardar Patel was of a similar view as 'when Kak [Prime Minister of the State] came to Delhi in July 1947, he saw Patel, who told him that he did not want the accession of Kashmir against the people's will.'[119] Even if the Maharaja had made up his mind to accede to India, the Indian leaders were literally coaxing him to not do so, and advising him to determine the will of the people, yet not appreciating the fact that the people of Kashmir were not a homogenous mass. There was great regional, ethnic, religious and cultural diversity.

The factor that had made Pakistan impatient was the announcement of the Radcliffe Award, which had allowed the Princely State of Jammu and Kashmir to have a direct though fair-weather link with the rest of India. The Award had three contentious districts to decide. One was the Chittagong Hills in Bengal and the other two were Ferozepur and Gurdaspur in Punjab. Because of the dense Muslim population along the Indus, it was a foregone conclusion that the river would go to Pakistan and the region between the Jamuna and Sutlej rivers being Hindu dominated, would remain with India. It was the middle portion which included Ferozepur and Gurdaspur that was problematic. Of the two, the fate of the latter was crucial for Jammu and Kashmir. Sir Cyril Radcliffe has been ceaselessly reviled in India as well as Pakistan for the manner in which the new borders were drawn, and because of the Gurdaspur award, he is often accused by Pakistani scholars and historians of showing favours to India because of Lord Mountbatten's friendship with Nehru. But in all fairness to Radcliffe, he was given too short a time to execute an unprecedented project.

Since, apart from the Partition of India, the province of Punjab too was to be partitioned, a separate Punjab Boundary Commission had been set up. This Commission was to report directly to Radcliffe and had two Muslim, one Hindu and one Sikh judge to assist it. The Hindu member was Mehr Chand Mahajan, who was to later become the Prime Minister of Maharaja Hari Singh. The judges were not given the mandate to interact with local leaders and people to listen to their pleas and were only to hear the cases. Invariably, in judging the cases, the Muslims stuck to each other as did the Hindu and Sikh judges. This left Radcliffe greatly handicapped as he had to hear inconclusive cases and had to give a verdict on boundaries that was entirely based upon his opinions, which needless to say, were not based on local knowledge of the terrain. Later on he was to say that he should have been given at least two years to do a just job of Partition.[120]

On the other hand, the Governor of Punjab, Evan Jenkins, who faced most of the heat of Partition, thought that twice as long was actually needed for this complex exercise. Gurdaspur was a curious case because if it, and Ferozepur, were awarded to Pakistan, as

Lord Wavell had pointed out in 1946, then Amritsar would have been surrounded on three sides by Pakistan, making its defence vulnerable. On this argument alone, Gurdaspur district needed to be given to India. But the statistics showed that of the four tehsils of this district, Gurdaspur, Batala and Shakargarh had a Muslim majority and Pathankot had Hindus in a slender majority. Thus on the face of it, a critic might accuse Radcliffe of favouritism but since other factors too needed to be taken into account, it can safely be said that it was the Amritsar factor that tilted the scales in India's favour. Conspiracy theorists however, especially those who argue for Pakistan, maintain that this happened because it was always the intention of Mountbatten to facilitate the accession of Jammu and Kashmir to India by influencing the Gurdaspur award. There is little doubt that he was aware that the accession of the State to India could only be possible if Gurdaspur was given to India. He had said to the Nawab of Bhopal and the Maharaja of Indore on 4th August 1947 that the State of Jammu and Kashmir was 'so placed geographically that it could join either Dominion, provided part of Gurdaspur were put into East Punjab by the Boundary Commission.'[121]

Another argument championed by the critics of Radcliffe was that the allocation of Gurdaspur and consequently Pathankot to India was done to facilitate the movement of the Indian army into Jammu and Kashmir. But these critics need to remember that the Indian army had moved into the valley by flying into it rather than taking the longer and arduous surface route. Moreover, in case the State had acceded to India without Gurdaspur, even then it would not have taken long for the Government of India to revive the old trade route that descended into the plains of India from Jammu-Basholi and Kangra districts. But in the meantime, the Maharaja had already ordered the cart road from Jammu-Samba-Kathua to be upgraded immediately because even if Gurdaspur was not awarded to India, the State could have an easier route from Kathua to Basholi and then on to Kangra.

In the end, except for Shakargarh, the rest of the Gurdaspur district went to India. This was more due to the need to safeguard the interests of the Sikhs, who would have been the biggest losers with the loss of even their Holy City of Amritsar along with the great material loss due to their displacement from west Punjab.

7

Before Accession

Meanwhile, communal violence and large scale killings in the border areas of Jammu and Punjab had started even as autumn was sending villages scurrying to finish preparations for the winter in 1946. This violence had begun soon after the Direct Action call of Jinnah. In the district of Hazara, aggressive patrolling by the Indian army was able to control violence by the middle of January 1947, but as subsequent events proved, once the British had announced their decision to withdraw from India and the Indian army too became a victim of the communal passions, violence was to return to these areas with a vengeance. What role the Jammu and Kashmir State Forces played in controlling violence on the Jammu and Kashmir side and helping out the civilian population in that hour of trial were deeply appreciated by the Punjab government, as has been noted earlier. Unfortunately, for reasons that can only be attributed to the deep rooted prejudice of later historians and commentators, the service rendered by these Forces has been completely ignored, perhaps deliberately, so that the focus remained on its failures and consequently on the saving of Kashmir by the Indian Army.

It is ironic that while first the British Indian Army and then the Indian Army has never been blamed for its inability to prevent and stop the violence and massacres that took place in Bengal and Punjab during the same period, the Maharaja and the State Forces have been repeatedly accused of complicity and participation in them without even making any effort to look at the challenges that were faced by them along the long border from the Northern Regions to Madhopur in the south of Jammu bordering Punjab, and the general nature of the situation in the State. It has been noted earlier that during the Second World War, the two mountain batteries of the State had been taken over by the British. Their brilliance and success in the war had been too noticeable for the British not to assimilate them in the Indian army. An infantry battalion had been disbanded and because of the economic constraints caused by the Emperor's War in far off lands, it was not feasible for the State to replenish these losses immediately. As if this was not enough, the State suffered because of the geographical constraints, as 'economically, administratively and even militarily, Jammu and Kashmir had always held closer ties with North-West India [now Pakistan] than with East Punjab or Delhi...As far as the State army was concerned, the old branch of Military Adviser-in-Chief in Army Headquarters had been wound up—and no direct or even indirect link existed between the Headquarters at Srinagar and Army Headquarters, New Delhi. Thus, no war diary or other record of the state forces was kept at New Delhi; there was no channel of direct communication. [Logistically, the J&K forces were mainly dependent upon the Rawalpindi arsenal.] It was for this reason that the Indian Army—and India as a whole—remained largely ignorant of the tremendous stresses and strains to which the J&K forces were subject for a period of months before the actual invasion by tribesmen.'[122]

The disconnect between the State and the state forces on the one hand and the Army Headquarters, New Delhi, on the other, was so glaring and dangerous that Lieutenant General L.P. Sen also commented in his book *Slender Was the Thread* that in early October 1947 a message was intercepted by the Army Headquarters, New Delhi regarding a battle involving Gorkhas at places called 'Sensa' and 'Owen'. But no action was taken by the authorities since the Defence Ministry could not locate these places in its records. In fact, they doubted the existence of these places since the *Compendium of Name Places* of the Survey of India did not mention any such names! It was much later that they realized that a minor war was already taking place along the border of Jammu when the name 'Poonch' also started appearing in these messages. When analyzing the events leading to the Indo-Pak War of 1947-48, these factors and the disconnect with as well as disinterest of the Indian army in the affairs and fate of the State Forces must be remembered. It is because of this disinterest and disconnect that their heroic role and the valiant manner in which they fought battles and saved thousands of civilians lives has largely gone unnoticed and unrecognized. Surprisingly, very few officers of the post 1947 Indian army have realized the odds facing the State forces. Major General Palit is one of the few exceptions to acknowledge that 'when Indian army intervened in Kashmir [at the end of October 1947] the state forces had already been fighting border operations for more than three months, fighting against heavy odds, large scale treachery and an almost total lack of direction from or even communication with their headquarters and their government.'[123] Therefore, it is only fair to make an objective assessment of the situation and tools that were available to face the cataclysmic period.

During the post-war period, the State forces were organized into the Army Headquarters located at Srinagar and four infantry brigades. The Jammu Brigade was located at the Jammu Cantonment and had a Training Battalion and 5 JAK, with its sub-units spread from Kathua to Bhimber along the southern border of Jammu. The Kashmir Brigade had its head quarter at Badami Bagh Cantonment, Srinagar with a Training School, 4 JAK (without two companies) at Domel on the border with Punjab (Pakistan), 6 JAK without two companies at Bunji (one company was stationed at the Headquarter, two platoons at Leh, two at Skardu, and two at Kargil), and 7 JAK with two companies at Srinagar, which were later moved to Poonch. The third was the Mirpur Brigade with headquarters at Dharamsala Jhangar. It had 2 JAK with outposts on the Naoshera border and the 3 JAK at Mirpur with outposts at the border. The Poonch Brigade with headquarters at Poonch had 1 JAK, which was spread out in Bagh area, 8 JAK at Poonch with elements of two companies at Srinagar, 9 JAK spread out in the Rawalakot area, two companies of 2 JAK, which was half Gorkha and half Muslim, the 4 JAK was half Hindu and half Muslim, and 6 JAK was half Sikh and half Muslim. In all, the strength of the State Forces was less than 10,000 soldiers and immediate steps were taken to re-raise the 7th Battalion that had been disbanded during the war and secure armaments so as to also raise a mountain battery.

A cursory glance at the composition of the State forces gives the lie to the malicious propaganda against the Maharaja of having an army consisting only of soldiers from Hindu and Sikh communities, particularly from the sub-community of the Maharaja. In fact, the construct of the State forces as on the eve of the 1947-48 war was similar to the one that Maharaja Gulab Singh had forged while making those conquests in the high Himalayan mountains, as well as when assisting the Lahore Durbar forces in their various battles all over Punjab and the Frontier region. That too had contained Muslim segments. An objective student of military history will not fail to notice that in their more than 100 years of history, the Dogra forces with these very elements had fought long and sustained operations from southern Sinkiang (Aksai Chin) to western Tibet, from Gilgit and Hunza to the valley of Skardu and Leh under the leadership of General Zorawar Singh, Lakhpat Rai, Baj Singh, etc. In an era when there were no high altitude warfare schools to prepare for such heights and adverse conditions, and in the absence of facilities and equipment that are available now, these soldiers had fought at a height of 15,000 feet in winter and summer. Fighting on behalf of the British in the jungles and swamps of Asia and the deserts and scrub lands of Africa, they had earned high praise and appreciation from the British field commanders. They had fought on behalf of the Empire against the Germans, the Turks as well as the Japanese. Thus, as far as the soldierly qualities were concerned they were second to none. But the problem in 1947-48 was that in the earlier battles and wars they knew who their enemies were; now they were faced with treachery within and sometimes fighting their former comrades.

It appeared that geography was taking some kind of revenge on the State for it became the strongest shackle in those times. After Partition, the State was effectively linked with only Pakistan. The main link for the Valley was from Srinagar through the Jhelum gorge at Baramula to Domel, from where the road bifurcated. One branch of the road went south to Kohala, from where it crossed the

Jhelum and carried on to Murree and Rawalpindi. The other crossed Jhelum at Domel and went onwards to Manshera, Abbottabad and Wah. In the south of Jammu, there existed both the rail and the road link from Jammu to Sialkot via Suchetgarh. Thus, the only connection to East Punjab and India was the cart road linking Jammu-Samba-Kathua and Madhopur in Punjab. This route was intersected by numerous tributaries of the Ravi, and when in flow, were difficult to cross since none of them had any bridge. In fact, Mehr Chand Mahajan has given graphic details of the challenges of the weather that he experienced on this track when he first went to the State in September 1947 for an interview with the Maharaja regarding his appointment as Prime Minister of the State. He wrote, 'I left Dharamsala on 10th September in heavy rain and started my journey to Kashmir. From Madhopur, I rode on horseback to Kathua, and then proceeded to the crossing where the road meets River Ujh. The wagon that had been sent for me stuck in the mud and would not move forward. So I walked part of the way, the rest I covered riding. The Ujh was in flood. My companions had arranged for a cavalry horse on which I was supposed to cross the river in flood. I sat on the horse banked by cavalryman on his horse on either side. The horses practically swam and I was drenched by the flood water. When we had managed to cross the river in this condition, I was taken to another military wagon which also stuck in the mud a mile or so from the river...'[124]

The State also did not have any external intelligence since that was the responsibility of the Government of British India and its Army Headquarters. It had no way of knowing what was happening across the new borders and what the Pakistan army was planning. This handicap was compounded by the fact that even the Army Headquarters at New Delhi was totally in the dark regarding Pakistan. General L.P. Sen has written in his book that when he took over the Military Intelligence Directorate, he discovered that all documents that were of material importance had been destroyed by the British before they relinquished charge. This indicated that even though many British officers were serving for India, their loyalties were not with India. This becomes abundantly clear from the book *Gilgit Rebellion: The Major Who Mutinied Over Partition of India* which states that the British plan to weaken the State of Jammu and Kashmir and India, and strengthen Pakistan was hatched by the Governor of the North-West Frontier Province, Sir George Cunningham, the British Agent in Gilgit Lieutenant Colonel Roger Bacon and the Commandant of the Gilgit Scouts Major William Brown, much before the British left.[125] It is not without significance that when the New Year Honours of the Emperor were announced, the list contained the name of Major William Brown though without any mention of the services rendered to the Crown. The British complicity was as clear as summer daylight. They had subverted not only in Gilgit but had also worked overtime in influencing the Muslim soldiers in other battalions of the State.

By April, 1947, the Maharaja was convinced about the evil intentions of the about-to-be created Pakistan. On the one hand he began trying to obtain help from India so that arms and ammunition could be stocked. On the other hand, he began mobilizing the resources that he had at his command. His soldiers, who had returned home after long battles during the World War and had been looking forward for a period of rest, now needed to make a big effort for the security of their State, homes and hearths. Therefore, Hari Singh took a whirlwind tour of Mirpur, Jhangar and Poonch regions, often sleeping in the field areas with the soldiers. His presence had greatly enthused them and it even had a calming effect on the population that was on the verge of civil strife. In the meantime, the planned and sustained raids into the State from across the border, often supported by the Pakistan police personnel and occasionally by active soldiers in civil dresses, had made one thing clear to the Maharaja, that these attacks were meant to draw out the State forces to the Jammu border, so that the main attack could be launched to grab Srinagar and the valley. But the problem was that even the border residents could not be left to their fates. This had put additional pressure on the forces that had never had the occasion to deal with such a challenge. Before 15th August 1947, the British were obliged to come to the aid of the State if it was threatened from outside. In return, the British had gained control over many policies of the State as well as over the number of battalions that the State raised. Since the supply of arsenal was only from Rawalpindi, Pakistan knew everything about the defence matters of the State.

In the past the State was not overly worried since its defence from external aggression had been the responsibility of the British. Now having not acceded to either India or Pakistan by 15th August 1947 it found itself in exactly the position that Lord Mountbatten had warned of. It was not only without the protection of any of the dominions but had become the victim of the predatory tactics of one of them. As part of a crafted plan to draw the State forces away from the borders of the valley, there was a lull in border incursions and violence in the month of September to the first week of October. The comparative quiet could also be a consequence of the aggressive patrolling that the Sate forces had undertaken in the Poonch region. Nonetheless now, with the wisdom of hindsight, some historians know that this period was used by Pakistan in organizing and training the raiders for the invasion of the valley in the not too distant future. Major General H.L. Scott, the Chief of the Staff of the State Forces submitted a note to Maharaja Hari Singh about the events that were likely to unfold.[126] He wrote:

> A survey of recent tendencies and events leaves little doubt that the Muslim Conference leaders intend to push forward their policy of union of the state with Pakistan by force if necessary. It is clear that in this respect they are finding ready support and assistance in the districts of Hazara and Rawalpindi...On the southern border of the State the Muslims massacred, driven [*sic*] out and looted the Sikhs and Hindus. The former having thus acquired a taste for massacre and loot are likely to be ready for fresh adventures. Even more dangerous than these are the many thousands of Muslim refugees that have passed into the district of Jhelum, Gujrat and Sialkot from the east. They have lost much and no doubt are prepared to recoup themselves at the expense of anyone they are in a position to attack...There are few indications that the Pakistani authorities are making efforts to restrain their people. In fact contrary may be said to be true. There can be little doubt that Pak Police and troops are not reliable.

Soon thereafter, General Scott relinquished his appointment, handed his charge to Brigadier Rajinder Singh and left for his home. In his parting advice, he had asked the Maharaja to strengthen the defence at the Domel-Srinagar route. But the problem was that he had himself spread the forces all along the border, manning every point, but nowhere strong enough to resist an attack in high numbers and with no plan for additional support of fully trained personnel. Realizing this, the State Army headquarters too put the period of lull to good use by reorganizing the forces to meet the ever increasing demands from the border forces. Auxiliary units were hastily disbanded to augment the strength of units and Colonel Bhagwan Singh, the ADC of the Maharaja was sent to Delhi to procure weapons for the impending war. Later he recalled:

> On October 10, 1947, the Maharaja called the author [Colonel Bhagwan Singh], who, had retired from service to the Gulab Mahal Palace, and after explaining that he was sensing an invasion from Pakistan, and was, therefore, in need of War experienced officers, asked him to rejoin service to which the author agreed. His Highness expressed the necessity of re-raising the Mountain Batteries and asked the author to put a scheme, which the author did the next day. The author was then sent to Delhi with a letter to Sardar Patel [Vallabhbhai Patel] and a list of guns, connected stores and some material for destroying Kohala Bridge, in case the need. The Sardar tried his best, but was unable to arrange anything under the set up then existing, with a British Commander-in-Chief and Supreme Commander still there. That the State had not acceded to India, seemed to be the excuse. The author explained that His Highness wanted no delay in accession, and desired that it should be brought about immediately, but the Sardar said "No, No, Not yet". The author, however, told him that the State Forces were already very highly committed and that they would not be able to hold the invasion if it came. The author returned with the assurance that the guns and the connected stores would follow.[127]

It has been suggested by some critics that Colonel Bhagwan Singh should have approached the Indian Defence Minister, Sardar Baldev Singh, instead, but they forget that he could not have gone to Baldev Singh directly because the Defence Minister was nobody to take any decision regarding the State, which at that point in time was independent and any such approach could have only been made either to the Prime Minister or the Deputy Prime Minister, which Sardar Patel was, and it was to him that Bhagwan Singh went. Another reason for approaching Sardar Patel was that in addition to being the Deputy Prime Minister and the Home Minister, he was also the States Minister and as such was responsible for dealing with problems of the princely states.

Even as the focus of everyone was on the Poonch and Kashmir sector, there were many critical battles, but of low intensity, that had broken out in the southern border of Jammu. Raids from Pakistan into Jammu and Kashmir State were conducted by irregular troops with the support of miscreants all along this border. This region had been quiet till the early days of October. From 6th October onwards the intensity of these raids increased, as if on cue, from the Pathankot border in Punjab to Akhnur at river Chenab. Now the raids were conducted by the regular soldiers of the Pakistan army with the support of local, armed villagers. Inexplicably, they were neither planned nor coordinated and were generally hit and run affairs. The purpose of these raids appeared to be to create confusion and was confined to looting, burning of villages, the molestation of women and in some cases their abduction, and the killings of civilians.

During this period 5 JAK was posted in this sector under Major Kripal Singh. The Battalion had its headquarter at Jammu but the headquarter company was in the Arnia area and distributed among the many border posts, barely a couple of kilometres from the border with Pakistan. This area was divided into three sectors—Ujh-Hiranagar, Ramgarh-Babiya and Ranbirsinghpura-Akhnur. Each sector was manned by a company of 5 JAK, with one company in the Pandorian Rest House on the Ranbir Canal, one company at the Mawa area of Samba, one company at the Suchetgarh barrier at the border and one company at Madhin in the south of Hiranagar, along with one company each of the garrison police stationed in Kathua and Ramgarh. The company at Suchetgarh consisted of recruits from the Regimental Centre who had less than six months of training. No sooner had this deployment been completed that on the night of 5th/6th October the post at Babiya manned by the

Gorkha Garrison Police was attacked by the enemy. It can be argued that this was the date when the war of 1947 started.

The fighting lasted about three hours and the Gorkhas, finding their position untenable, retreated with two casualties. But they returned the next day in company strength and after a hand-to-hand battle, forced the invaders to withdraw to their territory. On 18th/19th October, Bhimber and Manawar to the west of Akhnur was subjected to an attack, which was repulsed by a squadron of the cavalry. But when the next attack took place later that month on 27th October, it was supported by tanks, forcing the small state force, along with the civilian population to withdraw to Sunderbani. With this, the warning that Colonel Bhagwan Singh had sounded to Sardar Patel came true, since the commitment of meagre forces on such a long border had made their positions untenable.

The events were fast assuming dangerous dimensions for the people of the State. The Radcliffe Award had triggered a great deal of heartburn and anger in Pakistan and its supporters. Liaquat Ali Khan, the Prime Minister of Pakistan, was furious and went to the extent of accusing Lord Mountbatten of influencing the decision because of his friendship with Nehru while completely ignoring the fact that the Holy city of Amritsar could not have been exposed to the mercy and goodwill of Pakistan by giving Gurdaspur to Pakistan, for then Amritsar would have been surrounded by Pakistan on three sides. Pakistan, or for that matter historians favourably inclined to Pakistan, seem to conveniently forget this factor because of their disappointment and frustration at the decision to award Gurdaspur district to India, which thus gave Jammu and Kashmir to have a surface link with India. They believe that it was this factor alone that allowed Maharaja Hari Singh the freedom to make the decision in favour of India.[128] In doing so, they ignore that the repeated overtures of the Maharaja for help had been deflected not only by Lord Mountbatten but also by the Delhi leaders, including Sardar Patel. He was repeatedly told that accession to India could only take place if it was in consonance with the general opinion of the people, even though there was no mention of such a condition in the India Independence Act.

But even in this Alastair Lamb found proof of cunningness on the part of Nehru and the supposed gullibility of Mountbatten. He alleges that Mountbatten was completely dependent upon Nehru for his opinions about Kashmir, forgetting that Mountbatten's association with Maharaja Hari Singh went back to the time when Edward, Prince of Wales, visited India in 1921 and Mountbatten and Maharaja Hari Singh, then Yuvraj, had acted as his ADCs. That friendship of the youthful years could well have been rekindled. But Lamb focuses on Nehru and accuses him of giving a partial picture of the political scene of Kashmir to Mountbatten wherein the names, role and influence of the Muslim Conference leaders, Chaudhary Ghulam Abbas and Mirwaiz Yusuf Shah were missing. Lamb claimed that they had great influence, perhaps greater than that of Sheikh Abdullah and the National Conference in the valley.[129] In making such a claim, Lamb ignored the fact that during the elections to the Praja Sabha, there were five seats allocated to Srinagar, a place which was believed to be the epicentre of Mirwaiz's support. Despite that all his candidates were resoundingly trounced by the National Conference. So much for the claimed influence of Mirwaiz in the Valley! Thus, nothing could have been farther from the truth than the claim of their influence. Moreover, had they been so influential and confident of their support among the Muslims of the State, they would not have fled Kashmir when hostilities broke out between India and Pakistan (decades of scholarship has proved conclusively that the invading bands comprised soldiers of the Pakistan army and were not 'raiders', as maintained by partisans of Pakistan). Since historians subscribing to Lamb's view have always maintained that the 'rebellion' of Poonch was a secessionist movement and its 'brutal' suppression validated the invasion of the Kashmir valley by the Muslim tribes of the frontier region, by remaining there, the Muslim Conference leaders would have rallied the people to their cause just as Sheikh Abdullah did for his cause. Moreover, it should never be forgotten that the Mountbattens might have been intimate friends of Nehru but they were loyal members of the British establishment and had been specifically tasked with protecting the British interests in India, which they did with great care and diligence in such a sophisticated manner that India was re-conquered by them when the British left India. The last Governor-General of India, Chakravarty Rajagopalachari, wrote to Attlee, 'Lord Mountbatten has wound up Indo-British history in a manner which has secured for Britain a re-conquest.'[130] There could not have been a more powerful testimonial of the patriotism of Mountbatten than this tribute from an adversary of long decades.

Nevertheless, long before this, the Poonch situation had worsened because of multiple reasons, the communalism stoked by the Muslim League in neighbouring Punjab being the main. The reason for the discontent has already been discussed but the spin that has been sought to be given to it had many other dimensions. Some historians, like Alastair Lamb and Christopher Snedden, have argued that the Muslim Conference leaders like Chaudhary Ghulam Abbas and Mirwaiz Yusuf Shah exercised greater influence in the State than Sheikh Abdullah and the National Conference. However, they contradict themselves and concede that Sheikh Abdullah had the greater influence and the Muslim Conference was in a minority prior to the events of 1947. Snedden also concedes that because of the support extended by the Muslim Conference as well as Jinnah's Muslim League to the Maharaja during the 'Quit Kashmir' movement, the Muslim Conference and Jinnah had made themselves unpopular in Kashmir. In fact, Snedden quotes Mir Qasim, former Chief Minister and leader of the National Conference, and later the Congress, to note that Qasim believed Jinnah's unpopular and insensitive attitude 'killed the chances of Kashmir going to Pakistan'.[131] Thus it is clear that, whatever the reasons, the fact was that Chaudhary Abbas and Mirwaiz Yusuf Shah did not represent the State and that at no point in time were the people of the State willing to merge with Pakistan.

Much is often made by these historians of an indigenous war being waged by the native Poonchis against the Maharaja; much also has been made of the military skills among them. While enumerating the martial qualities of the Poonchis and the Mirpuris, Snedden reminds us that the region provided 31,000 soldiers during the First World War to the Indian army and close to 50,000 during the Second World War. The latter figure would suggest that they by far outnumbered the approximately 10,000 soldiers of the State army in 1947. This would also suggest that even after taking into account the number of casualties during the War as well as those who were still serving at the time of the so-called 'Poonch rebellion', these martial soldiers not only outnumbered the State army but were also more skilful in warfare, having been trained by the 'superior' British officers.[132] On another page[133] Snedden quotes Sardar Mohammad Ibrahim Khan that at Bagh there was a gathering of 40,000 ex-servicemen from the region during Maharaja Hari Singh's whirlwind tour of the Poonch-Mirpur regions and he was alarmed by the show of strength. Snedden further quotes his toxic sources as claiming that subsequently these ex-servicemen were disarmed and their weapons distributed among the Hindus and Sikhs. The claim is amusing for had it been so then would the Maharaja not have disbanded the Muslim soldiers in his army? The fact that they were not, and two Muslim companies of the 4 JAK were given the vital responsibility of guarding the strategically important bridge at Kohala, dispels any such notions. The same author has at another point used the fanciful claim of an unnamed Muslim who had migrated to Pakistan occupied Jammu and Kashmir (PoJK) and claimed that he heard the Maharaja not only ordering the massacre of Muslims but also going to the extent of himself killing a few.[134]

The sources used by these historians are usually based in PoJK and are people who have an axe to grind, having been appointed by Pakistan to high positions in the Government of PoJK. Alternatively, they are known champions of the Pakistani cause in the State, like former editor of Calcutta (now Kolkata)-based daily newspaper *The Statesman*, Ian Stephens, or the historian Alastair Lamb. The purpose of such claims is twofold—one, to prove that the events of Poonch had nothing to do with what was to follow in the valley, that is, the Pakistan sponsored invasion. The events, according to these people, were independent happenings because of local grievances that varied from prohibitive taxation to discrimination in the recruitment for the State army. To buttress this allegation, once again the authority of Sardar Mohammad Ibrahim is used, who claimed at one point that when 'immediately after World War II, the Maharaja was recruiting "Gurkhas, Sikhs and even untouchables"—but, it was alleged, not Muslims—for extra four battalions'.[135] This is a grossly misleading claim as only one battalion was being raised, which had the same composition as the earlier disbanded 7th Battalion. The second purpose was to absolve Pakistan and the Muslim League of any culpability in the events of Poonch, contrary to the other narrative so effectively presented by Brahma Singh in his book.

Another focus of these historians, as opposed to the communal violence in which all communities—Hindus, Sikhs and Muslims—lost lives in large numbers, is to accuse the Maharaja, the Maharani and the State administration of engineering and supporting Muslim massacres. However, while making such accusations, they fail to offer objective reasons other than continuing to dwell on the communal frenzy of the times. It has been said that the Maharaja ordered such pogroms so that Jammu could become a Hindu majority region. But they do not inform us about the advantages of such a planning to the Maharaja or the Jammu region. It is true that after a part of Jammu was occupied by Pakistan, the rest of Jammu did become a Hindu majority area but in the process it diminished the status of Jammu in relation to Kashmir because it yielded its majority. A cursory glance at the figures show that according to the Census of 1941, the population of the Jammu Province was 1,981,433 but was reduced to 1,572,887 in 1949 while in the Kashmir Province, the population which was 1,728,705 in 1941 rose to 1,899,438 in 1949. Thus any willful massacre would have been counter-productive for the Maharaja as well as the Hindus and Sikhs of the Jammu Province. Moreover, such a massacre could not have been possible in view of the fact that in 1947, the so-called 'Azad Kashmir' had, according to one claim, raised an army of 50,000 at Rs 10 per month.[136] Looking at the fact that the State had only 10,000 soldiers in comparison, this vastly superior number could have simply swamped the Jammu region by the sheer numbers, particularly after the Muslim soldiers and officers of the State forces had betrayed their oath and deserted.

What is true though is the fact that communal killings did take place and even cases of abduction of women happened at certain places in the Jammu Provinces. The accusation by PoJK leaders of that era, as well as Sheikh Mohammad Abdullah are, in fact, outrageous and need to be challenged objectively so that the name of an innocent person is not sullied for serving the political interests of some. It is a well-established fact that Muslims were given a fair representation in the State administration as well as among the advisors of the Maharaja. Among the Prime Ministers who held tenure during his reign were Mirza Sir Zaffar Ali, Mr Vijahat Hussein and Sir Abdus Samad Khan.[137] A substantial number of Muslims also occupied senior positions in the administrations, and Bhai Jaan (Sardar Abdul Rehman Effendi) and the Nawab of Palanpur were a constant feature of Hari Singh's court and life.

Malka Pukhraj, the legendary Dogri-Pahari singer from the State, who later migrated to Pakistan when communal tensions began to rise, has paid glowing tributes to the secularism and liberalism of Maharaja Hari Singh, and the congenial atmosphere that existed because of his personal conduct, in her autobiography, *A Song Sung True*. According to her, life in general, during his rule was marked by congeniality among the various communities, the sharing of festivals and tolerance for others. She has also mentioned the rising communal tensions caused by the vituperative reporting of some newspapers. In fact, she herself became the victim of vicious innuendos, which speaks volumes about the freedom of expression enjoyed by the media, and this had deeply troubled the Maharaja. Another fact that cannot be denied is that there were some courtiers who too had been carried away by the passions of communalism, creating a toxic atmosphere during those crucial years. Thus, there is no reason to believe that Maharaja Hari Singh was a communalist and could have ordered or instigated sectarian violence.

Had he been a communalist and distrusted and hated the Muslims to the extent of ordering their massacre, he would have first taken the precaution of at least disarming all Muslim soldiers and officers of the State forces. The fact that he did not take such a step is ample proof of his faith in the loyalty of the Muslims. Even at a time when reports had begun to pour in about the attempts being made to subvert the loyalty of the Muslim soldiers by communalists from across the border, and people affiliated with the Muslim Conference within the State, the Commanding Officer of the 4 JAK, Colonel Narain Singh, had been outraged by the suggestion of disloyalty by the Muslim soldiers and had assured the Maharaja of their loyalty.[138] The Maharaja had unhesitatingly accepted his assurance for he knew that any act expressing lack of trust of Muslims would send a wrong message among the rest of the battalions having Muslim soldiers. This was shortly before the invasion of the State took place on 22nd October, 1947, and much after the alleged ordering of massacres of Muslims in Poonch, as claimed by some sources in PoJK and partisans of Pakistan.

Apart from insinuations, wild allegations and nameless sources, there is no shred of evidence that the communal killings were sponsored, instigated or encouraged by the Maharaja or his administration. The fact of the Muslim soldiers having been put on normal duty is proof enough of the Maharaja not treating the Muslim soldiers, officials or the people, any differently in those testing times. Moreover, it is common sense that with the limited number of battalions, it would have been foolhardy to divert the soldiers to carrying out massacres, as has been made out by Pakistani sources and later, unfortunately, by Sheikh Abdullah, with disastrous consequences. Using the anonymous and interested PoJK sources to accuse the Maharaja and his forces of indulging in 'genocide' at a time when every able hand was needed to defend the borders and its people is not only outrageous but also abominable. It is a matter of record that the State forces fought with honour and professionalism in adverse circumstances. This, however, does not mean that there were no killings. There definitely were killings at Samba, Akhnur and Suchetgarh. This author has extensively talked to people who participated in one of them. Most of them were middle-aged men armed with swords, spears and match-lock guns, or young men, not young enough to be innocent but not too old to be recruited in the army or any other gainful employment. These young people mostly got recruited in the Indian army upon coming of age. A few among these young and middle-aged men were those who had single-barrel or double-barrel guns in their family. As narrated to this author by a participant, in a couple of places there were pitched battles between an armed Muslim family and the attackers, one being in Badhwani, Samba, and the other at the besieged Hiranagar fort. The first belonged to the rich family of a weaver by caste, but in reality a wealthy owner of handlooms and sheet printing trade. The other was a Tehsildar at Hiranagar who had young daughters in the family. In both families, no member survived, the women having been killed by their respective patriarchs.

Apart from these high profile killings, in the regional context, there were definitely fairly large scale killings on the Jammu-Suchetgarh road, when the convoy of Muslims, escorted to the border by a handful of soldiers, was overwhelmed by the Hindu-Sikh refugees by sheer numbers. A few armed Muslims had retaliated leading to a frenzy of killings. A similar incident took place on the Akhnur border. Just as the Suchetgarh border was the gateway for Muslims to Pakistan, it was also a gateway for Hindus and Sikh who were making their way to the safety of the State from Sialkot, as was the case with Akhnur. But these killings were nowhere near the scale that is alleged by some. These killings were tragedies that were so heart wrenching but not uncommon during that time of hate and madness. This had happened all along the East Punjab and West Punjab border in India. In that part of India, the Indian army was not trying to defend the borders from marauding raiders and yet it was either not used or it failed to maintain law and order. To blame the Jammu and Kashmir State forces for those killings without holding the Indian and the Pakistani armies and the leaders responsible for them, was not only unfair but was also indicative of a design that went beyond justice.

The killings at Samba, according to the information gathered by this author, were probably the handiwork of mischievous elements. What is known is that the Muslims of the region had been put together in a camp with the assurance that they would be escorted to the safety of Pakistan. But one night, a rumour was spread that a letter, written from Pakistan and addressed to the Muslims, was intercepted in which they were assured that help was on its way and soon armed Muslims from Pakistan would arrive to join hands with the local Muslims to annihilate the Hindus. This led to the tragic massacre. Again, it is farfetched to accuse the State administration of orchestrating it, as the meagre forces were busy guarding and fighting the hit and run raids from across the border. The administration just did not have the spare ammunition to expend on the Muslims for that would have depleted their own ability to fight the enemy. The accusers, including historian Christopher Snedden, put the number of people killed at Samba at 14,000 and this number could not have been killed by swords and spears alone because even the able-bodied youth capable of wielding weapons were sparse in number.

So why have Pakistan and its agents in PoJK shown persistence in making such an accusation and holding Maharaja Hari Singh and Lord Mountbatten guilty of massacres in Jammu and Kashmir and Punjab? It would be instructive to remember that it was an era that followed the Second World War and its aftermath. One of the consequences of the War and the defeat of Hitler's Germany was the Nuremberg trials that held senior members of the Nazi regime accountable for war crimes and crimes against humanity, including the holocaust. Inspired by this, Pakistan attempted to justify the invasion of the State from the north by pinning the blame on Maharaja Hari Singh. In fact, Pakistan also threatened the British government that it would prepare a case of genocide against Lord Mountbatten, holding him responsible for the Punjab massacres by influencing Radcliffe to change the boundary award at the last moment.[139] In view of these threats made in desperation, it is not surprising that having been thwarted in its effort to grab Kashmir by force, Pakistan was lashing out at all those it thought were responsible for Jammu and Kashmir State going to India—Maharaja Hari Singh, for having acceded to India and Lord Mountbatten for 'influencing' the Radcliffe award and giving Gurdaspur to India.

The largest massacres, according to Snedden's tally, took place at 'Maogoan' (Naogoan?), Samba and Akhnur Bridge, where, respectively, 25,000, 14,000 and 15000 Muslims are alleged to have been massacred.[140] How Snedden and others arrived at this figure is not known; they do not tell us how the 70,000 people who are alleged to have been killed were counted. But if they did their job as objective analysts and historians, as they claim to be, they would have to admit that a massacre of this magnitude was not possible given the number of able-bodied Hindus and Sikhs who would have been in the area at the time; most of them had been drafted in the border and civil defence efforts. The accusation that these massacres were carried out by the State Forces too defies reason as the meager Forces were locked in a battle of life and death on the borders or were engaged in tactical retreat while escorting the vast number of refugees. Add to this the fact that the narrative built by Pakistan sympathizers about Poonch also contradicts their own stand. Poonch had a Muslim majority of 90 percent. In addition, there were the 'rebels', constituting ex-British Indian Army personnel, former INA and other armed soldiers, numbering about 50,000 in all.[141] Together, they would have destroyed the small number of State forces in no time.

This is not to say that Muslims were not killed in the Hindu dominated Jammu region. In the insanity and savagery of Partition, every community that was in the majority in an area looted and killed people of minority communities. But the assessment of historians like Christopher Snedden that about 70,000 Muslim were killed in Jammu and Kashmir is not only vastly exaggerated but also malicious.

In this diversionary controversy what is forgotten is that the State was faced with an existential challenge and all possible support had been suddenly withdrawn, with the leaders of India being more interested in building their profile rather than providing relief to the Maharaja, his people and his State.

8

Strategic and Feudatory States

With the Indian leaders insisting that the Maharaja determine the will of the majority before taking any decision regarding the accession, the Maharaja wondered if it would be terribly wrong if he acceded to India. Was the dilemma just because the majority of the population was Muslim? Does history, culture and shared heritage count for nothing in the wake of the greed for power for the few demagogues? Kashmir has always been part of mainland India. Emperor Ashoka of the Mauryan dynasty built the city of Srinagar and ruled it for successive centuries. It was not that Kashmir had links to the outside world only through its north-western window. For centuries it struggled to gain control of the trans-Yamuna and Gangetic plains of India. Even Kannauj had been claimed, at one point, as a part of Kashmir.[142]

With such a rich and glorious past where was the need to be confined in the cocoon of an Islamic Kashmir of relative new origin and de-link a past that makes the valley so central to the spiritual being of Indians? Ideally, no blame was attributable to the Maharaja if he acceded to India. However, the leaders who were supposed to be the leaders of a modern India failed to provide leadership and guidance at that crucial juncture of history. He was acutely conscious of the events of Punjab and Bengal as a consequence of partition and was also aware of the strategic game that the treacherous English played. He suspected that they were leading the region towards making it a permanent theatre of confrontation and possible wars.

They had taken three hundred years to build their Indian Empire. In building it they had displayed too much arrogance, greed and cunning to have gained lasting friends in the region. Unlike the earlier invaders who came to India, made it their home and merged their identities in it, the English had remained aloof from the Indian way of life while not hesitating to milk the riches and siphon them off to England. Now the time for them to go had arrived. The Second World War had eaten into the vitals of Great Britain and after the terrible winter of 1946–47, it was on the verge of economic collapse. Rattled, it had taken a series of decisions that were so unlike a world power and the Attlee Cabinet had decided to drastically reduce its overseas responsibilities; it had abandoned its role of combating communism in Greece and supporting the economy of Turkey. It also opted to free itself of the thankless responsibility of mediating between the Arabs and the Jews in the Palestine Mandate. It left all the mess and responsibilities to the emerging world power from across the Atlantic Ocean. But of greater significance was its decision to dismantle the British Empire in India.

One can debate long into history as to what might have happened if the British had delayed their departure or somehow stalled the partition for another year or so. But the unpleasant fact remained that Mohammad Ali Jinnah had single-handedly made his two nation theory inevitable, for no one had the stomach for the ever-increasing communal violence all over the subcontinent. The Congress had not won a single Muslim seat in the United Provinces and had thus lost the claim of speaking on behalf of the Muslims. A lone Maulana Abul Kalam Azad was, for the world and for all intents and purposes, just what Jinnah derisively described him—a poster boy of the Congress. This probably explained the excessive indulgence with which Jawaharlal Nehru treated Sheikh Abdullah. In Punjab too the ideals of the Congress had collapsed with the resignation of the Unionist Ministry in the face of the violence unleashed by the Muslim League, rising support for it even among the hitherto secular Unionist supporters and the psychological and moral surrender to Jinnah. If there were elected Muslim Congressmen in the Frontier Provinces, then the credit went to the tall figures of the Khan brothers, Abdul Ghaffar Khan and Dr Khan Abdul Jabbar Khan, popularly known as Dr Khan Saheb. Moreover, the Congress leaders had grown old and tired and had not only lost the will in the face of rising communal tensions but were also impatient to get into the saddle of power.

Mahatma Gandhi was nearly isolated and had vainly tried to appeal to the leaders of the Congress, going to the extent of asking them to offer the prime minister's job to Jinnah in return for unity. However, for these Congressmen, Gandhi had outlived his utility.[143] The deed of partitioning the country had been sealed, but while the Congress leaders were only focused on the day when power would be handed over to them, the onerous task of taking the most difficult decision was the Maharaja's. It was the time to pay the price of being in power and it was also the time for him to prove his mettle and take a decision that would prove to be the wise one for the people of his State. Ideally, looking at the construct of the State, the subcontinent should not have been partitioned as it had deep historical, economic and cultural linkages with the whole of the region.

As the date of the partition and creation of Pakistan neared, Maharaja Hari Singh knew that for him, time was ticking away. Since the time of Maharaja Gulab Singh the British policy in Kashmir had been to use the State to keep the Russians out of the north-western corner of the Indian subcontinent. It had played many a games with his successors but now Lord Mountbatten wrote a letter to Lord Listowel, the Secretary of State, for India about the future of Gilgit Lease and its dependencies. He proposed that before the Paramountcy lapsed, the entire area of the Gilgit Lease be returned back to the State of Jammu and Kashmir. Accordingly, much before the lease period expired it was returned back to the State on 1st August 1947. It was the same day that Mahatma Gandhi had made his first and last visit to the Valley, and the State, having recovered all its territories, celebrated with lighting of buildings. That day the Maharaja probably felt satisfied as he had recovered the State that had been handed over to him by his ancestors. He had been cunningly forced to lease Gilgit in 1936 and now, in a dramatic reversal of fortunes, the British had been forced by circumstances to prematurely terminate the sixty years lease. In fact, he found it hard to believe that it was happening as Gilgit had been important for not only the British but the Russians and the Chinese as well. Gilgit and the northern regions, including Ladakh, were central to the rule established by the Dogras. At the heart of it all were the trade routes to Central Asia, the gold and other precious minerals, and the *pashm*, the undercoat wool from western Tibet, which was the raw material for the valuable shawl industry of Kashmir.[144]

No one was more aware of the strategic importance of this region than British, who had explored the routes and features of the region, its geopolitical and commercial significance. William Moorcraft[145] had travelled extensively in the region from 1812–1825, before his death in north Afghanistan. He had widely explored that corner of the subcontinent and beyond and had investigated the trade routes, natural resources and politics for the East India Company. He was the one who discovered for the British, the route to Chinese Turkistan from Ladakh by way of the Karakoram Pass which also led to Khotan, Yarkand and Kashgar. It was a route rich with commercial possibilities. But Moorcraft had also warned the British of the developing Russian interest in the Indian subcontinent, including that famous correspondence with the Lion of Punjab, Ranjit Singh. During his stay in Leh in 1820–21, Moorcraft had also noted the presence of official visitors from China. He had urged the East India Company to seize the opportunity being offered by the Ladakhis to intercede lest they are gobbled by the expanding empire of the Sikhs who had recently appropriated Kashmir and thus the market for their *pashm*.[146] But being what he was, Moorcraft had simultaneously approached the Government of the Manchu Dynasty in Peking (Beijing), which had been resisting the British advance from other directions as well.[147]

Soon thereafter the British had begun to play their games, pretending to be determining the borders from Lahaul to the northern most region of Panggong Lake, even though those belonged to Maharaja Gulab Singh and his progeny in perpetuity. The interference in the internal affairs of the State were not in accordance with the Treaty of Amritsar. It was then that they had for the first time discovered the Gilgit route passing through

Hunza to Kashgar over Mintaka, Khunjerab and other passes on the western side of Karakoram Range. They had also realized the commercial and geopolitical importance of the region as well as the fact that the Treaty of Amritsar made them dependent upon the rulers of the State of Jammu and Kashmir for guarding their interests. Ever since, there had been a school of thought among the British, under the garb of 'forward policy', to take Jammu and Kashmir under their direct control.[148]

The interest of the British in Maharaja Gulab Singh's kingdom, particularly Ladakh, had been aroused in his lifetime with raucous voices in the East India Company and England wanting a direct control of the kingdom, but simultaneously, alarming developments had been taking place towards the north and west of that region. The Tsarist Russia seemed to be too close to Afghanistan as they were fast approaching the Chinese Turkistan where, along with other parts of Central Asia, it was feared that the Chinese rule over its Muslim subjects was about to collapse. The resultant vacuum, the British felt, would be dangerous for their empire in India. In 1861, the British fears seemed to be coming true when Muslims in Kansu rebelled against the Chinese rule established only a century earlier by the Manchu Emperor. The region in any case had never really accepted the Chinese rule through Manchu Ambans over Turk and Mongol population. The region had remained in turmoil and uncertainty and many observers believed that it was a matter of time before it became a protectorate, if not part of the Russian Empire.[149]

Maharaja Gulab Singh's successor Maharaja Ranbir Singh was quick to understand the situation and found an opportunity to enlarge the diplomatic and commercial interest of the State if not its territories. Thus in 1864 he dispatched a garrison across the Karakoram Pass to Shahidulla (Xaidulla) on the caravan route from Leh to Khashgar and established a military post. Then he proceeded to contact the Amir of Khotan, Haji Habibullah Khan so that he could not only expand commerce with Eastern Turkistan but also protect his State and the trade caravans from raiding bandits. The garrison in Shahidulla was to ensure this as well as proper taxation collection on the trade route. By 1865 the British had become aware of Maharaja Ranbir Singh's new contacts in the region and the fact that he had expanded his kingdom by some 21,000 square miles. This he had achieved without violating the Amritsar Treaty of 1846 since he had expanded to the north and not west of Indus. The Treaty had not defined the boundaries to the north and he took full advantage of it. In the process a new route to Central Asia was discovered.[150] A route that did not have to cross the forbidding 18,000 feet high Karakoram Pass, which was usually well guarded by the Chinese.[151]

The British, while appreciating the strategic value of the new route did not want Maharaja Ranbir Singh to pursue any policy that was independent of their interest. It is true that the Treaty of Amritsar's Article I mentioned that the State of Jammu and Kashmir lay to the east of the river Indus. However, it did not say anything regarding the region that was north of it. Here, between the Indus, that flows generally in the direction of east to west in the State, and the great unexplored mountains lay the small states of Chitral, Hunza, Nagar, Gilgit, Punial, Ishkuman, Yasin and even smaller states like Chilas and Astor. Whoever controlled Gilgit had easy access to all these regions, routes and the mineral wealth like jade, which was in demand in Imperial China. The trade route here had existed ever since recorded times though always under threat from the bandits. That is why it was important for Maharaja Ranbir Singh to establish his garrison at Shahidulla. Moreover, Gilgit led to not only Chitral but also Afghanistan that was the scourge of Indian subcontinent since ancient times. By 1870 Chitral had accepted the Dogra suzerainty and the British too did not make any noise about it as it acted as a kind of buffer between Afghanistan and the Punjab. It was in Gilgit that they were really interested in. After a meeting with the Maharaja at Madhopur (Punjab), the Viceroy had managed to prevail upon him to accept arms and military assistance to achieve his ambition in the region of Dardistan in return for allowing a British representative to be stationed there. The proposal was accepted though there was no love lost between the two.

The British now were on the lookout for a chance to nail Maharaja Ranbir Singh and he in turn was too independent and smart to allow the British representative to control him. It was widely believed that he was in constant touch with the Russians and the Afghans but when there was a change of guard in Britain, with Gladstone taking over from Disraeli as Prime Minister, there was a policy reversal. Being less suspicious of the Russian designs, the Agency in Gilgit was withdrawn in 1881. But in the 1880s as the Anglo-Russian competition in Asia increased, Gilgit came to be known as the place where the three great Empires—the British, the Russian and the Chinese—met. The British once again grew paranoid of the Russians in the north-west frontier and the ruler of Jammu and Kashmir. After a sustained campaign against the new ruler, Maharaja Pratap Singh in England and India, he was accused of being in treasonable correspondence with the representatives of the Russians and the deposed heir of the Sikh Empire, Dalip Singh who was living an exiled life in England.[152]

It was ironic that a sovereign ruler with whom the British had entered into a treaty that made his State of Jammu and Kashmir an entity under the international law was being accused by the British of treason! These were the same charges that had been laid against the last Mughal Emperor, Bahadur Shah Zafar and the King of Burma before convicting them and sending them into exile—the former to Rangoon in Burma and the latter to Poona in India. But here the State of Jammu and Kashmir enjoyed an independent status and therefore had every right to be in correspondence with its neighbouring states. It is true that it had a special relationship with the British but its correspondence with Russia or any State on its borders was certainly not an act of betrayal. It is the duty of the rulers to ensure safe passage for its traders and that is what Maharaja Pratap Singh and his predecessors had done in the past. But now the British had reassessed their priorities and strategic interests and a lobby led by Lord Randolph Churchill, the father of the incorrigible imperialist, Sir Winston Churchill, had been stressing the need to not only annex the dependencies of the State of Jammu and Kashmir but the State itself!

Unable to do that, the British had devised a way around it. The tragic famine that had struck during the last years of Maharaja Ranbir Singh's regime in 1877-78 gave them the opportunity they were looking for. It is true that the famine was as much a result of the fury of nature as the insensitivity and greed of the state officials. It was to take years for the valley to recover from the tragedy, but in the meantime the administration had become worse. Maharaja Pratap Singh was stripped of all his powers and the entire State placed under the control of the Council of State, closely scrutinized by an Agent in Srinagar. The British had struck by symbolically bringing an end to the special status that the State enjoyed under the Treaty of Amritsar.

All this while, the defence of the Gilgit Agency had been the responsibility of the garrison that consisted entirely of soldiers from the Jammu and Kashmir State troops, numbering little over 2,000 and maintained by the State Treasury. Even when the Corps of Gilgit Scouts was raised in 1913 and its command entrusted to the British officer, half of its maintenance cost was borne by the State. At the time of the Hunza war it was the Dogra force that had saved the day when for all intents and purposes the much vaunted British army had wilted under the attack.

By then, in 1925 Hari Singh had become the Maharaja after Pratap Singh's death. Would he be as trustworthy and staunch a supporter of the British as his uncle had been? By 1934 the British believed that they had the answer. In fact they had put a question mark over his credentials after his frank speech at the First Round Table Conference. He had radical views about the future of the British in India and that was not appreciated by many British officials. Soon thereafter, a series of events had taken place in the valley of Kashmir that were enough for the British to pronounce that his administration was inefficient, oppressive and corrupt! They argued that with the Communist Soviet Union breathing down the Himalayas he might not be in a position to come to their aid and assistance.

Consequently, the Deputy Secretary in the Indian Foreign Office, Olaf Caroe, was raising an alarm that was further orchestrated by his minions. This, notwithstanding the extensive reports that the region was threatened by neither the Russians nor the Chinese owing to the mountain barrier between the subcontinent and Sinkiang, there was demand for taking over the Gilgit Agency. As a first, under the ruse of the financial crisis, the Maharaja was asked to bear two third of the maintenance cost of the Gilgit Scouts. Maharaja Hari Singh responded in 1933 with a counter proposal of taking the entire responsibility of the defence of the Gilgit Agency provided the system of 'diarchy' was terminated and complete authority reverted to the Wazir-e-Wazarat. As an alternative, in an ill-advised move, he said that the British take complete control and burden of the local administration and pay for it as well as defend the Gilgit Wazarat to the north of Indus and its dependencies. The Maharaja had made a last ditch effort to keep his hold over Gilgit.

The negotiations had begun and who else but his British Prime Minister Col Colvin represented him. The British had ensured that he was hamstrung by the domestic trouble that had plagued since 1931. To assist with the negotiations, also present was B.J. Glancy, the same person who had been earlier appointed to look into the grievances of Hari Singh's Muslim subjects. The British opted for the complete responsibility for the Gilgit Agency and its dependencies but Gilgit was somehow not ceded by the Maharaja. On 26th March 1935 he leased the Gilgit Wazarat north of the Indus and its dependencies to the British for a period of sixty years. However, the British were not to move their troops through the leased territory in normal circumstances and its defence would be the charge of the Gilgit Scouts. It was also made clear that despite the lease, the area remained part of the State and not only would the flag of the Maharaja fly there, but he would continue to receive certain public honours and mineral rights. In the September of the same year he had also demanded that the ban on cow slaughter, enforced in the whole State, be extended to the Wazarat too.[153]

It was this Gilgit, the pinnacle of the glorious campaigns of Dogras as well as the cause of so much hurt to them, that had been returned by the British on the eve of their departure from India. The past had not been easy for the Dogras. The control over the region had been difficult and demanding as was clear from the various documents related to them. It had been a part of the territories of Kashmir State from early times. Kalhan's Rajatarangini narrates vividly the detours of famous Kashmiri conqueror Lalitaditya (595–732 A.D.) in Gilgit and its adjoining territories. Similarly

Gilgit formed a part of medieval Kashmiri Sultan Shahab-u-Din's kingdom (1356–1374 A.D.). After the disintegration of the Shahmiri Sultanate these territories fell out, but Ghazi Chak had re-conquered or annexed such territories as had fallen off from the kingdom in the period between 1552 and 1562 A.D. In this attempt he attained marked success in recovering Skardu, Gilgit, Kishtwar, Pakhli and Mungli (near Pakhli), besides bringing into subjugation the Chief of the Gakkhars. In order to ensure efficient administration of these territories, he appointed experienced and intelligent governors to control them. After he took over Kashmir from the British in 1846, Maharaja Gulab Singh, subjugated Gilgit but he had to face repeated insurgency. In 1859 Maharaja Ranbir Singh sent a force led by General Hoshiar Singh, which ultimately tamed the resistance and the territory was permanently annexed to Jammu and Kashmir. Mian Jawahir Singh was appointed the first Wazir-e-Wazarat, who, according to the official assessment of 1916, assessed the revenue of the tract to be at Rs 7,842.

Even when Maharaja Hari Singh had been forced by circumstances beyond his control to sign the lease deed, he had been careful not to yield ground regarding the sovereign right over the territories. The lease deed signed on 26th March 1935 bears the signatures of the Maharaja on one side and British Resident in Kashmir, L.E. Lang on the other. Post haste, it was ratified by the Viceroy Lord Wellington on 3rd April 1935. Even while taking over the temporary administration of the territory, the British government made it explicitly clear that the territory falls within the boundaries of the Maharaja's domain and he continues to exercise sovereign right over the area. This was made clear by a reference to the provisions of the treaty itself, which read:

> Article 1: The Viceroy and Governor-General of India may at any time after the ratification of this agreement assume the Civil and Military administration of so much of the Wazarat of Gilgit province (hereinafter referred to as the "said territory") of the State of Jammu and Kashmir as lies beyond the right bank of the river Indus, but notwithstanding anything in this agreement the said territory shall continue to be included within the dominions of His Highness the Maharaja of Jammu and Kashmir.

> Article 2: In recognition of the fact that the said territory continues to be included within the dominions of His Highness the Maharaja of Jammu and Kashmir, salutes and customary honours shall be paid in the said territory by the administration on the occasion of the birth day of His Highness, Baisakhi, Dussehra, Basant Panchmi and on such other occasions as may be agreed upon by His Highness and the Viceroy and the Governor-General of India. The flag of His-Highness will be flown at the official headquarters of the Agency throughout the year.
>
> Article 3: In normal circumstances no British or British India troops shall be dispatched through that portion of the Wazarat of Gilgit province which lies beyond the left bank of the river Indus.
>
> Article 4: All rights appertaining to mining are reserved to His Highness the Maharaja of Jammu and Kashmir. The grant of prospecting licenses and mining leases will not be made during the period of the agreement mentioned below.
>
> Article 5: This agreement shall remain in force for sixty years from the date of its ratification and the lease will terminate at the end of that period.

The Maharaja had remained vigilant to the outward assertions and manifestations of his sovereignty even after conceding the lease. Consequently, the Kashmir flag continued to be hoisted along with the Union Jack on the portals of the Gilgit fort.

Hunza was another territory in that region that had been painstakingly made to accept the rule of law as enunciated from the capital of the State. It is bounded on the north by Barber range, many lofty and snow clad peaks as high as 25,000 feet. It is situated 8,000 feet above sea level and can muster about 5,000 fairly reliable fighting men, in any emergency. The State had often been hostile to the Maharaja of Kashmir and had often made attacks on Gilgit, either in alliance with Yasin or with some other petty state. But Maharaja Ranbir Singh (1856-1886 A.D.) had quelled the hostility and forced peace with the Raja of Hunza. Subsequently, a *Sanad* was granted by His Highness, the Maharaja of Jammu and Kashmir to Mohammed Nazim Khan of Hunza. It read:

> Whereas the State of Hunza has recently been in armed rebellion against my authority, and whereas in consequence thereof, Raja

Safdar Ali Khan, has justly forfeited any rights which he may have possessed as ruler of the State;

And whereas the said Safdar Ali Khan has fled from Hunza, and has not returned or made submission to me or to the Government of India and whereas, I nevertheless desire to continue the Chiefship of the said State of Hunza in the person of a member of the ruling family of the said State;

Now, therefore, I have, with the approval and the authority of Governor-General of India in Council, selected you, Mohammed Nazim Khan, to be ruler of the said State of Hunza.

The Chiefship of the Hunza State will be hereditary in your family, will descend in the direct line by primogeniture provided that in each case the succession is approved by the Maharaja of Jammu and Kashmir for the time being and by the Government of India.

An annual tribute of the following amounts, that is to say; 25 *tolas* of gold, equal to 16 *tolas* and 5 *mashas*, will be paid by you and your successors to the State of Jammu and Kashmir.

Further, you are informed that the permanence of this grant conveyed by the *Sanad* will depend upon the ready fulfillment by you and by your successors of all orders given by the Jammu and Kashmir State with regard to the conduct of relations between the State of Hunza and the States and tribes adjoining it, the administration of your territory, the prevention of raiding and man-stealing, the construction of roads through your country, the composition of such troops as you may be permitted to retain, and any other matters in which the Jammu and Kashmir State may be pleased to intervene. Be assured that so long as your house is loyal to the State of Jammu and Kashmir and to the British Government, and faithful to the conditions of the *sanad*, you and your successors will enjoy favour and protection.

A treaty was affected in August, 1870 between the Mir and the Kashmir Durbar, which read:

By the Holy Quran…

I am Raja Ghazan Khan, son of Raja Ghazanfar Khan and grandson of the late Raja Saleem Khan of Hunza. Whereas my father late Ghazanfar Khan remained under the control of

> Kashmir from a long time, especially the deceased Raja was obedient to the Maharaja, I also agree to remain obedient and present the tribute in the same manner. Hence I on my own accord, without force or pressure, depute my motabir, Wazir Fazal Khan and accept the following terms:-
>
> The following *Nazrana* will be paid by me to the Maharaja annually:
>
> Gold: 12 *tolas*
> Horses: 2
>
> In return, a *Khilat-Fakhira* and 2,000 Srinagari coins will be granted to me and also a *Khilat* to my Wazir.
>
> The revenue of Chaprot that has been fixed from old times will be paid annually at Gilgit.
>
> One *Motabir* of mine will always remain present in Gilgit and he will be paid thirty rupees per month by the State and one *Motamid* [*sic*] will yearly present to the Maharaja the annual *Nazrana*.
>
> The friends of the Maharaja will be my friends and his enemies will be my enemies.
>
> If a force be required in Gilgit, I shall place my troops at the disposal of the Maharaja for service and I shall not spare any effort in doing the service.
>
> As this agreement has been written, after swearing the Holy Quran, no change whatsoever will take place on my part.

The tribute was paid regularly and when Maharaja Hari Singh ascended the throne the Mir at Hunza went personally to Srinagar to take part in the coronation. He offered some presents besides the stipulated tribute, and received a robe in return. Even when Gilgit was leased out to the British in 1935, a procedure was adopted so that the Mir did not discontinue his offering of tribute to the Kashmir Durbar. The Mir was also in receipt of a subsidy of Rs 2,000 a year from the Kashmir Durbar.

The small territory of Nagar lies on the opposite side to Hunza, bounded on the north by the river Hunza, and possessing the same geographical and geological features. Since 1867 the State of Nagar had been paying a small tribute, to the Maharaja of Kashmir, receiving in return a present of larger value. The ruler there was difficult and it was with considerable force that he had to be brought around to give an undertaking in Persian in 1870 A.D.:

> We undertake to confer with Ghazan Khan, the Raja of Hunza that his son, as also the son of his Wazir should remain in attendance on the Maharaja of Kashmir and in case he does not agree, we shall send our forces against him.
>
> If any *Motabir* of Hunza comes for secret work into our State, we shall kill him.
>
> We shall ask Raja Ghazan Khan to handover the forts of Chaprot, and Nomal, if he agrees well and good: if not, we shall march against him and take their possession by fighting out.
>
> That one of us four, Shah Murad, Mohammad Shah, Mirza and Nadlu will always remain in attendance at Gilgit turn by turn.
>
> "Inter communication between the Gilgit and the Nagar subjects of the Maharaja and others will continue. If any loss occurs, we shall be held responsible.
>
> One real son of the Raja of Nagar and one son of the Wazir will remain always in the service of the Maharaja.
>
> Friends of the Maharaja of Kashmir will be considered friends and his enemies taken as enemies. In case, the Maharaja of Kashmir will demand any force, the same will be supplied without any hesitation well equipped.
>
> That in return for the *Khilat* granted to Raja Jafar Khan, annually, the following *Nazrana* will be presented:-
>
> Horses: 2
> Gold: 21 *tolas*
> Apricots: 5 loads.

Subsequently, a *Sanad* granted by His Highness the Maharaja of Jammu and Kashmir to Raja Jafar Khan of Nagar read:

> Whereas the State of Nagar has recently been in armed rebellion against my authority, and whereas in consequence thereof, You, Raja Jafar Khan, have justly forfeited any rights which you may have possessed as ruler of the said State:
>
> And whereas by reason of your submission, and in consideration of your promise to abide by the following conditions, it is thought

> desirable, as an act of clemency, to re-appoint you as ruler of the said State.
>
> Now, therefore, I have resolved, with the approval and authority of the Governor-General of India in Council, to re-appoint you, Raja Jafar Khan, as ruler of the said State of Nagar, and you are hereby appointed to be Raja of Nagar.
>
> The Chiefship of the Nagar State will be hereditary in your family, and will descend in the direct line by primogeniture, provided that in each case the succession is approved by the Maharaja of Jammu and Kashmir for the time being and by the Government of India.
>
> As annual tribute of the following amounts, that is to say:-
>
> 26 *tolas* of gold, equal to 17 *tolas* and 1 *masha*, will be paid by you and your successors to the State of Jammu and Kashmir.
>
> Further, you are informed that the permanence of the grant conveyed by the *sanad* will depend upon the ready fulfillment by you and your successors of all orders given by the Jammu & Kashmir State, with regard to the conduct of relations between the State of Nagar and the States and tribes adjoining it, the administration of your territory, the construction of roads through your country, the composition of such troops as you may be permitted to retain, and any other matters in which the Maharaja of Jammu and Kashmir for the time being may be pleased to intervene. Be assured that, so long as your house is loyal to the State of Jammu and Kashmir and to the British Government, and faithful to the conditions of the *sanad*, you and your successors will enjoy favor and protection.

Later, a letter from Zafar Zahid, son of Raja Jafar Khan, to the address of Dewan Kripa Ram, the Prime Minister of Jammu and Kashmir fully conveyed the relationship between the two:

> So long as there is breath in my body and head on my body, I shall not swerve from the sphere of your order. With your friends I shall cement friendship, your enemies I shall treat with vengeance and envy. In this work, I hold the Maharaja as my master and supporter and I believe he will think of my welfare, because I am always at his service and have just sent my tribute. The agreement which has been entered into and agreed by Mirza, Shah Murad and others is binding on me.

There is also a letter of August, 1870 from him to the Maharaja saying that he had sent Wazir Shah with his two sons namely, Alidad Khan and Habib Khan and that the Maharaja was pleased to fix an allowance for Habib Khan and appointed Alidad Khan as the ruler of Gilgit. That letter is acknowledgement of an order of the Maharaja, in which the above proposals are embodied. The conquest of Hunza and Nagar in 1895 by Pratap Singh stopped the occasional looting on the Karakoram. The Raja of Nagar had also paid tribute at the coronation ceremony of Maharaja Hari Singh in 1926 and had also entered into a fresh agreement to evolve modalities for paying his stipulated tribute to the Maharaja even after the lease of Gilgit to British in 1936.

Chitral had been the most recalcitrant of all the territories of the Northern most states. Located at the western fringe of Kafristan at an average height of 8,000 feet above sea level. It is adjacent to China and has been a centre of Buddhist learning. Records will show that since the year 1864 the Mehtar of Chitral, Aman-ul-Mulk used to send his *Nazrana* through his representatives, sometimes his brother, Makhmul Shah, to the Maharaja of Kashmir. In 1876 the Mehtar appears to have approached the Maharaja, with a view to seeking his protection against the threatening attitude of the Amir of Afghanistan, who had an eye on this territory. As a result, an agreement was made which ran like this:

> This agreement is made on behalf of myself and my children.
>
> I hereby agree that I shall ever endeavour to obey and comply with orders of the Maharaja and consider his well-wishers as my friends and his enemies as my enemies and in recognition of sovereignty, pay the following *Nazrana*:-
>
> Horses: 3
> Hawks: 5
> Hounds: 5
>
> One *Motabir* of the Maharaja will always remain at Kashgar and one in Yasin and they will be duly honoured and respected. Similarly, one *Motabir* of mine will remain in the Darbar of the Maharaja and another on behalf of the Hakim of Yasin in Gilgit for execution of orders.

> I shall receive a yearly subsidy of rupees 12,000 from the Maharaja in observance of the above conditions and if instead of the *Motabir*, any of my sons takes up the place, he will receive a separate allowance from the Maharaja.

In 1914 the Government of India acceding to the wishes of the Mehtar of Chitral, transferred the areas of Mastuj and Laspur to him by virtue of the agreement signed by him on 2ndApril 1914. The first clause of agreement runs as under:

> I acknowledge the suzerainty of the Maharaja of Kashmir and Jammu and in token thereof will resume the annual payment of following *Nazrana viz*:
>
> Horses: 3
> Hawks: 5
> Tazi Dogs: 6

Further, clause 8 reads as follows:

> In consideration of my acceptances of the above conditions, the subsidies now paid to me and certain officials *viz* Rs 12,000 a year by the Government of India and Rs 12,560 a year paid by the Kashmir Darbar, which he continued subject to the provision that the payment at present aggregating Rs 4,560 a year made by the latter to certain officials and headmen will gradually close as the present recipients die or are removed from Office.

The Mehtar too had attended the Raj Tilak ceremony of Maharaja Hari Singh in 1926. His difficult and complex nature had even then surfaced when after presenting his usual offering, he nursed a grievance on the matter of protocol. He had continued to correspond on the subject till as late as 1935.

Of all the regions it was Skardu that was of most strategic importance for both Ladakh and the Kashmir valley. Situated on the left bank of River Indus, Skardu is the principal town of Baltistan. It is bounded by river Shigar on the north, by Kiris and Parkuta on the east by, Tilail on the South and by Astor and Rondu on the West. They were all located in challenging and forbidding terrain but were of vital importance to the three worlds that met there. A slight lowering of the guards, and the floodgates were opened. Then there was no knowing of the impending fate.

Were the Maharaja to accede to India, how would it pursue the legitimate strategic interests in the region? The only proper road that led to that part was from Leh in Ladakh and the road to Leh started from Srinagar before it ran across the Zoji La Pass and then through Kargil. But how would one reach Srinagar from India if there was no direct link between India and the State? After the partition, the only routewhich was not a good one, was from Pathankot in the Gurdaspur District. Had the District of Gurdaspur gone to Pakistan, as many argued it should have, then Srinagar could not be accessed, nor could Leh or Gilgit. In those times of uncertain future, Maharaja Hari Singh had taken immediate steps to take charge of the territories and had dispatched Brigadier Ghansara Singh as the Governor of the Gilgit Wazarat. His kingdom was now complete. Appropriately, he had ordered the lighting of the buildings in the State. By a strange coincidence, 1st August 1947 was the same day when he was visited by Mahatma Gandhi.

9

The Gathering Clouds

August 1947 had brought some relief to the beleaguered Maharaja when the border raids eased, but that was shortlived as the situation in the border region brought new challenges. He knew that even though the State was dominated by Muslims in numbers, acceding to Pakistan was not an option. Pakistan had already displayed its policy with the uninterrupted killings and lootings of the minorities there. Unfortunately, no credible intent was shown to stop the bloodshed and Jinnah's speech to the Constituent Assembly of Pakistan on 11th August 1947, appeared hollow. As President-elect of the Assembly, he is believed to have made a solemn covenant with the people when he said:

> You are free; you are free to go to your temples; you are free to go to your mosques or to any other place or [*sic*] worship in this State of Pakistan. You may belong to any religion or caste or creed that has nothing to do with the business of the State As you know, history shows that in England, conditions, sometime ago, were much worse than those prevailing in India today. The Roman Catholics and the Protestants persecuted each other. Even now there are some States in existence where there are discriminations made and bars imposed against a particular class. Thank God, we are not starting in those days. We are starting in the days where there is no discrimination, no distinction between one community and another, no discrimination between one caste or creed and another. We are starting with this fundamental principle that we are all citizens and equal citizens of one State... Now I think that we should keep that in front of us as our

> ideal and you will find that in course of time Hindus will cease to be Hindus and Muslims would cease to be Muslims, not in the religious sense, because that is the personal faith of each individual, but in political sense as citizens of the State.[154]

It was a hollow and insincere speech. Even as he was addressing the Pakistan Constituent Assembly, the merchants of death and destruction were busy in the cities and the villages. In these conditions the only viable option for the Maharaja was to accede to India, since the State too was going through the same experiences of loot, plunder, abductions, rape and killings as in West Punjab. Accession to Pakistan, the Muslim majority of the State notwithstanding, with this experience was out of the question. But the leaders of free India, including Sardar Patel, were discouraging him from acceding to India. Nehru was more straightforward in demanding that administrative powers be devolved to Sheikh Abdullah. Patel was less forthright but he had told Colonel Bhagwan Singh, the emissary of the Maharaja who broached the subject with him on the Maharaja's behalf, not to accede at that moment as it was not the right time! All of them, however, suggested that the Maharaja should find a way of determining the will of the people. However, they were also clear in their suggestions that what they meant was the opinion of the Kashmir valley where, undoubtedly, Sheikh Abdullah was the most popular person. In other words, all the leaders in Delhi were telling him that the State's accession was dependent upon his handing over power to Sheikh Abdullah. It was in these circumstances, when the State was under increasing threat, that the idea of the Standstill Agreement looked appealing to the Maharaja.

If both India and Pakistan were agreeable, it would ease the pressure of taking an immediate decision on accession and, importantly, it would give time for passions to settle down. More than India, it was important that Pakistan agreed to it for that would have guaranteed unhindered import of basic and essential commodities like food and fuel. At the moment the communal frenzy had taken the sheen off the joy of independence. Punjab had been completely taken over by the fire of hatred and the lust for blood. Whole villages and towns had been forced to migrate in both directions, many people not even having the time to pick their documents or valuables. People carried and dragged whatever they thought they most needed to salvage for the exodus. These sights and the plight of the ramshackle refugee camps had been so pitiable that Nehru is said to have regretted the folly of having accepted the partition[155]. Even Jinnah had been shocked by the magnitude of the tragedy caused by it.[156] The Standstill Agreement would bring uninterrupted supply of commodities and give the Maharaja the time to wait till all the madness had passed. In this hope his Prime Minister, Janak Singh, who had replaced Ram Chandra Kak, telegraphically offered the Agreement to both India and Pakistan on 12th August 1947. Pakistan accepted the offer but India baulked, wanting some time to ponder over it and promising that soon an official from New Delhi would visit Srinagar for further negotiations. With Pakistan accepting it, the possibility of trade, communication and other essential services continuing uninterrupted was ensured.[157] For long it has been debated if New Delhi's desultory response was what probably effected a change of strategy in Pakistan. Despite the assurance, no one came from New Delhi to further negotiate the terms of the Standstill Agreement and it was probably during this period that Pakistan not only changed strategy but became more determined to have Kashmir at any cost, including force.

Till then it was possible that both Mohammad Ali Jinnah and Liaquat Ali Khan were complacent about the State's accession. They were confident that the Muslim majority district of Gurdaspur would inevitably become part of Pakistan, and therefore Jammu and Kashmir had no option but to join it. Nonetheless, now that the Radcliffe award had been announced and the Gurdaspur district divided, with three of its tehsils being awarded to India, a window of opportunity had been opened for Maharaja Hari Singh to realistically merge his State with India. Soon thereafter, Pakistan betrayed its first signs of impatience by violating the Standstill Agreement and disrupting the supply of essential commodities. Meanwhile, disgruntled ex-servicemen and Punjabi Muslims in Poonch, along with elements from Mirpur, not only armed themselves with the help of the Pakistan army, but were also joined by regular soldiers of the Pakistan army in mufti. The border of the State was truly volatile and Pakistan tried to use it as an excuse for the disruption of supplies, claiming that they were sent. However, lorry drivers were reluctant to enter the State as it was witnessing communal violence.

The life line of the State of Jammu and Kashmir was thus in the hands of Pakistan and all this while the leaders of the National Conference led by Sheikh Mohammad Abdullah made it clear that for them, at that point in time, the issue of accession was secondary. For them the transfer of power into their hands was of greater importance. They claimed that the issue of accession would have to be settled by them independent of the Maharaja. They argued that the fate of the people could not be decided by people who were not free and therefore till they were free of the 'thralldom' they could not possibly express an honest opinion in favour of acceding to India. So much for the national credentials of Sheikh Abdullah and his colleagues from the National Conference![158]

September was a new month and the pressure on the borders appeared to have eased. But, as later events revealed, it was a tactical ease since Pakistan was preparing for a more organized and sinister plan. It had begun to exert pressure on the Maharaja by orchestrating economic blockades to devastating effect. It withheld supplies of oils, petrol, food, salt and cloth, forcing the Maharaja to appeal to the Government of India for help. In the meantime, the Maharaja had continued to explore all the possibilities of help. Ram Chandra Kak, the Prime Minister of the Maharaja, had been asked to resign in the wake of the allegations that he was hobnobbing with Pakistan and been put under arrest. While Janak Singh Katoch had been given the temporary charge of Prime Minister, one Ram Lal Batra had been brought in from Punjab to be the Deputy Prime Minister. Significantly, the Maharaja was also in contact with Mehr Chand Mahajan, who was to be appointed as Prime Minister soon 'with the blessings of Sardar Patel, although it later became clear that he was not particularly popular with Nehru.'[159] In Delhi, Sardar Patel too had begun to take interest in the ongoing situation of the State and suggested to Maharaja Hari Singh to contact Mehr Chand Mahajan to offer him appointment as Prime Minister at that critical juncture.[160] Apparently, Maharaja Hari Singh and Maharani Tara

Devi had contacted Mahajan in the month of May in Lahore and the issues of the State were discussed. After the preliminary talks, because of the disturbed conditions no contact had been possible. But on 25th August, when Mehr Chand Mahajan was living in Dharamsala and was all poised to take oath as the judge of the East Punjab High Court, a special messenger from Srinagar arrived with a letter from the Maharani. She wrote:

> I hope you remember the discussion we had in Faletti's at Lahore in May last. In view of the conclusion arrived then, a telegram was sent to you which owing to the disturbed condition may or may not have reached you. I am, therefore, sending this letter through special messenger, Captain Harnam Singh. On receipt of this you should kindly come here immediately for interview with His Highness, so that after the same you may be able to take the necessary action for implementing the discussion we had and to which you agreed.
>
> Kindly intimate through the bearer the time and date of your arrival at Jammu so that conveyance may be sent for your journey up.[161]

Clearly, the Maharaja knew in May that accession to Pakistan was not an option and that in view of his strained relations with Prime Minister Nehru in the wake of his brief detention at Kohala border, he needed a person who could build bridges with Delhi, be loyal to him and secure favourable conditions of accession to India. Mahajan, in his judgment, was one such person. In response to the Maharani's communication, Mahajan wrote back that it would only be possible for him to come to Srinagar when the rains abated. However, on 7th September he received another communication from the Maharani. She was obviously insistent that despite the challenges of rains and dangers posed by the border raids, she was 'sending Harnam Singh again with necessary escort and a military car to bring you here. I hope you will be able to start immediately on receipt of this letter.' Accordingly, Mahajan left Dharamsala for Srinagar on 10th September. Obviously, the Maharaja was seized of the emergency that had arisen and wanted to follow the advice of Sardar Patel and appoint Mahajan as his Prime Minister at that critical juncture.

After due discussion a letter of appointment was given to Mahajan by the stop-gap Prime Minister Janak Singh on 18th September. He promised to join as soon as the Government of India released him. However, he could be released only after the intervention of Sardar Patel and after meeting Sardar Patel, Nehru, and Mahatma Gandhi who said that 'if possible the State should accede to India and that the administration should have a democratic set up.'[162] Mahajan also called upon Lord Mountbatten before he arrived in Srinagar on 12th October. In Delhi, when he had met Lord Mountbatten, the Viceroy had frankly told him that his position was unenviable and he did not know what advice he could give Mahajan. In addition, Mountbatten expressed his resentment against the Maharaja for refusing to meet him on the issue of accession. According to Mahajan, Lord Mountbatten was inclined towards the State's accession to Pakistan, though he said 'that as Governor-General of India he would be very happy if I advised the Maharaja to accede to India. He asked me to see Mr Menon in whom he had great confidence.'[163] Before his reaching Srinagar, Mahajan had already been informed by the Maharaja's Private Secretary, Nachint Chand, that Sheikh Abdullah had written a letter of allegiance to the Maharaja and had been released from detention. Sheikh Abdullah had written:

> It is about one and a half year's incarceration that—as long wished—I had an opportunity of having detailed talks with Thakur Nachint Chand Ji. What unfortunate things happened during this period in the State I need not mention. But this is now realized by every well-wisher of the State that many of the regrettable happenings of the past have been mainly due to the misunderstandings which appear now to have been deliberately created by interested people in order to achieve their own ends... He [Ram Chandra Kak, former Prime Minister of the State] painted me and my organization in the darkest colours and in everything that we did or attempted to do to bring Your Highness and your people closer...But God be thanked that all these enemies of Your Highness and the State stand exposed today.
>
> In spite of what has happened in the past I assure Your Highness that myself and my Party have never harbored any

> sentiment of disloyalty towards Your Highness' person, throne or dynasty. The development of this beautiful country and the betterment of its people is our common aim and interest and I assure Your Highness the fullest and loyal support of myself and my organization. Not only this but I assure Your Highness, that any party, within or without the State which may attempt to create any impediments in our efforts to gain our goal, will be treated as our enemy and will be treated as such. In order to achieve the common aim set forth above, mutual trust and confidence must be the mainstay. Without this it would not be possible to face successfully the great difficulties that upset our State on all sides at present. Before I close this letter, I beg to assure Your Highness once again my steadfast loyalty and pray that God may grant me opportunity enough to make this country attain under Your Highness' aegis such an era of peace, prosperity and good Government that may be second to none and be an ideal to others to copy.[164]

There was hope yet, and when Sheikh Abdullah, on his release, visited the Maharaja at Gulab Bhavan, he even followed the custom of the court by offering him a gold sovereign. Soon Mahajan had the first glimpse of Sheikh Abdullah, along with his Begum, who had sought a private audience with the Maharaja who insisted upon having Mahajan and Batra during the meeting. Sheikh Abdullah resented their presence and made it very clear that the appointment of a Prime Minister and a Deputy Prime Minister was wholly unnecessary and that the Maharaja should trust him and handover all administration. He would then behave like a dutiful son and a loyal subject, he assured. In the same breath as swearing allegiance to the Maharaja, he also said in so many words that he should only remain a constitutional head. Mahajan assessed him as a person who 'was out to gain power at any cost. To acquire it he would try to influence his friend, the Prime Minister of India, but would not disdain the use of any other means such as creating some kind of an uprising in the State.'[165]

As a first exercise, the new Prime Minister, Mahajan, apprised himself of the political situation of the State and discovered the complexities of the subject. He discovered that the leaders of the Muslim Conference and some influential religious personalities wanted the Maharaja to accede to Pakistan. When Mahajan met them, they told him in no uncertain terms that if the Maharaja acceded to Pakistan they would remain loyal to him and ensure that he remained an independent ruler in Pakistan! The feudatory states of Chitral and Hunza too sent similar messages and also threatened dire consequence if that was not done. The National Conference did not want to accede to Pakistan and one of the reasons was that there was no love lost between Jinnah and Sheikh Mohammad Abdullah. 'Both were thirsty for power and, therefore; there was no common meeting ground between them.'

Prior to Mahajan's taking over as Prime Minister, Jinnah had made repeated requests to the Maharaja to allow him entry in the State for reasons of health. He had also sent his British Military Secretary, twice with a personal letter to the Maharaja with the request that as advised by his physicians, he should be allowed to visit the Valley for rest and recuperation. Further, he was willing to come as a private citizen who would make his own arrangements. However, the Maharaja suspected that the real reason for his visit was to try to coerce him into a favourable decision of accession; to take possession of his territories and celebrate Eid in Kashmir as the Governor-General of Pakistan, including Kashmir. 'The Maharaja sent a polite refusal to all his requests emphasizing the fact, that he being the Governor-General of Pakistan could only visit the State if due arrangements could be made for his stay there by the State Government according to his status as head of a neighbouring State, and if proper security arrangements were possible. This the Maharaja said, he was not able to do in the circumstances that had arisen.'[166] In the opinion of Mahajan, if the Maharaja had allowed Jinnah to visit the Valley, he would have somehow created a situation in Kashmir leading to its accession to Pakistan, though the public stance of Jinnah was that accession was an issue, which entirely fell in the domain of the ruler of the State. To buttress this, the Maharaja was being constantly told that he was a sovereign and independent ruler and need not worry about either the National Conference, Abdullah or the will of the people. If he decided to accede to Pakistan, then Pakistan would ensure that not a single hair on his head would be touched. He was also being told that after accession to Pakistan, he need not delegate any power to the people and that he could rule his State as an absolute ruler.[167] But the Maharaja was not to be taken in by these promises and he was not prepared to put the lives of the Hindus of the State in grave danger by acceding to Pakistan.[168] At the moment, all that the State could do was to utilize the resources available in a way that it survives till the time a solution is found to the accession stalemate.

On the same day when Mahajan arrived in Srinagar, he set about his job and discovered the dire situation though he had some prior idea of it. One of the first tasks that he undertook was to take stock of what was needed for survival and wrote to Prime Minister Nehru of the assistance that was required. Pandit Nehru too responded on 20th October, partially assuring of it. He replied:

> I am aware of the difficulties Kashmir has had recently, more especially in regard to the attitude adopted by Pakistan towards it...we have the friendliest feelings towards Kashmir and its people and that we would gladly help to the best of our ability in providing Kashmir with the commodities...We are strongly of the opinion that no coercion should be exercised on Kashmir State and its people and that they should be allowed to function in their own way and to make such decisions as they think fit and proper...
>
> You will appreciate that there are some difficulties at present in establishing proper communications between India and Kashmir...In regard of sending necessary commodities to Kashmir, we should like to know what exactly you require. You are aware that the situation in India in regard to commodities is also serious one and many important articles are rationed because of short supply. It is not easy for us to spare them. Nevertheless, we shall try our utmost to send you anything that you particularly need...Could you kindly let me have some idea of what you require urgently.[169]

Even as Pakistan was peddling the excuse that the violence in the State and the rebellious conditions prevailing there were deterring lorry drivers from reaching their destination to unload commodities, a special emissary of Jinnah had come to the Valley and had been fomenting communal hatred. Pakistan had sent Major A.S.B. Shah,

Joint Secretary of Pakistan Foreign Ministry, responsible for matters relating to the State to Srinagar, apparently to discuss the subject of supplies, but in reality to coerce the Maharaja into acceding to Pakistan. By imposing the blockade, it had subjected the State to deprivation and not even a 'drop of petrol or an ounce of food' was allowed inside the State. Even those trucks that were bringing the provisions, and had been paid their full payment, were halted at the Sialkot border and Kohala. Though Major Shah had been discouraged from coming to Srinagar, he arrived and insisted on meeting the new Prime Minister Mehr Chand Mahajan. Pakistan was so confident of the ultimate fate of the State that Shah even had the gumption of offering Mahajan the blank Instrument of Accession that he had brought for the Maharaja to sign. But Mahajan raised the issue of blockade and asked him to get that lifted before he could even broach that topic with the Maharaja. Upon this Shah sent a telegram to Jinnah informing him of the development, but he arrogantly told Mahajan that the blockade would be lifted only after the State had acceded to Pakistan. When the Maharaja was informed of this he furiously responded that he would immediately order the construction of Bhaderwah-Kishtwar road to connect with Chamba and Dalhousie so as to connect with the plains of India. He was not prepared to accede to Pakistan for he knew what fate awaited them in Pakistan.[170] Thus Jinnah's proposal was turned down as it was abundantly clear that Pakistan had not denied that the blockade was a coercive tool to force the Maharaja into acceding. Pakistan was meddling in the affairs of the State, especially in the Poonch areas as a way of arm-twisting the Maharaja into acceding to the Dominion. Major Shah, according to Mehr Chand Mahajan then 'became a bit aggressive and he told me that my refusal to decide the question of accession immediately might result in serious consequences. When he said that, I blurted out that a threat of that kind would throw the State into the lap of India!'[171]

With the coming of Mahajan, supply began to trickle from India, but since the new route from Madhopur in Punjab was arduous, it was slow to reach Srinagar. Meanwhile, confident that the communal tensions were making the situation in the State untenable, Pakistan continued to press its tactics in the Poonch-Mirpur section and finally on 18th October, the Government of Jammu and Kashmir was forced to warn Prime Minister Liaquat Ali that if the deterioration in political and economic relations between the State and Pakistan were not halted, the Government of Jammu and Kashmir was fully justified in seeking 'friendly assistance'. Liaquat Ali retorted by accusing the State of trying to suppress the Muslims of the State who constituted 85 per cent of the population and claiming that they had expressed their will to join Pakistan. He accused the State of conspiring to stage a coup d'état against their declared will by joining India. He also warned the State of grave consequences that it would have to bear if it continued its policy of approaching India for support.[172]

Just before this, the Junagarh situation had developed. Even today, historians debate that there was a strong possibility that the situation in Junagarh was manipulated by Jinnah while New Delhi was grappling with the issue of empowering Sheikh Abdullah before accession of the State could be considered. Jinnah was already in touch with the Nawab of Junagarh and had managed to have Sir Shah Nawaz Bhutto, a prominent supporter of the Muslim League appointed as the Dewan of the State in May 1947. The cunning strategist that Jinnah was, he had seen the possibility of Junagarh becoming a pawn in the game to grab Kashmir. He could use it as a straight exchange for Jammu and Kashmir, where the final accessions were to be decided by the will of the people rather than the will of the ruler. Thus another dimension, not part of the Independence Act, was also added with the proposal of plebiscite.[173] On 30th September 1947 Jawaharlal Nehru accepted the idea of a plebiscite for Junagarh and invited Pakistan to submit the issue for referendum to the people of Junagarh under impartial auspices. Pakistan stalled, probably not ready yet for its move in Kashmir.

In Srinagar and New Delhi different moves were being made in the month of September and October. Sensing serious trouble on the borders, the State Forces had been scattered all over the State borders under instructions from the military commander Brigadier H.L. Scott. It was not without significance that Brigadier Scott along with Inspector General of Police Mr Powell resigned their offices a few days before all hell broke loose, as they were convinced that the Maharaja was not going to accede to Pakistan. Probably they had sensed or had some information about the impending invasion of the State by the Pakistan-sponsored raiders. Scattering of the troops could not have been of any help to the State as Pakistan had planned trouble all along the border inciting looting and burning of Hindu homes and villages. The State simply did not have the option of concentrating its forces and then launching an attack but the battalions posted at strategic points were so composed that in case of communal flare up among men in uniform, the task of the invaders would become that much easier.

In another parallel development when general amnesty was declared by the Maharaja and Sheikh Abdullah was released, not only did Sardar Patel express satisfaction and happiness but Sheikh Abdullah himself wrote a letter to the Maharaja on 26th September 1947. Hope, thus aroused, was further strengthened when Prime Minister Mehr Chand Mahajan received a letter dated 21st October 1947 from Sardar Patel, in which he informed him of his discussions with Sheikh Abdullah wherein he had gathered that he was genuinely anxious to cooperate and sincerely desirous of assisting the State in dealing with external dangers and internal trouble. But he had also conveyed to Sardar Patel that unless his hands were strengthened immediately in the public eye, he would not be able to contribute substantially. Sheikh Abdullah had played his first card and Sardar Patel also felt that what he was hinting at was understandable as well as reasonable. There was need for a responsible government in the State as witnessed in Travancore and Mysore. He also added that even though the Government of India was committed to giving maximum support to the State, the clouds were gathering and it was necessary that there be some measure of popular backing to the Maharaja, particularly from such community that represented overwhelming majority. Finally, Patel advised Maharaja Hari Singh to make a substantial gesture to win Sheikh Abdullah's support if India were to come to the help of his State. Without spelling the nature of the gesture, he qualified it by saying that he was not suggesting any radical step that might alienate the loyalty of the body politic that had lent him willing support till then.[174]

The Maharaja suspected that Sardar Patel was putting the precondition of handing over power of administration to Sheikh Abdullah for the support and assistance of the Government of India. With some of the narratives that came after the departure of the British and after the Indo-Pak conflict had taken a serious turn, it became obvious that the Indian leaders were not dealing with the issue of the State's accession with the seriousness it required. One wondered if India wanted the State at all.[175] The decision making was confusing, with Nehru more obsessed with Sheikh Abdullah's installation as head of the administration and Patel displaying little interest in the problem. Pakistan naturally took it as a sign of encouragement. Indian leaders also forgot that prior to Pakistan's creation there was a Congress government in the NWF Province with charismatic leaders heading it. But when the Islamic forces were unleashed during the referendum that was held in July 1947, the Muslim League had easily trounced the Congress and the Khan Brothers. Similar preparations were on for Kashmir too and yet Delhi failed to display the urgency that was then required. Not coveting the State, instead of becoming a virtue, turned into a nightmare.

Then, Prime Minister Jawaharlal Nehru wrote a letter to Prime Minister Mahajan, affirming that the issue of Kashmir was both a personal as well as public matter for him. He reiterated the importance attached to it by the Government of India and expressed concern at the reports that Pakistan was not only threatening Kashmir to accede to it but was approaching the leaders of the National Conference, assuring them of their best behaviour and everything short of independence in case the accession to Pakistan did happen. They had even promised to give them the right to secede. In light of this, the Prime Minister of India felt that it was imperative that Sheikh Abdullah, the most popular leader in his view, be asked to form a Provincial Government.[176] But he also suggested that in view of the circumstances prevailing, it would be undesirable for the Maharaja to make any declaration of adhesion to the Indian Union. This, he said, should be preceded by the installation of the popular Government.

Pakistan had fomented and assisted trouble in the border areas of Poonch, Bhimber, Kotli Mirpur and Muzaffarabad. It had not only made use of the communal frenzy but had sent its soldiers into those districts to organize assaults. Brigadier Scott had in his judgment already spread the thin resources of the State Forces from Gilgit to Sialkot border and with the loyalty of the Muslim soldiers now in serious doubt and the Treaty of Amritsar virtually defunct, the State was in grave danger of losing its identity. The State needed urgent help but the two stalwarts of the Congress who were shouldering the burden of creating a new India were more interested in seeing that power was first handed over to Sheikh Abdullah before the issue of accession could be countenanced. Sheikh Abdullah, on his part, had apparently also informed Pandit Jawaharlal Nehru of the overtures being made by Pakistan and the right to secede.

Maharaja Hari Singh had then undertaken a whirlwind tour of his Forces to motivate them for the oncoming storm in April, but with the worsening of the situation there was need for more effort. His new Prime Minister too became aware of the challenge as all along the 200-mile long border from Kathua to Bhimber, border raids were intensified by Pakistan. These raids were organized by local Muslims who had sent their women and children to the safety of Pakistan and would then invite Muslims from across the border for raids on the border villages. According to Mahajan, these raids were planned and organized by a large number of Muslim officers of the State, including those in the Police and Military. In retaliation, Hindus and Sikhs had started burning Muslim villages, killing them and looting their property.[177]

It was in these circumstances that the new Prime Minister decided to undertake a tour of the border areas from Kathua to Bhimber, Mirpur and Kotli. However, when he informed the Maharaja, he decided to take another hazardous tour of the border areas. Accordingly, he drew up a tour programme and they were to first go to Kathua on 20th October. But after leaving the palace, the Maharaja changed the itinerary and turned to take the Akhnur road that went to Mirpur. Mahajan politely protested as that would upset the whole programme as all the District officials had been informed accordingly. According to Mahajan, the Maharaja said, 'You are new to the State and it is much better in a situation like this not to follow the programme as the Pakistani raiders must have come to know of it and we may find ourselves in difficulty.' Thus they reached Bhimber where they had their lunch at the Dak Bungalow, which was situated just within two miles of border of Pakistan.

The Pakistani town of Gujrat too was within a few miles and there, they came to know later, a Minister of Pakistan had been camping. They also came to know that a raid on the Dak Bungalow had been organized for the next day when they were scheduled to reach, according to their original programme. The raid did take place the next day and the Dak Bungalow was destroyed![178] During the day they had witnessed the havoc that had been caused by the raiders and the beginning of retaliation by the Hindus and Sikhs. The next day they went towards the Kathua side, an area dominated by Hindus and saw a mixed bag. While the border villages suffered raids, considerable number of Muslim families were leaving their villages, bag and baggage, and driving their cattle towards Pakistan. At a number of places they were accompanied by State officers who were trying to render as much help as they could. But there were some places where they were also attacked and killed and what was happening in East Punjab and West Punjab came to be repeated here. The Maharaja and the Prime Minister tried their best to assure these Muslims but the continuous raids from across the border gave no chance of peace to prevail.[179]

Also, on the itinerary of the Maharaja was the 4 J&K Infantry at Kohala commanded by Lieut Colonel Narain Singh. It was a mixed battalion with half the strength constituted by Muslims. After his recent experiences and being aware of the importance of the Kohala Bridge, Maharaja Hari Singh wanted to know about the loyalty of the Muslim soldiers in the battalion and suggested that if the Commander had any doubt about it, then they could still be replaced by others. Lieut Colonel Narain Singh, a professional soldier who had spent much of his adult life among his soldiers was adamant about their loyalty and rejected the offer of replacement. He had responded that he had more faith in his Muslim soldiers than his Dogra brothers.[180] How dearly he and the State had paid for that assessment!

Treachery, as is its nature, raised its ugly head in the dead of night. The Muslim soldiers of the battalion, who had already established contact with the leaders in Pakistan, betrayed the trust of their Commander and struck on the night of 22nd October 1947. It had been the custom with the mixed forces of the State to exempt the Muslims from duty during Eid festival and vice versa during Dussehra. Consequently, the Muslims were on duty on behalf of the Hindus who were in a celebratory mood on the night of the 22nd, when the Muslims betrayed their oath of allegiance and sullied the name of soldiers. Significantly, the attack came from the flanks that were held by the two Muslim Companies. They immediately crossed over to join ranks of the invaders and then killed most of the Dogra soldiers including Lieutenant Colonel Narain Singh. Meanwhile, it was only at this stage that the media had fully grasped what was happening. The report of *The Tribune*, then being published from Ambala, described the conditions in the State as follows:

> ...With Mr Kak's help Pakistan had, completely cribbed, cabined and confined the National Conference and established its operational bases at strategic points like Srinagar, Pahalgam and Gulmarg. West Punjab and Frontier Pakistani crusaders, masquerading as pleasure seekers, had poured into the Valley and besides carrying on subtle poisonous propaganda were organizing stabbers' and fire raisers' squads...With the removal of Mr Kak from the seat of authority the ominous signs on the horizon disappeared...Then Pakistan drove a coach and six through the Standstill Agreement and stopped the import in Kashmir of essential commodities....For the non-Muslims ingress and egress at all the three Pakistan-Kashmir gates became impossible. While lakhs of Muslim refugees of Punjab passed along the Kathus road into Pakistan, no Hindu or Sikh could pass through Sialkot or Muree or Abbotabad [*sic*] into the State without being stabbed or fired at....Little feudal chiefs owing allegiance to the Kashmir Maharaja, were egged on to raise the standard of revolt. In border raids the victims were invariably Hindus and Sikhs. It is also its [India's] clear duty to provide with all the health-giving things—particularly petrol which is the sap of modern life—of which Pakistan has deprived it.[181]

When this report was written and printed in *The Tribune*, Pakistan had graduated to launching a military invasion of the State from Kohala with Srinagar as its target.

10

The Invasion

Major Shah had given an ominous warning of the hard times that were coming. But the problem was that the State could do little about that without support, at least in arms and ammunition, coming from India. On the other hand, India was adamant that devolution of power to Sheikh Abdullah should precede accession. The Government of India had decided that the National Conference leader enjoyed the popular support of the whole State, by which it probably meant that Kashmir was synonymous with the State. This was obviously resented by the Maharaja and surely would offend the people of Jammu, as it later transpired. The Maharaja was left with no other option but to prepare for the Pakistan-sponsored invasion with the tools available to him and hope that Delhi would recognize the nature of the threat and the tragedy that was building. So, he focused on his forces and did his best to recruit as many able-bodied men as possible. In hindsight, it is obvious that the leaders in Delhi had no inkling about the intentions of Jinnah and the Muslim League, or of what the League was planning. Arjun Subramaniam in his book *India's Wars: A Military History 1947-1971* writes that as early as the spring of 1947, when the Partition of the country became imminent, hard-core Muslim officers of the undivided Indian army had begun to conspire at Jinnah's residence at Aurangzeb Road, New Delhi. They 'put together an audacious plan to seize the princely state of Jammu and Kashmir through armed action...The plan in itself was pretty simple—train and push into the Kashmir Valley tens of thousands of warlike Pathan tribesmen from the constantly-at-war NWFP. Complemented by restive Poonch Muslims, who would spread across the Jammu province, the tribals had an added incentive of looting the prosperous towns of Srinagar, Rajouri and Poonch…It is interesting to know that prior to Partition, these very mercenary tribesmen from the NWFP had been bribed by the British with sixteen crores of rupees annually as legal gratuity to maintain peace on the frontiers. The new Pakistani regime could not afford such largesse and found it best to direct them towards the prosperous Kashmir Valley.'[182]

The only thing that the Maharaja anticipated was that the attack would come via the traditional route to the Valley, from the plains of Punjab. In the present circumstances, this strategy gave a twofold advantage—it was the shortest route to the summer capital of Srinagar, and the invaders, tribals from the north-western region, convinced by the propaganda of their planners, hoped that they might get the opportunity to loot and plunder. They also hoped that they might be welcomed by their co-religionists as their liberators from their Hindu ruler. The other two possible routes were the Poonch region, which again gave them the same advantage of religious affinity as in the Valley, and the Sialkot region, which was fraught with risk, as that area of the State was dominated by Hindus. Thus, it was known that the attack on the Valley would come from across the Jhelum, from the Domel-Kohala region. With this in view, the Maharaja had posted the 4 JAK to guard that strategic bridge.

The invasion of the Valley from Pakistan 'was planned with meticulous care and showed considerable strategic and tactical insight. The plan was first to split up the State's army into tiny groups by means of hit-and-run attacks all along the long frontier with Pakistan. In trying to control these apparently uncoordinated attacks, the defending force was compelled to distribute itself into garrisons of platoon strength spread very thin indeed along the entire southern frontier…distribution of the State army into innumerable tiny garrisons meant that it ceased to exist as a strong cohesive force able to offer battle to any strong invader anywhere along the frontier.'[183] In hindsight, it has become evident that the planning had been done and finalized over a period of time and there was a clear hand of not only those British officers who had opted to serve the Pakistan army but, even earlier, of those who had been serving the British Indian Army. Their English counterparts serving the Indian army after 15th August had also silently connived with their countrymen while the India officers were just not up to the challenge that the circumstances had thrown. But there is a clear suggestion of the involvement of General Douglas Gracey and the tacit support lent to him by Major General Scott of the State Forces. General Gracey, Chief of Staff of the Pakistan Army had proposed to the Maharaja to 'establish Pakistani pickets and patrols on the roads from Pakistan into the State via Domel and Islamabad in order to prevent Pakistani raiders from entering the State.'[184] It is difficult to believe that General Scott could not guess the motive behind the proposal though the Maharaja dismissed it out of hand. Nevertheless, this innocent-looking incident gives a peep into the minds of the Englishmen working on both sides of the border.

'Operation Gulmarg', as the invasion was code named by the Pakistani army, was planned and launched by the Army Headquarters of Pakistan. The orders to commence it were issued through demi-official letters marked 'Personal/Top Secret' and were signed personally by the British Commander-in-Chief of the Pakistan Army, General Sir Frank Walter Messervy. He, in tandem with his Chief of Staff, General Douglas Gracey, planned the entire operation of raising twenty *lashkars* (military force) from the frontier region and loaned officers from the regular army. To provide deniability, the officers and the junior-commissioned officers were shown as absent from duty. The task of recruiting volunteers for the *lashkars* fell on the old and experienced frontier man George Cunningham, who the British had brought back, even after his retirement, as Governor of the NWFP in July 1947 on Jinnah's request. Pakistan may have been the face of the Kashmir invasion, but the planning and leg work had been executed by the British officers. Whether this was a British policy or not is not clear, but the fact that George Cunningham was brought back barely a month before their departure gives reason to believe that the British were indeed making a last ditch effort to play some kind of a role in the 'Great Game'.

The fact that the demi-official letters were issued by the British Commander-in-Chief of the Pakistan army within a few days of Pakistan coming into being, was a proof of the complicity of the British officers. A plan like this could not have been visualized and implemented within such a short period. The evidence of the direct role of the Pakistan army in the invasion came from two sources. 'The first was Major Onkar Singh Kalkat, then serving as Brigade Major at Headquarters (HQ) Bannu Frontier Brigade Group, under Brigadier C.P. Murray. The Brigadier being away at Mirali outpost, Major Kalkat on 20 August 1947 received and opened an envelope market Personal/Top Secret, and found inside a letter from C-in-C, Pakistan Army, giving a detailed plan of "Operation Gulmarg". He hastily called up the Brigadier, and was advised not to breathe a word about it to anybody, or else he [Kalkat] would never be allowed to leave Pakistan alive. However, Pak Army got scent of Major Kalkat's knowledge of the "Operation Gulmarg" plan. Consequently he was put under virtual house-arrest in his residence. But the officer made a daring escape and reached Ambala on 18 October 1947. At night he boarded a goods train to reach Delhi post haste. The following day he met Brigadier Kalwant Singh, the acting CGS, Col Thapar, the acting DMO, and Sardar Baldev Singh, the Defense Minister and told them about the Pakistani plan for "Operation Gulmarg". But this did not cut ice with them. While Major Kalkat was in East Punjab to search out his family, which had arrived in India from Mianwali with the help of the local Deputy Commissioner, "Operation Gulmarg" had already started on 22 October 1947, exactly according to the plan that he had informed [the authorities about]. The Indian authorities now realized their folly in showing indifference to Kalkat's invaluable information, and traced him at Amritsar only on 24 October. He was taken to Prime Minister Nehru, who shouted at the Defense Minister and the acting DMO for not taking necessary action in the light of Kalkat's revelation.'[185]

The second source was a journalist, G.K. Reddy, who on 21st October 1947, took a trunk call and found it was from 'Lt Col Alavi, [the PRO of GHQ, Pakistan Army] to API [a news agency] Lahore. Alavi, not suspecting he was talking to anyone but a Muslim, clearly stated that the attack on Ramkot [J&K Border Post in Kohala region] would begin that night. The subsequent progress of the invasion would be given to API Lahore by GHQ Rawalpindi every evening on phone, but must be published as communiqué from "Azad Kashmir Government" under Palandri date line; Palandri being given out as HQ of the "Azad Kashmir Government". After escaping from Pakistan, Reddy gave out his story which was published in *Blitz* weekly of Bombay dated 9 June 1948.'[186] Apart from the information that came from these two sources, the fact that even though there was a strict control over rations and petrol, the supply was still reaching the raiders from official sources, was an indicator of collusion.

In the State, whatever preparations could be made in the face of the odds, hopes had really been pinned on the 4 JAK as it was the crack Regiment and pride of the State Forces. It had been tasked to hold the Domel front where the headquarters of the battalion were located. As noted earlier, it was composed of Dogra and Muslim forces in equal proportion. All troops, barring three companies plus one platoon of the B Company, were stationed at the Battalion headquarters. The A Company plus a platoon of B Company (all Dogras) and a detachment of three-inch mortars were in the Kohala area. The C Company, consisting of all Muslims, was manning the strong defences at Lohar Gali, except for one platoon, which was stationed at Ramkot. The B Company (Dogras), without two platoons, was at Kupwara, with one platoon at Keran. The D Company (Muslims), without two platoons, was at Domel, with one of the detached platoons at Ghori and the other platoon at Dhub. A platoon of the Dogras of the headquarters company was at Battika, and another mixed platoon of the Headquarters was at Kotli. A Muslim platoon of the garrison police company was holding Tithwal. One section of the medium machine guns of the 8 JAK was also under the command of the 4 JAK at Muzaffarabad. Thus the main strength of the JAK forces was focused on Domel, where the two roads approaching from Murree and Abbottabad to Srinagar converged.

The 4 JAK had all the credentials to defend the Muzaffarabad-Domel area. The river Jhelum takes a huge turn from its northwesterly direction to swing southward towards the plains of Punjab. On its south bank, at its confluence with River Kishenganga, is Domel. The main road from Srinagar, which follows the south bank of the Jhelum, crosses over to the north bank at the Domel bridge and then goes two miles north to Muzzafarabad. The south fork of the road from Srinagar travels south from Domel along the east bank of the Jhelum for about twenty miles to Barsala before crossing over to Pakistan via the Kohala bridge. The 4 JAK, the crack battalion of the State Forces, was tasked with defending this sector when it was evident that Pakistan was bent upon seizing the State by force.

The battalion thus posted was the best that the State had. It had gone through intensive training in jungle warfare at Raiwala (Dehradun) and additional training in the jungles of Ranchi before it was earmarked for operations on the Burma front. It had served with distinction during the Second World War. In fact during the war, Admiral Lord Louis Mountbatten, Supreme Commander of the Southeast Asia Command, had visited five Indian Infantry Division and then sent this message to the Officer Commanding of the 4 JAK: 'I was impressed by the representatives I saw of 4 Battalion, Jammu and Kashmir Army, and was glad to have such a good account of them from your General.' When the hostilities of the Second World War came to an end, on 15th September 1945, the 4 JAK received orders to return to Jammu and were warmly seen off by the GOC 505 District, Major General A.H.J. Snelling with the message: 'On leaving the District, we thank you for the magnificent work you have done while here and the excellent results achieved. On returning to your own country, we wish you all good fortune and ever greater triumphs'.

In Jammu, the Battalion was enthusiastically received by Maharaja Hari Singh, the Staff of Army Headquarters and the officers and other ranks of the Jammu Brigade, after five years of service outside the State. During the overseas service, it had earned 2 OBE, 1 MBE, 5 MC, 3 IDSM, 1 OBI Class I and 1 OBI Class II. Pleased by the performance, Maharaja Hari Singh had awarded fifteen days of bonus pay to all officers and other ranks of the unit, and within a week of its return, the whole battalion was sent on paid leave![187]

The danger that now threatened was known even to Major General H.L. Scott, the Chief of Staff of the JAK Forces. As early as 22nd September 1947, he had written a note to the Maharaja on the overall military situation, saying, 'A survey of recent tendencies and events leaves little doubt that the Muslim Conference leaders intend to push forward their policy of union of the State with Pakistan, by force if necessary. It is clear that in this respect they are finding ready support and assistance in the districts of Hazara and Rawalpindi. There can be little doubt that a close alliance is intended if not already formed between [the] Conference leaders and the excited fanatical agitators across the state border to the west. On the southern border of the State the Muslims have massacred, driven out and looted the Sikhs and Hindus…Even more dangerous than these are the many thousands of Muslim refugees that have passed into the districts of Jhelum, Gujrat and Sialkot from the east. They have lost much and no doubt are prepared to recoup themselves at the expense of anyone they are in a position to attack…There are few indication that the Pakistani authorities are making efforts to restrain their people.'[188] Soon thereafter Major General Scott relinquished his appointment and left the State via Rawalpindi for England. Such were the circumstances in the State of Jammu and Kashmir when paramountcy lapsed. The Government of India, the successor to the British Empire was not only baulking but was ignoring the Maharaja's offer to accede, unless its condition of transferring power to Sheikh Abdullah was met.

The fate of the 4 JAK, the betrayal, the perfidy, and the ugliness of communalism was redeemed in ample measure by the heroics displayed by those who had survived that early onslaught and those ex-servicemen and civil volunteers who joined hands to lead the refugees to safety. It is easy to blame Lieutenant Colonel Narain Singh, the Commanding Officer of the Battalion for his monumental folly of trusting his Muslim soldiers in times when forces far too strong for the gallant soldiers were at work. The stresses and strains that the Maharaja and the State Forces were going through even during the pre-invasion days. They were never registered in New Delhi or was ignored in order to build pressure on Maharaja Hari Singh. It is possible that those who studied the messages at the Army Headquarters did not believe what they read. It has been noted earlier that the names like Owen and Sensa, which were mentioned even in early October could not be found in the *Compendium of Places Names* drawn up by the Survey of India. It was only when the name Poonch came to be mentioned in the dispatches that it was realized that a minor war was already being fought on the border of the State of Jammu and Kashmir and Pakistan.[189] The heroics of the State forces notwithstanding, the fact of the matter was that they were ill equipped and ill prepared for such an eventuality. Adding to its woes was the fact that logistically, they were mainly dependent upon Rawalpindi, and the Chief of Staff, Maj. Gen. H.L. Scott, a British officer, had been pressing for release and probably did not have heart in the work during those crucial days.

Actually, much before Maj. Gen. Scott submitted his note, the hostilities had already begun in mid-July 1947 when thousands of Sikh and Hindu refugees were driven from the districts of Rawalpindi and Jhelum. These hapless and ragged groups were chased by large and armed groups. The aim was to harass and loot and then incite the local disaffected Muslim population.[190] The major incidents on the Jhelum front took place by mid-August when, among the hordes of invaders, many could be seen in the Pakistani Army uniforms. Riots had also broken out as early as December 1946 in the area of the Black Mountains in the Hazara district that bordered Muzaffarabad. The Muslim tribes of Hazara made a determined and brutal attack on the Hindus and Sikhs of the area and succeeded in driving them out of the region. An Indian Army column had been sent there in January 1947 but by then the non-Muslim population had been killed, raped or driven into the state.

The Commandant of the 9 JAK, Lieutenant Colonel Chattar Singh, tasked with the defence of the region, knew that he had a challenge on his hands. He had realized the enormity of the challenge when the next crisis hit the region with a political event over which neither the State had any control nor should it have been affected by it in normal times. But since these were abnormal times, in March 1947 when the Khizir Hyat Ministry fell in Punjab, rioting broke out, also engulfing not only Jullundur and Amritsar but also Murree and Rawalpindi. As arson and looting became the order of the day, columns of refugees began pouring into the Mirpur district of the State, crossing the Hill Begam ferry. On a tour of the area, Lieutenant Colonel Chattar Singh noticed that the Muslim troops in the State forces, belonging to the tribes of Chib, Kesab and Gabhar, were not only getting restive but were disinclined to obey the orders of the Company Commander, Captain Dil Mohammad, a Khoja from Poonch. They certainly did not like the idea of providing succour to the non-Muslim refugees. In fact, so intense was their antipathy to their task that they would often gleefully point to the columns of heavy black smoke signalling the sacking and looting of another village or town by their co-religionists.[191] It was not an isolated observation that Lieutenant Colonel Chattar Singh had made, for he found the experience repeated in the areas of Bhimber, Saligram, Owen Pattan, Lachman Pattan and also Rawalakot. Could this mean that the Muslim soldiers of the Forces had been subverted? Maharaja Hari Singh had visited the area between 21st and 25th April and recently on 20th October. Though arriving in a car at Akhnur he travelled to Chichian, Hill, Mirpur, Jhangar, Pandar, Kotli, Hajira and Rawalakot and his encouragement did wonders to the morale of the troops, at least that of the Hindu forces.

Serious trouble had begun to brew since the day India attained independence on 15th August 1947. The non-Muslim population of Gujrat and Jhelum was subjected to large scale massacres and with it came another wave of refugees across the border from Chichian to Manawar. The massacres though were not the end of the matter for a much more sinister plan had begun to unfold in the district of Mirpur and other areas. Posters began to appear on the walls, leaflets were distributed and gatherings at mosques were subjected to communal propaganda. The Muslim population was being incited to rise against the Maharaja and there was no mistaking that the agents of Pakistan were active in the region. With most of the State troops committed to the border and the Pakistani agents succeeding in inflaming the communal passions of the local Muslims, looting, burning and massacre of the unprotected Hindu and Sikh population became synonym of Jehad. More troops were rushed to all these sensitive spots where the refugees from the different parts of Punjab came converging. The Pakistan army was not providing any help to them and the Indian army was not in a position to come to their aid. Moreover, India had communal riots of its own, thus leaving the State not only to defend its borders but also to deal with an internal situation that was worsening by the day. Civil machinery had virtually ceased to exist. The State Forces were stretched to defend the borders and help maintain some kind of law and order. However, the refugee population was enabled to reach places where their lives were secure. For this, three crack Dogra battalions were tied down in the Poonch region. Now there were no reserve units either in Srinagar or Jammu. Probably this was the game plan of Pakistan. In view of the evolving situation, all the penny packet troops were reorganized into a Brigade during the first week of October. As a consequence, the Mirpur-Poonch Brigade at Jhangar was re-designated as the Mirpur Brigade and Lieutenant Colonel Krishna Singh was promoted as Brigadier and given charge, and Lieutenant Colonel Hiranand was handed over the command of the 1st Battalion. Outlying posts, under the Poonch Brigade, too were withdrawn and concentrated mainly at Bagh, Rawalakot and Poonch.

The betrayal by the Muslim troops of the State Forces had begun on a smaller scale, though there were still a few who remained loyal to the State. The contradiction first manifested when armed gangs from the Pakistani tehsils of Murree, Kahuta and Gujjarkhan began mounting increasing pressure and the Poonch Brigade decided to withdraw the border posts of Saligram and Owen Pattan to Sensa. The withdrawal from the Saligram picket had barely been finished on the night of 5th-6th October, when 500 Pakistanis in the Pakistan Army uniforms and distinctive *mazri* (handloom cotton cloth) shirts of the tribesmen attacked Owen Pattan. The two platoons of the Gorkhas of the 2 JAK Battalion, who were manning the post, were asked to surrender. But under the leadership of Subedar Dhan Bahadur, they not only refused but gave stiff resistance. Meanwhile, the garrison commander at Sensa sent out a platoon of Muslims to cover the withdrawal of Sensa, but tragically the platoon turned treacherous and joined hands with the enemy. By morning the post had been run over and the Gorkhas slaughtered, with a few being taken prisoners. This was the first major attack from Pakistan and the first serious setback for the State Forces.

Another setback was met on 9th October when the news of the attack on Owen Pattan reached Kotli. A platoon under Captain Mohammad Hussain was ordered to proceed to Sensa and contact Lieutenant Raghubir Singh Thapa, the Company Commander, and push for Owen Pattan. Captain Hussain did reach Sensa only to discover that it had been surrounded by the enemy. Even then Captain Hussain managed to contact Lieutenant Thapa but both found that the enemy pressure was too much to reach. Therefore, they were forced to withdraw to the Tharochi Fort. But on 12th October, 'a strong column of two companies of 2nd Battalion, under the Commanding Officer Lieut. Colonel Abdul Hamid Khan was sent out…to recapture Sensa and push on to Owen Pattan. The column was accompanied by many Hindu/Sikh refugees from Sensa in the hope of recovering their lost property. The column met with some opposition on the way but it was easily overcome and it reached Sensa the same day. Here the enemy was found to be occupying the Dak Bunaglow with the Pakistani Flag hoisted on the main building. Colonel Hamid Khan immediately launched an attack and drove the enemy out of Sensa. To everyone's joy some Gorkhas of the Owen Garrison, who were being held prisoners at Sensa, got freed during the attack and joined the rescue Column. The Column then advanced towards Owen but it found its way blocked by a very much reinforced enemy. Not only was an advance to Owen not possible but the Column also found it difficult to hold on to Sensa, and two days later Captain Hamid was forced to fall back on Tharochi.'[192] By 10th October the force had managed to reach the Tharochi Fort, twenty-two miles west of Jhangar after re-establishing faith in the professionalism of the State army. It was a fort of strategic importance as it commanded control over the surrounding areas and had been first occupied by Maharaja Gulab Singh.

On the night of 11th-12th October, two companies of the 2 JAK launched an operation to recapture Sensa. The A Company consisted of Gorkhas and was led by Captain Prem Singh, while C Company from Rajouri was led by Captain Rahmat Ullah.Both Companies were under the overall command of Lieutenant Colonel Abdul Hamid Khan. The task was to capture Sensa and then proceed to Owen. On 12th October, Sensa was captured but the march to Owen did not make headway as the enemy was well entrenched on the way. After two days of fierce fighting the troops were forced to fall back to the Tharochhi Fort, which then came under several sustained attacks from the enemy. The assault, under cover of medium machine guns, was repulsed many a times but ultimately it was decided to abandon the fort. However, as the garrison was preparing to leave on the night of 16th-17th October, it received orders that the fort was to be held at all costs. Meanwhile, Colonel Hamid Khan fell sick and Captain Rahmat Ullah Khan was left in command of the Tharochi Fort.

On 21st October, the main garrison of the Tharochi Fort was ordered to withdraw to Jhangar, leaving two Gorkha platoons of the B Company under the command of Lt Raghubir Singh. The rest of the garrison, led by Capt. Rahmat Ullah Khan, moved but encountered the enemy at Juna, fifteen miles west of Jhangar. It was there that they were stuck as the enemy fire pinned them down. With no communication with any one, a Gorkha soldier finally managed to reach Jhangar on 25th October to inform the Brigade Headquarters that the garrison was heavily engaged at Juna. In his anxiety to extricate the column, Brigadier Chattar Singh dispatched two platoons of Gorkhas of the A Company of the 3 JAK with rations and ammunition under Brigade Major Nasrullah Khan. He received explicit commands to reach Juna, extricate the column and thence move to Tharochi Fort to deliver the ammunition and ration to the garrison. Major Nasrullah Khan, upon reaching Juna, took command of the column and in the evening called a meeting of the Muslim Officers and JCOs. Later, the Gorkha soldiers were ordered to rest, only for the Muslim officers and the JCOs to fall upon them and slaughter. Only two Subedars and thirty other soldiers managed to escape to narrate the perfidy and the manner in which Captain Pritam Singh, the Gorkha Company Commander was led into a hut and strangled to death by the Muslim officers and the soldiers of his own battalion.

With the fall of Owen Pattan and Sensa, it was Kotli's turn to be threatened. Anticipating an attack, a platoon of the 3rd Battalion under Lieutenant Ishri Singh was dispatched from Mirpur to reinforce the garrison at Kotli. However, on the way it was ambushed and only thirty men of the platoon and Lieutenat Ishri Singh escaped. When this news reached the Mirpur Brigade, Brigadier Chattar Singh felt helpless as there were no more troops at Jhangar to send. He, therefore, requested the Army Headquarters at Srinagar for additional troops to defend Kotli, which was left with only one Muslim Company of the 2nd Battalion. Meanwhile, he collected some forces and machine guns to reach just in time to avert Kotli from being run over by the enemy.[193] This restored the confidence of the Hindus and Sikhs who were then preparing to abandon the place. On its part, the Army Headquarters sent reinforcements who arrived after a forced march of fifty-six kilometres. However, they could not dislodge the enemy from the surrounding areas and the forces were compelled to take up positions in Kotli. Word had spread about their arrival and with some confidence restored, the Hindus and Sikhs from the rural area, came to the safety of Kotli. The Army Headquarters, apart from sending two companies, had also sent some old muzzle-loading rifles that were lying in the military stores. These were distributed among the Hindus and Sikhs after they had been organized into two platoons. By some coincidence, Revenue Minister Colonel Baldev Singh Pathania had also arrived in Kotli and since the surrounding heights had been occupied by the enemy for sniper shots, the veteran in him was aroused. He stayed back with the garrison to inspire and provide leadership in that hour of trial.[194]

These events also find place in the narrative of the events in Mehr Chand Mahajan's book. He wrote: 'After assuming office of 15th October, I had sent Colonel Baldev Singh Pathania and our military adviser, Colonel Kashmir Singh, to Poonch and Kotli to help our small military force there, and to inspire confidence in the citizens. Colonel Baldev Singh remained at Kotli to give heart to the citizens at great personal risk while Colonel Kashmir Singh returned to Srinagar to apprise the Maharaja about the military situation in Poonch and in Kotli…we decided in the afternoon of 25th that the raiders be given a receding battle. Every effort was to be made to ensure that our depleted forces suffered as few casualties as possible. An all-out effort was to be made to check the advance of the raiders to the town of Srinagar. The Maharaja instructed me to fly to Delhi if I could secure a plane. There had been some loose talk of invoking help from Kabul. Some had even suggested surrendering to Pakistan *if* Indian help was not available in time. All of us however were agreed that we should do our best to save Srinagar.'[195] Since there are only two authentic eye-witness accounts, Dr Karan Singh's and Mahajan's from the civilian point of view, this is an important account of that crucial period, and later descriptions of those critical days need to be tested on this touchstone. Mahajan also described the atmosphere that prevailed in Srinagar on that fateful day of 25th October. He recalled that since the morning that day, panic stricken batches of officials and citizens came to him. While he assured them that the raiders would be driven out, he also added that if they wanted to leave Srinagar, the government would provide some assistance, if they arranged their own transport and would also try to get some transport too. Many who approached him were officials who were waiting for the annual Durbar move to the winter capital of Jammu. Though the leader of the National Conference, Sheikh Abdullah left for Delhi on 25th October, his party workers not only discouraged people from leaving Srinagar but also deflated tires of the cars that were moving out of the city. A day earlier, on the 24th, the Deputy Prime Minister left for Delhi carrying a letter of accession to India from the Maharaja, and personal letters to Pandit Jawaharlal Nehru and Sardar Patel, asking for military help in men, arms and ammunition. Mehr Chand Mahajan also wrote to them, asking them to save the State from Pakistan's unprovoked aggression.[196]

Meanwhile, on the battle-front, another crisis evolved. The forces at Rawalakot had seriously depleted since many had been sent to other places for help. The enemy, becoming aware of this, found it an opportune time to launch an attack. The attack came on the night of 19th-20th October, with the support of mortars, medium machine guns and light automatic weapons. Despite that, this attack was repulsed and heavy casualties inflicted upon the opposition. In the morning, the Rawalakot was littered with the dead bodies of the enemy and the State Forces were able to collect a large number of rifles to help build up its own stores. The weapons used by the enemy during the Rawalakot attack, left no doubt about the direct complicity of the Pakistan army since otherwise they could not have been procured. All these attacks along the border went on to demonstrate that contrary to popular perception, the attack on the State had taken place much before the popularly accepted date. Perhaps the Kashmir factor played such a dominant role in the mind that people found it hard to accept that an attack on southern Jammu too constituted an attack on the State.

In those uncertain and challenging times, the most onerous responsibility lay on the 4 JAK. It had to defend the State borders with the same grit, determination, bravery and above all camaraderie that had been its hallmark during the five years of service outside the State, especially during the Burmese campaign. Its Commanding Officer Lieutenant Colonel Narain Singh had a fierce pride in his battalion, which he had served for a long time. The Battalion was of mixed composition, with half the force consisting of Dogra Hindus and the other half of Poonchi Muslims. This battalion too was stretched out with the A Company, consisting of Hindu Dogras with Lieutenant Labh Singh as Company Commander, and one platoon of the B Company of Dogras posted on the southern fork of the road in the Barsala-Kohala bridge area. The C Company, consisting of Muslims and under Captain Mohammad Azam Khan was posted at Lohar Gali and Ramkot on the Abbottabad road. The D Company consisting of Muslims and under Captain Gaznafar Ali Shah was at Domel with one platoon at Ghori and one at Dhub. The rest of the B Company under Captain Prabhat Singh was away at Kupwara, with one platoon at Keran and a company of the Garrison Police consisting of Muslims at Tithwal. In addition two mixed Companies were formed from the Headquarters Company and located at Bhattika and Kotli on the west bank of Jhelum south of Domel.

The area where the 4 JAK was positioned was quiet compared to what the State Forces had encountered in the Poonch and Mirpur sectors. The Battalion was not on 'operational alert' but was always battle ready. However, the Army Headquarters at Srinagar had begun to see ominous signs on this front too. By 15th October, the refugees, both Sikhs and Hindus from Abbottabad and Manshera, had been coming from this area and they brought disturbing news. A few might have been inclined to dismiss their news as untrustworthy, coming as it was from those who had been rendered homeless and destitute. Traumatized and hallucinating, perhaps they were the ravings of people who were unable to reconcile to the loss of the dear ones. But they were adamant that a large force of Pakistani tribesmen, mainly Afridis and Waziris and numbering more than 6,000 had concentrated in the Abbottabad-Manshera area, and had planned to reach Srinagar at the earliest by the Domel-Srinagar axis. The refugees were certain that they had decided to invade the Valley.[197] In fact, the Government of India too had received such reports earlier as Dewan Shiv Charan Lal, Deputy Commissioner of Dera Ismail Khan, Punjab, had reported to New Delhi while on leave, indicating the impending invasion. He had also reported that it was supported by Pakistan Government.[198]

It was disturbing news and Lieutenant Colonel Narain Singh decided to check its veracity. He had a dedicated team of officers and troops who had gone through the fire together for long years in the jungles of Burma. Each one of them had stood by one another. With the half of the troops being Muslim, it was easy for him to depute them to find if there was any truth in the rumours. His Muslim company commander at Lohar Gali assured him that what he was being told by the Army Headquarters was nothing but alarmist rumours created by traumatized refugees. The commander assured that he had verified from credible sources that no such tribesmen had gathered in concentration. Lieutenant Colonel Narain Singh chose to believe what his Muslim officers told him. Was there any reason for him to disbelieve them? Or, even suspect them? It would have been terrible if they were to know that their Commanding Officer did not trust them because they belonged to a different religion! He was, from his perspective, right in ignoring the rumours brought by the overwrought mind of the refugees.

However, the Army Headquarters in Srinagar had begun to worry. Intelligence reports suggested that the Muslim officers and men manning the forward posts on the Manshera road had been congregating in mosques, ostensibly for prayers, but in reality for secret rendezvous with the agents of the enemy. While the Army Headquarters did try to convince Lieutenant Colonel Narain Singh to verify the reports from independent sources, it was all in vain. Singh repeatedly asserted his trust in his Muslim officers and troops, even more than his Dogra brothers and assured that he had tested their mettle in good measure during the campaign of Burma. He shot down the proposal to disarm them or to withdraw them to Srinagar during those critical times on some pretext by retorting that such an act would be a grievous insult to the battalion and that as long as he was the commanding officer he would not allow that to happen!

Blinded by his loyalty to his command and subordinates, Lieutenant Colonel Narain Singh abandoned caution that was needed in those treacherous times. He refused to see that the circumstances that prevailed in Burma were different. There, the enemy was clearly identifiable and all troops of the 4 JAK, irrespective of their religion or class, were facing a common threat and enemy. The bonds of unity had only grown when both communities rubbed shoulders in the muddy trenches to conquer the common enemy. However, the situation had changed. The Muslim soldiers were all from Poonch, which had become the extended arm of Pakistan and had been causing great concern since August. Nonetheless, drawn by his destiny, Lieutenant Colonel Narain Singh obstinately refused to see this reality.

The Muslim officers and men of the 4 JAK had actually already been in league with the Pakistanis. Detailed information regarding the garrisons at Domel and Muzaffarabad had been passed on to them and when the occasion came, they defected.[199] Thus, during the night of 21st-22nd October, when the Pakistani tribesmen crossed the border into Kashmir, guides from the C Company at Lohar Gali led them to Muzaffarabad and Domel. The troops there were not alert and were sleeping as they believed that security was being provided by the Muslim troops deployed in the forward positions. There were more than 5,000 tribesmen, heavily armed with rifles, light machine guns, mortars and grenades. The defence had no chance and soon after occupying the defensive positions of the battalion, they swarmed the civilian inhabitants of Muzaffarabad and Domel, killing, raping, looting and burning. Aided by their Muslim allies from the 4 JAK, they attacked the battalion's quarter guard and massacred the troops. One of the first to fall was Captain Ram Singh, the Adjutant, who had tried to organize some defence.

Not all was lost, though, in that single fell stroke. A medium machine gun section of the 8 JAK had been left behind in Muzaffarabad when it had passed the city on its way to Chirala from Srinagar. It was located on a high ground and under the command of Havildar Bishen Singh, they repulsed the enemy throughout 22nd October. But by the time evening descended, it had become obvious that the defence of the city was futile and that the city had simply disintegrated. The town, its bazaars and rows of houses were up in flames and the thick black smoke rose ominously over it as the tribesmen began looting, burning, killing and raping women. The Hindu population was particularly targeted.[200]

Soon another Havildar, Nar Singh Dev, a straggler who had managed to escape Domel reached Muzaffarabad and told Havildar Bishen Singh of the sacking of Domel. The two decided there was no hope of holding out for long even on that commanding height that the medium machine gun section occupied. As darkness descended, Havildar Bishen Singh could see the mile long convoy of headlights of vehicles. At midnight, Havildar Bishen Singh gave the order to pull out and after dismantling the machine guns led his troops and a large column of refugees towards the hills to the north. He eventually succeeded in bringing them back safely via Tithwal, Nastachun Pass and Sopore to Srinagar. He, indeed, was the hero of the hour and the saviour of hundreds of lives. Soon the Headquarters Company located at Bhattika too fell victim to treachery.[201] The Company was not under attack but on hearing sounds of firing from the direction of Muzaffarabad and seeing clouds of smoke billowing above the town, Subedar Hukma Singh attempted to contact the Battalion Headquarters by telephone and radio but got no answer. Meanwhile, Subedar Mir Waiz, in command of the platoon at Ghori, rang up urgently and asked for help as, he said, the post was under attack. Subedar Hukma Singh decided not to believe and excused himself by saying he had no troops to spare for the relief operation. That same night, most of his Muslim troops deserted the platoon. The next day was spent waiting for some communication. There was no word. By evening the post was surrounded by about 500 of the enemy, who attacked with mortar and automatic fire. The enemy thereafter had retreated into the hills in order to continue attacking under the cover of darkness. The intense firing had taken heavy toll on the ammunition of the platoon and forced the Subedar to withdraw and try to reach the Battalion Headquarters. They pulled out quietly at midnight to move westward towards Ghori along a track. But during the withdrawal, a Muslim signaller, Sepoy Lal Din slipped away from the column. He went across to Ghori to inform Subedar Waiz about the Bhattika platoon's plight and location. The dawn saw the platoon surrounded and engaged by the enemy in a battle. Among the enemy many were from the platoon of Subedar Waiz! With the ammunition expended, Subedar Hukma Singh had no option but to surrender. They were taken prisoners, marched down to the river, stripped to their underwear, lined up and shot in cold blood. Only one escaped. Sepoy Sansar Singh, who plunged headlong into the torrential stream, managed to emerge on the far bank, a mile downstream to make his way towards the Srinagar road.[202]

The 4 JAK had more heroics in store yet. One of its outposts at Kotli, on the west bank of the Jhelum and about four miles south-west of Domel, consisted of eight men led by Naik Sant Ram. He had heard the sounds of firing on the morning of 22nd October but had no information from the headquarters on the wireless. The able-bodied Hindus and Sikhs of the villages had been issued muzzle loaders earlier and Naik Sant Ram called them up to help bolster defences. They were soon attacked by raiders and hostile villagers but the two attempts made by the enemy were repulsed. However, when ammunition began to run out, Naik Sant Ram had no option but to withdraw the post. After engaging the enemy in running battles, they reached the Jhelum and crossed it by the suspension foot bridge, before quickly dismantling it after the last civilian refugee had crossed it. As they moved towards Domel, they ran into raiders coming from south of Domel. Sensing danger, and with a large number of women and children accompanying them, Naik Sant Ram decided to escape westward through the hills and forests to Garhi. They reached that safety in the early hours of 23rd October. By a coincidence, Naik Sant Ram and his gallant eight men encountered Brigadier Rajinder Singh who was rushing a relief column towards Domel with the explicit instruction of fighting 'till the last man, last bullet'. The civilian population was dispatched eastward along the road but Naik Sant Ram and his men joined the relief column that was on a mission that could stave off dismantling the hundred-year-old legacy.

11

Heroic Retreat

Apparently, the invaders faced only a brief resistance as the initial attack had succeeded because of the betrayal by the Muslim soldiers and some officers. It appeared that the invaders would make a short work of the State Forces. But that did not turn out to be the case as the Barsala-Kohala area demonstrated. Lieutenant Labh Singh, who was commanding his company, galvanized his force by including a handful from the garrison police and some veterans and able-bodied men from the local Hindu and Sikh population. They launched operations inflicting heavy casualties on the enemy and in the process captured many prisoners and seized sizeable arms and ammunition.[203] In fact, Lieutenant Labh Singh and his brave soldiers demonstrated quick thinking, decisive decision-making as the situation emerged and inspiring leadership. This only gave a glimpse of what the State Forces could have achieved if the magnitude of the challenge had not been so unequal, if it had not been outnumbered, or if treachery had not struck them. The sector also demonstrated the will of the common people in the face of adversity.

The southern front of the Barsala-Kohala area was manned by Lieutenant Labh Singh, his Company of Dogras, a few from the garrison police, and when the situation so demanded, some ex-servicemen from among the Hindus and Sikhs of the villages. The young Lieutenant forged a team that carried out offensive operation, inflicting heavy causalities on the enemy and seizing arms and ammunition when defending and retreating. He also succeeded in successfully withdrawing his men when the need arose. When the need did arise, he led a remarkable operation of leading thousands of refugees to safety. The deeds of the A Company rank high in bravery and importance as they thwarted Pakistan from achieving their goals by setting their time table in disarray. Lieutenant Labh Singh also went beyond the call of duty in wartime to lead the civilian population—men and women, young and old—to safety and for that alone his story ought to rank high in the annals of military history. Nowhere in the world is there a parallel to this heroic act as the armies are known to abandon the civilian population in order to pursue their military and strategic needs. The civilians are expendable and their wastage considered an acceptable fact of war—collateral damage in modern day expression.

It was at 2.30 p.m. on 22nd October, that a signaller from the Battalion Headquarters passed a wireless message about the attack by the tribesmen and subsequent slaughter, but did not mention if there were any orders for the Company from the Commanding Officer. At that point in time, number 3 Platoon of the A Company, under Jemadar Suraj Prakash was guarding the bridge of Kohala, number 4 Platoon of the B Company under Jemadar Romal Singh was at Bagla Sikhan and the A Company with one platoon less was at the Barsala Dak Bungalow. Besides these regular troops, there was a newly raised platoon of the Garrison Police consisting of ex-servicemen, mostly Sikhs of the local area. This platoon too was posted at Bagla Sikhan. When Lieutenant Labh Singh learnt of the invasion, he thought it prudent to move his Company Headquarter from Barsala Dak Bungalow to a strategically better location where defensive positions had already been prepared in anticipation of the invasion. Since nothing happened for the next two days, he thought that in their eagerness to reach Srinagar, the raiders had bypassed his position. Thus, for the next three days the Company waited and waited for some message but even the wireless set remained ominously silent. Lieutenant Labh Singh had no means of knowing either of the large scale perfidy that had struck the Battalion or the fact that a large section of the local population had joined forces with the raiders in plundering, killing and raping.

It was only on 24th October that the first footsteps of the

outside world were heard by this Company. A British Brigadier and a Lieutenant Colonel of the Pakistan Army came to Kohala and sent for Lieutenant Labh Singh. He was informed that 6,000 tribesmen were on the rampage in the Valley and that Baramulla had already been sacked. They also claimed that even the Maharaja and his government had fled. Finally, disassociating the Pakistan army from the carnage that was taking place, they asked him to surrender all weapons except personal arms so that he could be taken in custody for safe escort to Rawalpindi, where some Sikh and Gorkha troops of the Indian Army were also waiting to be repatriated to India. Lieutenant Labh Singh did not think long before refusing the offer saying, 'A Dogra soldier would prefer to die fighting than to seek Pakistan's protection'. Jemadar Suraj Prakash, who had accompanied the company commander was pleased to hear the retort and himself added before leaving, 'Good-bye, Sir. We shall meet again if we live'. However, seething within for having failed to trap the Dogra troops, the Brigadier gave vent to his frustration by saying, 'You won't live, Sahib. Take it from me'.[204] The platoon unanimously endorsed the stand taken by the Company commander and resolved to lay down their lives fighting rather than surrendering either before Pakistan or some British officer in its pay. But this episode was proof of the British officers being involved in the 1947-48 war, effectively participating in aggression against a 'country' that had been till the other day under, a dependency of the British Crown.

Lieutenant Labh Singh came to know of the events of that fateful day at Domel only on 25th October when three men of the local Garrison Police, who had been located in the Domel area, reached him after escaping the fate that befell Lt Col Narain Singh and others. They did not have to wait long for the next move of the enemy, for by 8.30 p.m. that evening, they saw a convoy of lorries coming down the Murree road to Kohala. A detachment of the A Company at the bridge reported troops in uniform getting off the lorries. Soon reports of the looting and burning of non-Muslim homes began reaching them. The raiders were operating from the north and driving the refugees southwards. The morning of 25th October, brought the news of the raiders having worked their way to the south, indicating to Lt Labh Singh that the enemy was trying to encircle the A Company's area. The raiders were by then working in the north, east and south while Pakistani troops were occupying the west, on the bridge of Kohala, across the Jhelum.

There was no time to lose and Lt Labh Singh realized that no useful purpose would be served in holding on to the present position. On the contrary, he would be falling prey to the plan of eliminating his Company by the Pakistani Army at Kohala and the raiders from Domel. Therefore, he decided to abandon his positions by the last light of the day. But before he could abandon the position, he received the news from the 4th Platoon at Bagla, which was located two miles to the north-east of the bridge. They reported that a large number of refugees had been driven to that village by the raiders who were now preparing to attack. Without a second thought Lt Labh Singh dispatched the 2nd Platoon to reinforce the 4th Platoon from the B Company of Jemadar Romal Singh. But since the enemy, sensing a big kill at Bagla, continued to build in strength, Lt Labh Singh decided that all his forces should first deal with the imminent threat at Bagla. However, he had to reckon with the fact that the enemy had occupied the Topa Ridge that overlooked the village and the Dana Gali feature. The refugees could not possibly be rescued if the enemy continued to perch on the commanding heights. Therefore, Lt Labh Singh decided that the dominating heights be captured in a pre-dawn attack the following morning. Ex-servicemen of the Indian Army, employed in the Garrison Police Company and able-bodied refugees from the local villages were mobilized to be used both as guides as well as soldiers. The Topa Ridge was attacked with one ex-serviceman Naik Makhan Singh acting as the guide. The raiders were exhausted by the exertions of the day-long looting and plunder and were fast asleep when the attack was launched at 2.15 a.m. It was easily captured though Dana Gali offered some resistance as the raiders there had been warned. Nonetheless, that too was captured after a three-inch mortar was brought to support the assault.[205]

Five refugees, who had volunteered as guides and one ex-serviceman were injured, but the A Company made a rich haul of 8,000 rounds of 303 ammunition and twenty-one hand grenades. More importantly, a number of 'tak-dums'[206], the Pathan-made rifles were captured and issued to Sikh refugees. The captured Subedar also informed that he had retired from the Baluch Regiment and had been called up to join as volunteer for a raid with 300 men under his command. He was leading a mixed force of raiders that consisted of Pathans and Punjabis and Kashmiri Muslims.[207]

Early on 27th October, a new and unexpected situation evolved just when this column was preparing to advance to Awera. A group of about thirty Sikhs arrived, having been sent by Havaldar Balwan Singh of the 5th Garrison Police Company, who along with a few other men had escaped to Mandhari after the Hindu and Sikh elements of his platoon had been killed by the Muslims. But on reaching Mandhari, Balwan Singh had found that a large number of Hindu and Sikh refugees had gathered there from the surrounding villages. Havaldar Balwan Singh had taken charge of the large group but with only swords, muzzle-loaders and a few rifles, it was a matter of time before they were over-run by the invaders. Immediate help was needed to extricate them and escort them to safety. After sending some ammunition for immediate use, Lt Labh Singh led a column to Mandhari, reaching there at about 2.30 p.m. Their arrival was a huge relief and after securing the flanks, Lt Labh Singh had about 9,000 refugees under his protection, as more refugees had arrived. They were then organized in a column and led towards Chikar Gali. The enemy allowed the column of refugees to move, either because it was not aware of the movement or did not want to be involved in a fight at night. But early in the morning this group was attacked by about a 100 local Muslims supported by about thirty Pakistani soldiers. The attack was repulsed and then a counter attack launched under Jemadar Romal Singh, with the support of a strong and determined group of Sikh refugees. The fighting continued till 5.30 p.m. when the enemy was put to flight, leaving behind seventeen dead, seven rifles, thousands of rounds of ammunition and some food. From the platoon, Naik Bharat Singh, Lance Naik Hans Raj and five Sikhs from among the civilians, lost their lives.[208] By then winter had set in and the old and the children were the worst affected. However, since not moving was not an option, everyone pushed forward. For three days the huge column under Lt Labh Singh's care waited while, with the help of the local people, the hill features were cleared of the snipers and the chances of being ambushed eliminated. Inspired and determined the column displayed exemplary will to survive and despite casualties to the troops as well as the refugees, they boldly fought their way through Chikar to reach Nanga Pir, the last high ridge before Bagh, about eight miles to the north.[209]

Tired and believing that they had survived the ordeal of the past many days, the troops, while waiting for the whole column to close in, set about cooking the first hot meal in days. However, before they could eat they noticed two parties of the enemy approaching their position from two opposite directions of the ridge. About the same time when the column of refugees had begun to arrive, the enemy open fired upon them with rifles and machine guns. The troops of Lt Labh Singh responded and repulsed them but the enemy took up sniping positions before another attack. This went on for the entire day and night. Before the day break when platoon commanders and refugee leaders were summoned to the Company Headquarters for consultations; the JCO reported that there was very little ammunition left. Everyone realized that if no progress was made and time allowed to pass, not only would the ring around them tighten but the raiders would get reinforcements as the word of the possibility of a large kill spread. The only option was to break out.

The refugees, however, were not trained to face a crisis situation. Their faith in humanity had already been diminished after their former neighbours had reduced them to destitution after robbing them of their honour and property. After days of living in uncertainty and fear, they had thought that they had reached safety. This early dawn conference sent down jitters and a few among them having already lost faith, imagined the worst. Someone sent the word across that since danger had increased and ammunition was running low, the troops were planning to abandon them and escape. Before order could be restored, many Sikhs had unsheathed their swords, killing their women, particularly the young, lest they be carried away to be converted or sold by the raiders. Desperation and hopelessness had taken a heavy toll, indeed.[210]

Even Lt Labh Singh was getting desperate. The incident had

shaken everyone and he decided that the only course was to take a chance with a desperate break. Who would expect that the troops of the 4 JAK, after having been dealt a number of cruel blows and losing their Commanding Officer to treachery, could launch a daring offensive and lead everyone to safety? They had been on the run with thousands of refugees, consisting of old men, women and children, who had not had a proper meal since leaving Barsala. Lt Labh Singh and his men decided to follow this course in the hope of taking the enemy by surprise. Before launching the attack, Lt Labh Singh ordered the mortars to be destroyed, since all were completely fatigued and exhausted and there was none among the refugees to carry them and their ammunition. His troops were to be used in the attack and the protection of the long refugee column. Thus prepared, about sixty men of the A Company backed by a large group of Sikh refugees made a decisive charge at the enemy on 30th October. The supporting fire came from a platoon's machine gun and the enemy ran helter-skelter, leaving behind some dead, six Pathan rifles, one 303 rifle bearing a JAK number and some ammunition. A number of valiant Sikh refugees too were killed.

No sooner had the enemy begun running, than the column of refugees who were hitherto orderly, got excited at the hope of reaching the safety of Bagh. They broke rank to move down the ridge towards Bagh. This posed a challenge of a different kind to Lt Labh Singh. He decided not to stop them. Instead he focused on organizing a rear guard with three platoons along the three sides of the ridge. He was sure the enemy would return. It did, and the rear guard engaged the raiders. The troops raced backwards to catch up with the last of the refugee column and withstood the ambushes and the frontal assaults. By 3 p.m. all had reached Bani Pasari which was still three miles short of Bagh. Here, the 'the enemy was still hesitant to get too close to the Column and instead sent his agents to the camp in [the]guise of sympathizers to gauge the strength of the troops.'[211]

Meanwhile, it had been decided that the column would spend the night at Bani Pasari because of the pitiable condition of the refugees. Lt Labh Singh called a meeting of his subordinate commanders. Soon, a person, resembling a Sikh, approached the troops. He had brought along with him one Mohamed Yakub and introduced him as the *lambardar* (headman) of the village. It was also vouchsafed that he was a loyal servant of the State and had helped many Hindus and Sikhs to escape to Bagh. Both made the assertion that till a day or so ago there were a number of troops of the Maharaja in Bagh but since then they had heard neither the firing nor noticed any activity. However, they claimed to have heard rumours that the Maharaja's troops had withdrawn to Rawalakot. Fortunately, Lt Labh Singh was not to be fooled and therefore subjected both to intense questioning to finally discover that Bagh, where he and the thousands of refugees were seeking safety, was full of Pathans.

Moreover, behind Lt Labh Singh's back, another drama had been enacted. The man who claimed to be the *lambardar* and had claimed to have helped a few refugees, had won the confidence of some by distributing stocks of flour. He had also 'told them that if they collected some money and gave it to the leader of the Pathans, they would be given safe passage to Bagh. Desperate and demoralized, the leaders of the refugees agreed. Two thousand rupees were collected and one of the refugee leaders crossed over to the enemy and handed over the amount. On being questioned by the Pathans about the state of the Dogra troops, the refugee leader told them all that he knew—particularly about the rumours and that the ammunition had finished and many of them had deserted, therefore, the force consisted of not more than 40 or 50 unarmed personnel—most of them having thrown away their weapons.'[212]

Pleased with the news and the prospect of having thousands herded for their onslaught, the Pathans waited till the dawn of 31st October, and then surrounded the area. Firing a few rounds in the village and confident of not facing any resistance, the leader of the Pathans entered the perimeter of the village along with thirty raiders. Another fifty or sixty raiders remained huddled on a high ground, not knowing that they were facing the Platoon of Jemadar Suraj Prakash. The Dogra troops knew that they were running short on ammunition and therefore were determined to make every bullet count. When the leader of the raiding Pathans entered the village, he shouted for the Maharaja's soldiers to surrender.

Smug and confident, he had not noticed the defensive positions in the bushes and thickets. The first shot was fired by the orderly of Lt Labh Singh, Sepoy Beli Ram that neatly targeted the Pathan leader between the eyes. On cue, a hail of bullets followed and not a single raider escaped. Simultaneously, Jemadar Suraj Prakash and his 2nd Platoon charged towards the rest of the body of raiders who fled but in the process a large number were killed.[213]

As luck would have it, soon after, a detachment of Dogra troops from the Bagh garrison appeared, cheering the morale of the camp. Colonel Maluk Singh had heard of Lt Labh Singh's column and had sent a party to his help. That day, Lt Labh Singh's column finally reached Bagh at 2.30 p.m. Many among the refugees broke down, for in safety it was time to mourn the dead and lament the fate of those who had survived. For Lt Labh Singh, it was time to prepare for other operations. The war for saving the State of Jammu and Kashmir had just begun.

12

The Saviour of Kashmir

The scale of the invasion, the tragedy of the 4 JAK and the thrust towards the summer capital had pushed the State Army towards disintegration and this required the urgent attention of the Ruler. To meet this situation, he sent for his most trusted commander. When the Chief of Military Staff was summoned by Maharaja Hari Singh, he found the Maharaja in his army uniform. All signs were of a critical moment seizing history and Brigadier Rajinder Singh prepared himself for whatever was to come next. He had taken charge when Major General H.L. Scott had relinquished his office to lead a retired life. It was common knowledge that the Maharaja was not inclined to accede to Pakistan and this had probably hastened Major General Scott's decision to press for his retirement. He had been the longest serving Chief of Staff of the State and had overseen the modernization of the State army. But now he had left the State Army at a time when his experience and knowledge was most needed. In a way, his departure from the State was good because his heart was not in this war for reasons already delineated in the earlier chapters. It was now for the Dogra Maharaja, and his officers and soldiers, to face the challenge of defending their State.

When the storm had finally hit Kashmir on 22nd October, it was not like any other day for the Chief of Military Staff, Brigadier Rajinder Singh. It was the day of Dussehra and to give an impression of normalcy, the annual Durbar too had been held,[214] even though it appeared a little surreal. Till that morning it was believed that the border of Kashmir was safe as all the focus of the invaders had been on the Poonch-Mirpur region. This belief was shattered 'when the Officer Commanding 4th Battalion spoke to the duty officer at Army Headquarters on wireless and informed him of the catastrophe that had befallen his troops. The Battalion Headquarters was at that time under attack by the enemy and Colonel Narain Singh could not pass anything beyond an urgent request for reinforcement, before going off the air.'[215]

It was under these circumstances that Maharaja Hari Singh had summoned Brig. Rajinder Singh. He told him that he had already entered into informal discussions with the Government of India regarding accession and for sending troops to defend the State, but there were, unfortunately, some road blocks that were hindering accession, and therefore, help was needed. He did not need to elaborate on them as the Brigadier could guess what they were. However, the more pressing task was immediate, and within the power of the State. As the Chief of Staff, Brig. Rajinder Singh was to 'organize a reinforcement column which he [the Maharaja] would personally lead into battle to stop the enemy's advance.'[216] This holding operation was to be done till the time that help arrived from India. Brig. Rajinder Singh stood there stunned at the words for he thought they implied that the officers of the State Forces were not capable of stopping the enemy! Gathering his wits he vehemently argued against any such move. Pointing to the serious consequences of it and asserted that as long as Dogra soldiers like him were there to sacrifice their lives, the Maharaja did not have to take such an enormous risk. He reminded that his ancestors too had shed their blood in building this marvel of a State, and emotionally recalled the various battles in the high mountains they had fought and recorded achievements that were unparalleled in the history of the Indian subcontinent. Even the mighty Mughals who came from the cold climates of Central Asia had become so soft by their third generation that they had failed to hold on to the north-western frontiers and the Dogras from the lower Shiwaliks and plains had overcome the adverse and alien climatic conditions to wage battles at heights of 15,000 feet, and prevailed. This legacy of the Dogras would not be allowed to be obliterated without a battle unto death by soldiers like him. It was only after the repeated assurances of personally leading the reinforcement column to stop the enemy that Brig. Rajinder Singh could dissuade the Maharaja from going to the front. His task was to hold the enemy on the Muzaffarabad-Uri road until the arrival of the Indian troops. It was then that he was commanded by the Maharaja to defend the Muzaffarabad-Uri road till the 'last man, last bullet', and then directed to mobilize all combat personnel that were available in the Badami Bagh Cantonment and set out for the front. Evidently the Maharaja was not fully aware what the leaders in Delhi were thinking at that moment and what was guiding their decision making. Yet he was confident that help from India was on its way if it did not wish to see a tragic turn in his State. Anything less than armed help from Delhi, would amount to giving a nod to Pakistan to purge the State, killing or forcing the Hindus and Sikhs to convert.

The crisis situation had arisen because of the sacking of Muzaffarabad and the consequent beastly treatment of the civil population by the raiders. Brig. Rajinder Singh, as Chief of Staff knew that there were no reserve battalions in Srinagar as those Battalions that had been there had already been sent to Chirala in Jammu region in view of the SOS received in the first week of October. However, a force of about 100 soldiers of various ranks was collected from the various details in Badami Bagh. Finally an assortment of two platoons from the 8 JAK and one from the 1 JAK, a few personnel from the 7 JAK, who had been on line communication duties between Kohala and Baramulla, a few personnel from the JAK Training School—both, trainees and staff—a detachment of three-inch mortars and a medium machine gun, had been gathered.[217] Three officers, Captain Prithi Singh, Captain Khazan Singh and Captain Nasib Singh were deputed with this force.

This reinforcement column left Srinagar at 6.30 p.m. in civil buses and trucks and after halting briefly at Baramulla to contact civil authorities and give necessary instructions, reached Uri at midnight. Not surprisingly, it was a town on tenterhooks but with the arrival of the troops and their taking up of defensive positions, some confidence was restored among the nervous inhabitants. During the night, they set about organizing and constructing defences, which were reasonably set by morning. Early next morning, on 23rd October, a small force of two platoons was sent forward under the command of Capt. Prithi Singh. They met Subedar Munshi Ram and three men of the 4 JAK near Chakothi, who confirmed the fall of Domel. However, they could neither inform about the fate of Lieutenant Colonel Narain Singh and his officers, nor how the enemy had succeeded in breaking through the defences of Lohar Gali and Ramkot. As the column moved, it came across a stream of refugees fleeing from Muzaffarabad and Domel. It was about half a mile short of Garhi when they heard the first sounds of firing. Upon sighting the enemy, the forces de-boarded the buses. The enemy too had sighted this column and a number of buses, hurrying towards Uri, also arrived. Captain Prithi Singh's column engaged them but they were facing superior numbers and during the encounter, one soldier was killed and Capt. Prithi Singh too was injured. They believed that the enemy, with overwhelming numbers, was working to get around them. Therefore, it was decided to move the forces back by six miles and take up positions at village Hattain, where they could build proper defensive positions with the aim of delaying the advance of the enemy. However, the forces at Uri too realized that the enemy, using its numbers was preparing for a double blow. It was planning to bypass the Uri positions of the JAK forces by crossing the Jhelum over the footbridge at Garhi and going along the north bank to reach Srinagar. They would climb the mountainside from south to proceed along the Pir Kanthi ridge and then descend towards Uri. If the enemy succeeded in doing that, then Brig. Rajinder Singh's mission would have failed as Srinagar would have fallen soon after. If the Maharaja were to fall in the hands of raiders, and therefore Pakistan, everything would have been lost.

The enemy strength was estimated to be more than 5,000. The sheer numbers was making the situation untenable and it was then that Brig. Rajinder Singh sent a message to the Srinagar Brigade Commander Brigadier Faqir Singh, suggesting that all available soldiers at the Brigade Headquarters be dispatched immediately to the front; additional supporting weapons and ammunition be procured somehow and sent to the battle theatre; one Company from Poonch be directed to march immediately via Haji Pir so as to join at Uri; and, the Company of the 4th Battalion posted at Kupwara be immediately moved to Baramulla and then Uri.[218]

But soon, at Hattain too, Brig. Rajinder Singh realized, after another unequal engagement that taking a stand there was not practical. So, it was thought prudent to rejoin the main body at Uri where he and his column reached by nightfall. As this column was preparing for a stand, it was joined by a platoon of infantry, with one section of medium machine guns and one section of three-inch mortars, which had been sent under the command of Captain Jawala Singh in response to the request of Brig. Rajinder Singh. After sending Brigadier Rajinder Singh to defend the Muzaffarabad-Uri road, Maharaja Hari Singh had taken over the command of the Army Headquarters at Srinagar. He sent for Capt. Jawala Singh of the 1 JAK and told him to mobilize whatever troops he could find in the barracks of Badami Bagh and proceed immediately towards Uri with a written message of 23rd October, for the Chief of Staff. It read:

> Brigadier Rajinder Singh is commanded to hold the enemy at Uri at all costs and to the last man. Reinforcement is sent with Capt. Jawala Singh. If Brigadier Rajinder Singh is not contacted, Capt. Jawala Singh is commanded to hold the enemy at all costs and to the last man. He will do his best to contact Brigadier Rajinder Singh.[219]

Capt. Jawala Singh reached Uri and delivered the message. However, found the place swarming with the enemy. There was danger of being overrun and annihilated, and giving the enemy a free run to Srinagar. The next morning, on 24th October, Brig. Rajinder Singh decided to blow up the steel-girder bridge on Uri Nallah just ahead of the forward defences. It was a sturdy bridge and it took the Pioneer personnel of the force about two hours to prepare a suitable demolition plan. Finally, the bridge was sufficiently blown up to prevent vehicular traffic from crossing without carrying out major repairs. Six miles away at Chakothi, the battle was unfolding in its deadliest form. The enemy, supported by three- and two-inch mortars and medium machine guns, and armed with modern weapons launched an offensive in huge waves. However, the medium machine guns of the JAK forces were deadly and the enemy retreated.[220] After regrouping, the column was threatened with another offensive attack but that too was contained, though barely. By now the enemy appeared everywhere, on the ridges, along the slopes, across the river and on the road between Chakothi and Uri. It had crossed over to the north bank of Jhelum by a foot-bridge, which was intact. But this was a clear sign that the enemy was getting help and guidance from local people, either a deserter from the State Army or some sympathizer of Pakistan. Whatever the reason for the evolving tactics of the raiders, Brig. Rajinder Singh was facing a dilemma. He had given his word of honour to his Maharaja that he would defend Uri and the Maharaja had also given him written order to defend till 'last man, last bullet'. However, if he interpreted that order literally, he would be stuck at Uri, either killed or bypassed, and the raiders would reach Srinagar before help arrived from India.[221]

Because of the sheer numbers, Brig. Rajinder Singh knew that the enemy would easily breach the thin defensive positions. Thus, he had a choice to make. He could follow the order to the letter and stick to the defence at Uri, or, to fall back on Mahura and establish fresh defensive positions to stop the raiders from marching on to Srinagar, and redeem the pledge made to Maharaja Hari Singh. Finally, he opted for a strategic retreat and the 'first vehicle of the retreating Column reached Mahura at about 2230 hours on 24th October…But mistaking it for the enemy the staff of the power house cut off the electric supply and the whole of Srinagar was plunged into darkness. That was the Dussehra night and the Maharaja in order to prevent panic among the people was going through the usual practice of celebrating the festival, as if nothing was amiss. When the lights went off it was believed that the enemy had captured the Mahura power station. The Maharaja had by that time just completed the formalities of the Dussehra Durbar and the dinner that was to follow was held in the normal manner with the help of the Palace generator.'[222]

Fortuitously, the raiders not only halted at Uri for the night but also refused to go further without their vehicles as without them they would have nothing in which to carry back the loot that they had been promised. The partial damage caused to a steel-girder bridge earlier had been enough for checking their progress to a certain extent. In the end, that had turned out to be the difference between saving Srinagar and the Valley and the utter rout that had loomed over it, and giving some more time to the leaders to sort out the conditions of sending help. Meanwhile, all the reinforcement promised by Brig. Faqir Singh too had arrived along with the medium machine gun section of the 5 JAK and two detachments of three-inch mortars. They had arrived just in time to be ready for the first enemy attack that began at seven in the morning on 25th October. Brigadier Rajinder Singh also ordered Capt. Jawala Singh and Capt. Nasib Singh to take a demolition party to destroy the two bridges at Boniar on the river Jhelum so that the enemy was prevented from crossing them. This goal was achieved by 4.30 p.m. but before that quite a number of enemy pockets had crossed and occupied the hills and spurs overlooking the stretch of road between Mahura and Rampur.[223]

The attack came from those of the raiders who had crossed the footbridge at Garhi and had moved along the north bank. It was repulsed but a few casualties were suffered, including Capt. Nasib Singh and Subedar Rasila Ram, who were injured. The enemy too realized that it would not succeed in a frontal attack and therefore decided to reach the rear and establish road blocks to prevent withdrawal and encircle the State forces. Thus they continued their journey on the track north of Jhelum to cross to the south by foot bridges. It was decided to once again withdraw to Rampur and establish new defensive positions there. Accordingly, near the Pathar ruins at Rampur, trenches were hastily dug and the perimeter occupied. The night was spent raising high walls around the trenches so that they were not picked up by the fire from the spurs and ridges.

As expected, with the break of day on 26th October, the enemy began firing. Groups of tribesmen could be seen all over the hillside and this brought the three-inch mortars of the column into action. Combined with the effective firing of the machine gun section, the enemy was not given any chance to launch an organized assault. But obviously, the raiders were not just a band of brigands; they were well trained in tactics of warfare. So, once again, the earlier strategy of outflanking and then occupying vantage points behind the State Forces was implemented, so as to cut off any possibility of retreat. The raiders were in nine buses and trucks and this meant that if the defenders were not to be isolated and then picked off, then they had to rush further back before the enemy. Brig. Rajinder Singh, therefore, gave orders to withdraw to the Seri ridge, west of Baramulla. This withdrawal, though, could only be organized by midnight of 26th-27th October.[224]

The enemy, however, had closed in and it became difficult for the defenders to make a break, as they had done on earlier occasions. This was further complicated by the fact that the enemy had already reached the rear of the defenders and had established a roadblock. As Brig. Rajinder Singh's party approached the roadblock it discovered that it was also covered by enemy fire. The only option left was to make a daring attempt to rush through it. It was decided that the troops from the two leading vehicles were to clear the roads of trees while the two behind them provided covering fire. The first roadblock was successfully cleared, but as the penultimate vehicle, in which Brig. Rajinder Singh was sitting, neared Diwan Mandir, the moment proved fateful. His driver was hit, bringing the entire convoy to a halt and making it an easy target of the enemy. Then as Brig. Rajinder Singh got down to occupy the driver's seat, he too was hit in the leg. Major Brahama Singh notes: 'We have it on the testimony of Captain Khazan Singh who was in the same vehicle as Brigadier Rajendra Singh, [*sic*] that he and his men offered to carry the Brigadier on their backs but the Brigadier appreciating that carrying him would hinder the withdrawal, asked him [Captain Khazan Singh] to leave him there, and themselves rush to the next defensive position. That was the last that was seen of this gallant son of Jammu.'[225]

Mehr Chand Mahajan too gives a similar account in his book, where he wrote, 'After dinner as I was about to leave for my residence, the Captain who had come away [after getting injured] from the scene of fight reached the palace. He told us that the State forces under the command of the Dogra Chief of Staff had met the raiders at Garhi...He gave a very optimistic account of the first clash of the State forces with the raiders and told us that they were being driven back. In the early hours of the morning I received a telephone call from the electrical engineer at Mahura as well as from the Dogra Chief of Staff. The Chief told me of his decision to retreat for taking up a position on the Srinagar side of Uri town, as it had not been possible to destroy the bridge situated on the Garhi side of Uri. He was confident of stopping the raiders.'[226] Regarding the fate of Brig. Rajinder Singh, Mahajan wrote, '…an officer came from the front and informed me that the Dogra Chief of Staff had been wounded and was lying on the road with six or seven bullets in his body. He had ordered the rest of his troops to retreat to a position of vantage but did not wish to leave the place where he lay. Though fatally wounded, he was determined to give a fight as long as he was alive.'[227]

Meanwhile, though injured, Capt. Jawala Singh had managed to climb on a vehicle and make a break to reach Seri. He discovered there that only four vehicles had managed to break through and the one carrying Brig. Rajinder Singh was not among them! Other accounts suggest that Brig. Rajinder Singh had been seriously wounded at that roadblock and had ordered his men to hide him under a culvert and to reach Baramulla to join the defences.[228] Thus he remained, a pistol in hand fighting till the last bullet. When the Pakistanis crossed over his dead body, he had redeemed the pledge that he had made to his Supreme Commander.

The saga of Brig. Rajinder Singh's martyrdom has also been described in Ministry of Defence's account of the 1947-48 war operations: 'The defenders under Brigadier Rajendra Singh [*sic*] dug in at Uri. Soon the raiders arrived and launched wave after wave of attack, supported by LMGs [Light Machine Guns], MMGs [Medium Machine Guns] and mortars. After fighting for several hours, the defenders fell back to Mahura during the night of 24/25 October. There the fight continued on 25 October, and the handful of defenders held the overwhelming enemy force at bay the whole day. The raiders redoubled their attack on 26 October and managed to reach within 45 meters of the defenders' positions; but they were halted and could make no progress the whole of day. By then Brigadier Rajendra Singh's [*sic*] small force was running short of ammunition and it feared encirclement. During the night of 26-27 October, therefore, the defenders retreated towards Baramula [*sic*]. In the course of this retreat, a number of roadblocks were encountered and cleared after stiff engagements. The tiny band, however, was being steadily decimated by casualties, and finally it came to a roadblock covered with intense enemy fire. There the gallant band fought and perished almost to the last man. Brigadier Rajendra Singh [*sic*] was himself killed fighting bravely. He was awarded the Maha Vir Chakra for his supreme gallantry and devotion to duty. He and his handful of men held up thousands of the enemy for four most valuable days and thus undoubtedly saved the entire valley of Kashmir from sack and pillage by the raiders.'[229]

Colonel Bhagwan Singh, brought out of retirement by the Maharaja at that critical juncture, described the events leading to, and the aftermath of, the martyrdom of Brigadier Rajinder Singh in the following words:

> The Maharaja sent his Chief of the Military Staff, Brigadier Rajendra Singh [*sic*], to get first hand information about the situation. He found the company position at Garhi within overwhelming numbers approaching from all directions. As the Company was without an officer, he decided to stay on and sent the situation report to the Palace through a Motor Cycle dispatch rider, describing withdrawal from Garhi inevitable. But the Maharaja commanded him not to withdraw under any circumstances and fight there to the last man, last round. It was Maharaja's this Command and its unflinching obedience by Brigadier Rajendra Singh [*sic*] that saved Kashmir. These gallant men put up a heroic fight for three days. Brigadier Rajendra Singh [*sic*] was himself killed and almost all others were either killed or wounded badly. The way now was clear for the raiders advance to Baramulla. They burnt the Mahura Power House, and repeated the atrocities of Muzaffarabad at Baramulla. Out of the population of 15,000 about 5,000 survived. Even the Saint Jospeh's Convent Church and Hospital were not spared. Nurses and patients were brutally killed.[230]

The attack on Kohala was not a local and isolated event, for simultaneously, Pakistan had invaded Skardu too. With the wisdom gained by hindsight, today most of the analysts acknowledge that it was Domel, the gateway to the Kashmir Valley, and Skardu, an important staging point in the 'Great Game', that the British wanted Pakistan to gain possession of, as they were vital cogs in the strategy of the imperialists who still did not believe that their dominance in international affairs was over. In this game plan, Mirpur and Poonch played an important strategic role in scattering the State Forces all along the border of the State from Leh down to Madhopur. Also, the presence of thousands of ex-servicemen from the British Indian Army was used to create the impression of a local rebellion and used as a ruse for Pakistan and its people coming to the 'help' of their co-religionists in their fight against the Hindu ruler.

There might be critics who suggest that Brigadier Rajinder Singh did not follow the order of his Commander-in-Chief in letter, as he abandoned the original position where he was supposed to make a 'last man, last bullet' stand. But he was there when the Maharaja sent for him and gave him the background to the effort that was to be made. The purpose was to buy time for Delhi to decide on his request for help, or a decision on accession. He need not have made that clarification to Rajinder Singh, but if he did, then there was a purpose. It was meant to convey to him the importance of buying time, or else the Maharaja would not have sent his Chief of Staff on such a suicidal mission. Brigadier Rajinder Singh had understood the message clearly and that is why he used his judgment to choose the places where a defensive stand could be taken with minimum loss of life. The four days that he had given to his Maharaja, and to Delhi, to reach an agreement regarding sending help to the State, was all that had mattered in the end. The fact that in the end this extraordinary soldier and officer, one of the finest examples of character, grit, clarity of thought, and gallantry had needed to make the supreme sacrifice, was unfortunate, but then not all stories have a fairy tale ending.

In Delhi, unmindful of the sacrifices being made by the soldiers of the State Forces, Prime Minister Jawaharlal Nehru continued to humour his friend Sheikh Abdullah in the hope that he would be instrumental in exposing the hollowness of the Two Nation theory.

But even as vital days were being gained, negotiations about help to the State from New Delhi continued to flounder on the rock of Sheikh Abdullah and the technicalities of democratic transition. New Delhi had come to know of the fall of Muzaffarabad on 24th October. In response to Maharaja Hari Singh's request for military assistance, all that New Delhi did was to direct the commanders of the Indian Army to 'examine and prepare plans for sending troops to Kashmir by air and road'. It also sent staff officers of the Army and Air Force along with V.P. Menon on a flight to Srinagar to consult with the Kashmir government and the military headquarters.

The Defence Committee met only on the morning of 25th October, and was chaired by the Governor-General, Lord Mountbatten to consider the Maharaja's request. It only decided to alert the Indian Army and not to take any further action till the egos were humoured and technicalities satisfied. There is reason to believe that since the top commanders of the Indian army were all British, they were inclined to delay any decision on help so as to give sufficient time to Pakistan to grab the whole of Kashmir. That would have neatly fitted in the defence plan for Pakistan prepared by their Chief of Staff, General Messervy and his number two, General Douglas Gracey. The misfortune of India and Kashmir was that those British officers, who chose to stay back and serve the Indian Army, did not display any loyalty that the British in the Pakistan Army displayed. The fact was that the British officers in India and Pakistan were still pursuing the British geostrategic interests in the region, and were, therefore, focused upon ensuring that Pakistan gained control over as much of Kashmir as possible, if not the whole of it. Therefore, they were also in contact with one another and exchanging views. The Indian officers had come to know of their duplicity, but since the ultimate decision was with the civilian government, they could do little. This became clear as the Kashmir war progressed. According to the biography of Field Marshall Cariappa, he had to fight 'two enemies, Army Headquarters headed by Roy Bucher, and the Pakistan Army headed by Messervy.'[231] There is reason to believe that General Scott, the Chief of Staff of the Jammu and Kashmir Armed Forces, too had worked in tandem with his fellow British officer in India and Pakistan.

While the British Generals of the Indian Army baulked, Lord Mountbatten, the Governor-General of India, too played upon the idealism of Nehru and argued that unless the State acceded, the presence of the Indian Army in Kashmir would be considered as an act of aggression by the international community. So even as time was ticking for the State, the Government of India was still pondering over the subject. Nevertheless, they sent V.P. Menon to assess the situation. Colonel Sam Manekshaw, later Field Marshal, was also sent to gauge the military situation of the State. The fact that a Colonel was sent to assess the military situation in war-conditions, was indicative of the kind of assessment that was being made. When V.P. Menon had evaluated the circumstances in Srinagar, he realized the gravity of the situation and advised the Maharaja to leave the summer capital immediately so that he could be at hand for consultations in Jammu.[232] He himself left at day break. The Defence Committee once again met on the morning of 26th October, where Lord Mountbatten reiterated that India could legally move troops only after the Instrument of Accession had been signed.

All this while, what were Sheikh Mohammad Abdullah and his colleagues from the National Conference doing? Two of his trusted lieutenants, Bakshi Ghulam Mohammad and Ghulam Mohammad Sadiq, the same duo that had carried the tale of atrocities against Muslims and Islam to Jawaharlal Nehru when Sheikh Mohammad Abdullah had launched the Quit Kashmir movement, had been sent to Pakistan to hold talks with the leaders there.[233] Sheikh Abdullah himself was enjoying the hospitality of his friend, the Indian Prime Minister in New Delhi, far removed from the storm that had broken in Kashmir. Prime Minister Nehru in his letter to Mehr Chand Mahajan, dated 26th October 1947, said that 'I think it is important for Sheikh Mohammad Abdullah to go to Srinagar immediately as the situation there requires urgent handling and his presence will be helpful. I am suggesting him therefore to go straight to Srinagar tomorrow morning'. What he avoided mentioning was that he was suggesting to Sheikh Mohammad Abdullah to take a ride in the plane that was to carry the first Indian Army soldiers to Kashmir!

Meanwhile, both Bakshi and Sadiq who had reached Pakistan, were unable to meet either Governor-General Mohammad Ali Jinnah or Prime Minister Liaquat Ali Khan. They were probably not considered worth meeting because the operation for grabbing Kashmir had already been set in motion by that time. But the fact was that the Kashmiri leaders had failed to read the mind of the Pakistani leaders and they found that the double game that they had wanted to play had failed to cut any ice with Pakistan. It is not inappropriate to imagine the contempt that the martial Muslims from Punjab and the Frontier area had for the martial qualities of the Kashmiris! In any case, Jinnah was by then already boasting that he had Kashmir in his pocket as the invaders had reached Baramulla. That was when V.P. Menon had advised Maharaja Hari Singh to leave Srinagar, and he drove with a caravan carrying families of the officers who had already moved to Jammu for the annual Durbar move.

13

The Politics of Accession

The State had been in serious danger of being overrun till Brigadier Rajinder Singh had held off the raiders for those four crucial days. Even on 25th October when he was repeatedly taking new defensive positions while gradually retreating, the Maharaja had been making desperate overtures to the Government of India to accept the Accession under his signature or provide help. By then the option of warding off the aggression if arms and ammunition had been provided was no longer there since there was hardly any time to raise and train new battalions. By then, nothing short of accession and intervention of the Indian Army would have served the purpose. But even at that late stage, both Nehru and Sardar Patel insisted upon immediately beginning the process of devolution of power to the people by appointing Sheikh Abdullah, Head of Administration. Ironically, the Indian leaders, the commentators and historians have routinely blamed the Maharaja for taking the State to the brink of catastrophe by refusing to concede to their pre-condition for help. They have not been asked what would have happened if the process of democratic devolution of power had started after the accession had been accepted. Did they fear that the Maharaja would go back on his words? After all, there was no such condition in the Instrument of Accession that all the rulers had signed and in all other states the process of constitutional evolution of government had *followed* the accession and not *preceded* it.

In order to comprehensively understand and appreciate the events of that period that deeply influenced the future, it has to be acknowledged that not only the political leadership of India but also the Indian Army approached the State and its Forces with irrationality and prejudices. Applying a different yardstick for the accession of the State to India by its leaders is a prime example, but unfortunately, the Indian Army too has not been free of that prejudice. It is a fact that the officers of the Indian Army treated the State Forces and their officers with barely hidden contempt. Only recently, since the early 2000s, have the surviving officers of the State Forces started speaking of the hurt that was caused to them. It is surprising that it did not register among officers of the Indian Army that their Army was compelled to absorb all the ranks of the surviving JAK forces not because of some political or administrative necessity, but the fact that the same 4 JAK that had suffered treachery in 1947 had given a befitting reply to the Pakistan Army when they confronted each other in Hussainiwala in 1956. All other officers and ranks from other States' forces had been absorbed only after screening; the JAK forces were the only exception to this. Their valiant defence of Hussainiwala in 1956 made this screening unnecessary and redundant. And yet the prejudice continued. This prejudice becomes more pronounced when the officers of the Indian Army write their memoirs about 1947-48 operation in the State. This, unfortunately, also reflects in the Defence Ministry's account of those operations.

By 24th October, it had become clear to the Maharaja that the aggression on his borders was unprecedented in numbers and in scale and that unless India came to the help of the State, the Valley would be occupied by raiders, and hence Pakistan. In order to avert this fate, Mehr Chand Mahajan recalled that the Maharaja sent the Deputy Prime Minister, R.L. Batra to Delhi on the same day 'carrying a letter of accession to India from the Maharaja and a personal letter to Pandit Jawaharlal Nehru and another to Sardar Patel asking for military help in men, arms and ammunition. I also wrote to both requesting them to save the State from Pakistan's unprovoked aggression.'[234] Batra had met, both Jawaharlal Nehru and Sardar Patel, but both were not interested in getting the Instrument of Accession signed. The situation, between the time when Colonel Bhagwan Singh had called upon Sardar Patel and

Batra's visit, had changed little. Batra was told that unless the administrative power was transferred to Sheikh Abdullah, India could not justify sending help. That was the evening of 24th October. It was the same day when Pakistan, having occupied the areas of Muzaffarabad, Mirpur, Bhimber and Kotli through its agents, had declared the establishment of the so-called State of 'Azad Kashmir', along with a Government that was headed by Mohammed Ibrahim Khan as President and included Mirwaiz Mohammed Yusuf Shah as Education Minister. Mirwaiz was one of the first to give up his exalted position of Mirwaiz of the Valley and flee to Pakistan and has been hailed by some historians as being more influential in the Kashmir Valley than Sheikh Abdullah.

The insistence of Delhi upon the Maharaja's transferring of power to Sheikh Abdullah was nothing new. Prime Minister Nehru had made Sheikh Abdullah and his National Conference central to his plans for Jammu and Kashmir's accession to India. As early as 10th October 1947, Nehru is on record having written to Sheikh Abdullah on this subject. 'What should be done in Kashmir is for you to determine. I have impressed upon all the advisers of the Maharaja who have seen me that the only hope for Kashmir and for him [Maharaja Hari Singh] is to obtain your confidence completely and follow your advice,' he wrote. Nehru also followed up with Mahajan, to whom he wrote on 21st October, just a day before the organized offensive to capture the Valley was undertaken by Pakistan backed raiders. He wrote:

> It is clear that the only proper solution of the Kashmir problem today lies in the fullest cooperation between the Maharaja and the people of Kashmir as represented by the National Conference. The cooperation can only come when the people feel they are more or less running the show.
>
> That is why I suggested to you the urgency of taking some step like the formation of a provisional government. Sheikh Abdullah, who is obviously the most popular person in Kashmir, might be asked to form such a government. In law there need to be no major change and the Maharaja's powers might therefore continue. But in practice the burden would fall on the new interim government.

Since an all out effort to check the advance of the invaders to Srinagar needed to be made, the Maharaja did not wait for Batra to return but asked his Prime Minister to arrange a plane for him to go to Delhi the next day, on 25th October. In order to avert devastation of the civil population of the Valley and thickly populated Srinagar, he also contemplated surrendering to Pakistan if Indian help was not available. But just as they were groping with the issue, Menon arrived on a plane. Probably the efforts of Batra had managed to rouse Delhi a little bit, but even at that late stage Menon arrived only to assess the situation and take Mahajan to Delhi. In his memoir, Mahajan has recalled that he reminded Menon that before his taking charge of the office of Prime Minister of the State, Prime Minister Nehru had assured him military assistance whenever he wanted. But all that Menon could tell him was that no decision could be taken till Mahajan went to Delhi. Then he and Menon went to the palace to inform the Maharaja of the latest development, who immediately approved his departure. He further told them, 'that he had decided to send the Maharani and the Yuvraj, who was bed-ridden owing to a fracture of his hip-joint, to Jammu. His Highness did not want to leave Srinagar. He wanted to remain in the city on post of duty, and do his best to protect it from the invaders.'[235]

However, Menon and Mahajan advised him to also leave for Jammu, with Menon arguing that it was better for him to stay at Jammu from where, in the circumstances, consultations, when required, would be easier. Maharaja agreed to this but before leaving at about 2 a.m. on the morning of 26th October, he had to make many arrangements. Delhi leaders, under the influence of the National Conference stalwarts used this fact to spread the canard of his abandoning Srinagar along with his favourites. Even today, many commentators do not realize that those events took place at that time of the year when the annual movement of the Durbar—capital—took place to reopen in Jammu on the first Monday of November. As part of this annual exercise, some staff had already moved to Jammu to oversee the smooth functioning of the annual move and its reopening on the fixed day. However, their families were still in Srinagar therefore the Maharaja also arranged for their departure for Jammu as he thought that he was morally responsible for their safety. His leaving Srinagar for Jammu was later used by Sheikh Abdullah and his colleagues for a vilification campaign against him, and he had to repeatedly protest to Sardar Patel. He also referred to these facts in his Memorandum to the President of India. Recalling the events of those fateful days in the Memorandum, he wrote:

> In the third week of October 1947 Lord Mountbatten was of the opinion that it would be dangerous to send any troops to the help of the State unless the State first offered to accede particularly as such accession would be temporary, being prior to a plebiscite. No final decision was, however, taken on the vital questions by 25th October 1947 but Mr V.P. Menon was asked to fly to Srinagar to find out the situation there. He met me at Srinagar and I made him realize the urgency of the situation and that unless India helped immediately, all would be lost. It was then that on the strong advice of Mr V.P. Menon who said it would be foolhardy for me to stay in Srinagar when raiders were as near as Baramulla, then I left Srinagar with my wife and son. I also ignored the Letter of Accession which Mr V.P. Menon took back with him.
>
> None of my officers fled. The families of some of the officers left for Jammu as the Government used to move to Jammu at the end of October and open at Jammu on the first Monday in November.
>
> On the other hand, it was Sheikh Abdullah who fled from Srinagar and did not return till the Indian troops had started coming into Srinagar.[236]

This issue was also commented upon by Dr Karan Singh in the following words:

> ...his move to Jammu on the night of 25 October 1947 in the wake of the tribal invasion [on the insistent advice of V.P. Menon] was seized upon by the Sheikh to attack and malign him in bitter and brutal fashion. It was presented to the country and the world that here was a cowardly ruler who fled his capital in the dead of night along with his family, jewels and courtiers, leaving his people to face the fury of the approaching onslaught. A barrage of vituperative propaganda was launched by the National

> Conference leaders, and was echoed by newspapers in Delhi and other parts of the country. The irony of the situation lay in the fact that Sheikh Abdullah himself had flown to Delhi on 25 October… and did not return until after the Indian Army arrived.[237]

Later, Lieutenant General L.P. Sen too has mentioned this incident when he narrated a conversation between him and Deputy Prime Minister of the State, Bakshi Ghulam Mohammad. It gives an idea of how strong the opinion of the National Conference was on this issue:

> During the conference I had noticed a definite tinge of bitterness in the hearts of the three men in the room, and as Bakshi Ghulam Mohammed [*sic*] who, unable to restrain himself, brought the reason to the surface.
>
> "Brigadier," he said, "may I ask a question?" I answered in the affirmative. "What," he continued, "would you do to a commander who left his troops and ran away?"
>
> "Court-martial him," I replied, "on a charge of cowardice."
>
> "Well, that's just what our Maharajah has done," he said slowly. "He is the Commander in Chief of the State Forces, and when the tribesmen arrived at Mahura he collected all his valuables, loaded into all the trucks he could lay hands on, and bolted with his family to Jammu."
>
> The Maharajah of Kashmir had not "bolted", as Bakshi had put it. Bakshi Ghulam Mohammed's [*sic*] statement was not wholly accurate. The Maharajah might have been the Commander in Chief of the State Forces, but he was the titular head and not the executive commander. That position was held by the Chief of Staff, who, unfortunately, had been killed at Diwan Mandir. Nor had the Maharajah "bolted", as Bakshi had put it. He had been persuaded for political reasons to leave Srinagar and take up residence in another part of his State. Had he remained in Srinagar and fallen into tribal hands, his functions as the Maharajah would have been dictated to him.[238]

It also needs to be remembered that Lt General Sen had this conversation with Bakshi, and two other dignitaries of the National Conference, at a time when they were unanimous in their opinion regarding the need to vilify the Maharaja, and hence a campaign that became a 'must do' for the leaders of that party to express their solidarity with Ṣheikh Abdullah and degrade the Dogras. Lt General Sen, then Brigadier of the 161 Brigade, has made quite a few comments that are disparaging of the Dogra army, including the claim that when the headcount was made in the Badami Bagh Cantonment, Srinagar in December 1947, 1,854 fully trained soldiers of the State forces were found to be hiding when every hand was required to help out Brigadier Rajinder Singh and his brave troops.[239] Both Major General D.K. Palit as well as Major Brahama Singh have categorically stated that when Brigadier Rajinder Singh called the Srinagar Brigade and requisitioned additional troops, every available soldier, including trainees who had not yet learnt to fire properly, and some non-combatants too were marshalled to create a platoon. Moreover, with an effective strength of just over 8,000 troops, absence of nearly 2,000 soldiers would have been impossible to be missed, unless Sen was accusing the Dogra forces of cowardice. Nevertheless, it was laudable of him to put the record straight as far as Maharaja Hari Singh's departure from Srinagar was concerned.

The next morning, on 26th October 1947, Menon and Mahajan flew to Delhi. Upon landing, they immediately drove to the Prime Minister's residence where Sardar Patel was also waiting. As the situation required, Mahajan requested them for immediate military aid 'at any terms' as Srinagar was in imminent danger. Even at that late stage, Nehru said that 'even if the town was taken by the tribesmen, India was strong enough to re-take it.' Apparently he did not understand the extent of the damage that would have been caused after the tribal takeover and as a result of the struggle to re-take it, and the difficulty and human cost of fighting an urban war. Then he said that it was 'not easy on the spur of the moment to send troops as such an operation required considerable preparation and arrangement, and troops could not be moved without due deliberation merely on [Mahajan's] demand.'[240]

Mahajan claims in his book that he remained adamant on his demand and the Prime Minister remained stuck to his point of view. Finally, exasperated by the refusal of the Prime Minister and his inability to grasp the gravity of the situation, as a last resort, Mahajan said, '…"give us the military force we need. Take the accession and give whatever power you desire to the popular party. The army must fly to Srinagar this evening or else I will go to Lahore and negotiate terms with Mr Jinnah." When I told the Prime Minister of India that I had orders to go to Pakistan in case immediate military aid was not given, he naturally became upset and in an angry tone said, "Mahajan, go away." I got up and was about to leave the room when Sardar Patel detained me by saying in my ear, "Of course, Mahajan, you are not going to Pakistan." Just then a piece of paper was passed on to the Prime Minister. He read it and in a loud voice said, "Sheikh Sahib also says the same thing." It appeared that Sheikh Abdullah had been listening to all this talk while sitting in one of the bedrooms adjoining the drawing room where we were...Prime Minister's attitude changed on reading this slip.'[241]

After that the plans to airlift the forces to Srinagar began to be drawn and Nehru asked Mahajan to go back to Srinagar but he insisted upon staying in Delhi till the aerodrome officer of Srinagar had confirmed the arrival of the planes and troops in Srinagar.

Before leaving for Srinagar, Mahajan met Nehru again and requested him to give him in his own hand the conditions on which help was being sent to the State at such a crucial juncture in its history. The first term was, the Maharaja should accede to India with regard to subjects: defence, external affairs and transport. This the Maharaja had already done. The second was that the internal administration of the State should be democratized and a new constitution was to be framed on the lines of the model already set out for the State of Mysore. The third condition was that Sheikh Abdullah be taken into the administration and made responsible for it along with the Prime Minister. The Maharaja agreed to all those terms. Considering all these facts, if the judgment of history is that at that crucial moment the Maharaja 'vacillated', then history must also record that Sheikh Abdullah and Nehru, because of their stubborn refusal to accept that only the Maharaja had the powers to decide the accession issue, very nearly pushed the State over the precipice into the net of Pakistan.

When the need arose, Maharaja Hari Singh willingly made the sacrifice, which Sheikh Abdullah was not prepared to make.

In this context, the final exchange between Nehru and Mahajan needs to be revisited and analyzed. Even after conceding that the ruler was under the delusion of the prowess of his army and hugely underestimated the danger from the raiders, his primary concern was the safety of the people of his State—the Muslims as much as Hindus. In the end, if he capitulated to Delhi, it was for the safety of the Valley and the capital city of Srinagar. On the other hand, Nehru and Sheikh Abdullah, both, displayed a lot of brinkmanship and insensitivity to the threat as both did not know how Brigadier Rajinder Singh had held off the raiders for four crucial days so that they may arrive at the desired conclusion. Had he not been there, Srinagar could have fallen before India even reacted. It was quixotic of Nehru to say that Srinagar would be retaken if captured by the raiders. The army commanders would have known the difficulties and the cost of such an operation in an urban area. Finally, one suspects that Sheikh Abdullah sent that slip only after hearing Mahajan saying on behalf of the Maharaja that power be given to whosoever Nehru wanted to, but military aid be given to the State. This was what Nehru and Abdullah had wanted all along during that period. Moreover, if the Maharaja had really approached Jinnah and presuming that he would have agreed, then the dream of Sheikh Abdullah to drive out the ruler of Kashmir would have remained a fanciful dream.

Batra had appraised Delhi of all the events and the critical situation on 25th October 1947. It was placed before the Indian Defence Committee that was presided over by Lord Mountbatten and included many British officers as its members. The Committee wasted considerable time in deliberating the legal position and authority of India to intervene unless the State was a part of India. Even at that critical time, the British decision makers could only decide, to send V.P. Menon to Srinagar to investigate and assess the situation! Sheikh Abdullah, in the meantime had fled Srinagar and was in New Delhi enjoying the hospitality of the Indian Prime Minister.

From the objections raised by the British-dominated Defence Committee to the deference shown to those views, it was obvious that even when the future of the State of Jammu and Kashmir was hanging by the thread, the British had been able to sufficiently influence the national leaders to put the condition of 'accession first', and transferring power to Sheikh Abdullah before help could be sent. Much credit needs to be given to Menon who, on reaching Srinagar and assessing the situation, had urged the Maharaja to leave his summer capital immediately in the larger interest and future of the State. Security of the ruler of the State was of paramount importance for his falling into the hands of enemy and Pakistan would have been catastrophic for the Dynasty, the State and also India. It was also very essential that instead of staying in a place of uncertainty he should be in the safety of his winter capital Jammu, so that he could be easily available when required for consultations. By then it was clear that the only option available to him was accession to India, and at that point in time it did not matter whether he remained the ruler or not, since whatever condition might have been laid by India, the priority was to save the Valley from the barbarity of the invaders. By then, the Valley too had come to realize that the people who had come from across the border were the modern day avatars of the same marauders who had been coming to the Valley from across the north-west frontier to loot, kill and deprive them and their womenfolk and honour. The news that had come in the past two days dispelled the theory that communal passions had caused all the tragedy in the subcontinent for the invaders had not spared even Muslims in Muzaffarabad and Baramulla. So buying time till communal passions cooled was no longer an option. Even the so called 'third option' had been taken out of the equation as Pakistan had already played its hand to grab Kashmir by whatever means.

Some historians and commentators have condemned the holding of the Dussehra Durbar under the shadow of looming tragedy and presented it as an example of Nero fiddling as Rome burned. But, as Mahajan, the Prime Minister at that time, and the person who was there, vouchsafed that the Maharaja had held the traditional Dussehra Durbar in the city palace on the Jhelum as had been the custom so that a semblance of peace and calm was maintained. But there was tension and uncertainty as the air was thick with rumours throughout the day and he had thought of scaling down the Dussehra celebrations. However, he also knew that doing that would have only caused panic. It was in such an atmosphere that all hell had broken loose with the lights going out. Not only the palace but the entire capital city of Srinagar had been plunged into darkness. That was the moment when in confusion the employees at Mahura Power Station had switched off the lights. Immediately there were dark suggestions and rumours about the imminent arrival of the invaders. Delhi had finally fallen in the trap of its own making, as it had gone along with Lord Mountbatten in adding a new dimension to the India Independence Act by adding the ascertainment of the will of the people in States. Now Delhi had no option but to go along and insist upon determining the will of the people.

It was being obliquely suggested by Delhi leaders that history would judge Maharaja Hari Singh for his procrastination, but equally, powers in Delhi too would be judged by the same yardstick for their obduracy in insisting that Sheikh Abdullah was the most popular leader of the State and not just the Valley. Even Mahatma Gandhi had been taken in by the propaganda driven myth of his being the leader of the State. Ironically everyone ignored the fact that the Maharaja's willingness to sign the Instrument of Accession had been consistently rebuffed even by Sardar Patel. At a time when the arrival of the raiders in Srinagar looked imminent, Menon, who was there to have a first-hand understanding of the threat and danger, as measure of abundant caution had asked the Maharaja not to remain in Srinagar. He was the first to realize the consequence of his falling in the hands of Pakistan.

It was then that the Maharaja began to make arrangements for moving to Jammu. Additional vehicles and buses had to be arranged for transporting the families of those employees who had gone to Jammu in the advance party that arranges the reopening of offices. Contrary to the propaganda of the National Conference every item of the palace that was usually left there during the winter, remained there in 1947 too. Not a single jewellery or artifact from the palace was taken from Srinagar. It was some decades later that it was discovered that the Maharaja's fabulous wealth in the *Toshkhana* had remained in Srinagar and yet commentators have not regretted the deliberate misrepresentation of facts and continue to repeat unfounded charges. Moreover, it should be remembered that the

Maharaja always kept his personal wealth separate from the State and never took anything from the State unless it was needed for some State function. That night there was the additional problem of the Yuvraj, since his leg was still in plaster and it was obvious that he could not travel in a car. Therefore, a station wagon was altered to adjust his wheel chair and amidst apprehension of attack on the highway, the caravan had begun moving well past midnight in the early hours of the day.[242]

In later years, the Maharaja had regretted adhering to Menon's advice for he was made to pay a very heavy price and had to bear the brunt of a no holds barred malicious propaganda of fleeing the capital to leave the Kashmiris to face the raiders. But that night, he had chosen to listen to the pragmatic advice and had driven his car with his old, and probably the last trusted friend, Victor Rosenthal at his side. The two military ADCs sat on seats behind them. It was dawn when the car reached the top of Banihal Pass. He had slowed down to look below at the valley that had already embraced autumn. For as far as he could see, there was bare and empty expanse of the Valley, with the trees having shed leaves and the farmers gathering their harvest. The onset of autumn is always a sad affair with occasionally a russet maple leaf reluctantly parting from the tree. It would be months before life would again throb in this blessed land. He had driven on, halting at Kud and a few more places before the caravan finally reached Jammu. That was when he had involuntarily said, 'We have lost Kashmir!'[243]

Menon flew to Delhi the next morning only to return the same day to Jammu, when the Maharaja signed the additional papers of the Instrument of Accession and also instructed Prime Minister Mehr Chand Mahajan to assure Delhi that he was willing to hand over administration to Sheikh Abdullah in return for military assistance of India. Along with the Instrument of Accession, he wrote a letter to Lord Mountbatten, the Governor-General of India, informing him:

> I have to inform Your Excellency that a grave emergency has arisen in my State and request immediate assistance of your Government.

As Your Excellency is aware the State of Jammu and Kashmir has not acceded to either the Dominion of India or to Pakistan. Geographically my State is contiguous to both the Dominions. It has vital economical and cultural links with both of them. Besides my State has common boundary with the Soviet Republic and China. In their external relations the Dominion of India and Pakistan cannot ignore this fact.

I wanted to take time to decide to which Dominions I should accede, whether it is not in the best interest of both the Dominions and my State to stand independent, of course with friendly and cordial relations with both.

I accordingly approached the Dominions of India and Pakistan to enter into a standstill agreement with my State. The Pakistan Government accepted this arrangement. The Dominion of India desired further discussion with representative of my Government. I could not arrange this in view of the developments indicated below. In fact the Pakistan Government under the standstill arrangement are operating Post and Telegraph system inside the State.

Though we have got a standstill agreement with the Pakistan Government, that Government permitted steady and increasing strangulation of supplies like goods, salt and petrol to my State.

Afridis, Soldiers in plain clothes, and desperadoes, with *modern* weapons, have been allowed to infilter [*sic*] into the State at first in Poonch and then in Sialkot and finally in mass in the area adjoining Hazara district on the Ramkote side. The result has been that the limited number of troops at the disposal of the State had to be dispersed and thus had to face the enemy at several points simultaneously that it has become difficult to stop the wanton destruction of life and property and looting. The Mahura Power House which supplies electric current to the whole of Srinagar has been burnt. The number of women who have been kidnapped and raped makes my heart bleed. The wild forces thus let loose on the State are marching on with the aim of capturing Srinagar…as a first step to overrunning the whole State.

The mass infiltration of tribesmen drawn from the distant areas of the NWFP coming regularly in Motor Trucks using Mansehra-Muzaffarabad road and fully armed with up-to-date weapons cannot possibly be done without the knowledge of the Provincial Government of NWFP and the Government of

> Pakistan. In spite of the repeated appeals made by my Government no attempt has been made to check these raiders or stop them from coming to my State. In fact, both the Pakistan Radio and Press have reported these occurrences. The Pakistan Radio even put out a story that a Provincial Government has been set up in Kashmir. The people of my State both Muslims and non-Muslims generally have taken no part at all.
>
> With the condition obtaining at present in my State and the great emergency of the situation as it exists I have no option but to ask for help from the Indian Dominion. Naturally they cannot send the help asked for by me without my State acceding to the Dominion of India. I have accordingly decided to do so and I attach the Instrument of Accession for acceptance of your Government. The other alternative is to leave my State and my people to freebooters. On this basis no civilized Government can exist or be maintained. This alternative I will not allow to happen so long as I am the Ruler of the State and I have life to defend my country.
>
> I may also inform Your Excellency's Government that it is my intention at once to set up an Interim Government and ask Sheikh Abdullah to carry the responsibilities in this emergency with my Prime Minister...[244]

Lord Mountbatten replied on 27th October 1947 and added another dimension to the situation, and made it even more complicated than it was. He wrote:

> In the special circumstances mentioned by Your Highness, my Government have decided to accept the accession of Kashmir State to the Dominion of India. Consistently with their policy that, in the case of any State where the issue of accession has been the subject of dispute, the question of accession should be decided in accordance with the people of the State, it is my Government's wish that as soon as law and order have been restored in Kashmir and her soil cleared of the invader, the question of the State's accession should be settled by a reference to the people...
>
> My Government and I note with satisfaction that Your Highness has decided to invite Sheikh Abdullah to form an Interim Government to work with your Prime Minister.[245]

The Government of India's official version of the sequence and events leading to the military support given by it to the State was given in the White Paper in February 1948. It stated:

> ...A large number of States acceded to the Dominion of India, and copies of the Instrument of Accession, as well as the Standstill Agreement governing the administrative arrangements between the States and the Government of India until the new Constitution should come into force in India, are appended. The State of Jammu and Kashmir announced its intention of negotiating Standstill Agreements with both India and Pakistan. In fact, however, the State signed a Standstill Agreement only with Pakistan and entered into no agreement with Government of India, prior to its accession on October 26th, 1947...On the 24th of October, 1947, the Government of India received the first request for military aid from the Government of Jammu and Kashmir State. At that time the Government of India had no agreement, military or political, with the State. A document signed by the British Chiefs of Staff of the Indian Armed Forces states that on the 24th of October information of the capture of Muzaffarabad was received by the Commander-in-Chief in India. No plans for sending troops to Kashmir had up to that time been considered by the Indian Army. On the 25th the Government of India directed the preparation of plans for sending troops to Kashmir by air and road. Indian troops were sent to Kashmir by air on the 27th, following the signing of the Instrument of Accession on the previous night.
>
> The accession was legally made by the Maharaja of Kashmir, and this step was taken on the advice of Sheikh Abdullah, leader of the All-Jammu and Kashmir National Conference, the political party commanding the widest popular support in the State. Nevertheless, in accepting the accession, the Government of India made it clear that they would regard it as purely provisional until such time as the will of the people of the State could be ascertained.[246]

With this curtains had been drawn to a history that had begun in 1846. The hundred years of its life had been witness to many periods of trial and trepidations, which were sometimes marked with the conspiracies to depose the rulers and absorb the State into British India. Finally, circumstances, in which the forces of history had turned out to be too powerful to be repelled or tided over, had prevailed. But Maharaja Hari Singh could derive the satisfaction from the fact that by acceding to India he had saved the lives, properties and honour of at least those Hindus, Sikhs and Buddhists who had not been affected by the early onslaught of the raiders and the Muslim communalists. In acceding to India, he had proven that he was as concerned about the safety and welfare of the Muslims of Kashmir as he was of the Hindus of Jammu. It is hard to believe that Pakistan would have called off the raids if it had been able to take control of the Valley for it needs to be remembered that Pakistan was dissatisfied with the partition of Punjab and Bengal as it wanted both of them to be its part because of the Muslim majority. Without them, Jinnah had called Pakistan 'moth-eaten'. Therefore, Pakistan did covet the Buddhist Ladakh and Hindu Jammu. Had he yielded to the demand of Delhi and decided to handover administration to Sheikh Abdullah, then the raiders would have been in Srinagar in a day or two. But in that final hour, he had redeemed the promise that he had made to the people of the State on his accession of being even-handed in justice. On the other hand, Sheikh Abdullah and Nehru had indulged in the most dangerous game of brinkmanship. Even on the morning of 26th October when Mahajan had been pleading for help in the face of danger from the raiders, Sheikh Abdullah and Nehru had stuck to their demand of installing Sheikh Abdullah in power along with the accession before help could be given to the State. Probably Nehru was not fully apprised of the threat to Srinagar by Sheikh Abdullah, who could not have been unaware of it as he had arrived in Delhi only on 25th October. He had shown little concern for the fate of the Valley and remained focused on somehow grabbing power with the support of Nehru. Finally, when he sent that message to Nehru, supporting immediate military help, it was only after he had heard Mahajan say that Nehru could take all the powers he wanted in the State and give them to anyone he chose, and that Mahajan was under the instructions to fly to Lahore to surrender to Jinnah and save the Valley from destruction if India still baulked at giving military aid. Sheikh Abdulla knew that in that case Jinnah would render him superfluous to his scheme of things for then he would have found his old loyalist Chaudhary Ghulam Mohammad or someone else placed in the seat of power. The Maharaja's Memorandum to the President of India was self explanatory as he had summed up every aspect of the crisis, and if it is studied dispassionately and with an open mind, the reader can get answers to all the questions relating to the delay in taking a decision on accession. The Srinagar airfield, in the meantime, had been upgraded and equipped with new facilities in preparation for the arrival of the planes carrying personnel of the Indian Army. Among those who were waiting in Delhi for the Indian Army to fly to Srinagar was Sheikh Abdullah.

When the first troops of the Indian Army landed in Srinagar, among those present at the airfield was Colonel Bhagwan Singh, the ADC of the Maharaja. In his words, 'Buses had been kept waiting at the aerodrome to avoid delay in moving them to the front. Lieut Col Rai, commanding the Indian troops, issued orders for one Coy to stay at and defend the aerodrome, and the other to move with him to the front. Considering that Colonel [Dewan Ranjit] Rai was not in the picture, the author suggested to him to move with both his Coys to the front as the enemy was advancing in great strength and that the aerodrome was safe until the arrival of more troops, but he ignored the suggestion. On joining the last State troops at Pattan he, however, realized how correct I was, and immediately called the other Coy to the front leaving the aerodrome unprotected. Later, he was killed while withdrawing to Shaltang on the outskirts of Srinagar where a big battle was fought. Another battle was much later fought at Badgaum in the aerodrome area, when some more troops and some armoured cars had arrived by road, which marked the beginning of the raiders' retreat and destruction.'[247]

14

The Defence of Poonch

Understandably, the Valley was the focus of attention for everyone in New Delhi, more so because Delhi hardly understood the region. Therefore, it remained unaware of the equally serious threat that had already taken shape in Poonch. Even Lieutenant General L.P. Sen, later admitted that though the names of Owen and Sensa kept coming up in the intelligence interception of messages, the Army Headquarters in Delhi, unable to find these names in *Compendium of Places Names*, could not identify them. It was much later in the third week of October when the name of Poonch started coming up, that it realized that the State Forces had been fighting a war since mid-August![248] Another reason for this apparent apathy of Delhi was the mutually vitiated atmosphere of antagonism between the Maharaja on the one side and the combine of Jawaharlal Nehru and Sheikh Abdullah on the other. While Nehru remained in denial of Muslim communalism, Sheikh Abdullah became an impediment in his understanding of the situation.

It also took the Indian Army quite some time to understand the construct and geography of the State and realize that the State was not just Kashmir but also Jammu, and that it was the composite State of Jammu and Kashmir. Within the first few months of the war, the Indian senior officers came to understand that the threat to the State was as much from the Poonch and Sialkot region as from the Domel-Uri-Baramulla sector. If Pakistan had succeeded in making deep inroads from the Poonch sector, or if, it had made headway from the Sialkot sector then Jammu too would have fallen, and with it, the Valley would have been completely cut-off from the rest of the country as supplies by air would have been very limited.

Since the inhabitants of Poonch were predominantly Muslims and had close links with the district of Rawalpindi, it had emerged as the pivot on which depended the carefully crafted plan of Jinnah and the British officers, even before Pakistan had come into existence. It has been noted earlier that a secret understanding existed between Churchill and Jinnah.[249] It has also been noted that most of the British officers of the Indian army were sympathetic to the cause of Muslim League as they believed that Pakistan alone could help their home country's strategic interests in the region. We also know that in case of Jammu and Kashmir not acceding to Pakistan, General Douglas Gracey had drawn up a plan to push the borders of Pakistan as far away from its strategic locations as possible.[250] The alternative was to forcibly annex the State. It was for these reasons that fomenting trouble in Poonch was imperative for Pakistan. All this while, India suffered a huge handicap because a large number of British officers either opted for Pakistan or left for home. As a result of this, junior Indian officers of the Indian Army had to be rapidly promoted to higher posts and being less experienced and not fully trained for higher command, remained deferent to their superior British officers for a long time. As a consequence, a number of decisions regarding the conduct of the war affected the ultimate fate of the State and the Indo-Pak relations. How this challenge was dealt with by the middle rung officers of the State and Indian Armies was best demonstrated in the battle for Poonch.

Poonch town had till then remained peaceful as far as the battle was concerned. Like many places dominated by the Muslim population in the subcontinent, the spread of the Hindu and Muslim population was along the rural-urban lines, with Hindus in majority in the town and countryside being dominated by Muslims. For this reason, Poonch was a safe haven for the Hindus and Sikhs of the region. As the outposts held out against the raiders, the enemy had remained focused on the borders. The town was also the Headquarters of the Poonch Brigade, but the troops had been away, manning and defending the outposts. Only a few odd sub-units of the battalions and the personnel of the GPC were located there for local protection. To tell the truth, there was woeful shortage of troops and till the battalions began withdrawing to Poonch, no effective defence mechanism could have been organized for Poonch.

As noted earlier, the Muslim Conference leaders had already established contact with Muslim League in Rawalpindi and its rural branches along the Jhelum.[251] It is strange that when trouble broke out in Poonch warning bells did not ring in New Delhi. On the contrary, the National Conference, the Congress and the media in India preferred to believe and propagate that what had begun as non-payment of taxes by the Muslim population of Poonch, had morphed into a rebellion against the autocratic rule of Maharaja Hari Singh. Consumed in their hatred for the Dogra rule they refused to see that at the end of the day Poonch was a part of the Jammu and Kashmir State and any threat to it was a threat to the entire State. They also did not see that this could be a well-planned move of the Muslim League to gobble up the whole of the State. Poonch, thus, was a calculated and orchestrated move by Mohammad Ali Jinnah to discredit the rule of Maharaja Hari Singh and demoralize both those supporting him and the common citizen.[252]

But at that moment, while Poonch was strategically important for the long term plans of Pakistan and also for the State, for its immediate survival. Lying on the north bank of Poonch river, it has an elevation of 3,400 feet and is dominated by a ring of peaks, the highest being a feature lying to the north of the town rising steeply to a height of 7,700 feet. It was connected to the Srinagar-Domel road from Uri over the Haji Pir Pass. It was also connected to Jammu via Kotli, Jhangar, Naoshera and Akhnur. From Pakistan, Poonch could be accessed by means of two foot bridges, one west of Palandri and the other to south-east at Lachman Pattan and four ferries. As early as mid-September, serious trouble had manifested itself when pressure from the infiltrators across the Jhelum had increased. Located at that time in Srinagar, the 8 JAK, was ordered to move to the Poonch area along the river and on 20th September. The A Company led by Devraj Kotwal moved via the Haji Pir Pass to Lachman Pattan to relieve a Company of the 1 JAK of Captain Prithi Singh so that it could reach Srinagar in time to take part in Brigadier Rajinder Singh's operation to save Uri. On 2nd October, the B Company of the 8 JAK too reached but could not be sent to Palaṇdri because the situation in Poonch itself had begun to deteriorate. Meanwhile, the 7 JAK that was located in Chirala had been surrounded by a strongly armed hostile column and was under mortar fire,Ttherefore, the 8 JAK was to go there as reinforcements under Lieutenant Colonel Maluk Singh, the C Company under Captain Kirpal Singh and the D Company under Captain Mahattam Singh. They were to move to Chirala and assist with the withdrawal of the garrison there to Rawalakot via Bagh. On 4th October, they reached the village Hill where they stopped to cook meal and interact with a platoon of the ill-fated 4 JAK. Though unable to gather any information regarding the presence of the raiders and hostile forces, they could see all the tell-tale signs of enemy activity with the smoke still rising from the burnt houses in the villages. From nowhere the refugees too began to appear and soon about 250 of them gathered at Hill. That afternoon when the column of the 8 JAK began its march towards Chirala, the refugees followed them.[253]

Since the first village that fell on the way was found deserted, the 8 JAK grew suspicious of the situation and from then on moved tactically. It was only on reaching Salian that the troops encountered the enemy in the form of heavy firing. Reacting swiftly, the C Company under Capt. Kirpal Singh attacked the spur from where heavy fire was being directed and took control. Who the enemy was became clear from the facts that among the dead were bodies of men from the North-West Frontier and Punjabi Muslims from Murree. The column could make progress only the following day when the D Company had opened the route after an offensive on Salian was launched. From Salian to Chirala, the route was dotted with the hostile forces with not a single ridge or spur not being occupied by them. In the heavy fighting that ensued, the combined might of the C and D Companies inflicted considerable casualties on the enemy but also suffered a lot, as a number of ponies were hit, forcing the abandonment of dry rations. Nonetheless, the 8 JAK managed to reach Chirala at 5 a.m. on 6th October, just in time, for the garrison there had run out of ammunition and rations.

Next day all of them were to withdraw to Bagh.[254] The troops, like elsewhere, were not only to conduct an orderly withdrawal but also ensure that the refugees who had come under their protection in those difficult circumstances also reached the destination safely. When on 8th October the troops at Chirala moved out along with the 250-odd refugees, they were soon joined by hundreds of other refugees who had been hiding in the jungles. Finally, when the trek to Bagh began it was found that the main track was constantly under sniper fire. Therefore, the column commander decided to take a less travelled but circuitous route to Arja. With old and children among the refugees in tow, the progress was slow and the column halted for the night at Riavla village.[255] However, along with a JCO and four other ranks the company commander of the D Company, Capt. Mahattam Singh had been hit on the first day. After a fierce fight, they finally entered Arja and Bagh on 9th-10th October, respectively.

Bagh, situated on the right bank of Mahl river at a height of 3,400 feet, is surrounded by even higher forested mountain peaks. Hindus and Sikhs constituted its population though the Muslims dominated the surrounding areas. It was connected with both Kohala to the west and Poonch towards the south east by pony tracks. With the communal divide having taken place much earlier because of the influence of the Muslim League and Punjabi communalists, it had been under constant attack by local armed bands. The garrison though had held out even though it was isolated and no movement in or out was possible. Adding to the problems of the garrison was the ever increasing number of refugees from the surrounding areas. Soon a critical situation arose, with the civil authorities running out of food stocks and medicine. On 19th October, Srinagar responded by sending the message that it would be sending supplies, medicine and ammunition from Chakothi on 21st October, and the casualties would also be evacuated. The elation at Bagh over the happy news was short lived for soon the wireless informed them on 22nd October, of the attack on Muzaffarabad and Domel. The beleaguered garrison was informed the same evening of the difficulty in sending relief as there was heavy concentration of enemy positions between Chakothi and

Garhi. Therefore, the garrison was advised to fight on its own—to the last man and last round.[256] By now the only ammunition left with the troops was the one in pouches. Even air dropping was ruled out as it had been tried in Rawalakot with limited success but high risk to the aircraft. By 28th October, the situation had worsened with many soldiers having totally exhausted their ammunition, but still the troops held on. On 7th November, a sustained attack from the enemy brought it to within 700 yards of the perimeter. It was then that Lieutenant Colonel Maluk Singh decided to abandon Bagh. By now there were about 20,000 refugees in Bagh. Leading them to safety was a far greater challenge and it was decided that if they were to be guided to safety then the route through the Toli Pir Pass should be taken. The advance guard did a commendable job when it quietly crept up the pass to surprise the enemy. Having killed the enemy, they safely negotiated the pass along with the long column of refugees. On 8th November, the column had made way to Kholi Draman and amidst occasional to sporadic enemy fire finally reached Poonch on 9th November. Another battalion, the 9 JAK too had been sent from Badami Bagh Cantonment, Srinagar to Poonch in September. Under command of Lieutenant Colonel Ram Lal, it had its headquarters at Rawalakot along with the A and B Companies. Major Somant Singh's C Company and D the Company under Major Prakash Chand Katoch were sent to Tain and Thorar respectively and a platoon of the D Company was sent to Mang.

The first onslaught was repulsed by inflicting many casualties, but the 9 JAK posts too had suffered heavily. Consequently, the Commanding Officer at Rawalakot decided to reinforce the outposts. As the enemy was concentrated at Thorar, Lt Col Ram Lal himself led the troops consisting of the B Company of the 9 JAK along with its support and Headquarter Companies and the A Company of the 1 JAK from Palandri led by Captain Vakil Singh. Lt Col Ram Lal also decided to withdraw the C Company from Tain to strengthen his column. Thus after two days of heavy fighting, the column managed to break through the enemy lines to first reach Thorar and then Mang. It was only upon reaching these places that Lt Col Ram Lal realized the magnitude of the problem. The garrison had exhausted its rations and was saddled with the responsibility of looking after 5,000 refugees from the neighbouring areas, both within the State and from across the border where communal frenzy had taken a heavy toll. In addition, it had suffered heavy casualties. Thirteen of the troops were dead and twenty-seven wounded. Considering the situation, Lt Col Ram Lal decided to withdraw the military personnel and the refugees to Rawalakot.[257]

Rawalakot had by then become the gathering point for all the sub-units along the border. On 12th October, Major Khajoor Singh and his company had joined it from Bagh. Captain Kotwal's A Company of the 8 JAK had originally been sent to Lachhman Pattan but under intense enemy pressure had first gone to Paladari to join the A Company of the 1 JAK and then finally reach Rawalakot. Even the C Company of the 8 JAK, under Capt. Kirpal Singh, had arrived there from Bagh. While Lt Col Ram Lal was still out on 19th-20th October, the enemy launched a well-planned attack on Rawalakot supported by three-inch mortars and medium machine guns. The attack was repulsed but in doing so heavy casualties had to be endured. It had also entailed expending much of the ammunition. Lt Col Ram Lal and his column from Thorar had reached just in time or there would have been terrible consequences for Rawalakot and its occupants. Taking stock of the situation, he decided that it was prudent to withdraw the whole force to Poonch rather than wait for death and destruction after the ammunition was completely exhausted.

Lt Col Ram Lal decided to withdraw in two phases. On 27th October, he sent a column from the 9 JAK, commanded by Major Amarnath Lakhanpal and consisting of the B and D Companies of Major Ram Prakash and Major Arjun Das. The B Company of the 8 JAK went along with them to Hajira with 3,000 refugees. Their task was to escort the refugees to the safety of the Hajira garrison and then collect ammunition and supplies to bring back to Rawalakot. On reaching Hajira they found that a battle had already been raging on the perimeter. This situation became easy on their joining force. Finally, the refugees were escorted to safety. In another development, Lieutenant Colonel Shiv Ram Silwal was sent by the Army Headquarters to take command of the 9 JAK from Lt Col Ram Lal. He was at that moment present in Hajira as he had not been able to move forward earlier because of the operational situation. Now he assumed command of the 9 JAK column and also the battalion.

Back in Rawalakot, situation had taken a bad turn. Lt Col Shiv Ram Silwal received information of a heavy attack and the urgent demand that the column return immediately. He decided to respond quickly, and without collecting the supplies the column set off for Rawalakot. The enemy was waiting for just this move and its determination to prevent the link up. But the 9 JAK too was equally determined to reach Rawalakot as soon as possible. However, it took them three days and nights, mostly without food or water, to evade the ambushes and road blocks that had been put all along the way. To their dismay on reaching Rawalakot, they realized that without supplies and ammunition it would not be long before the either abandoned the post or were decimated by the ruthless enemy. The daily rations for the men were already reduced to half a chapatti per day! The position of ammunition was so precarious that some of the posts had actually sent out raiding parties at night to fight for ammunition from the enemy posts and patrols! By now this situation was known to Srinagar as well as New Delhi. In response a sortie of the Royal Indian Air Force aircraft free dropped 1,000 rounds of ammunition. However, only 600 could be retrieved, of which more than half had been damaged beyond use.[258] Holding on to Rawalakot was impossible. Rawalakot had to be abandoned to fall back on Poonch.

Lt Col Silwal decided to withdraw to Poonch by crossing over the Toli Pir Pass since he had anticipated that the track to Hajira would be full of strongly entrenched enemy expecting the Rawalakot column to retreat to Hajira. Rawalakot was abandoned on the night of 9th-10th November. Along with the troops there were about 6,000 refugees, thirty stretcher cases of soldiers and civilians, and a large number of sick and wounded. The enemy made many a determined assault but the State Forces fought valiantly to hold on and finally reached Poonch. The progress had been excruciatingly slow and there were about forty casualties, many were women and children.

After this, only the posts of Hajira and Madarpur were holding out ahead of Poonch. The enemy was now converging on them. At Hajira there was a mixed bag of sub units that consisted of the JAK garrison. They were under the command of Capt. Vakil Singh of the 1 JAK who had a total strength of two companies. The garrison at Madarpur consisted of one platoon of the 8 JAK under Jemadar Jaimal Singh. The raiders were anticipating an easy kill with all the other forces in the region having withdrawn to Poonch. But on the night of 13th-14th November, a strong column set out from Poonch to rescue the two garrisons. By 15th November, and they too reached Poonch.[259]

Poonch town had till then remained peaceful as far as the battle was concerned. With the outposts holding out the raiders, the enemy had remained focused on the borders. The Brigade Headquarters was located there but the troops stationed therein had been in the forward areas, defending the outposts. Only a few odd sub-units of the battalions and the personnel of the GPC were located there for local protection. The fact was, there was a woeful shortage of troops till the battalions began withdrawing to Poonch. No effective defence mechanism could have been organized earlier. Fortunately, till then the town of 10,000 had enjoyed smooth civil administration under the Poonch Wazir, Pandit Bhim Sain and the Superintendent of Police. The situation of civil supplies was also satisfactory, though the town had been cut off from Srinagar and Jammu after the fall of Haji Pir Pass and Kotli respectively. Theoretically, the town could last a siege for several months. But the situation changed dramatically with the rapid fall of the strongholds of the JAK forces like Palandri, Bagh and Rawalakot. As they fell, the troops retreated to Poonch. Along with them came a stream of refugees, both from the outer regions as well as from Pakistan, from where the Hindus and Sikhs were forced to flee. By the time Hajira and Madarpur outposts were withdrawn, the influx of refugees had swelled to disconcerting proportions.

There was a fourfold increase in civil population. The existing stocks were no longer sufficient. Since the army too had to be catered to, the Poonch garrison had increased by nearly four battalions. The existing food grains were not likely to last more than a few weeks even after reducing the rations critically.[260] With this ground situation, 'began the defense [*sic*] of Poonch which lasted sixteen months, one of the most gallant efforts of the JAK forces. Everywhere else the war was being fought mainly by Indian Army troops; only at Poonch did the garrison consist of predominantly State forces. The command of the brigade later devolved on the Indian Army; and two infantry battalions—1 (Para) Kumaon and 3/9 Gorkha Rifles—joined the garrison, but the JAK battalions continued to play a crucial role in the defense of Poonch.'[261]

The raiders, in the meantime, had sensed a kill. The heights of the surrounding areas had been occupied by them. Poonch, though, was in no mood to give up. The JAK forces were determined to fight valiantly, to prolong the battle in the hope of the Indian Army arriving in that sector too. The Indian Army had effectively taken complete charge of the Kashmir Valley and it was responsible for all the operations. It was only the Poonch garrison that was defending itself and the town on its own. The garrison at that point consisted of Brigadier Krishana Singh, the 1 JAK led by Lieutenant Colonel H.N. Dubey but without one Company, the 8 JAK commanded by Lieutenant Colonel Maluk Singh, the 9 JAK Infantry commanded by Lieutenant Colonel Amarnath Lakhanpal, the A Company along with a platoon of the B Company of the 4 JAK Infantry under the command of Lieutenant Labh Singh, two Companies of the 7 JAK Infantry under the command of Major Amarnath Sharma, one Company of the AT Regiment and one Company of Garrison Police.

The immediate challenge for the garrison was to organize a defence but unfortunately a tactical mistake had been made when it was decided to occupy the immediate heights surrounding the town. The enemy had occupied higher positions and was therefore able to immobilize the forces. A heavy price was paid as one by one all the commanding heights had to be attacked and captured to defend the town. In the meantime, equally desperate but heroic effort had gone into saving Srinagar. First, Brigadier Rajinder Singh and his column and then the 1 Sikhs of the Indian Army had fought valiantly to hold the enemy at bay. Gradually the tide had begun to turn and on 12th November, when 161 Infantry Brigade succeeded in capturing Uri. It was a remarkable achievement for the enemy had to be pushed back all the way from the doors of Srinagar.

Historians will debate in the future, trying to pin responsibility on the persons who halted the push of the Indian Army towards Muzaffarabad, and wonder if there was any design behind it.[262] Design, surely there was, as the biography of Field Marshall Cariappa mentions. He had to fight 'two enemies, Army Headquarters headed by Roy Bucher, and the Pakistan Army headed by Messervy'. The impact of the understanding between Bucher and Messervy was that by December 1947, 'Bucher made an effort to get the Defence Committee to accept the evacuation of Poonch, which, according to British thinking, had to be left with Pakistan. However, Nehru was able to shoot down this proposal despite the support Bucher received from Mountbatten. On the other hand, the commander-in-chief succeeded in getting shelved the push from Uri to Domel to clear the Jhelum Valley till the next spring. He also succeeded in getting dropped the plan to destroy the bridges across the Kishan Ganga river, which would have cut off Muzaffarabad from Pakistan.'[263]

However, there is another version of the saga for the battle for Jhelum Valley and Poonch. Though it should be conceded that Brigadier Sen, being in the field, had no means of knowing what was going on in the Army Headquarters, Delhi. It is acknowledged that with heavy odds against them, the State Forces had fought to their utmost limit even when they were vastly outnumbered. How unequal the battles had been for them is best judged by the fact that when Brigadier L.P. Sen arrived in Srinagar on 29th October to take command of the 161 Brigade, he made an assessment of the military situation in the Valley and concluded that contrary to the plans of the Army Headquarters in Delhi, the Valley required more than a brigade if the raiders were to be defeated. 'He felt that the area was much too large and the enemy far too superior numerically for the three battalions of a brigade...He made a bid for a full infantry division strength in the Valley immediately. The requirement was more or less accepted by the Government of India...'[264]

In those early days, the defence of Poonch was under Srinagar and Brigadier Sen made a bold attempt to send help to Poonch by crossing over the Haji Pir Pass. After capturing and consolidating positions at Uri, the 161 Brigade was ordered to halt its progress towards Domel and Kohala, hold Uri and prepare to send a column towards Poonch along the Haji Pir so that the Poonch garrison could be reinforced. The plan was that the column from Uri would move towards Poonch to link up with the 50 Para Brigade from Jammu that was to come towards Nowshera and Rajouri. Of the three battalions with the Uri Brigade, two were to cross over the Haji Pir, leaving one battalion behind to defend Uri. After the link up at Poonch, one battalion was to return back to Uri. The battalion left behind in Poonch was to work under the 50 Para Brigade in the Mirpur-Poonch sector. The 50 Para Brigade had arrived in Jammu in late October but at that time the priority was to save the Valley, therefore, it had been asked to remain in Jammu for keeping the communication lines open between Jammu and Srinagar. It was to play only a supportive role to the 161 Brigade.[265] However, while the plan to rescue Poonch was in the offing, someone had forgotten to send the message to Poonch. Thus, when on the night of 20th-21st November, a detachment of the JAK forces, which was guarding a wooden bridge across Batar Nullah about eleven miles north of the town, saw a number of lights on the Haji Pir Pass, they assumed that a serious and big assault on Poonch by the enemy was imminent. In response, the bridge was hurriedly burnt and it was much later and with great difficulty that the 1 Para Kumaon could march into Poonch to establish the linkup.[266] 'This slip-up on the part of some staff officer, somewhere, caused... some heartburning between the State Forces and the Indian Army for some time before it was discovered that the Poonch Brigade had not been included in the distribution list of the Jammu & Kashmir Force [Indian Army] operational order, directing the move of 161 Brigade.'[267] That probably was the outcome of the disdain that the Indian Army officers nursed for the State Forces making them to execute the operational plan by themselves without including the State forces present in Poonch.

No sooner had this happened that the Indian Army and the State Forces had to deal with a delicate situation. The Indian Army had begun to take charge and it was decided that Lieutenant Colonel Pritam Singh of Indian Army be made the commander-in-charge for the defence of Poonch. But since the Indian Army had continued with the colonial practice of a British Indian Army officer not serving under an officer of the State Army, he could not be placed under the command of the State Forces. Therefore, Brigadier Krishana Singh of the JAK had to relinquish command, which he did willingly. But apart from that small matter of protocol, there were enormous challenges that emerged as the time passed. Not the least of challenges was the need to expand the ring of defensive positions and then arrange for ammunition and supplies. First of all the positions of the enemy that were using three-inch mortar had to be pushed beyond their hitting range of the civil inhabitants. In response, the Pakistani Army sent in mountain guns. Thus the defensive ring had to be further expanded, often beyond a ten-mile radius. But a more serious problem in the form of shortages of ammunition and supplies stared the garrison. Strength wise the Brigade could now withstand any scale of attack but realistically this could only happen if the ammunition was made available to it. Moreover, the besieged population had to be fed.

Both the problems were solved with ingenuity, in a creative and daring manner. It was decided to construct an airstrip a mile west of the Poonch Fort. Galvanized by the arrival of the Indian Army, the refugee population too had come alive. Thousands among them volunteered to work with the troops and within a fortnight, on 12th December a Beechcraft, flown by Air Commodore Mehr Singh with Air Vice Marshal Mukherjee in the passenger seat, landed there. Within the next fortnight it was worthy for the landing of Dakotas. With that, an air-bridge had been created, giving the Poonch Brigade and the population some much needed relief. [268] After being isolated for about two months, Poonch had once again established contact with the rest of the State and India. The seriously wounded and the ill were then evacuated to Jammu. But the supply situation remained critical.

The fair weather airstrip, constructed after demolishing some of the army barracks, connecting two football fields and filling up the bed of seasonal *nullah*—rivulet—was only 700 yards long. On the one side was a ten-foot embankment and the other nothing but the gushing waters of river Batar. Even in the lightest of showers the runway would become slippery and dangerous for the aircraft.

As a result, even during the dry weather of those trying months, aircrafts could land barely thrice a week. As a result, on an average only thirty to forty tonnage of supplies could be ferried by the aircraft. In addition, on fair days, and if the aircraft could be made available for Poonch, there were some air drops that made it to fifty to sixty tons. It was just enough to meet the demands of the civil population, which had increased manifold, and the administrators needed fifty tons and a minimum of fifteen tons for the military garrison—that too at half rations. In addition, the garrison needed fifteen tons of ammunition and store, again at half-contact rates. In the meantime, the airstrip had radically changed the situation and the enemy responded by bringing in three-inch mortars to forward positions to fire at it. After a Dakota had been damaged by mortar fire, the A Company of the 9 JAK led by Captain Jagdish Singh and the C Company led by Captain Kirpal Singh were sent out to establish a picket on the lower slopes of a feature. This effectively stopped the enemy from subjecting the aircraft to mortar fire.

However, at a dominating height, about a mile and half to the north-east of the Poonch Fort, the enemy was still in a strong position. Captain Sewa Nath of the 1 JAK's C Company led a column that also consisted of Subedar Kharood Singh Salathia and the B Company. It was a bloody hand-to-hand fight that ensued when they reached the top of the wooded spur as there were about ninety of the enemy. After a fierce struggle with bayonets, eleven prisoners were taken in and thirty bodies counted. Many of the wounded and the dead had been carried away by the enemy. The State Forces too suffered with one JCO and three soldiers killed, and four wounded. The next few weeks were spent in capturing the never-ending 'next' high point of the mountains. But while earlier the JAK Forces had nothing except their courage and determination, now they had the support of the strafing from the Spitfires of the Royal Indian Air Force.

The battle for Poonch was far from over and the decisive turn came only after the induction of the Indian Army in the area was completed by mid-January, 1948. By then, the more the situation improved the more difficult it appeared to become. More than 5,000 refugees had been evacuated by the aircraft that brought rations, but there were still 30,000 mouths to feed. The level of rations had become precarious once. The Army was sharing its rations with the civilians and often it was a horse-meal gruel that was served in certain parts of the town. It was a desperate situation that needed a desperate measure. Fresh into the battlefield, the Brigade Commander decided that as far as food grains were concerned the garrison would have to fend for itself by raiding the surrounding villages occupied by the raiders and the Pakistan Army for procuring food grains. To overcome this situation, the army, under the directions of Brigadier Pritam Singh decided to launch 'harvesting operation'.

From Poonch town, the flat ridge across the river to the south-east, climbing up to the heights of Khanetar Gali could be seen. It was covered with vast expanses of ripening corn that was ready for winter harvesting. The Brigade Commander decided to harvest the bounties of the Khanetar Ridge. Therefore, on 1st-2nd March, the A and C Companies of the 8 JAK and supported by the 1 Kumaon, crossed the Poonch River bridge and then crept along a *nullah*. From there began such a steep climb that the mules carrying the three-inch mortars and medium machine guns had to be left behind. The column was accompanied by Lieutenant Colonel Maluk Singh as well as a company of the 1 Kumaon that had climbed a separate spur and was to extricate the other column and porters, should the need arise at break of day. However, the enemy was ready in considerable strength and had to be chased away after heavy fighting to another spur from where they kept up the machine gun fire. In response, the D Company of the JAK too had to be summoned upon whose arrival the enemy was routed, leaving thirty of them dead. Finally, under Major Angrez Singh, the C and D Companies of the 8 JAK captured Khanetar village. Even there the enemy was well entrenched and after a day long battle Major Angrez Singh ordered the destruction of the enemy bunkers and ammunition dumps. It was only after this that the column of refugees arrived to harvest the corn. The grain thus collected was about six tons.[269]

In between, the operation to expand the defensive ring continued. Often the enemy attacked, using 3.7 howitzer and three-inch mortars but that was repulsed easily with negligible casualties as the soldiers had dug in effective bunkers. At other times, to counter the enemy fire, that had acquired higher degree of sophisticated weapons with each failure, there had to be operations to gain control of superior heights to neutralize the enemy or at times to push it out of the dominating positions it was occupying.

In one such operation, a composite battalion, consisting of the 1, 8 and 9 JAK battalions under Colonel Hira Nand Dubey, was formed. The feature to be captured was occupied by about 150 of the enemy and was well defended with anti-personnel mines and booby traps. It was only after two attacks and heavy losses that the enemy could be dislodged. Jemadar Sarda Ram was posthumously awarded the Vir Chakra, while fourteen other ranks were killed; two officers, Colonel Hira Nand Dubey and Captain Balwant Singh; and nineteen other ranks were wounded. However, with the capture of this slope, Poonch suffered no further attacks from that direction.

By now the command control structure in Jammu and Kashmir had changed, with the Headquarters of the JAK Forces being abolished and in its place two separate divisional headquarters had been created. The Jammu Division was to be responsible for operations south of the Pir Panjal and the Srinagar Division for the Valley. Initially, the Poonch Brigade had been placed under Srinagar but soon it was realized that logistics demanded that it be placed under Jammu. Meanwhile, the 3/9 Gorkha Rifles was engaged in an action that was to prove of far-reaching consequences. After a fierce bayonet fighting at three successive defensive lines of the enemy at point 4036, it had succeeded in reaching the top but had suffered heavy casualties and were finding it difficult to evacuate the wounded in the face of sniper firing down the slopes. Lieutenant Colonel Maluk Singh was asked to attack and dislodge the enemy from that spur. The A and B Companies of the 8 JAK were led by the guides of the 3/9 Gorkha Rifles and the assault began on 19th May 1948. Taken by surprise, the tribesmen escaped down the hill, leaving three dead. It was only after this that the wounded could be escorted to Poonch for which Brigadier Pritam Singh himself had come along with a Company of Kumaonis.

It was during this time that the position of the Poonch Brigade could be said to have been secured. Not only had the situation of ammunition and supplies improved but more than 10,000 refugees had been evacuated by air. After this the Brigade Commander organized operations in which the first two Companies of the 8 JAK and one Company of the 1 Kumaon did a sweeping movement in the Suran valley to the south near Mendhar. The purpose of this was to establish contact with the two Punjab from Rajouri, which had come up to meet the Brigade column. This task was successfully achieved on 15th June, making it the first overland contact of the Poonch Brigade with the outside world. For nine long and testing months it had remained cut off not knowing if there would ever be some light at the end of the tunnel. There had been many times when the situation had become hopeless. With no food and bullets, the end appeared near and yet the officers and the troops of the JAK Forces had found reserves of hope even in that darkness. Often courage, indomitable will and innovation had been the only strength but that had been enough to carry them through one crisis after another. History will record how, while the Government of India was focused on saving only Srinagar and the Kashmir Valley, the valiant soldiers of the JAK Forces fought and laid down their lives to live up to the rich legacy of their ancestors. It is also a wonder, the at the length of time that they survived, for even after the Indian Army had reached there it had taken many months to secure the safety of Poonch.

15

Gilgit—The British Conspiracy

Up in the northern frontiers, more engrossing, but tragic, drama was being played out. Treachery was at its worst but, as if to convince mankind that life is not entirely made of betrayal and back stabbing, it was being counter balanced with the heroic saga that personified courage, sacrifice and devotion to duty. This was being done by the soldiers who could not help recall, that deep within the snowy peaks of the mountains, a century ago, lay the blood of countless Dogra soldiers who had relentlessly fought the enemy as well as adversity.

The northern frontiers have always been pivotal to the security of not only the State, but also the whole of Indus and the Gangetic plains. Whenever laxity has crept into their defence, the enemy has clawed its way into the valley of Kashmir. In the modern era, since the nineteenth century, these geostrategic regions had assumed great importance for the security of the British Empire in India. The Russian bear, first in the form of Tsarist ambitions and then as the Soviet Union, had become a phantom that appeared to be leaning over the snow-capped mountains. The British, therefore, had assumed strategic responsibility, for the region though this was a region for which they never had to use force or fight wars. It was only by virtue of their interpretation of the Treaty of Amritsar, 1846 that they assumed the right to interfere in the affairs of the State.

The Gilgit Agency had first been established in 1889 during the rule of Maharaja Pratap Singh and had a force of its own, the Gilgit Scouts. But soon, when the Russian threat receded, its importance also diminished. But, as part of the moves of the 'Great Game', Maharaja Hari Singh had been forced to lease out the Gilgit Agency to the British in 1935, for it commanded control of the mountain passes to the North-West Frontier Province (NWFP) and Central Asia. In ancient times Before the Common Era, Alexander the Great had trodden these mountains along with his army. Since then many predators had followed his footsteps. Skardu and Kargil, two other entrepôts of the region along with Gilgit, were on the way to Leh from Gilgit. The Gilgit Agency had become a focal point of British military and political influence. As a consequence, it had a wireless station installed, and built an all-weather airstrip suitable for heavy aircraft. The roads linking the Agency with the NWFP were good, making for excellent roads and communication network. Gilgit Scouts, with strength of over 600, were well trained, well-armed and equipped, and officered by the British. It was composed of eight Companies of eighty Scouts each, with two Companies each of Hunza and Nagar and one Company each from Yasin, Gupis, Punial and Gilgit.

Till 1935, the Scouts were mostly irregulars who were called up periodically by the British for training. The rest of the period they were allowed to spend at home. But from 1935, when the British managed to secure the sixty years lease, they converted it into a permanent force. Obviously, the regular pay and the prestige that followed for the Scouts, greatly enhanced the British magnanimity and power in the region. The local Scouts were made officers only in exceptional circumstances, otherwise they could rise only to the rank of a junior commissioned officer. It was through the tool of the Scouts that the British had established their image of a benevolent and just ruler. In fact, they had succeeded in creating an aura around the Political Agent with his voice becoming next only after God. Their specific task was to maintain internal security in a region that was prone to lawlessness and rebellion at the slightest excuse. It also formed the first line of defence in the event of hostilities and prevention of infiltration of borders. Gilgit Agency having been leased out to the British for sixty years had come again in the complete domain of Jammu and Kashmir after the British relinquished control over it on 1st August 1947. The same day, when the Union Jack was lowered for the last time, Brigadier Ghansara Singh, who had been posted at the Srinagar Army Headquarters, hoisted the State flag after he had been appointed as its Governor.

It has been noted in earlier chapters that a large section of the British establishment was loath to leaving India but was also convinced that if its departure and the partition of India was inevitable then the entire State of Jammu and Kashmir should be part of Pakistan. Military leaders had their reservations about the strength of Pakistan but believed that with the support of the western powers, it would be better if the passes and the trade routes to Central Asia were controlled by Pakistan. With the wisdom of hindsight, it can be safely concluded that to achieve this goal, they carefully executed their connivance in helping Pakistan secure them. Their point-man was William Alexander Brown who had already served tenures in the Frontier Corps of Scouts and South Waziristan before being posted in the Gilgit Agency. He had also acquired a fair degree of proficiency in Pushto and other local dialects. In June 1947, Brown was posted in Chitral as Acting Commandant Scouts when on his way to Chitral he met Lieutenant Colonel Roger Bacon in Peshawar, then the Political Agent in Gilgit. Bacon informed him that the Viceroy, Lord Mountbatten had decided that the 1935 British lease of Gilgit Agency was going to be terminated and that the Agency 'with 99 percent Muslim population, was going to be returned to the Hindu rule of Dogra Maharaja, Sir Hari Singh... it was put to him that he would be a suitable candidate for the position of Commandant of the Gilgit Scouts, during and after the period of transition. William Brown, while fully appreciating the difficulties and dangers involved, and angry that the British could so callously return without any preparation or warning the Muslim people of the Gilgit Agency to by no means congenial Hindu rule, volunteered for the task even though it meant leaving the British service and become in effect a mercenary employed by the Maharaja of Jammu & Kashmir.'[270] This was the first move of the British to handover Gilgit to Pakistan.

In the set up of the Agency, the most important person among the British was the Political Agent and then the Commandant of the Gilgit Scouts. It goes without saying that the Political Agent was always in a position to fairly judge the traits of all British officers working there and, therefore, Lt Col Bacon must have zeroed in on Brown after carefully judging his abilities and character during his earlier tenures. Brown's philosophy was that the 'peace and tranquillity of an Agency entirely depends on the good relations between the Political Agent and the Commandant Scouts…A Commandant has therefore to be more than a parade ground soldier. He must be politically minded as well, and a diplomat who can pass on ideas without appearing to be usurping the Political Agent's position.'[271] Bacon had identified the right person for the job.

In another move, when it became clear in July 1947 that the partition of India was inevitable and Pakistan would be created with the NWF Province as one of its constituent, the Governor designate Mohammad Ali Jinnah requested the colonial government to again requisition the services of Sir George Cunningham as the Governor of NWFP. He had already served two terms and had happily retired. However, he was pulled out of retirement during those crucial days. Later, after accomplishing his mission in Gilgit in 1948, Major Brown was taken in the Frontier Constabulary with the benign help from Cunningham. Even later, the former Governor of NWFP secured him a job in the Imperial Chemical Industries as a Sales Executive in Pakistan. Thus, the British had the right people for their plan in the right places—Brown in Gilgit, Bacon in Peshawar and Cunningham as Governor, when the British conspiracy of 1947 unfolded.

The British had left no stone unturned in fanning communalism in Indian subcontinent and the State was no exception. In 1944, the then Political Agent in Gilgit, Lieutenant Colonel E.H. Cobb, had revived a custom that was long buried and was only in the fading memory of folktales. It was believed that there lived a king in those lands, who had come from Kashmir and was a Hindu. He was a cannibal who enjoyed the meat of young kids and therefore demanded the people to supply him with that food. Ultimately, fed up of the tyranny and cruelty, the people devised a plan to overthrow the king. They created a huge pit at the gate of his fort and filled it with burning wood. Then they managed to draw him out. Thus as soon as the king rushed out in anger, he fell straight into the fire pit and met his death. The king, Sri Badat, was the last Hindu ruler of Gilgit. For many years after his death, the people celebrated his death by burning his effigy at the annual festival of Nauroze. But gradually this custom had been given up. However, Lt Col Cobb revived it in 1944, thereby reminding them of the tyranny and inhumanity of a Hindu ruler.

Upon taking charge of the Gilgit Scouts, now Major, Brown went about the task of walking down the road-map that he had drawn in his mind. As a first step, he enlisted Captain A.S. (Jock) Matheson as his deputy and sent him to the strategically important Chilas as the Assistant Political Agent. Then he carefully began identifying key men for the job and tactfully removing those whom he could not trust implicitly. This he did by touring each and every significant place of Gilgit and ensuring the personal loyalty of every Scout. In this he took full advantage of the uncertainty in the minds of the people regarding their future. The fact was that they had come to accept the political power of the Dogra rulers, even if it was headed by a Hindu family. The Dogra rulers were perceived to be independent and since the sovereignty in Gilgit was shared with the British, as a result of the appointment of a Political Agent, and they were largely left alone in internal administration, they had no reason to complain. However, during the period of the Agency control, the British had succeeded in creating their image of 'benevolent and just' rulers. The Agency had craftily used the tool of the Scouts to discipline the people and usually the Commandant of the Scouts exercised judicial powers, civil and criminal, to dispense justice. Since they did not have any personal axe to grind, they were viewed as impartial and just and the offenders accepted the punishment. In this they were greatly helped by the perceived respectability that a serving or former Scout had whenever he visited the Commandant. Parallel to the Commandant Scouts was the Political Agent who had taken to the practice of holding 'Durbars' and inviting selected people over to his 'court', sometimes to hold consultations. This created a special class of people who were beholden to the British for this honour.[272] Thus, even if the common citizens considered the British as outsiders, the privileged position of the Scouts created an aura around them.

All this, however, was to be swept under the carpet by the overwhelming influence of communalism and by 1947, the Hindu-Muslim divide had come out in the open. This was aggravated in Gilgit with the sly suggestions from the British and therefore the people were not very sure of their future. It was in this context that the local rulers of Hunza, Nagar and Chitral had approached the Maharaja to either declare accession to Pakistan or independence and had also warned of serious consequences if either of the two options was not followed.

During his visit to Chilas, Major Brown talked about the whole plan with Captain Matheson. He also knew that nothing could be left to chance and every doubt should be eliminated before fixing the date of executing the conspiracy. There were significant bottle-necks that needed to be ensured. His whirlwind tours and talks had assured him that Hunza, Punial, Yasin and Kuh Ghizr were under his complete control. Since they represented six of the eight Companies of the Scouts, he knew that it would be easy to get the remaining two also on board. Only the 6 JAK Battalion was a challenge, but since it was composed of mixed forces, with Dogras, Sikhs and Muslims, they too could be neutralized through some stratagem. There was no doubt that the Dogras and the Sikhs were implicitly loyal to the Maharaja and the Muslims too had been hitherto extremely loyal to the Maharaja. They were also well trained and disciplined.

Meanwhile, on 1st August 1947, when the lease of Gilgit Agency was to revert back to the State, Brigadier Ghansara Singh arrived in Gilgit as the Governor designate, along with Chief of Staff, Major General H.L. Scott. The Governor-designate indeed was a baffled man and to his utter dismay, he found that the British officers present for the ceremony of lowering of the Union Jack one last time and unfurling the State flag as it used to be before 1935, were sullen and almost non-cooperative. As it was, he knew that he had arrived in Gilgit without the much needed bureaucratic support of Srinagar. In his account of the events of Gilgit, he recalled in a booklet, *Gilgit Before 1947*, that 'It was essential for me that before departure for Gilgit, I should have a wide range of discussions with the Prime Minister [Ram Chandra Kak] and fully understand the existing situation and threat…I strongly objected to the retention of British Officers in Gilgit Scouts as they would unnecessarily create problems and hamper in the independent disposal of cases…The Prime Minister refuted the idea. It was decided that Major General H.L. Scott would go with me to see my requirements on the spot and report to the Government.'[273]

Brigadier Ghansara Singh, who took charge of Gilgit from Lt Col Bacon on 1st August 1947, has also given a description that suggests internal subversion had been done by none other than the Prime Minister of the State Ram Chandra Kak. As Governor-designate of Gilgit, he had called upon Kak on 20th July 1947 and was to proceed to Gilgit the next day, but a plane could not be arranged. It continued like that for the next few days till he received a message from his Prime Minister telling him to leave for Gilgit immediately and reach within two days. Kak was not prepared to listen to any excuse for the delay in departure till Brigadier Ghansara Singh approached General Scott whose intercession with the Maharaja, finally managed a plane for him. General Scott too was to accompany him.

Finally, when both reached Gilgit, the Governor-designate found that the atmosphere was by no means friendly as immediately after taking over, he learnt that all the British officers had opted to serve Pakistan. The civil employees presented him with a list of demands, including raise in salaries; otherwise they threatened to quit. He also realized that a local political crisis was also waiting to be resolved. In one of the last acts as Political Agent, Lt Col Bacon had put some leading men of Yasin in prison for revolting against the local Raja. About 300 locals from Yasin came to the Governor seeking the release of their local leaders. It came to the knowledge of the Governor that the revolt had been supported by the Mehtar of Chitral who, taking advantage of the period of uncertainty, wanted one of his close relative installed in place of the reigning Raja. Recognizing that this was an unpleasant and mischievous legacy of the departing British, the Governor-designate sought the help of Punial in quelling the revolt. But this episode gave clear sign of hope that the local people had no grouse against the Dogra rule and that this was all a part of the communal politics that had burst out in the open.[274]

By then, he had got hold of the full picture of the challenges that awaited him. The most worrying of all the situations was the news that came filtering down to the Governor about the 6th Kashmir Infantry that had been sent to replace the 5th JAK Infantry. It was a mixed battalion, with one-third soldiers Sikhs, one-third Dogras and one-third Muslims. The Sikhs were still under training and had not yet fired in the field, the Dogras were also new to the job, whereas the Muslims were fully trained. The leading Company was commanded by Captain Hussain Khan. In hindsight, it was a clear case of choosing an incorrect battalion for a difficult challenge. Later, Brigadier Ghansara Singh was informed that no sooner had the Muslim Company crossed Bandipur in the Valley than they had started shouting slogans hailing Pakistan. Raja Noor Ali Khan, the Revenue Assistant of Gilgit, sent a similar report informing that such slogans had been raised from the Astore area too. Lieutenant Colonel Abdul Majid Khan was asked to investigate these reports but he affirmed that only religious slogans had been raised.

Earlier, when Major Brown called upon the Governor, the Subedar Major of the Gilgit Scouts, along with all other Junior Commissioned Officers, categorically told him that they wanted to serve Pakistan. They also said that they would be willing to serve the State only if their demands were met. However, more serious damage was done to him by Major General Scott, who subverted the authority of the Governor by interceding to assure them that their demands will be sympathetically considered. The Governor had no chance to make the statement that he was in-charge in Gilgit and all decisions will be taken only through him. Major General Scott's intercession conveyed the message that the Governor was only a dummy and that all decisions will happen only through the British. He had been further weakened by the fact that he did not have any civil staff to assist him whereas earlier the Agent had the support of a number of British officers and other administrative staff members. He only had one member of the medical department with him, Dr Hans Raj Gupta and Revenue Assistant, Raja Noor Ali Khan. By then it had become clear that neither the Scouts nor the civil administration was in a mood to cooperate with the new Governor representing the Maharaja. Brigadier Ghansara has also claimed that he wrote a demi-official letter to Prime Minister Kak, and upon his removal, to Prime Minister Janak Singh as well as Deputy Prime Minister Batra about the situation, warning that if the State acceded to India, the Province was likely to join Pakistan.[275] There was no doubt in the mind of the Governor that the British had used their time in Gilgit in consolidating their say and had completely destroyed the trust in the Dogras that had existed before 1935. The team of Lt Col Bacon and Major Brown had completely eroded Gilgit's confidence in the Maharaja. Major Brown knew that with the Gilgit Scouts at his command, and the loyalty of the feudatories to Dogra ruler doubtful, all he needed to do was to execute a well-conceived plan.

In the meantime, Srinagar directed the Governor to administer the new oath of allegiance to all the Scouts on a date of his choice. The Governor duly forwarded the direction to the Commandant Scouts for early action. Major Brown in his autobiographical account has dwelt at great lengths with the subject and it soon becomes obvious to the reader that he is trying hard to rationalize the treachery that he committed. He recalled that the Subedar Major of the Scouts advised him not to hurry the oath and to wait 'until the Kashmir regime is functioning properly here, for the whole world to behold. By that time the Scouts will have appreciated the benefits of Kashmir administration…Anyway we have all sworn an oath of allegiance to you, Sahib, and since you are under contract to the Maharaja of Kashmir, it follows that we too hold fealty to His Highness.'[276]

It becomes abundantly clear that the Subedar Major was only cautioning Major Brown and not ruling out the possibility of the oath ceremony. What followed was extremely bizarre for he gives a detailed account of the situation at Chilas bazaar and nothing is left to doubt that he was exercising executive as well as judicial powers in stamping his authority over the civil population. It is difficult to swallow the fact that even when the Governor was present in Gilgit, Major Brown, a mercenary in the service of the Maharaja in the Gilgit Scouts was exercising all the constitutional powers of the Governor without his concurrence. But this fitted well in his scheme of things, as it continued the aura of the British and consolidated the loyalty of the Scouts to his person. But the civilian interaction with Major Brown at Chilas only underlined the fact that the Governor had been sent to Gilgit only to fail in his mission. Brigadier Ghansara Singh was convinced that Prime Minister Ram Chandra Kak deliberately subverted his mission and that the Maharaja was never given a full account of the developments, as the episode of his getting the plane to arrive in Gilgit showed. Even then it was only after Major General Scott had interceded to inform the Maharaja of the problem that a plane had been made available to him. The fact that he had been sent without support staff to carry on the administrative work also indicated a deep rooted conspiracy for creating a difficult situation in Gilgit.

But back to the swearing of oath of allegiance, Major Brown was party to a plan to cover up treachery. In his account he absolves himself of all the guilt by claiming that he was not informed of the plan. He described the oath ceremony as follows:

> The Quran Sharif is always kept wrapped up in cloth. The cloth bundle was duly produced and placed on the table. I do not suppose for on[e] instant that the cloth contained a Quran Sharif, but probably some other book of similar size. I did not mind, however. The Governor would not know, and I was not supposed to know so I could assure him, in all good faith, that the oath had been taken. All I wanted was for this wretched ceremony to be completed in seemingly satisfactory way to all concerned without a showdown on the part of the Governor or the Scouts. And, of course this was the answer, for the oath to be taken on a copy of the *Oxford Dictionary*.[277]

A similar oath taking ceremony was held in Gilgit and Gupis and it cannot be a coincidence that similar kind of charade was carried out. To any reasonable person this would have been highly implausible. Only Major Brown remained ignorant of it! In fact, Major Brown was doing exactly what was expected of him by his masters behind the scene and carrying out the plan that he had drawn. During one of his conversations with Captain Matheson, he frankly shared the debate of accession with him and Captain Matheson came out frankly with his views and therefore the likely course that ought to be followed. His observations were:

> The big question of the moment is which side of the fence is the Maharaja of Kashmir going to jump? If he has the sense to jump toward Pakistan, good and well. But if he accedes to India... [then] the question is what are we going to do? Are we going to support the Kashmir regime as we are duty bound to do? If we do, surely we shall be acting against our own democratic sentiments, which could never agree with the hundred thousand Muslim inhabitants of the Gilgit province being forced against their wills to become members of the Indian Union. Or shall we actively join and naturally lead the revolution in favor of Pakistan which will undoubtedly take place...Further, my sentiments dictate that I am bound to support any movement, the object of which is to make the Gilgit Province, and Kashmir for that matter, an integral part of Pakistan.[278]

Between the two, there was such a strong bonding of views that all that they needed to do was to draw out a plan of neutralizing the 6 JAK Infantry for Major Brown knew that if he did not manage desertions from the State Forces, there would be battle on hand, even if all the Scout companies were under his complete control. He also knew that the critical factor that could work in favour of his scheming was treachery and he worked on that aspect. Finally, after carefully plugging each and every loophole, he and Captain Matheson, prepared the details of the Plan:

> 1. The operation was to be called DATTA KHEL and would be put into immediate effect as soon as I signaled this code word to Jock [Captain Matheson] in Chilas.
> 2. It was impossible as yet to fix a day for the *coup d'etat*. I would watch development carefully in Gilgit and the burden of choosing the correct day would lie on me, as soon as I had decided that the time had come. The day would be called D day and subsequent days D+1, etc.
>
> On D day in Gilgit I will act as follows:
>
> (1) put the Governor and his staff under protective custody;
> (2) put all Hindus and Sikhs in a refugee camp under guard;
> (3) cut all telephone links;
> (4) takeover the civil wireless station;
> (5) set up my own administration of the entire Province;

> (6) signal the Prime Minister of the North West Frontier Province in Peshawar, to the effect that there had been a revolt in Gilgit in favor of Pakistan and with the request that he should inform the Pakistan Government;
> (7) take whatever steps I considered necessary to uphold the new regime.
>
> 4. In the meantime Jock will take similar action in Chilas as relevant, but the responsibility of dealing with 6th Kashmir Infantry also lay on him. If the Muslims of the battalion turned out to be loyal to the Maharaja, the action would be as follows: A fighting patrol of three platoons of Scouts would move out from Chilas and move with all haste to the Raikote bridge…move to Bunji…their arrival will coincide with the start of the operation in Gilgit and Chilas, which would be at night. They would then make a lightning surprise attack on the quarter-guard, rifle *Kotes* and magazine of the 6th Kashmir Infantry……They would liquidate the sepoys on duty on the quarter-guard, and secure the rifles *kotes*, and magazine…The battalion would therefore be *hors de combat* now, and could easily be made prisoners *in toto*. At the same time as this attack was being carried out, a fighting patrol from Gilgit would liquidate the 6th Kashmir Infantry picquets at Jaglote and Partap Pul…Scout picquets would then be posted on the bridges at Chamogarh, Partab Pul, Ramghat and Raikote… if on the other hand, the Muslims of the Kashmir Infantry were prepared to forego their allegiance to the Maharaja and join us, then we would leave the task of crippling the rest of the Battalion on them…[279]

By then the administration had come to a standstill. Effectively, the Governor had absolutely no support and he was groping for some support. He candidly recalled in his booklet that 'At this time I was sitting like a dummy at Gilgit. I had no powers to operate the Budget, no powers of a District Magistrate, no powers to operate criminal offences in the Agency. I had no controlled articles such as cloth, sugar or kerosene oil for the public…Telegrams were sent incessantly to the Foreign Secretary and the Prime Minister but no replies were sent to my queries…'[280] The Governor had been rendered helpless but Major Brown, in his book has spared no opportunity of mocking him for idling away time, sitting in his rocking-chair and puffing away the *hookah*—the hubble-bubble. Major Brown wrote in his book, 'After lunch I went along to see the Governor. He was sitting on the verandah on his leather-covered armchair, he was still wearing the olive-green uniform, he was still puffing away at his hubble-bubble and he did not have a care in the world.'[281] In fact, he was deriving sadistic pleasure at the helplessness of the Governor, particularly when he had been instrumental in creating that toxic environment. With no staff member to attend to administrative work and no support from the Scouts, the Governor had been made powerless and severely handicapped.

The partisans will for long debate if the deeds of the Gilgit Scouts amounted to rebellion or was it an act of betrayal or a coup? It was true that for long the Agency and the Gilgit Scouts were being administered from Peshawar but this did not justify the decision of the British officers of the Scouts to transfer their allegiance and loyalty to Pakistan. In fact, it is doubtful if they did what they did out of loyalty for Pakistan because there is strong evidence to suggest that ever since creation of Pakistan had emerged as a distinct possibility, the British strategists within the army and bureaucracy, in connivance with a select band of politicians, had wanted this region to be part of Pakistan. The Scouts had been raised for guarding the northern borders of the Agency so that an effective defence could be mounted against the designs of the Soviet Union from across the mountain passes. Since the region was vital to the geostrategic policies of the British, they had brow beaten Maharaja Hari Singh to hand over its administration to it. This in no way meant that the sovereign right over Gilgit had been surrendered to the British, and, even less, that the Gilgit Scouts and the officers manning it had been given the right to decide the future course of the Agency. Moreover, it was inappropriate for the key military officers to conspire the handing over of Gilgit to Pakistan as they had no business deciding the allegiance of a princely state to one or the other dominion.

It was then that the full impact of the treachery of the British officers unfolded. The Jammu and Kashmir government had naively believed that all British officers were of honourable conduct and had blundered in retaining them even after they had expressed their choice to opt for Pakistan. A few days before the storm broke out, Brigadier Ghansara Singh visited Bunji with the object of finding out for himself what support he could expect from the 6th JAK Infantry. It was here that a Kashmiri Pandit employed at the Buji Telegraph office informed that one Major Sher Ali of the 4th JAK Infantry had joined hands with the Pakistani troops after the fall of Muzaffarabad. He had taken Baramulla and had mentally prepared himself for martyrdom along with his other colleagues. He had half a mind, while at Bunji, to slip away to safety but the soldier in him forbade from such a cowardly act.[282] By the close of the third week of October, Major Brown was ready to strike whenever the Maharaja had made his decision to accede. If he acceded to India, he would strike according to the plan. Finally the decision had been hoisted upon him when the Pakistan army-supported raiders invaded the Valley and the Maharaja acceded to India. The Governor came to know of the development upon his return to Gilgit.

On 30th October, Brigadier Ghansara Singh ordered Lieutenant Colonel Abdul Majid Khan to immediately proceed to Gilgit from Bunji with as large a force as was possible. But he was, however, ill and therefore dispatched Captains Ehshan Ali and Hussain Khan of the D Company. But to the horror of Brigadier Ghansara Singh, in a repeat of what had happened at Domel and Muzaffarabad, these officers on arrival in Gilgit on the morning of 31st October, joined the forces of Major Brown and the Gilgit Scouts. Brigadier Ghansara Singh knew that his death was as certain as that of Lieutenant Colonel Narain Singh of the 4th JAK and, therefore, had to make the choice to face death at the hands of either the Scouts or the Muslim soldiers of the 6 JAK. 'I had a great problem, I had to weigh the two, i.e., the Gilgit Scouts and the 6th J&K Infantry. I knew the attitude of the Mohammedans of 6th Infantry will be more destructive than that of the Gilgit Scouts. The Mohammedans of 6th Infantry knew what had happened in East and West Punjab...After critical examination of these pros and cons, I decided that I should depend on Gilgit Scouts as they had not seen disastrous actions of East and West Punjab. The second consideration was that it will bring no credit if we died at the hands of our own Mohammedans,' he shared later.[283] In the end he probably decided that death at the hands of the Scouts would be less barbaric since they were under the command of a British officer.[284]

The vital decision, however, was taken by Major Brown, who on the night of 31st October, with Lieutenant Haider Khan, son of Colonel Sher Ali, a pensioner of the State forces, and a treacherous deserter from the 6th JAK along with 100 Scouts, surrounded the Governor's residence. Inside were Brigadier Ghansara Singh, his orderly and driver who had a revolver, rifle and a gun between them, collectively manned three rooms and fired at the besiegers. Soon, the residence was subjected to light machine gun fire for the rest of the night. Having demonstrated his intention, in another diabolical move Major Brown sent a delegation of two Hindu officials, the Naib Tehsildar, Pandit Mani Ram and a police inspector with the ultimatum that either the Governor surrender within the next fifteen minutes or the non-Muslim population of the area would be massacred. Thus cornered and faced with dire alternatives, The Governor recognized the futility of resistance as there was no hope of any help reaching them. Those who were supposed to uphold the sanctity of their oath had turned betrayers and any resistance would only mean the massacre of the innocent civilians and his colleagues' along with him. Finally, it was a tame end to a glorious saga of the Dogra operations and campaigns in the Gilgit region. There had been many setbacks in the past and thousands of the Dogra soldiers had perished in these snowy and alien mountains chasing a dream of conquest and glory. In the end, they had been felled by a combination of treachery, conspiracy and betrayal by their own.

These events have been called a 'revolution', as Brigadier Ghansara Singh has done or, 'rebellion' as Major Brown termed it. But in reality it ought to be simply termed as 'coup d'état', for that is what it was. According to the definition provided in Brittanica.com, the essential elements of a revolution or rebellion are participation of the people in the overthrow of a legally constituted government or State along with the army. But a coup is purely a military action carried out by a section of the military. In Gilgit there was no participation of the people since there is evidence that when one of the Scouts thrice volunteered to shoot Brigadier Ghansara

Singh, the civilian population interceded to have his life spared.[285] However, young non-Muslim females were subjected to the same treatment that has been the custom of Islamic invaders. They were forcibly converted and married. 'Captain Mohammad Khan married a Kashmiri Pandit girl at pistol point while many male Sikhs and Hindus were shot at the slightest pretext.'[286] Even otherwise, it has been noted that except for Hunza, Nagar and Chitral, other regions had cooperated with the Governor. However, one question has remained unanswered. The Governor had been put under arrest on 1st November 1947 but the Pakistan flag was raised only on the third. This gap has never been satisfactorily explained though according to the elaborate plan to execute the conspiracy, immediately after the coup, the representative of Pakistan in Peshawar was to be informed of the development. There is no reason to believe that Pakistan was reluctant as it had almost succeeded in capturing Srinagar.

Meanwhile, after the surrender of the Governor, Major Brown became the de facto Governor of the Gilgit Agency and organized the ceremonial raising of the Pakistani flag on 3rd November. 'A provisional government was formed of which the leaders were Major Brown, Capt. Ehsan Ali, Capt. Mohammad Khan, Capt. Sayeed, Lieut. Haider and Subedar Major Babar Khan. Interestingly, no local Raja or any member of the public was included in this set up.'[287] In fact, in hindsight it can be said that on that date the first military rule was set up in Pakistan! The same day, Brigadier Ghansara Singh was told to sign a telegram to the Jammu and Kashmir Government informing that the control of Gilgit had been handed over by him to Pakistan. When Brigadier Ghansara Singh objected that the control was not 'handed over' but 'taken over', he was again threatened that in case he failed to sign on the dotted line, the non-Muslim population would be massacred. In this he was persuaded by the Commandant of the 6 JAK Lt Col Abdul Majid Khan, who himself had been taken prisoner for refusing to betray the State and the Maharaja.[288] Meanwhile, Major Brown had ordered Capt. Matheson, his second in command, then at Chilas, to occupy Astore so that the retreat of the B Company of the 6 JAK consisting of Sikhs was blocked from Bunji. Simultaneously, the defecting Muslim soldiers of the 6 JAK attacked Bunji to overrun one of the Sikh outposts at Janglot. A few soldiers swam across the Indus to inform the garrison of what had befallen them. The garrison retreated to Astore, but Capt. Matheson and his Scouts were lying in wait, so it tried to retreat to the hills. But after spending a fortnight of torture by snow and being without provisions the Sikhs surrendered and were taken prisoners.

By the end of November, with the arrival of Sardar Mohammed Alam, Pakistan had officially assumed control of the administration of Gilgit. At that time the total value of the treasury of the Agency, the Toshkhana and other stores was approximately Rs 3,000,000. Recruitment drive was one of the first priorities of the new dispensation and it resulted in the enlistment of about 2,000 local inhabitants who were armed, trained and equipped by Pakistan. In addition, small arms and artillery pieces too arrived from Pakistan as preparations were made for further territorial acquisition in the area. Soon, 'Civil and Military officers of the regular Pakistan Army poured in. One Colonel Mohammad Aslam Khan, son of Brigadier Rehmat Ullah Khan, pensioner of J&K State Forces arrived with two other regular officers. In short, Pakistan Civil and Military Officers took over the administration. There was never any Azad Government in Gilgit...as soon as Pakistan officers reached they transferred Major Brown and Captain Matheson to Peshawar and took over command of both the Scouts as well as the Mohammedan troops of the State.'[289]

All this while, for three months Brigadier Ghansara Singh was confined in a dimly lit room, without any sanitary facilities in the Gilgit Scouts Lines. He was allowed neither books nor papers, and was given the barest of rations from which his own cook prepared meagre meals twice a day. For heating his quarters during the bitter winter months, he had to pay for the fuel, a proposition made more difficult by the fact that his back pay had not been cleared. In his own words, 'I was kept in one room continuously for three months. There was one W.C. and no bath room in it. My servants, one Sardar Makhan Singh, his son Roshan Singh and one Sohan Singh were put with me in the same room. I was not allowed to get out of my room. I did not see the sun...I could not take bath for three months as there was no arrangement. During daytime I was all alone as my orderlies were allowed to sit outside in the sun; I was given no books or any paper. My orderly had one Ramayan which I would read all the day...my orderlies were not allowed to talk or contact anyone.[290] After this period of incarceration he was moved to comparatively habitable quarters where he had bathing facilities and was also permitted to smoke. In view of his failing health, he was also provided with milk and vegetables, allowed to walk within the compound and also correspond with his family. Eventually he was taken to Pakistan and released at Suchetgarh on 15th January, 1949 after the ceasefire between India and Pakistan.[291] It is worth mentioning here that upon his arrest, Major Brown had personally opened and searched the luggage of Brigadier Ghansara Singh and had taken away his secret records, one double barrel twelve-bore gun, one rifle, one service revolver, one pistol, 4,000 cartridges and one new fishing rod of extremely superior quality. When the new Political Agent, Sardar Mohammad Alam Khan, took charge in Gilgit, Major Brown is believed to have handed over all the confiscated items. However, on enquiry by the arrested Governor, and he was told that Major Brown had not handed over the fishing rod, the service revolver and the 4,000 cartridges. So much for the much acclaimed 'honourable' conduct and character of a British officer!

Finally, there should be no ambiguity about the capture of Gilgit not being a coup d'état that was organized by the British military establishment. According to Major Brown's account, before sending a wireless message to Khan Abdul Qayum Khan, Prime Minister of NWFP requesting him to 'approach higher authority' for further action and instructions, he had given the 'text' of the message considerable thought. He had also assured that till the time he received instructions for future, he 'can carry on meantime'. His considerable deliberation was because, 'it was most necessary to guard against an impression arising that I had performed the coup d'état at the instigation of the British government, so that the latter might once again stake a claim in this all important part of Central Asia...In order to prevent faction feeling and internal friction, however, it was important that the honour of staging the revolt against Hindu Rule should be equally distributed between the influential and useful participants, whose vanity and prestige would be much enhanced, if their names were put up to Pakistan Government as having struck a blow for Islam in faraway Gilgit.'[292] Interestingly, he also sent a personal message to Colonel Bacon, who was then the Political Agent of the Khyber Pass and his headquarters in Peshawar because, 'I knew he would be of utmost assistance in explaining the conditions of the little-known Gilgit Province to Frontier Premier and to the Pakistan Government. He was the only real authority on Gilgit in Pakistan at that moment."[293]

Major William Brown had an uncertain time in Pakistan but that too raises some questions. In June 1947, he had been persuaded by Lieutenant Colonel Roger Bacon to resign his commission and opt as a mercenary for service with the Gilgit Scouts. The fact that the Maharaja of Jammu and Kashmir, through his Prime Minister Kak, had been prevailed upon to take him as the Commandant of Gilgit Scouts along with Captain Matheson, who too had resigned his commission for this uncertain venture in Gilgit, is a giveaway of the conspiracy. What was the motivation for this is not very clear. The years that followed prove that he was no Lawrence of Arabia in the high Himalayas. He claimed that he had excellent bonding with Gilgit and Pakistan but within two months of the takeover of Gilgit by Pakistan, he was shunted out of Gilgit and transferred to the Frontier Constabulary, the Police force of NWFP. Clearly his career in the army was over for him and he left policing within the next two years.[294] But before leaving the Constabulary he had been honoured by his own country when the King of England, instead of frowning upon him for leading a coup against one of his Dominions, awarded him the MBE (Military). An entry in the 1948 *London Gazette* reads: 'The King has been graciously pleased on the occasion of his birthday to give orders for the following appointments to the Most Exalted Order of the British Empire to Brown, Major [acting] William Alexander, Special List [ex-Indian Army]." The citation did not clarify what merited such an honour but it must be presumed that within the British military establishment there were those who approved of what he had done in Gilgit to ensure that this region went to Pakistan rather than India.

16

The Saga of Skardu

Unknown to everyone, while a glorious saga of conquests and consolidation in these regions was coming to a rather tame end in Gilgit, another chapter of courage, indomitable will and fidelity to the oath of a soldier was about to be added in Skardu. No sooner had a regular Political Agent arrived in Gilgit from Peshawar, the new authorities embarked upon consolidation of power. It is difficult to believe that Sardar Alam Mohammad Khan, the Political Agent did not understand that the Scouts, the only military power in the region, were firmly under the control of Major Brown and Captain Matheson. Both the officers had served the purpose of their parent country and Pakistan well, but now they needed a force that owed loyalty to Pakistan. But before his departure from Gilgit, Major Brown prepared a blueprint for the future defence of the region because he was certain (mistakenly, as it turned out) that India would make efforts to regain Gilgit. Therefore, 'the task of paramount importance on our hands was the preparation of the plans for increasing the strength of the Scouts to 1500 and equipping them in such a way that they would be an independent Corps d'Elite of Central Asia, capable of stemming all aggression against the Agency.'[295] They were to be used for the defence of the whole region as, sooner or later, India was expected to send its forces to regain control over the region.

Therefore, it was time to get over the euphoria of Gilgit and focus on the future dangers. In this the most important consideration was Skardu in Baltistan. Lying some 90 kms from the Gilgit Agency borders, on the Silk Route to Central Asia, this was another place of great importance along the Srinagar-Kargil-Gilgit route. It was a small garrison town consisting of a fort, perched on a high oval shaped mound, surrounded by a cluster of small hamlets on the banks of Indus. The approach to it from Gilgit was through Haramosh and was difficult to negotiate but open throughout the year. Therefore, Skardu was the perfect launching pad for any offensive by the State Forces or the Indian Army for regaining Gilgit; and, if Pakistan desired to defend Gilgit, it was imperative that it seized control of Skardu. No delay could take place for both, India and Pakistan. Lieutenant Colonel Sher Jung Thapa, the commanding officer of the 6th JAK, though not an ethnic Dogra but a Gorkha from Kangra, had served all his life in the JAK Forces and knew the geography of the region. Therefore, immediately after taking stock of the situation in Skardu, he requisitioned reinforcements from Srinagar. The new authorities in Gilgit knew, and certainly Major Brown feared, that in view of the developments in Gilgit and after the desertion of the Muslim soldiers of the Battalion at Bunji, the possibility that the Commandant of the 6th JAK would disarm the remaining Muslim platoon in Leh and put them under detention, was real.[296] This would deprive the expected raiders from Gilgit the advantage of having a fifth column in Skardu.

Major Brown also assessed that 'if, by the spring, the Pathan tribesmen had been unable to advance from Uri towards Srinagar, they would undoubtedly try a by-pass and advance up the Kishenganga Valley via Tithwal. In the event of this being successful, they would naturally hold the Gurez Valley which would prevent India sending a force against the Agency by the Burzil Route. The only route left to them then would be from Srinagar over the Zoji La into Ladakh and thence from the upper Indus through Skardu to Haramosh. This strengthened our contention that Skardu must be secured and held.'[297]

With the Gilgit Scouts having established complete control over Gilgit, Astore and Bunji, Pakistan, therefore, focused its attention on the small garrison of the 6 JAK along the northern frontier regions of Skardu, Kargil and Leh. These garrisons were under the command of Sher Jung Thapa, then a Major, and were headquartered at Leh.

Pakistan, with the expert advice and guidance coming from their British officers, the two turncoats in Gilgit knew that Pakistan could not depend upon the Gilgit Scouts as they were, at the end of the day, a militia force that would not stand a chance against the well-trained and better-equipped soldiers of the State Forces. Therefore, they used Muslim deserters of the 6th JAK since they were in no position to return to their homes in the State and had all the incentive to prove their loyalty to their new country.[298]

The news of what the Muslim soldiers had done to their fellow soldiers and the generally communally charged propaganda of hostile elements had also found receptive audiences in the Muslim dominated area of Skardu, but still, of the five Rajas—Rondu, Khaplu, Shigar, Karmang and Skardu—only Rondu had openly expressed his preference for Pakistan. Nothing could be said with confidence about the others. Leh being predominantly Buddhist was considered to be safe and, therefore, Lt Col Thapa was ordered to proceed to Skardu with all the available forces that could be spared from Leh and Kargil. He arrived in Skardu on 3rd December, with a total strength of two officers, two JCOs, and seventy-five other ranks, of whom three were Muslim wireless operators.

On reaching Skardu, which was captured by General Zorawar Singh in 1834, Lt Col Sher Jung Thapa found the situation not very promising. Religion-based loyalties seemed to have taken firm shape but even then the Wazir-e-Wazarat Amar Nath had held a meeting of the five Rajas to remind them of their allegiance to the Jammu and Kashmir Government and to ascertain the extent of support each was willing to commit to provide rations for the soon to be arriving troops. Of the five Rajas, by not attending the meeting, Rondu had made his inclination clear. He was, in fact, already in touch with Gilgit. He had been urging an early attack on Skardu and promising his full cooperation in that eventuality. Lt Col Thapa's own troops were under a cloud of suspicion as Captain Nek Alam of the C Company had intercepted and forwarded to Army Headquarters, Srinagar two letters from Captain Hussain Khan, a deserter from the 6th JAK in Gilgit. The letter urged Muslim troops at Skardu to take and hold the garrison until the arrival of troops from Gilgit. On 4th December, Capt. Nek

Alam, on receiving information from local sources, proceeded to the nearby villages and rescued four Sikh survivors from Bunji, the rest having been taken prisoners and taken to Gilgit.

A hurried military reconnaissance indicated that a winter attack could only come via Rondu, which had, unfortunately, already committed itself to Pakistan. Lt Col Thapa, in anticipation of such a move, established two outposts on either side of Indus at Tsari about twenty miles north-west of Skardu. The Muslim platoon commanded by Capt. Nek Alam was on the far side of the river and that of Sikhs under Captain Krishan Singh, on the near side. By thus positioning his small force, Lt Col Thapa hoped that he would have a timely warning, through the runners, about any enemy attack and the garrison would hold on to its position till help arrived from Srinagar. He was acutely aware of his precarious position and had immediately requested Srinagar for reinforcements. By then more than a month had passed since the State had acceded to India and according to the Instrument of Accession, the Defence of the State fell in the domain of India. But inexplicably, no urgency was shown by India or even an appreciation of the importance of the region. Everyone, from politicians to Military commanders, seemed to be in the State, with the single objective of saving Srinagar and the Valley. Gilgit and Skardu were not even on the fringe of their horizons. The region seemed to be the problem of the Maharaja alone. By this time, all available reinforcements in Srinagar had already been mustered and dispatched to Poonch and it was not considered wise to withdraw the garrison at Kargil to be sent to Skardu. Even then, Srinagar rummaged every possible option of manpower for raising a Skardu relief column of two Companies composed of orderlies, bandsmen and store men. Commanded by Captain Prabhat Singh, the column, of about ninety strong, minimally equipped soldiers, left Srinagar on 13th January 1948, and covered the first twenty-five miles to Kangan by bus. The rest of the 200 miles were traversed to the accompaniment of frostbite, trench foot, insomnia and breathlessness caused by the high altitude. The column crossed the 3,353 metres high of Zoji La Pass on 30th January. The troops had been split up in sub-units to make advance in batches in view of the limited accommodation available at the halting stations en route.

The 5 km climb from Baltal to the Pass was not only stiff but also extremely hazardous as they had to walk over the ridges and across the tracks that had been obliterated by heavy snow. Each soldier had to carefully tread over the footstep in front for fear of falling and getting buried in the snow. Finally, they reached Skardu after braving snow storms and blown bridges on 10th February, just in time for the first attack.[299] This is that time of the year when the Zoji La Pass, and all the tracks, is covered in snow and many tracts are frozen. Now, Lt Col Thapa had a force of 161, including thirty-one Muslim, apart from a few officers. Among the Muslims were three who operated the wireless telegraphy.

By February, three months after India Army had landed in Srinagar, the attackers were ready for their offensive. The first attack on the garrison, by approximately 600 strong enemies was led by Major Ehsan Ali, earlier Captain, Captain Mohammad Khan and Lieutenant Baber Khan of the Gilgit Scouts who became the first Scout to be a Commissioned officer in Pakistan. Lt Col Thapa was taken by surprise since he was convinced that the two outposts in Tsari on both the banks of Indus would warn of the impending attack. Obviously, these posts had also failed to blow up the river-crossings, making it easier for the enemy to move forward. The last message that the garrison received from Tsari was on 9th February, 1948. Unknown to the garrison, the attack on the Tsari occurred on the night of the 9th-10th and not surprisingly, the outpost was over run, survivors captured and Captain Krishna Singh and his Sikh troops murdered in cold blood.[300] Till then Captain Nek Alam had remained loyal to the State. However, he too succumbed to the pressure of communalism and reports of the establishment the 'Azad Kashmir Government', and occupation of large tracts of the State by Pakistan. As result, the Muslim troops under him on the northern side of Indus at Tsari, crossed over to the attackers.[301]

The first attack on the Skardu garrison, on 11th February 1948, was met with cool courage and determination and the element of surprise notwithstanding, it was repulsed. The second attack was well supported by more fire-power and it was renewed with Bren guns, mortars and medium machine guns. The 130-strong garrison responded gallantly and succeeded in not only repulsing but also taking one of them prisoner along with one medium machine gun, four rifles, one two-inch mortar and several boxes of ammunition. While retreating, the enemy took out their frustration on the civilian population killing several, including the Wazir-e-Wazarat, Amar Nath. The garrison suffered grievously in trust during the night when the Muslims in the fort, thirty-one troops as well as the three wireless operators, defected. Fortunately, the commanding officer had been wise enough to take possession of the wireless set and having worked as the brigade signals officer, was able to put it to good use.[302] The temporary withdrawal of the attackers was a welcome relief for the garrison because during that period another reinforcement of seventy men, commanded by Captain Ajit Singh arrived on 13th February. Another group reached on 15th February. At this point there were 285 in the garrison, but they were still too inferior in numbers compared to the enemy who had the added advantage of easy access to additional man power. To meet the challenge, Srinagar authorized the garrison to raise a platoon of labour with rations and pay commensurate to those of the State Forces. Lt Col Thapa used all his ingenuity to make maximum use of the resources and man power but the killing of the Wazir-e-Wazarat had added a few problems he could have done without. By now the garrison was also saddled with the security of refugees—229 non-Muslims and nineteen Muslims—the former being taken in the fort and the latter kept at the perimeter. The garrison just bided its time hoping for sufficient reinforcements to arrive.

Srinagar responded again. This time, dispatching a column, under the command of Brigadier Faqir Singh on 16th February, that consisted of three platoons of infantry, including elements of the 7 JAK, two medium machine guns, two two-inch mortars and a wireless set. It was a baffling move since he was the Brigade Commander of Srinagar and only a small force had been sent under such a senior officer. But there is a clear indication that this move was made by the Indian Army since 'the obnoxious practice of the British days seems to have been revived by attaching one officer of the Indian Army, Major Coutts, to the column as a sort of Special Officer of the bygone days. The men of the column were totally ill-equipped and ill-clothed for operations...'[303] It crossed the Zoji

La pass under the severest winter conditions on 24th February. So severe were the conditions that the wireless set became inoperable thus snapping all contact between Skardu and Srinagar; it therefore had to be left behind. The column reached Kargil safely and was reinforced there on 8th March, by one platoon of the A Company of the 6 JAK, to set out for Skardu.[304] It had been delayed since many porters had deserted and new had to be hired. On 16th March, it reached Gol and marched towards Skardu in high spirits. The morale was high as they were close to their destination after having braved the arctic conditions. But ten miles out of Skardu, as the column passed through the narrow defile of Thergo, it came under fire from light and medium machine guns from the surrounding and dominating ridges. Thirty-two of the troops were killed and many wounded, including Brigadier Faqir Singh. At nightfall the column retreated to reach Totli and then back to Kargil where the medical facilities were limited. Brigadier Faqir Singh was ordered to hand over charge to Major Coutts, the Special Officer of the Indian Army attached to the column, and return for medical treatment.[305]

With the limited resources that the State had its disposal, it was the classic case of 'so near yet so far'. The tragedy of the column and the defenders of Skardu was further heightened by the fact that the next day, Lt Col Thapa himself and Lt Ajit Singh, along with two companies had come out of Skardu to meet the reinforcement column but because of miscommunication, they set out a day too late and had to grievously suffer for the error as they too were ambushed. With the wisdom of hindsight, some military historians have raised many questions over the tactics and leadership of Brigadier Faqir Singh. While certain questions can be raised, a lot of them remain in the realm of 'ifs' and 'buts'. What if the wireless set had not broken down on the way and Brigadier Faqir Singh informed Skardu or Srinagar the exact date of his arrival in Skardu? Surely then the enemy would have been sandwiched between the two columns of the State Army. What if the column from Srinagar had 'moved tactically and secured the heights before moving through the defile or if after extricating itself from the area of the ambush it had stayed at Gol [rather than racing all the way back to Kargil] and then made fresh attempt to reach Skardu [after having learnt from earlier mistakes] the course of history might have been different…One must nevertheless wonder what advice Major Coutts had been offering to Brigadier Faqir Singh all this time.'[306]

Another aspect of this failed mission was that Lt Colonel Thapa had earlier sent out look-outs in the region and had been informed that the attacker too were scouting the region and would definitely ambush the approaching column of Brigadier Faqir Singh and since his wireless set was working, he had informed Srinagar accordingly with a request for an aerial attack on the enemy. Unfortunately, this request was not accepted.

The tragic episode affected the morale of the Skardu garrison for it had been banking heavily upon the arrival of the Brigadier and had in anticipation sent a platoon to engage the enemy. This platoon barely managed to escape ambush and had to retreat after a running battle for the last five miles of the march. The enemy was now brimming with confidence having successfully scuttled reinforcements. Conversely, the garrison was in greater difficulty. The fort had about 800 inmates including refugees and all of them had been subsisting on rations calculated to supply eighty men since the month of August. Additional rations were rummaged from the local bazaar and the vacated homes of the refugees but they were highly insufficient. They were reduced to three *chhataks* of flour, half a *chhatak* of lentils and no ghee to cook in.

After the failure of the reinforcement under Brigadier Faqir Singh, the A and B Companies of the 7 JAK under the command of Captains Davinder Singh and Durga Singh were sent to the garrison. At Kargil they joined hands with Major Coutts and the remnants of the previous columns, and awaited the arrival of more reinforcements from the 5 JAK that had been air lifted to Srinagar. Some elements of the battalion had been detained at Ransu and Banihal to guard the Srinagar-Jammu road while the rest reached Srinagar from where B Company proceeded on foot to Parkutta. Captain Tajram Thakur, commanding the D Company as well as a platoon from the A Company also moved in but was held up at Parkutta as the enemy was well entrenched on both sides of the Indus. It was only on 31st March, that reinforcements regrouped at Parkutta under Major Coutts and were designated the Biscuit Column. The remainder of the 5 JAK, under Lieutenant Colonel Kirpal Singh, on reaching Bagicha encountered Lieutenant Colonel Sampuran Bachan Singh, the Indian Army Adviser to the Biscuit Column who had been recalled to his unit and when Major Coutts returned to establish headquarters at Kargil. Lt Col Kirpal Singh then took command of the Biscuit Column. Thus the two designated advisers from the Indian Army were safely taken out of the active theatre. At this point, some of the columns were still in the vicinity while others were on road to Skardu.

Meanwhile, in another move, the Indian Army, leaving the Gilgit-Baltistan sector and the State Forces to their fate, made a dash for Leh, Ladakh. According to the *Operations in Jammu & Kashmir 1947-48* by Ministry of Defence, Government of India, the official account of 1947-48 operations says:

> After the departure of Lieut. Colonel Sher Jung Thapa for Skardu in November 1947, it appears that only 33 men of the State Forces were left at Leh. The platoon was responsible for defending a region many thousands of square kilometers in area, containing monasteries which were rumored to hold fabulous riches. Its population was non-Muslim and unwarlike. By attacking Ladakh, therefore, the raiders could obtain wealth and women, and destroy 'Kafirs', all without serious fighting. These facts were sure to attract them irresistibly, and people both in Ladakh and Kashmir immediately appreciated it. For the moment, Leh was sheltering behind Kargil and Skardu, but Kargil could be by-passed and *Skardu could not be expected to hold up the raiders from Gilgit for long.*[307] (Emphasis added)

The Indian Army had landed in Srinagar on 27th October 1947 and even before three months had passed it had already given up on Skardu and the region, which the British were so anxious to hand over to Pakistan. The Indian Army had finished and sealed the job that Major William Brown and the Gilgit Scouts had started. Thus ignoring the needs of Skardu they left the garrison to its fate. As early as 16th January 1948, Brigadier L.P. Sen, Commander of the 161 Infantry Brigade, informed the Headquarters of Jammu and Kashmir Force that he proposed to send a small detachment of troops to Leh. Officers and troops from the 2 Dogra volunteered for this mission to 'raise, organize and train local militias' there. But before they had moved, the news of attack on Skardu had reached Leh, where it created panic and a desperate telegram was sent to the Prime Minister of the State for immediate help. According to this version of the events, the telegram by the Officer Commanding of the detachment left at Leh, emphasized 'the virtual certainty of their being killed, the treasury and ammunition looted and the people massacred by the raiders, unless the detachment was permitted "to move to a place out of reach of the enemy".'[308] The urgency and response of the Indian Army to the pleas of Leh were in sharp contrast to the pleas of Skardu, an equally, if not more important place.

On 16th February, a small column of Indian Army, composed of two officers, one Viceroy's commissioned officer, two non-Commissioned Officers and eleven other ranks of the Indian Army, along with one Officer and two Viceroy's commissioned officers and fifty-six other ranks of the State Force, led by Major Prithi Chand of 2 Dogra, set out from Srinagar for Leh. The first group reached on 8th March and was closely followed by the group consisting of State Forces. On 25th February, Leh was placed under the operational command of the Z Brigade of the Indian Army. Even today, understandably, the retired officers of the Indian Army take pride in this feat performed under extreme conditions, completely ignoring that a month earlier, when Indian Army had turned its attention the other way, the valiant soldiers of the State Forces had already achieved the feat of crossing the Zoji Lal. Had the Indian Army displayed a similar urgency for Skardu, the State might still have retained that passage into Central Asia for India.[309] The whole of April passed without any sign of the enemy but once Kargil fell on 10th May, as will be seen, the whole scenario changed.

Dras and Kargil should never have been allowed to fall because their fall would effectively cut off Leh and whatever hope there might have been for Skardu would disappear. Also, the dash to Leh would have come to nothing if Pakistan would have been in firm control of the Dras-Kargil road to it since then the rear of the Indian forces there would have been deprived of the land route.

The beginning of April brought hectic activity in the theatre with the Army realizing that tragic consequences were waiting ahead. A constant stream of reinforcements began to flow on way to Skardu even as the Indian Army remained focused on making preparations for any possible future attacks. Even at that critical stage, the Indian Army could not spare its forces for Skardu since, it was argued that all its 'units were fully occupied in the bitter fighting of Uri and Poonch sectors'.[310] So, all the available troops of the 5 JAK and the 7 JAK were collected and sent to Skardu. As noted earlier, the 5 JAK, of seven Officers and 400 men, had arrived at Srinagar after having been pulled out of the southern Jammu sector. It would be recalled that raids had begun in this sector from across the border even before the British had pulled out of India. Sustained raids had also taken place at a number of points from the second week of October. The defence of that sector was, in fact, vital for the State as it could throttle all communications to Kashmir as well as the Jammu-Poonch region. Therefore, this sector was now entirely manned by the units of the Indian Army.

The first group from the new reinforcements, consisting of one Officer, one Viceroy's Commissioned Officer and forty other ranks reached Kargil on 1st April. They were soon followed by another party of three Viceroy's Commissioned Officers and thirty other ranks. With this strength Major Coutts was ordered to make Kargil a firm base. He was also ordered to move one Company to Bagicha and another to Parkutta to convert them into 'defended bases'. Another column, with thirty-seven combatants carrying three-inch and two-inch mortars, Bren and Sten guns and plenty of ammunition, was led by Lieutenant Colonel Sampuran Bachan Singh of the Indian Army, who had been till recently a Major, and two IC of the 1 Sikh. It was named the 'Sugar Column', with instructions to relieve Skardu, leave the majority troops there to strengthen the garrison and return with the civilians. 'For this purpose, he [Lieutenant Colonel Sampuran Bachan Singh] was made the commander of all the State Forces in the Kargil. He was also informed that two companies of 7 J&K Infantry and a section of MMGs were already in Kargil under Major Coutts and that one company of 7 J&K Infantry with a section of 2-inch mortars was just then reaching Kargil. Major Coutts was to act as Staff Officer to Lieut. Colonel Sampuran Bachan Singh.'[311] A cursory analysis of the manner in which this relief operation was being planned is a clear evidence of the inability of the Srinagar Headquarters to comprehend the challenges of geography, people and the general climate of the State. One also suspects that the earlier attempt and subsequent failure to reach Skardu under Brigadier Faqir Singh, had neither been appreciated nor taken seriously, and had been dismissing as an example of incompetence and lack of professionalism among the State Forces. After all, the State Force had sought help from the Indian Army after having failed to defend its borders!

Two more batches of the 5 JAK, consisting of seventy officers and men, followed Lieutenant Colonel Sampuran Bachan Singh. The last one under, the command of Lieutenant Colonel Kripal Singh, had sixty-nine men, mortars and guns. Lt Col Kripal Singh was the designated as the commander of the relief column while Lt Col Sampuran Bachan Singh was to be left between Kargil and Skardu to defend and hold local positions. All this while the defence of Skardu was becoming more untenable, and in view of this Major Coutts was ordered to advance from Kargil towards Skardu. When his party had reached 14 kms beyond Bagicha on 14th April, there was a stream of relief columns between Srinagar and Skardu and at various stages. After 17th April, Major Coutts found that the villages were silent and deserted and began to find various reasons for not moving any further, particularly without 100 pack ponies and wireless sets as well as the harsh weather conditions. 'Two days later, he reported that the raiders had surrounded his column, and were sniping it from the heights. Supplies of ammunition were wanted immediately and he concluded with the hope that though his troops were raw, they 'definitely should hold' the attacks. To this, Headquarters 163 Brigade replied that his troops were certainly better than the irregulars opposing him, and he should explain how his stock of ammunition was expended in a single short engagement.'[312] On 20th April, six of Major Coutts' force were killed, and two light machine guns and three rifles had fallen into enemy hands. The Indian Army's historian concedes here that the raiders were 'fully trained' and had the full support of the locals.

With the non-availability of porters and pack ponies, Major Coutts' force had carried only bare minimum ammunition. Looking at the situation, Lt Col Sampuran Bachan Singh was ordered to hurry-up to Parkutta, where Major Coutts was relieved to see him arrive and hand over the command.

But in between there had been a crisis of command and control. While Lieutenant Colonel Kripal Singh had been made the commander of this relief column, two officers of the Indian Army—Lieutenant Colonel Sampuran Bachan Singh and Major Coutts—were also attached. This obnoxious practice of the British, of attaching an Indian Army Officer as advisor to State Forces, had been continued by independent India's army. The result in this particular operation was that the 163 Brigade was passing all orders to the two officers of the Indian Army, who kept Lt Col Kripal Singh in the dark. Consequently, instructions often passed by them would contradicted his, which therefore hampered the entire operation. Unable to suffer this confusion any longer, Lt Col Kripal Singh approached the higher command, which after deliberations decided on 4th May that he would be the sole in-charge of the operation to save the starving Skardu. Lt Col Sampuran Bachan Singh was asked to return to Srinagar and Major Coutts was advised to remain with the column but only as an observer. In the end, Lt Col Sampuran Bachan Singh could not complete his journey. He was caught up in the web of the raiders and while fleeing, only reached the relative security of Leh.

In the meantime, the raiders of Skardu had followed a successful tactical strategy. Their strategy also dispelled the suggestion that their action was unorganized, and primarily, local. It was apparent that trained minds were behind their operations and they took full advantage of the presence of deserters from the 6 JAK among them, as they were well conversant with the region and trained to lead men. Moreover, the deserters had a natural flair for fighting in the mountains, of ambushing, sniping and a tactical sense of the ground. After taking control of Gilgit, and thereby, the nerve centre of the region where airplanes could land and stocks stored for the winter, the enemy buckled down to the task of making use of the winter for the control of Skardu. With the passes closing, the raiders made Skardu their next target because it was at a comparatively low height of 7,000 feet. Thus, the raiders had made the optimum use of the opportunity. However, they had not bargained for the grit and determination of Lieutenant Colonel Thapa and his equally determined soldiers. The raiders had to change their strategy once the first relief under Captain Prabhat Singh reached Skardu in the dead of winter. On the prowl along the route between Kargil and Skardu, they tired to tire out those that were besieging the garrison. However, as news began to spread that a stream of columns of relief were between Srinagar, Kargil and Skardu, the enemy in a bold move decided to seize Kargil and Dras so that those who had crossed Kargil might be completely cut off, and those behind were unable to move forward. By the end of April, this is where the struggle for Skardu had reached when Lieutenant Colonel Kripal Singh was made the sole in-charge of the relief column. By then the situation had begun to worry the Western Command because the raiders had begun to surround Kashmir from all the sides—north, north-west, south and east. For the first time since landing in Kashmir, the Indian Army realized the gravity of the situation in the Baltistan region though by then the initiative had been seized by the enemy.

In the meantime, Lieutenant Colonel Kripal Singh could never bring his complete battalion forward. Only his Battalion Headquarters moved forward. The two supporting companies, under Captain Rachhpal Singh and Captain Kashmir Singh, remained stuck in Sonamarg and Dras for lack of porters and ponies. In fact, they were never able to join their Battalion. While Captain Kashmir Singh was forced to take-up a defensive position at Dras, Captain Rachhpal Singh got involved in action in the Zoji La-Machoi area.[313] Under such circumstances, the commanding officer, requested Lieutenant Colonel Prithi Chand of the Dogras at Leh to send his ponies and Buddhist porters. Tragically, the day they arrived in Kargil, it was attacked and a number of them were killed.

What had actually happened was that by then the enemy had lost their patience combatting the doughty resistance of the Skardu garrison. They also knew that the waiting game had run its course and further delay might give an opportunity to Indian Forces to finally bring across their arsenal and control the Kargil-Skardu route. But it also knew that there was little chance of any immediate relief arriving for the garrison from Srinagar. They had therefore decided to launch 'Operation Sledge', the code name for the Ladakh offensive. Having failed to capture Skardu, 'the enemy, in order not to waste any more time had decided to invest it [Skardu] with a portion of his force and with the remainder launch the first phase of "Operation Sledge". He had the twin aim of the destruction of the State Force troops that were trying to reinforce Skardu and cutting the Indian line of communication at Kargil and Dras to isolate Leh which was the objective for the next phase. Consequently on 10 May while a simultaneous attack was launched on Parkutta, Kargil and Dras, Lieut. Colonel Kripal Singh's column was ambushed at Mirpigund with devastating effect.'[314] This happened even as the Raja of Totli pledged his loyalty and cooperation and provided 400 porters to Lieutenant Colonel Kripal Singh. He also assured that the enemy was not in significant numbers in the area. However, when the column of the State Forces reached the bend of the river at Mirpigund, it was ambushed by heavy small arms and mortar fire from the other side of the river. The porters panicked, dropped their loads and disappeared. Urgent request for reinforcements from the 7 JAK were of no avail as that battalion too was encountering similar attacks.

For six days, Mirpigund was the scene of intense firing before it abated. The enemy was superior in numbers and had greater capacity to absorb losses and hits than the 5 JAK, and in the light of the fact that there were no replenishments of either men or ammunition, further progress became obviously difficult. Adding to the woes, the villages were deserted and hence neither rations nor porters were available. Those that were available were of dubious loyalty. In a short time, as the fortunes of the State Forces ebbed, the attitude of the civilian population changed. Sensing the overwhelming superiority of the Pakistan-backed troops, it had begun to actively aid them by acting as informers regarding the movement, number of troops and equipment of the JAK forces. There were also rumours that the brother of the Raja of Shigar had been posing as a porter to spy on the state troops.[315]

On 14th May 1948, the columns of the 5 and 7 JAK heard that Kargil had fallen on 9th-10th May. Their mission now was to recapture the town. In preparation for the attack, the Biscuit Column fell back to Olthing Thang and destroyed all the heavy equipment that could not be carried without the porters, including wireless sets and heavy arms. They then began the march to Bagicha, and to avoid the enemy patrolling on the much-frequented tracks, the column took the less-travelled cross country route. But by now the locals had completely aligned themselves to the enemy who succeeded in getting information about their movement. The column was frequently harassed but it closed in on an apparently deserted village of Kharmang on 19th May, at 2 p.m., only to be ambushed by automatic and mortar fire. Pinned down in a hopeless situation, the column suffered the loss of sixty dead and equal number wounded. It was only under the cover of darkness that the column broke through the enemy lines to reach Bagicha, but without three platoons, they had to take a different route through the hills.[316]

Obviously the morale was low, the strength depleted and with the heavy weapons destroyed, the column was in no position to launch an attack on Kargil. Lieutenant Colonel Kirpal Singh decided that he should bypass Kargil and proceed to Dras. Once again the same strategy was adopted and the column moved through the less traversed mountains than the tracks. They barely had anything to eat with only *sattu* (a mixture of ground barley) for rations. It also ran into the blinding fury of a snow storm on their way Tohunwas. There they found twelve stragglers from the missing three platoons. The remainder had either been killed or wounded seriously in their attempt to break through the enemy lines and escape at Kharmang. On 23rd May, the Biscuit Column reached Kiniyal, where they got minimal rations from the villagers.[317]

The column then arrived at Franshot with the intention of crossing the Shingo River by footbridge. However, they found it destroyed. Meanwhile, the enemy patrol too had been sighted and thus an attempt to repair the bridge was given up. The next day a section forded the river with the intent of making repairs from the other side but was sighted and mowed down. The column gave up hope of crossing from that point and moved up stream to Gultari where on 29th May, the A and B Companies of 7 JAK as well as fifteen men of the 5 JAK had a safe passage before the cradle bridge collapsed, killing three. The column was now divided and moved on towards Dras. Those who had crossed Shingo advanced at 14,300 feet height of Marpo La and the rest, commanded by Lieutenant Colonel Kirpal Singh crossed Kuroghal Gali at 13,647 feet. However, in crossing the pass and reaching Badoab on 3rd June, thirty-nine lives were lost.[318] The village was inhabited by Muslims who not only provided food to the troops but also the accurate information about an enemy ambush at a track junction beyond the village. With the help of the local Muslim guides, the enemy was ambushed and routed. By now the column had reached the limits of human endurance, physically as well as mentally. But upon reaching Sonamarg on 7th June, they were rejuvenated as they found the much needed help from the Indian Army that was stationed there.[319]

The two Companies of the 7 JAK that had succeeded in crossing the cradle bridge at Gultari were less fortunate. Under constant fire from the enemy entrenched on heights and unable to find the tracks, they did reach Dras, only to find that it was occupied by the enemy. After more than twenty-four hours, these men, with their ammunition exhausted and without the strength or the means to find an escape from the mountains, were taken prisoners. At Kargil, by the end of April, the garrison had been critically reduced, consisting of only one platoon commanded by Captain Lachhman Das Silwal and twelve wounded and sick in the dispensary. In early May the enemy began its attacks in earnest, which were repulsed but it had become clear to Capt. Silwal that he and his men were in no position to withstand a sustained attack. On the night of 9th-10th May there was a determined attack, supported by three-inch mortar fire. After resisting for twenty-four hours, being outnumbered and finding the situation untenable, the garrison broke the engagement in the dead of the night to flee over the unexplored mountains, along with Hindu civil officials, and found their way to Kokernag after a trek of several days.[320]

Dras was garrisoned by two platoons of the C Company of

the 5 JAK and came under attack on 10th May. This garrison had resisted the enemy attacks for more than three weeks now, and had suffered heavy casualties. That day the enemy was more determined than ever before and cut the telephone lines with Machoi where one mixed company was defending Zoji La. With no reinforcements in sight and all ammunition exhausted it was decided to abandon Dras to join forces at Machoi. It succeeded in breaking through the enemy lines but was pursued and attacked at Pindras, six miles near Dras. The contact lasted more than an hour and half before the enemy withdrew to again launch sporadic attacks, till the column's fire power was exhausted. Meanwhile, the commanding officer, Captain Kashmir Singh, his JCOs and the majority of the other ranks had been killed. The forty survivors attempted to escape through the hills but were eventually captured.

The fall of Kargil and Dras meant that Skardu, which had till then successfully resisted incessant attacks for more than four months, could not even entertain the hope of getting reinforcements. Now the enemy strength, buoyed by the success, was increasing by the day while inside the fort, the garrison was not only dwindling but sick and exhausted, physically and materially to such a state that there were orders to shoot only to kill so that the dwindling supplies of ammunition could be conserved. On 14th March, a JAK ambush inflicted heavy casualties on the enemy patrol but could not consolidate the position as there was constant fire from the enemy occupied at Point 8853. The odds were heavy but the garrison was not prepared to give up. On the contrary a careful plan was laid out for the defence, with double-roof bunkers constructed against mortar fire. Soon, on 28th March 1948, in the early hours of the morning, the enemy launched a determined attack supported by heavy fire from Point 8853. There was fighting throughout the day with many attacks repulsed. By dawn the next day, there were more than twenty dead of the enemy while JAK force had four dead and ten injured. The pickets, School and Raja, commanded by Captain Ajit Singh and Jemadar Priar Singh displayed exemplary courage and once Capt. Ajit Singh and his men defended their picket for three days even after being cut off from the garrison. The fight now was virtually eyeball to eyeball with the enemy positions within a distance of fifty yards. The enemy had also forced vigorous night patrolling as it had begun to penetrate the gaps in between the defence lines.

In another development, on 16th May, after the fall of Kargil and Dras, Srinagar cabled orders for the Skardu garrison and refugees to withdraw to Olthing Thang along with as many arms and ammunition as possible so that an attack to capture Kargil could be launched. Finally, those who were taking military decisions were beginning to understand the geography and the strategic importance of the places that they were only familiar with as names. While the capture of the whole of Baltistan would have meant a loss of an area of strategic importance but that did not pose any threat to the life of the people as they were Muslim. But the capture of Ladakh would have meant a large scale massacre of the Buddhist population and the plundering of their monasteries. However, this order to Skardu only betrayed more ignorance on the part of the senior commanders of the Indian Army, particularly Major General Thimayya, and not surprisingly, Lieutenant Colonel Thapa, vigorously opposed the proposal. The message of Srinagar had been explained in detail:

> First. Enemy pressure on Skardu and L of C between Skardu Kargil increased considerably recently. Enemy attacked and captured Kargil 12 May. Enemy now reported Bod Karbu with intention advancing Leh. Second. Garrisons at Skardu Parkutta Totli and other places on L of C Kargil was to temporarily withdraw from above places as early as possible and come at Olthing Thang NJ 1804 with a view to recapture Kargil. Third. Withdrawal will be carried out as follows. A. Skardu Garrison to fight its way back to Olthing Thang as soon as possible. Every effort will be made to bring back all arms ammunition and civ population. Arms ammunition and equipment which cannot be brought will be destroyed. Parkutta and Totli. Comd 5KI will make every endeavour to withdraw Parkutta Grn. To Totli. While Grn will then fight its way to Olthing Thang and establish firm base there. Efforts will be made to contact Lt. Col. Sampuran Bachan Singh and Maj Coutts and help come their detachments at Olthing Thang. Arms and equipment which cannot be brought will be destroyed.[321]

Obviously, the order had been issued by looking at the map without the knowledge of the ground, and opposition to it was swift and precise by Lieutenant Colonel Thapa, who responded:

> Though message not clear due to some mistakes probably in transmission I gather intention is to withdraw and conc [*sic*] on Olthing Thang with a view to recapture Kargil. May I bring to your kind notice. One. Two days after war we were attacked in Skardu we said we could not hold Skardu and then it was easy to withdraw as enemy had not occupied line of withdrawal and plenty transport available. JAK forces ordered to hold last man last round. Two. We are holding for more than three months. Are left with no mortar ammunition and other ammunition practically exhausted. With that we have to fight back about 80 miles route all held by enemy in well prepared positions and having all supporting weapons with plenty ammunition. Three. We have wounded stretcher cases. In addition some indoor patients and male and female and young all unfit to move. No coolies to evacuate above. Four. Two routes open for us to follow one through Gol-Parkutta and second via Satpura. Both very strongly held by enemy in great depth. Simply impossible to pass through. If moved then 50 percent casualty of troops and not less than 80 percent refugees certain. Five. Not single coolie for ration etc. Six. There are no troops at Kargil Olthing Thang Bagicha. Major Coutts having reached Leh. Troops at Totli Parkutta are one strong battalion and have not been able to clear opposition and reach here. We are hardly two companies with no mortar ammunition and cannot fight back such a long distance all vital points held by enemy. Seventh. Troops from Srinagar could come much quicker than collection of scattered garrisons here and recapture Kargil. If SF troops not available IA troops be pushed. Suggest and request. A. Ammunition be dropped immediately. B. More troops be pushed from Srinagar to capture Kargil. C. Troops in Totli area may not be withdrawn. If our withdrawal is imperative suggest troops at Totli Parkutta be pushed here and we will all fall back collectively. Lastly to avoid disaster of this garrison and refugees request you please reconsider your orders.[322]

The request was acceded to and the orders cancelled. Air dropping of ammunition too was arranged but it proved ineffective as the planes had a limited capacity and the dropping zone was so narrow that a lot of ammunition fell into the hands of the enemy. But on 2nd June, two Tempests of the Indian Air Force strafed Point 8853, inflicting heavy casualties and in the process cheering the spirits of a garrison that was demoralized by malnutrition, malaria, dysentery and general hopelessness. On 17th June, Sepoy Amar Nath, captured by the enemy at Parkutta, approached the garrison bearing a white flag and a message to Lieutenant Colonel Thapa from Colonel Shahzada Mata-ul-Mulk, commander, Azad Central Forces, Skardu. The written message tried to convince the garrison of the futility of resistance and the assured benevolent and good treatment of the surrendered forces. It was unanimously rejected and even though the means to resist the enemy were fast depleting, the garrison prepared for further battle. It duly came on 12th August 1948 and so exhausted the garrison energies and ammunition that the last box of ammunition was also expended. 13th August passed by slowly and as night fell, those of the garrison who could and wished to, were allowed to slip away from the Fort in small groups. In his last act as the Commanding Officer of the Skardu garrison, Lieutenant Colonel Sher Jung Thapa, the man who had inspired his men to withstand a siege that was one of the longest in war annals, sought permission to surrender from the Headquarters in Srinagar. He was granted permission, which was conveyed to him by Colonel Shri Ram Oberoi of the Srinagar Division on behalf of Major General K.S. Thimayya, DSO. It was 14th August, 1948—a year after Pakistan had come into being.

The garrison on 14th August 1948, consisted of Lieutenant Colonel Thapa, four Officers, one JCO and thirty-five Other Ranks apart from the civilians. The end is best described in the words of General Thimayya:

> My strategy was to save Ladakh was to hold on to Skardu at all costs so that Pakistani forces may be prevented from reaching Kargil and Leh. Fortunately, I had the right man in Skardu to fulfill this mission. No words can describe the gallantry and leadership of Lieutenant Colonel Sher Jung Thapa who held on to Skardu with hardly 250 men for six long months. It is one of the longest sieges in the annals of war. While ordering him

> to defend Skardu to the last man last round, I had promised to send him reinforcements and supplies. Unfortunately, neither could reach Skardu. I also tried to air drop more rations and ammunition but these were merely helping the enemy. At the end of six months, when he completely ran out of ration and ammunition, I asked him to surrender. My General Staff Officer, Colonel Shri Ram Oberoi, gave this order to the gallant officer in August 1948. Thapa's response is etched in my mind and I can never forget it. He said, "I know that I cannot hold out without rations and ammunition. General Thimayya has failed me. I know the fate my troops will meet after surrendering to the enemy. I cannot do anything now against the enemy but I will certainly take revenge in my next birth." It is officers of this stamp who make great armies and great nations.[323]

What followed was what had kept the garrison going even in the most trying conditions. They had known that not only no mercy would be shown but terrible reprisals would follow for holding out for so long and frustrating the enemy. The garrison had, therefore, held on in the hope that somehow help will reach them. It had not, and now frightening scenes followed.

Many years later, Brigadier Sher Jung Thapa described what followed:

> We used our last box of ammunition. Everyone knew our plight and there was panic and chaos all over. The women started committing suicide by jumping into the Indus and poisoning themselves in order to save their honour. There was an instance when a girl jumped thrice into the Indus to kill herself but each time the waves carried her to the shore. My troops fought under very adverse circumstances and held Skardu for six months and three days. Then was left with no alternative but to surrender. The surrender was followed by mass murder. All Sikhs were shot dead. Captain Ganga Singh, my Adjutant, was tied laid on the ground and shot. The only Sikh who escaped was Kalyan Singh, my orderly who was staying with me.[324]

The enemy had been frustrated for more than six months and it took it out on the men and women within the fort. The forty non-Muslim refugees were the first to be killed and then began general murder and rape. Many women in the garrison committed suicide. All Sikhs were put to sword and that now infamous radio message boasting 'All Sikhs killed, all women raped' was sent. Lieutenant Colonel Sher Jung Thapa and his orderly Kalyan Singh were spared probably on the instructions of General Sir Douglas Gracey who was the Commander-in-Chief of the Pakistan Army. Thapa had had his college education at Dharamsala and being an excellent hockey player, frequently played with stalwarts of the 1 Gorkha Rifles, Regimental Centre, Dharamsala. In the hockey field, he had become a close friend of Captain Douglas Gracey, Adjutant of the 1 GR RC, who encouraged Thapa to join the forces of Jammu and Kashmir State as an officer. L. Col Thapa's old association and friendship with the now General Gracey came to his rescue; otherwise he would have met the same fate as that of the other prisoners of war who were killed by the Pakistani Army. It also indicated how closely the Pakistani army's top brass was involved in the war that was being waged in the State of Jammu and Kashmir.

The valley of Kashmir was now under serious threat from north as well as east. The line of communication between Srinagar and Leh passing over the Zoji La and through Kargil, stood disrupted. There was also real danger of the enemy walking into Ladakh unless reinforcements were sent urgently. However, what has been most regrettable is that military historians are yet to objectively analyze the failures in Gilgit and Skardu. While the blame for the Gilgit loss can be solely attributed to the then Ruler, Maharaja Hari Singh, his Prime Minister Ram Chandra Kak and other military advisors, the failure in Skardu has to also be attributed to the Indian Army in general and the then Major General K.S. Thimayya. Major General Thimayya shared the common trait of other officers of the Indian Army of not treating the officers and soldiers of the State Forces with the respect and seriousness that they deserved. As soon as the 1 Sikh of the army had landed, they had been received by Colonel Bhagwan Singh of the State Forces who advised him not to leave any soldier for the defence of the airport for it was not threatened, but it had not been heeded. Lieutenant Ranjit Rai had no means of independently verifying the strength of the enemy yet he dismissed the advice and his first push was immediately beaten back. In the process he had lost his life. Lieutenant Colonel Thapa had suggested to Major General Thimayya that he be allowed to withdraw to Kargil but was turned down and when the situation had become irretrievable he had been ordered to evacuate Skardu along with civilians! He had the last word when he told Major General Thimayya that he had failed him.

Operations in Jammu & Kashmir 1947-48, the official word of the Defence Ministry has also erroneously concluded that the failure is attributable to lack of leadership among other officers of the State Forces. But it has to be said that almost all Battalions of the State Forces were well trained and all were the proud inheritors of a legacy. They were aware of the responsibility that history had put upon them but unfortunately the odds were overwhelmingly against them. In that region across the Zoji La, the officers of the State Forces held fixed defensive positions in Skardu and Dras. While in Skardu they held out for more than six months, at Dras also a small band of soldiers kept the enemy at bay for about four weeks. It was only in Parakutta and Totli that they failed miserably because they had no defensive positions and were hounded by the enemy from the front and rear. The local population had turned hostile, cutting them from the supply of even the barest essentials. Finally, out there in the open, being ambushed anywhere and everywhere, they had become demoralized. So had Lieutenant Colonel Sampuran Bachan Singh and Major Coutts of the Indian Army who found safety in retreating all the way to Leh. Skardu was a collective failure and accordingly needs to be acknowledged. The State Forces and its officers need to be judged by comparing the kind of support that the Indian army needed to cross the Zoji La in November 1948. This had been done thirteen months after its landing in Srinagar. Finally, it needs to be asked, why the Indian Army not make a move towards Skardu after it had taken control of the Zoji La Pass, Kargil and the route to Leh. After the tanks had crossed Zoji La, one can imagine the kind of panic they would have created among the raiders occupying the road to Skardu. That would have eased the pressure on Leh too. But obviously, Skardu had been, in all probability, written off. The million dollar question is, by whom, the Army or the political leadership?

17

The Political Battleground

Even while the State Forces were fighting a lonely battle for survival in Skardu, another war, equally deadly in intent and having far reaching consequences, was being waged by Sheikh Abdullah with the support of Nehru. Sheikh Abdullah was determined not only to end the Dogra Dynasty but to humiliate it and liquidate the Dogras as a power centre. It has been noted earlier that Maharaja Hari Singh had signed the Instrument of Accession in extremely complex circumstances, but whatever the circumstances, the matter should have ended there. But Lord Mountbatten had added a rider to its acceptance, and the Government of India too had accepted it on the condition that the issue would be subject to the approval of the people. As discussed earlier, it had not been clearly stated why it had become necessary to add a clause that was not part of the India Independence Act and, therefore, technically, had no legal validity. But to be charitable to Lord Mountbatten, he also had a burning desire to establish that every decision being taken by him reflected the democratic credentials of the British in general and the Dominion of India in particular. 'It is my Government's wish,' he had written to the Maharaja in response to the signing of the Instrument of Accession, 'that as soon as law and order has been restored in Kashmir and her soil cleared of the invaders the question of the State's accession should be settled by a reference to the people...'

Which people and how they would decide was left for the future, but everyone understood that for Prime Minister Jawaharlal

Nehru 'the people' under reference were Sheikh Abdullah and his National Conference. Jammu and the Dogras, who had in the first place created that State, had no existence on his horizon. By that time, Sheikh Abdullah was riding a crest of popularity wave in the valley and Nehru applauded and supported him in everything that he did. How strong the bond between the two was, is best illustrated by the reception that Nehru was given in Srinagar when he visited November 1947. In a public welcome organized in the present day Lal Chowk, an emotional Sheikh Abdullah had recited the Persian couplet of Amir Khusro:

> *Mun tu shudam tu mun shudi, mun tun shudam tu jaan shudi*
> *Taakas na goyad baad azeen, mun deegaram tu deegari*
>
> (I have become you, and you me, I am the body, you soul; /
> So that no one can say hereafter, That you are are someone, and me someone else)

After reciting this couple, Sheikh Abdullah had turned to Nehru and embraced him to the thunderous applause of the Kashmiris; one a Kashmiri Muslim whose ancestors had embraced Islam not too long ago and the other a Kashmiri Pandit, whose ancestors had migrated to escape the religious persecution unleashed by successive Muslim rulers.

This was a period when for Nehru, Sheikh Abdullah could do no wrong, even when it had been proven during the Quit Kashmir movement against the Maharaja, that through the National Conference Abdullah was feeding malicious falsehoods to Nehru. Yet, Nehru had continued to repose absolute trust in him. They were friends, indeed, but there was no mistaking the fact that Nehru had genuinely come to believe that in the peculiar circumstances of Kashmir, with its Muslim majority, it was absolutely essential that Sheikh Abdullah be fully involved in the government of the State. No one had the inclination to wonder if Kashmir was the only identity of the State of Jammu and Kashmir or question the wisdom of considering Sheikh Abdullah as the sole spokesman of the State? His opinion was accepted as the opinion of Dogras of Jammu and Buddhists of Ladakh, in the process, ignoring that the Dogras, in particular had visceral antipathy for him. Historically, even the Ladakhis had no reason to trust the Kashmiris. Its history is full of chapters filled with the invasion of that Himalayan region by Kashmir rulers during different periods. Moreover, there was that historical grudge that the grandeur and vastness of the Ladakhi kingdom had been shrunk by the perfidy of the Governor of Kashmir during the negotiations for the Treaty of Tingmosgang in 1684 to end the Ladakhi-Tibet war. Therefore, hoisting of the Kashmiri leader upon the Dogras and Ladakhis was deeply resented though in that uncertain period of transition and turmoil this could not manifest in reasonable political idioms.

Not surprisingly, the first shot was fired by Prime Minister Nehru, on 13th November 1947. Barely a fortnight after accession, he wrote to Maharaja Hari Singh about the desirability of involving Sheikh Abdullah in affairs of governance. He said:

> As I pointed to you, the only person who can deliver the goods in Kashmir is Sheikh Abdullah. He is obviously the leading popular personality in Kashmir. The way he has risen to grapple with the crisis has shown the nature of the man. I have high opinion of his integrity and his general balance of mind. He has striven hard and succeeded very largely in keeping communal peace. He may make any number of mistakes in minor matters, but I think he is likely to be right in regard to major decisions.
>
> But the real point is that no satisfactory way out can be found in Kashmir except through Sheikh Abdullah. If that is so, full confidence must be placed in him. There is no half-way house between full confidence and half and half affair which has little advantage and many disadvantages. Even if a risk has to be taken in giving full confidence, that risk has to be taken. There is no other way so far as I can see it both from the short-term point of view and the long-term one. Sheikh Abdullah is earnestly desirous of co-operating and is amenable to any reasonable argument. I would suggest to you to keep in close personal touch with him and deal with him directly and not through intermediaries.[325]

That 'Sheikh Abdullah is earnestly desirous of co-operating' appeared to be so, at least, on the face of it, particularly in the backdrop of Sheikh Abdullah having assured the Maharaja in his letter written from the jail before his release that he was assuring

His Highness of his steadfast loyalty and prayed to God that under His Highness' aegis such an era of peace, prosperity and good governance be ushered that it may become an ideal for others to follow.[326] But once the Instrument of Accession had been signed and Sheikh Abdullah brought into the mainstream, pressure began to be built on the Maharaja for bringing about changes as a matter of urgency. While Sheikh Abdullah showed little concern for the situation on the war-front, Jawaharlal Nehru also displayed little appreciation for the priorities during war-time. Apparently, both had no empathy for the people—Hindus, Sikhs and Muslims caught in the war—and were more obsessed with the transfer of power to an unelected person. Nehru's letter of 13th November 1947 had made that clear. By that date, even the Valley had not been fully cleared to give full security to the people, let alone Jammu that had become a blur in the consciousness of Delhi.

On the issue of devolution of administrative power to the people, the Maharaja had a different opinion, which he had shared with Mehr Chand Mahajan before he had taken up the office of Prime Minister of Jammu and Kashmir. On the advice of the Maharaja, Mahajan had called upon Mahatma Gandhi during his visit before the accession of the State. Gandhi had told him that he desired that the Maharaja accede to India and that the administrative setup be democratic. During Mahajan's visit to Nehru, he too had emphasized on the need of a democratic administrative setup. To this the Maharaja had responded that the question of reforms in the State should be left to him. Hari Singh wrote: 'The one thing that is vital from the point of immediate necessity of the State is the ability of the Government to choose its own time for the orientation and association of the people for their own betterment, security of life and property and full development. You should be able to convince the persons concerned about this aspect of the case before you arrive here. A visit to Delhi, of course, will be necessary.'[327] Apparently, Mahajan had not been able to convince Nehru, who was apparently giving more importance to democratization than pushing the invaders out of the State. It is very hard to justify his insistence to transfer power to Sheikh Abdullah because of the non-democratic nature of the whole scheme. Being a non-elected leader of a political party that had its presence only in Kashmir Valley, the setup being suggested as desirable by Nehru was as undemocratic and unrepresentative as the Maharaja's rule. Vehement opposition to the Maharaja's rule was only from Sheikh Abdullah and the National Conference and this was understandable since not too long ago he had launched the Quit Kashmir movement against the Maharaja, which was supported by Nehru as well. Moreover, opposition to Sheikh Abdullah in the Jammu region was as strong as that of Sheikh Abdullah for the Maharaja in Kashmir. In view of this, the insistence of Nehru in hoisting his friend in a position of greater responsibility was hard to swallow. The letter of 13th November had set the agenda for the future, the bitter harvest of which was to be reaped many decades later.

Soon after, Nehru, through the letter of Gopalaswami Ayyangar, Minister without Portfolio, written on 9th December 1947, had advised the Maharaja to establish close personal touch with Sheikh Abdullah and involve him in matters of governance. In view of the critical situation that had befallen, Nehru wanted the Maharaja to take into consideration Abdullah's views regarding the changes needed in the existing constitutional and administrative set up in the State. Obviously, what was being sought of the Maharaja was the unconditional transfer of all power to Sheikh Abdullah in the name of the people of the State. Maharaja Hari Singh felt that while the woes of the people of his State were increasing by the day, not only was he being asked to make sacrifices that no other ruler of the British India was asked to make, but the primary task of ridding the State of the raiders was far from being achieved. In fact, there were times when he would wonder if the Instrument of Accession had any sanctity, as he candidly wrote to Sardar Patel on 31st January 1948 about the unsatisfactory military progress, continued influx of refugees and deadlocked Security Council deliberation.

> ...a feeling comes to my mind as to the possible steps that I might take to make so far as I am concerned a clean breast of the situation. Sometimes I feel that I should withdraw the Accession that I have made to the Indian Union. The Union only provisionally accepted the Accession and if the Union cannot recover back our territory and is going eventually to agree to the decision of the Security Council which may result in handing us

> over to Pakistan then there is no point in sticking to the Accession of the State to the Indian Union. For the time being it may be possible to have better terms from Pakistan but that is immaterial because eventually it would mean the end of the Dynasty and end of Hindus and Sikhs in the State. There is an alternative possible for me and that is to withdraw the Accession and that may kill the reference to the UNO because Indian Union will have no right to continue proceedings before the Council if the Accession is withdrawn. The result may be return to the position the State held before the Accession. The difficulty in that situation however will be that the Indian Troops cannot be maintained in the State except as volunteers to help the State. I am prepared to takeover command of my own Forces along with the Forces of the Indian Army as volunteers to help the State. I am prepared to lead my Army personally and to command, if the Indian Union agrees, also their troops. I know my country better than any of your Generals will know it even during the next several months or years and I am prepared to take the venture boldly rather than merely keep on sitting here and doing nothing.[328]

By this time the Maharaja had been frustrated, not only by the lack of progress of the Indian Army in the Jammu sector and the loss of Gilgit, but also the inability to make any headway in providing any relief to the Skardu garrison. Some progress had been made in the Valley but there had been no large scale pushing back of the raiders. This situation was further aggravated by the reference of the subject to the Security Council which, may or may not, rule the Accession in India's favour. He was also not satisfied with the internal political situation though he left that to the judgment of Sardar Patel and asserted that he was prepared to be the constitutional head of the State in future. He had added in the letter:

> ...I am quite willing to give Responsible Government but I am not prepared to go beyond the Mysore Model because I am not satisfied that the leaders of the National Conference are for the time being very fit administrators or command the confidence of the Hindus and Sikhs or even a large section of the Muslims. I must therefore keep certain reserved powers of which you are already aware and I must have a Dewan of my choice as a member of the cabinet and possibly as a President.

> Another alternative that strikes me is that if can do nothing I should leave the State [short of abdication] and reside outside so that people do not think that I can do anything for them. For their grievances they can hold the Civil Administration responsible or the Indian Forces who are in-charge of the Defense of the State. The responsibility will then clearly be of either the Indian Union or the Administration of Sh. Abdulla [*sic*]. If there is any criticism those responsible can have it and the responsibility of the suffering of the people will not be mine. Of course I well anticipate that—as people started saying when I left Kashmir only on Mr. Menon's advice that I had run away from Srinagar—they will say that I have left them in their hour of misery but it is no use remaining in a position where one can do nothing merely to avoid criticism. Of course if I go out of the State I will have to take the public into confidence and tell them the reasons why I am going out.[329]

Meanwhile, another problem had added to the woes of the State. The refugees had been bringing harrowing tales of atrocities committed upon them in their own homes. Traumatized and in tatters, many among them had lost their equilibrium. Moreover, often when they saw the Muslims in Jammu enjoying normal life, the beast in them would awaken to seek revenge for the rape, murder and plunder that they had suffered. The new political dispensation that was emerging in the State pinned all the blame of the violence against the Muslims on the State Forces for it was alleged that they had not only failed to control such violence but had aided and abetted it. Such aspersions were cast against the Maharaja also and even Mahatma Gandhi was manoeuvred into becoming an accomplice to such propaganda.

Sheikh Abdullah had gone about this in a roundabout manner and his moves and motives had become visible to Mehr Chand Mahajan much before everything came out in the open. Even before the Accession, Abdullah had told the Maharaja, when he called upon him and his wife in the middle of October 1947, that it was wholly unnecessary to have outsiders as Prime Minister and Deputy Prime Minister. He also assured that he would serve the Maharaja and the State like a dutiful son if the Maharaja would bestow all powers in him. Mahajan could see that here was a man who desired to wrest control of all power and if thwarted, he could go to any length. This came out in the open when a local paper of the State prominently carried the news on 15th December 1947 that Sheikh Abdullah has demanded full powers for his Ministry and also the termination of the services of Mehr Chand Mahajan. The ink of this news had hardly dried when Mahajan had the first taste of the tactics of Sheikh Abdullah. In the wake of the invasion by the raiders, and after the Indian Army had landed in Srinagar, Sheikh Abdullah had organized a Kashmiri Volunteer Corps and had, therefore, written a letter to Nehru, seeking supply of .303 rifles for them. Accordingly, the Rifles were sent to the Commander of the Indian Forces who was warned by Mahajan not to handover the weapons without ensuring that they could not only be handled but also taken care of properly by those who were issued those weapons. This, understandably, caused some delay and immediately Sheikh Abdulla complained to Nehru that they had been supplied to the volunteers of Rashtriya Swayamsevak Sangh (RSS) instead of National Conference volunteers. As on earlier occasions, Nehru did not wait to make inquiry and wrote a very nasty letter against Mahajan to the Maharaja who asked him to give a reply. Commenting on the incident, Mahajan replied that he 'had not received a single rifle from him, the rifles sent were in the possession of the Officer Commanding the Indian Forces in the State who had not given a single rifle to RSS. I challenged the Sheikh to prove his allegations. Pandit Nehru promptly withdrew the allegations. He expressed regret and said he was sorry to learn that he had been misinformed.'[330]

Not content, Sheikh Abdullah then tried to poison the mind of Mahatma Gandhi against the Maharaja and his Prime Minister by telling him that the Maharaja and Mahajan had been instigating the killings of Muslims in Jammu. It worked with Mahatma Gandhi too, and during one of his post-prayer speeches he charged both of them of those killings. This was widely circulated by the newspapers and Mahajan had to forcefully refute the allegations in a letter. He wrote:

> I have the report of the post-prayer speech delivered by you and printed in the *Hindustan Times* of 27th of December 1947, which contents a passage to the following effect:

"He [Mahatmaji], had heard of murders of numberless Muslims and abduction of Muslim girls in Jammu. The Maharaja must hold responsibility for this. The Dogra State forces were under his direct control. He had not become the mere constitutional head and, therefore, he must be held responsible for all the acts, good or bad, of people under his rule. Sheikh Abdulla had been to Jammu and tried to allay passions…Gandhiji would advise the Maharaja to step aside along with his Minister in view of what had taken place in Jammu and give the fullest opportunity to Sheikh Abdulla and the people of Kashmir to deal with the situation."

It seems to me that the speech has been made on false representation of facts…It is undoubtedly true that a very large number of Hindus and Sikhs were killed and their women abducted. It is also true that a considerable number of Muslims were killed and a number of their women were abducted. The wave of insanity that prevailed in the East and West Punjab took hold of the State territory and with its vast area, limited resources, a scanty number of troops and police, with practically no means of communications, it was not possible for any human agency to meet this unexpected and sudden trouble but I can assure you that no efforts were spared to stop it and it was actually stopped in a much shorter time than it was stopped anywhere else.

After 30th October…killings continued. Since then the Muslims suffered the most in parts of Udhampur and Reasi Districts and in parts of Kathua and Jammu Districts. Two convoys of Muslims under military protections were attacked. Both these convoys were being evacuated under the command of an Indian Brigadier. The Indian military took very strong action against the attackers and killed about 100 to 120 of the attackers with my full approval and the approval of His Highness as were definitely of the opinion that a very strong action was needed to stop the process of mutual killing started by the communities. The Muslim population in a part of the Reasi District on the side of the Chenab, in Bhadarwah and Kishtwar and in Rajouri area became very aggressive after 30th October. In these parts the Hindu and Sikh population has been practically wiped out and a very large number of their women have been abducted and are in the possession of local Muslim population. In the Mirpur District, the Hindu and Sikh population has been exterminated…

> Even at this present moment, though aggression on the part of Hindus has completely stopped, the Muslim population is still out of control...In the circumstances stated above, all that can be said is that on the reasoning employed by you, whatever communal trouble took place between 15th and 30th October, the responsibility for it, in the absence of extenuating circumstances, is on the Government of His Highness. After the 30th October up to date whatever has happened or is happening and whatever loss of life, whether of life or property or abduction, the responsibility is on the Dictator and his Government as he has been in complete control of the administration...[but] in view of the extent of territory no effective steps could be taken to completely stop the mutual killings. Sir Dalip Singh, Agent of the Government of India, was here during a part of this period. His word on this subject will undoubtedly be a word of independent observer and may I request that you should call him and satisfy yourself whether the Government did not do all that was humanly possible...if they were unsuccessful in their efforts it was mainly due to circumstance out of their control.[331]

Mahajan also offered that the Maharaja and he were willing to be put on trial before an impartial tribunal along with all the heads of the Governments of East Punjab, West Punjab, Delhi, Bihar and West Bengal where similar massacres took place. He confidently claimed that the Maharaja and he would emerge from such an ordeal better than the others. Such a claim did not mean that he was justifying the killings and abductions that took place in the State but only wanted the Mahatma to judge them with the same yardstick with which other Governments had been judged and should not be singled out for condemnation. He also challenged that he was 'prepared for the investigation on the question of the number of Hindus and Sikhs killed and the number of so called massacre of Muslims and about the abduction of women of both communities.'

Mahatma Gandhi, during the course of his post-prayer speech had also said that the amity that had been maintained between the different communities in Kashmir was a ray of hope and lauded the people (and apparently the leader—Sheikh Abdullah) for re-instilling hope in humanity. But Mahajan said in his letter that as far as the Kashmir Valley was concerned 'more than 30 per cent [Sikhs] of them had been finished'. Their houses had been burned and women abducted and this had happened in Poonch, Bhaderwah, Kishtwar and a part of Reasi. Similar sufferings were undergone by Muslims in Jammu, Kathua and parts of Udhampur and Reasi, which was equally condemnable but on a far lesser scale than the sufferings of Hindus. Finally, Mahajan wrote:

> His Highness has always treated all his subjects equally and with complete impartiality but in spite of this if he is told that he is responsible for the killings of the Muslims in Jammu Province he naturally feels hurt.
>
> May I submit that it was a condition of helplessness in which the administration of the State was placed owing to the partition of India which brought into existence a purely Muslim State that was responsible for all that happened. The award of the Boundary Commission and the sudden unexpected departure of the British created an extraordinary situation and whatever happened was due to this curious sequence of events and was also due to the Pakistani mentality to annex the State to Pakistan... His Highness, as ruler, however, accepts full responsibility for the killings of Muslims by Hindus and Sikhs and vice versa whether these killings were done by the State subjects or by the refugees from West Punjab who themselves had suffered enormously at the hands of Muslims there. He does not agree with you that the responsibility would not have been his if he had been a constitutional ruler; he feels that the responsibility for all the troubles would have been his whether these troubles took place when I was in-charge as Prime Minister or whether Sheikh Abdulla [*sic*] was in charge as Head of Administration because both these appointments were made by him and whatever powers are vested in me or Sheikh Abdulla [*sic*] are vested by him. The ultimate responsibility remains with the administration of which he is the Head, whether constitutional or otherwise.[332]

Mahatma Gandhi did not respond to the rebuttal directly but sent a message through Raj Kumari Amrit Kaur[333] mentioning how he would like to meet Mahajan. Both met and had a free and frank exchange of views during which Mahajan again reiterated his hurt at being singled out for condemnation for the killings of Muslims without uttering a word of sympathy for the aggrieved

Hindus and Sikhs of Mirpur and other places. To his credit Gandhi acknowledged his mistake and expressed sympathy for those who had suffered in those places in his next speech.[334] Mahatma Gandhi's comments were not only unfair but also used as a weapon by Sheikh Abdullah. They inflicted such a deep cut that they continue to find space in all future discourses on the subject and has led many scholars to search for population figures to validate them. It was also becoming clear that while Sheikh Abdullah had willing ears in Delhi—via Gandhi and Nehru—they were only weak listeners. Both, Gandhi and Nehru, were very sensitive to the subject of killings of Muslims in India. Violence against them in some way validated the 'Two Nation' theory, which they loathed accepting. But while condemning the Hindus and Sikhs they ignored the human factor that overcomes reason and good sense in such an environment. Sheikh Abdullah and his National Conference repeatedly accused the Maharaja of having the blood of Muslims on his hands. This had been cleverly combined with the circumstances of the departure of the Maharaja from Srinagar on the night of 25th-26th October 1947. It was presented as if he had fled his capital to save his life. Thus, he was painted as a cowardly ruler who left his people to the mercy of ruthless invaders to save his life, as well as a ruler who was complicit in the killings of his innocent people. With each succeeding day such brutal personal attacks to malign on the Maharaja increased. It was said that he 'fled his capital in the dead of night along with his family, jewels and courtiers, leaving his people to face the fury of the approaching onslaught. A barrage of vituperative propaganda was launched by the National Conference leaders, and was echoed by newspapers in Delhi and other parts of the country. The irony of the situation lay in the fact that Sheikh Abdullah himself had flown to Delhi on 25 October, two days before we left Srinagar and did not return until after the Indian Army arrived.'[335]

There were many in the country who were willing to believe in this malicious propaganda since they needed to have the guilt of loss of humanity pinned on someone. Maharaja Hari Singh became the perfect target on whom the blame could be laid. He was a Hindu and in his State the Muslims enjoyed considerable numerical superiority. Therefore, if the Muslims had been massacred, there must have been official complicity. By claiming that Maharaja Hari Singh had failed in performing his duties as a protector of life and property of his people, they had drawn away the attention from all those who had failed in both East Punjab and West Punjab, Delhi, Bihar and Bengal. Conversation about those massacres had to be stopped by finding someone guilty so that no questions were asked of Nehru and Patel who were in Delhi and others who were in charge in other States. In his voluminous work *The Punjab—Bloodied, Partitioned and Cleansed*, author Ishtiaq Ahmed has brought out in great detail the role of various rulers, of big and small States in Punjab and the use of various agencies of the governments in that act of cleansing.[336] The fact that it took almost seven decades for some scholar to work diligently to dig out incidents on both the sides of the border indicates to the conspiracy of silence that prevailed effectively and absolved all others of similar accusations for so long.

Sheikh Abdullah regularly and publicly used the jibe of abandoning Srinagar along with his family, jewels and courtiers against the Maharaja to rile him, and the allegations of him fomenting communal violence against the Muslims of Jammu to hurt him. But he studiously maintained a dignified silence though he not only felt hurt but also seethed in anger. Sheikh Abdullah had some complex about Jammu, probably aware that he was friendless there, and the only support that he had, came from a few left-leaning activists among the Hindus. Therefore, for quite some time, after being appointed Administrator of the Emergency Administration, he avoided coming to Jammu though he had wasted little time in occupying the Residency in Srinagar upon being appointed. It was after a great deal of persuasion from Prime Minister Mahajan that he finally arrived in Jammu along with a retinue of fifteen people. According to the Prime Minister, he had made his arrangement of his stay with a private citizen and Mahajan had to persuade him to move to a Government Guest House. During his stay he also called upon the Maharaja and discussed certain matters during which, 'he suggested that it would be a very good thing if India and Pakistan were made to recognize the State as an independent unit like Switzerland, both Dominions guaranteeing this independence. The Maharaja nodded assent.'[337] In fact, it was this ambition that motivated and drove Sheikh Abdullah. On the face of it, the Maharaja shared this ambition but for different reasons. He believed that because of the demography and geography of the State, peaceful existence between the competing ideas of India and Pakistan would be difficult for it, and, therefore, he was searching for a middle path. But for Sheikh Abdullah, though never articulated, a neutral existence would have been a means of maintaining the Muslim supremacy in the State. It was obvious that his secular credential had a limited purpose of gaining support from the New India that had rejected the 'Two Nation' theory and religion-based State. All through his career, decisions were taken on the basis of establishing this supremacy, and in the name of secularism and socialism many mainstream leaders of India became his most ardent supporters.

Among his early supporters after the accession was the Socialist leader Achut Patwardhan who came visiting the State. He also met Prime Minister Mahajan and suggested that he and Sheikh Abdullah should have a free and frank talk about the State and the situation. He also added that in the interest of Kashmir, Mahajan should give up his office and leave Sheikh Abdullah in complete charge of the State administration. Mahajan told him that he had come to the State at the invitation of the Maharaja and would not quit without his order but he, nevertheless, reached out to Sheikh Abdullah for a frank discussion. During the course of the meeting, Sheikh Abdullah tried to bully and browbeat Mahajan into submitting to his suggestion about leaving the State. Having failed in his mission, he again accused Mahajan of being a party to the deaths of some Muslim personnel of the State who were being evacuated by the Indian Army from Kotli. The fact was that they were rebels from the State Forces and were being escorted to Jammu after being disarmed but had become rowdy on the way and killed in the firing in an effort to control them. Mahajan claimed in his book that he had no knowledge of this incident till informed by Sheikh Abdullah. Commenting on the issue, Mahajan wrote, 'Though the Sheikh boasted that he was a nationalist, really he had a communal outlook on things. Any harm done to the Hindu population or their property did not affect him at all, but the slightest injury to a Muslim touched the very core of his heart.'[338] He also took up the matter to Nehru who had to be explained that the concerned army Commander had already ordered a court of enquiry. There were other examples too when he intervened on behalf of the Muslims to the determent of the State. The most prominent among such cases was that of Chaudhary Ghulam Abbas[339], who had been put under arrest for his pro-Pakistan activities. He had been the founder of the All Jammu and Kashmir Muslim Conference along with Sheikh Abdullah and was a rabid communalist. However, Abbas and Abdullah had later parted ways. Sheikh met him a number of times in jail and then insisted upon his release. At that time, considerable number of people from Mirpur had been kept in a camp by Pakistanis in the Pakistan-Occupied-Jammu area. After negotiations it had been agreed that transport be sent to fetch them and these buses would carry a certain number of Muslims released from the State prisons. Accordingly, the first group of people was repatriated from Mirpur but for the return-trip, neither the captives were released nor the bus returned. The said arrangement had been agreed to on the assurance of Sheikh Abdullah who had held a number of meetings with Chaudhary Ghulam Abbas and it was believed that Abbas will ensure that all captives were released. 'On this promise Abbas was set free, but as soon as he reached Sialkot, he made a thundering speech full of venom against India and the Sheikh.'[340] So much for the much touted claim that Sheikh Abdullah represented not only Kashmir Valley but the Jammu region too!

The Accession was not final at this stage since India had made it provisional and subject to the will of the people. But still all this while, and notwithstanding the war and the resultant problems that were being faced by the State, the Government of India was holding consultations with the Maharaja to draw a road map for the future constitutional setup in the State. It had been suggested by Nehru that the Mysore model be applied to the State wherein certain powers were retained by the Maharaja. These powers were to be exercised through his Dewan who would also sit during the Cabinet meetings. To be fair to the Government of India, it must be said that political and constitutional developments were happening at such a fast pace that the Government of India had realized that the Mysore Model had become inadequate. It was causing more problems than facilitating smooth functioning of the administration. In view of this, Prime Minister Nehru desired that the Maharaja should become a constitutional and ceremonial head. This was not appreciated by the Maharaja since he found the representative credentials of Sheikh Abdullah deficient. Impulsive and impatient, Nehru was a man in a hurry and was not prepared to countenance resistance. Gradually things were moving towards a showdown and the first sign of Nehru having run out of his patience came when one day while Mahajan was in Delhi and with him, Nehru called Sir Gopalaswamy Ayyangar and suggested that Mahajan should resign from his office in the State and let Sheikh Abdullah have a free run in the State. The stalemate, however, continued and even the intervention of Sardar Patel and the Maharajas of Patiala, Jamnagar and Jaipur could not convince the Maharaja to let Mahajan go.

After some time, 'Pandit Jawaharlal sent his personal representative Mr Brij Lal Nehru, to the State. Mr Brij Lal met the Sheikh in Srinagar…He came to Jammu and met me at the residence of Kanwar Sir Dilip Singh who was then India's Agent in the Jammu and Kashmir State. He started talking in a very presumptuous manner and suggested that His Highness should be advised to abdicate. I told him that he had no business to indulge in such talk. Being merely a personal representative of the Prime Minister, he had no business to make such a suggestion,'[341] recalled Mahajan in his memoir. This was another example of Sheikh Abdullah canvassing support from anyone who showed some interest in the affairs of the State or came there in any other capacity. He had set his eyes on removing Maharaja Hari Singh from his monarchical perch and force him out of the State to finally fulfil his goal of the Quit Kashmir movement against the Dogra rule.

As far as the Maharaja was concerned, he had placed all his trust in the hands of Sardar Patel and believed that Patel would recognize that all his political and socio-economic reforms ever since his coronation had been for the greater good of the people. He also expected Delhi to appreciate the fact that his land and other reforms had usually benefited the Muslim peasantry more than the Hindus and hence he could not be accused of being discriminatory. In fact, he was among the early Princes who had begun the process of devolution of powers to the representatives of the people and his reforms were acknowledged as being far ahead of his times.[342] He was also supportive of the concept of the Responsible Government but was not prepared to go beyond the Mysore model that had been implemented by the Government of India, for he believed that Sheikh Abdullah did not represent all the segments of the society. However, he also did not think that he and his colleagues were capable of either winning the confidence of the people or administering them. The Maharaja, therefore, wanted certain powers reserved for himself to be exercised through a Dewan chosen by him and who would be a member of the Cabinet. He would also have preferred the Dewan to be the President of the State.

In the meantime, the Pakistan-supported invasion of the State by the raiders had been referred to the Security Council. But Pakistan's effective advocacy of its defence had converted the whole issue into a dispute over who had a just claim over the State. Gopalaswami Ayyangar had led the first Indian delegation to the Security Council and Sheikh Abdullah too was a member of the delegation who also made a speech, which turned out to be directed more against the Maharaja than advocating India's case. The Pakistan side, led by Sir Mohammad Zafarullah, spoke more with passion than reason. They focused on the Muslim angle in State to hijack the debate. The Indian delegation had proved highly ineffective. Thus, the issue before the Security Council had become a dispute about the Accession and this had brought in the element of determining the will of the people of the State. Since this entailed holding a plebiscite, Sheikh Abdullah had found a very useful weapon to blackmail and intimidate the leaders in Delhi. Failure to win the plebiscite was not an option for Delhi for that would have meant that the Two Nation theory stood validated and that India was a Hindu nation. Therefore, Delhi decided that constitutional changes needed to be made at an urgent basis.

Throughout the month of February, hectic parleys took place in Delhi. Mehr Chand Mahajan too was called to Delhi for that purpose as another Security Council meeting was to be held in March or April 1948. Delhi was desperate to strengthen its case at that point and concluded that the best course was to appoint

Sheikh Abdullah as the Prime Minister of the State as a gesture of devolution of power to the people. Therefore, after exhaustive consultations between Ayyangar, Mahajan, Nehru and Patel, a draft of the Proclamation that was to be issued by the Maharaja to appoint Sheikh Abdullah as Prime Minister was drawn up. On 1st March 1948, Ayyangar wrote to the Maharaja:

> Messrs V.P. Menon and Mahajan are going to Jammu this afternoon to discuss and finalize with you the draft of the Proclamation which Your Highness has to issue for appointing Abdullah as Prime Minister and others on his advice. The draft has been very carefully considered by myself, Panditji and Sardarji, and we are of the opinion that the whole of it should be accepted by you. Anything less would not satisfy the requirements of the present situation.
>
> As a friend of yours, I consider it most important that Your Highness must make a very big gesture in order to rally the maximum percentage of the population of the State behind you with the help of Abdullah. Things are moving very fast and we have yet to fight a great battle at Lake Success.[343] I have already stated during the discussions at Lake Success that Your Highness had only been waiting for Sheikh Abdullah to return from America to convert the Emergency Administration into an Interim Council of Ministers with Abdullah as Prime Minister. I am leaving Delhi for Lake Success the day after tomorrow, and it would be a great strength to the cause that I have to plead there on behalf of Kashmir if this Proclamation is issued before I leave... It is further very important that everything that has happened in the past should be forgotten and forgiven and that Your Highness should take Sheikh Abdullah into your fullest confidence. In fact, I was almost going to suggest that you should give up your usual reserve, come out in the open and put yourself at the head of your people, both Muslims and non-Muslims, for the purpose of consolidating and strengthening the large volume of support for preserving the integrity of the State and maintaining its accession to India, which thanks to Sheikh Abdullah and Indian Army, you have already behind you.[344]

The truth was that the Proclamation had been presented to the Maharaja as a *fait accompli* and his role was no more than that of a signatory. The wise men of Delhi, no doubt under the influence of Sheikh Abdullah, and jittery by the fact that the Congress had lost a referendum in the NWF Province even though Khan Abdul Ghaffar Khan and his brother had convincingly trounced Jinnah's Muslim League not too long ago because of the ability of Muslim League to rouse communal passions. Apparently, they were not sure that in case a plebiscite was held, the Kashmiris would vote in favour of India. The events of the past two years in the subcontinent had shaken their confidence and, therefore, they were banking upon strategy rather than ground reports. Even the person upon whom they were reposing so much faith and trust needed the crutches of office to prove to the Kashmiris that their future was secure in India. Alastair Lamb, a historian whose discourse on the subject borders on hostility towards India, is of the opinion that during those early months when the plebiscite was being hotly debated, if India had agreed to hold it under the conditions that were acceptable to Pakistan, it 'might possibly have won' as 'in the early stages of Kashmir problem when the memory of the horrors of the tribal invasion of October 1947 was still fresh in the minds of the local population' the chances of communalism triumphing over security and honour, would have been small.[345]

Even more importantly, Delhi had turned a blind eye and deaf ears to the activities and speeches of Sheikh Abdullah and had, therefore, made a serious error in judgment about his reliability. Delhi should have suspected that even if Sheikh Abdullah had become instrumental in winning the plebiscite that would not have necessarily meant a vote for union with the State. He had made that abundantly clear as early as October 1947, before he took up the office of Administrator of Emergency Administration, when he declared:

> Our first demand is complete transfer of power to the people of Kashmir. Representatives of the people in a democratic Kashmir will then decide whether the State should join India or Pakistan. If forty laks [4,000,000] of people living in Jammu and Kashmir are bypassed and the State declares its accession to India or Pakistan, I shall raise the banner of revolt and we face a struggle. Of course, we will naturally opt to go to that Dominion where

> our own demand for freedom receives recognition and support. We cannot desire to join those who say that people must have no voice in the matter.[346]

Delhi had made a mess of the whole situation by their muddled thinking, poor presentation of their case at Lake Success and the initial error of conditional acceptance of accession. At home, it had handed unwarranted advantage to Sheikh Abdullah for pursuing his goal enunciated during his speech of October 1947. Abroad, it had allowed others to dictate in a subject that should have remained an affair between the Ruler and the Government of India. Prisoner in its own web, Delhi wanted the Maharaja to bail it out of the difficulties. Therefore, Nehru and Patel had approved the draft of Proclamation and presented to Maharaja Hari Singh for issuing it. He issued it on 5th March 1948 and it read:

> ...It is now my desire to replace the Emergency Administration by a Popular Interim Government and to provide for its powers, duties and functions, pending the formation of a fully democratic Constitution.
>
> I accordingly HEREBY ORDAIN AS FOLLOWS;
> 1. My Council of Ministers shall consist of the Prime Minister and such other Ministers as may be appointed on the advice of the Prime Minister. I have by Royal Warrant appointed Sheikh Mohammad Abdullah as the Prime Minister with effect from today.
> 2. The Prime Minister and other Ministers shall function as a Cabinet and act on the principle of joint responsibility. A Dewan appointed by me shall also be a member of the Cabinet...
> 4. My Council of Ministers shall take appropriate steps, as soon as restoration of normal conditions has been completed, to convene a National Assembly based upon adult suffrage, having due regard to the principle that the number of representatives from each voting area should, as far as practicable, be proportionate to the population of that area.
> 5. The Constitution to be framed by the National Assembly shall provide adequate safeguards for the minorities and contain appropriate provisions guaranteeing for the freedom of conscience, freedom of speech and freedom of assembly.

> 6. The National Assembly shall, as soon as the work of framing the new constitution is completed, submit it through the Council of Ministers for my acceptance.
>
> 7. In conclusion I repeat the hope that the formation of a popular Interim Government and the inauguration, in the near future, of a fully Democratic Constitution will ensure the contentment, happiness and the moral and material advancement of my beloved people.

The Maharaja had done all that he had been asked by Delhi but neither he, nor any alert observers could have missed the tone and tenor of Ayyangar's letter of 1st March 1948 wherein he had claimed that support for 'consolidating and strengthening' of unity of the State was largely due to the efforts of Sheikh Abdullah and the Indian Army, as if the siege of Skardu did not exist and the areas of Mirpur and Poonch had been retaken from Pakistan, and that the State Forces and the Dogras had made no contribution. But setting his own opinions and emotions aside, the Maharaja had done what Delhi said was for the good of the people of the State and integrity of the country. Sheikh Abdullah, by then, had already begun to arbitrarily exercise powers and did not display the courtesy of acknowledging his appointment as Prime Minister as early as possible since Ayyangar had told the Maharaja that in view of the impending discussion in the Security Council, such an appointment was urgently needed. Abdullah's letter of acknowledgement was written only on 24th March 1948, wherein he wrote:

> The situation in Jammu and Kashmir is, as you are well aware, a difficult one and requires the most careful handling. The emergency continues and has to be dealt with as such till normal conditions are restored. The burden of Prime Minister in these circumstances will be a heavy one. He cannot function effectively without the fullest cooperation of his colleagues and the people as well as, of course, Your Highness. I have consulted some of my colleagues, who were available and have come to the conclusion that it is my duty in these circumstances to undertake this burden. I trust that in heavy work ahead I shall have Your Highness' full help and cooperation. I appreciate the spirit in which you have made the offer of the Prime Minister to me and on my part I assure Your Highness that I shall fully appreciate it.[347]

While signing the Proclamation, the Maharaja had insisted upon one change, to remain the Commander-in-chief of the State Forces, and Sardar Patel had agreed to this. He had insisted because he was certain that if he relinquished that command and handed it over to Sheikh Abdullah he will lose no time in being vindictive towards the Forces that largely consisted of Dogras. Simultaneously, Mahajan had approached Sardar Patel to seek his help in convincing the Maharaja to relieve him from the service of the State, which the Maharaja did with a heavy heart. In any case since the new setup had vested almost all powers in the Prime Minister and there was a provision for appointment of a Dewan, Mahajan had occupied that post with reluctance. One of his abiding regret was that he was unable to convince Nehru in treating Maharaja Hari Singh with the consideration that was due to him. The Government of India had offered a better deal to the Nizam of Hyderabad who had publicly declared his intention to remain independent and had given loan to Pakistan at a time when it was at war with India. He also thought that if Nehru and Patel had stuck to the Mysore model for the State and allowed the Maharaja to have a Dewan, the course of events in the State would have been different, since then monarchy would have gradually faded as in other bigger States, and the State of Jammu and Kashmir too would have been merged with the Indian union as the others States had been merged. With Mahajan functioning as an effective Dewan and the reserved powers retained by the Maharaja in those early days, Sheikh Abdullah would not have become the autocratic ruler that he became soon after the departure from the State of, first Mahajan and then the Maharaja.[348] Mahajan has also summed up Sheikh Abdullah the public figure, as 'an ambitious person prepared to go to any length to achieve his ends…To me he looked like a demagogue who could control Kashmiri crowds.'[349]

18

Despair of a Maharaja

It is a matter of conjecture what course the history of the State, the country and, indeed, the subcontinent, might have taken if Sheikh Abdullah had been true to the averments before Maharaja Hari Singh and the promise that he aroused among his friends in Delhi, Nehru in particular. A very congenial environment had been built in which there was scope for him to work within the limits of the Proclamation that appointed him as the Prime Minister of the State. By all accounts, the Maharaja had been content playing the role of a constitutional head and he and Nehru had made genuine efforts during that early period to exchange views, mend fences and work in cooperation. Dr Karan Singh has noted in his autobiography, 'Evidently Jawaharlal did make an attempt to strike some sort of equation with my father, as there are a number of long letters during the period 1947-8 in which he tried to make certain points about the prevalent political situation. But the tension between my father and the Sheikh came in the way of any real understanding developing.'[350]

There is no denying the fact that the Maharaja and Sheikh Abdullah belonged to two worlds that were poles apart. One belonging to an order that had already entered its sunset years, and the other, brash and looking forward to hastening the demise of the old order. In addition, Sheikh Abdullah, a product of the newly awakened Muslim community, was also influenced by the Muslim 'nationalism' that was bred in the Aligarh University of his era. He also nursed, genuine and imagined, grievances against the monarchical order. But one cannot help but wonder how much he was driven by the fact that after centuries of Muslim rule, the State had come to be ruled by a Hindu dynasty. The fact was that Sheikh Abdullah represented the Kashmiris, who were numerically in a majority and Maharaja Hari Singh represented the smaller number of Dogras who were extremely proud of being the architects of the State of Jammu and Kashmir and, for the first time in history after Chandragupta Maurya, to have expanded the boundaries of India. In reality, both represented the demographic, religious, cultural and geographical fault lines that underlined the challenges of the State. For a century, the Dogra dynasty had maintained a balance between the two regions by not allowing any interference in the religious and local affairs of the Kashmiris, and maintaining the supremacy of the Dogras in the armed forces.

But whatever the grievances of Sheikh Abdullah might have been, when he was appointed the Prime Minister he was faced with the serious challenge of existence and had the burden of guiding the State towards a Constituent Assembly that would frame the constitution for a democratic society. In March, when he became Prime Minister, the situation was that the garrison of Skardu was still holding out in the hope that help will reach it from Srinagar and India. Poonch too was under siege, Muzaffarabad had been lost, Mirpur and Kotli was lost, and Ladakh threatened but not in immediate danger. The meagre State Forces had done their best in delaying catastrophe and were still in the forefront at many places. The Proclamation had made it clear that the new constitutional government had been established under the Jammu and Kashmir Constitution Act of 1996, that is, Vikram Samvat, equivalent to 1939 A.D. and in accordance with that constitutional provision there were reserved subjects that would not fall within the purview of the Prime Minister and the Cabinet. It had also been stated, and agreed to by all concerned that a 'Dewan appointed by me [the Maharaja] shall also be a member of the Cabinet', and that the reserved subjects would be dealt by the Maharaja through his Dewan. It must also be added that till the time a new Constituent Assembly was convoked and a new Constitution framed and passed, the Constituent Act of 1939 was supreme since Section 5 of that Act declared:

> Notwithstanding anything contained in this or any other Act, powers, legislative, executive and judicial, in relation to the State and its Government are hereby declared to be and to have always been inherent in and possessed and retained by His Highness…[351]

However, Sheikh Abdullah displayed neither, patience, as his friend Nehru had displayed during the framing of the Constitution of India, nor reticence that is a virtue among the statesmen. There were early warnings, which Nehru chose to ignore, that here was a demagogue who could not be relied upon. Abdullah fired the first shot by demanding that the Maharaja hand him over the administrative control of the State Forces. This was one subject that the Maharaja guarded zealously and perhaps that motivated him to demand control. The Forces symbolized all that the Dogras had achieved during the preceding 125 years as they had not only contributed in all the campaigns of Maharaja Ranjit Singh but had also undertaken independent campaigns to carve out a State in a strategically important region. Not surprisingly, Sheikh Abdullah's suggestion was sternly objected to by the Maharaja but he was not deterred and suggested that even if the Maharaja was to remain the Commander-in-chief of the Forces, their operational and administrative control be transferred to the Indian Army; though the operational control had been already handed over to the Indian Army the day it had landed in the State. But Maharaja Hari Singh was reluctant to handover the administrative control because he did not wish to merge the distinct identity of a Force that had captured the Imperial Chinese flag in the battle of Mantalai in 1841. It was then that a frustrated Sheikh Abdullah launched a barrage of malicious propaganda against the State Forces in general and the Maharaja in particular, and also accused them of having their 'hands dyed in blood' of the Muslims.

In reply to a memorandum written on the subject by Sheikh Abdullah, the Maharaja made two significant points:

> I have given careful thought to the suggestion made in the above memo. It appears that there are certain aspects of the question which have not probably struck you. I am, therefore, asking you to reconsider your opinion after giving your earnest consideration to the following:

> (1) Firstly in case the administrative control is transferred to the Union Government as suggested by you the Pakistan propagandists will make political capital out of it and make a plausible case that the State has been completely annexed to Indian Union by taking over complete Military control. Such an impression should not be permitted to be created.
> (2) Secondly, the Pakistan suggestion that at the time of Plebiscite the Forces of Indian Union should be sent away may to some extent be forced upon us. In case the administrative control of the State Forces is handed over it will be difficult for us to make out a case for the retention of the State Forces because administratively there will be no distinction between the two.[352]

The logic did not register with Sheikh Abdullah and he made an unfair and frontal attack on the State Forces, accusing them not only of killing civilian Muslims but of all sorts of crimes and misdemeanors in a letter to Prime Minister Nehru. He also insisted upon the complete takeover of the State Forces by the Indian Army so that its identity ceased to exist. It was ignored that the time period of the said 'massacres' took place, no unit of the State Forces was anywhere near the region where those 'massacres' were supposed to have taken place. All such units were engaged on the front. It was also obvious that he was oblivious to the threat that the State was facing a war that was still going on and a large part of the State had been occupied by the enemy. It needs to be pointed out that at that moment, the Valley had been liberated of the raiders and only that part was under Pakistan occupation, which had greater affinity to Punjab than Kashmir. Perhaps, this suited Sheikh Abdullah who did not have the same degree of control over those regions. Failing in his efforts to make India take complete control of the State Forces, in a mean act, he informed the Maharaja that as of 16th August 1948, the State administration would not pay the salaries and allowances of the State Forces.[353] For the record, it was on 14th August 1948 that the gallant garrison of Skardu surrendered to Pakistan, but there was no word of lamentation and sorrow over the loss or a word about the gallantry of the State Forces or even of the fact that a disproportionate number of its soldiers had been killed performing the duty of soldiers.

The Proclamation had left nothing for the imagination regarding the areas of responsibility of the constitutional head and that of the Prime Minister, but Sheikh Abdullah had embarked upon a mission to render the Maharaja humiliated and the Dogras marginalized. The propaganda against Maharaja Hari Singh was at the core of his strategy. All this while, Nehru as well as Patel, had made no effort to stop Sheikh Abdullah from maligning him, not even when in his letter of 31st January 1948 to Sardar Patel, the Maharaja had appeared to be in a state of despair and was toying with the option of withdrawing the Accession letter. In response to that letter, apart from other subjects, Sardar Patel dealt with his state of mind, with one of the paragraph saying, 'I fully realize what an anxious time you must be having. I can assure you that I am no less anxious about the Kashmir situation and what is happening in the U.N.O., but whatever the present situation may be, a counsel of despair is entirely out of place.'[354] But soon thereafter, the Maharaja had been visited by V.P. Menon and Mahajan with a letter from Ayyangar, along with the draft of the Proclamation for his signature. The letter showed desperation by India over how things had been going in the Security Council and the wise heads in Delhi thought that only dependence on Abdullah could take them out of the hole they had dug for themselves and the country. Sheikh Abdullah too had realized this weakness of Delhi and hence he became bolder in his efforts. On 5th March 1948, the Proclamation appointing him as the Prime Minister of the State, had been issued and by 20th April the relationship between him and the Maharaja had worsened to such a degree that the Maharaja had to write a letter to Sardar Patel. He had no other option because he could not bring himself to such a level where he had to publicly contradict his own Prime Minister or indulge in a slanging match with him. So he wrote:

> As I have mentioned to you and to Mr. Menon and Mr. Shankar also once or twice, there is one aspect of propaganda against me which has distressed me beyond words, particularly as it affects not only my position as a Ruler but my personal honor. I refer to the wild and baseless allegations that are being made against me that I left the Capital at the dead of night and removed truckloads of furniture and other belongings. I would

have ordinarily dismissed these allegations but to my great regret and profound shock, they have found expression in some of the utterances of my present Prime Minister. I would invite your attention to the speech which Sh. Abdullah made before the Security Council in which he said the following words:

"The Maharaja in the dead of night left the Capital along with his courtiers and the result was absolute panic. There was no one to take over the control. This is the manner in which the administration changed hands and we were de facto in charge of the administration. The Maharaja later on gave it a legal form."

How entirely divorced from facts this allegation is would, I am sure, be borne out by your Secretary Mr. Menon at whose instance I reluctantly left Srinagar for Jammu. The other allegation that truckloads of belongings were removed is absolutely false and fantastic. The fact is that some lorries carrying the families of those officers who had already moved to Jammu on Government work and families of my servants followed me. I felt morally responsible to afford transport facilities to these families. All my household effects which usually remain permanently in Srinagar have been and are still there...

You might ask why I am resuscitating this matter after so much lapse of time since the speech was made, but apart from the fact that those allegations are still being persisted in and are being given credence under continuous propaganda, the speech of my Prime Minister is being distributed in a pamphlet form headed "Kashmir: Appeal to World Conscience". I hope your Ministry will succeed in giving a lie to this propaganda by means of an authoritative pronouncement or communiqué explaining the correct facts and by persuading Sh. Abdulla [*sic*] to make amends for the lapse which he has made.

While I am on this subject I should also like to refer to one important aspect of the propaganda which is being carried on against me on the lines that I was a despotic and autocratic ruler, that the popular movement was directed against Dogra tyranny and that the present position has been reached as a result of fight put up by the people against me and my regime...by presenting me as an unmitigated autocrat it is perhaps not realized that they merely help Pakistan propaganda. I should have thought that they would themselves realize the expediency of countering this

> propaganda of Pakistan rather than keep fresh old animosities, for, as some knowledgeable persons have told me, the justification of Poonch and Mirpur revolt can be sought in the pages of some of the publicity material issued by the Ministry...I hope that instructions from you to Sh. Abdulla [*sic*] on this point would go at least some way in repairing the damage done.[355]

It is not known what efforts were made by Sardar Patel to convince Sheikh Abdullah to refrain, if not retract, from indulging in such propaganda, or, even convince Nehru to exercise his influence over his friend to stop it, but the fact was that Sheikh Abdullah was beyond the control of Delhi. He knew that Delhi had put itself in a corner at the international level and had to depend upon his goodwill. He used Nehru during his struggle against the Dogra rule; he had also used him effectively in wresting power from the Maharaja and planting himself as the sole centre of power in the State. After that, it was only a hypothetical conjecture as to what might have happened if the Maharaja too had been as power hungry as Abdullah, and what would have been the consequences if he had chosen his powers of a monarch and decided to dismiss Abdullah from office. After all, the only constitution applicable in the State was the Jammu and Kashmir Constitutional Act, 1939, wherein the ruler was the repository of all powers whether executive, legislative or judicial. He made all the appointments in all the three organs and had the authority to dismiss or remove any member of any State organ.[356] Even Adarsh Sein Anand has conceded that the ruler of Jammu and Kashmir might have lagged behind the princely states of Cochin and Mysore in devolving power to the people, yet he was far ahead of others in democratic reforms.[357] By not adopting the same confrontational attitude that Sheikh Abdullah had, by exercising his constitutional powers, he proved that he was capable of putting aside a personal pique and work for the welfare of his people and the interests of his country. Not enough credit has been given to Maharaja Hari Singh for maintaining public silence over the issue. His sense of dignity and duty towards his country too remained unappreciated even by Sardar Patel. In the environment that he had built rather than being restrained, the malicious and vituperative propaganda continued unabated and the Maharaja was constrained to write a memorandum on 3rd December 1948 to his Prime Minister:

> PRIME MINISTER
>
> I would like to draw your attention to the malicious propaganda which is being carried on against my person inside the State and outside. I presume this has come to the notice of the Prime Minister and the Ministry but I find that no steps have been taken either to counteract or ban such activities. I am sending herewith some copies of extracts of the speeches of some of the Ministers and National Conference Leaders which also offend in the same manner.
>
> I am sure you will agree that it is most improper both on the constitutional and moral grounds for Ministers to indulge in this kind of propaganda. I put it to you that it should be as much a concern of my Government as of myself to ensure that the person of Constitutional Head of the State, his dignity and position are fully respected and that any tendency to the contrary, from whatever quarter, is dealt with promptly and severely. I hope you will take suitable action immediately to counter these tendencies and this propaganda...[358]

Needless to say that Sheikh Abdullah did not reply nor was any action taken because he was the leader of the pack. But it is difficult to understand why the Government of India gave so much of latitude to him though there were certain objections of the Maharaja that had nothing to do with his honour or dignity. He raised the issue that the propaganda against him regarding Poonch and Mirpur was a cannon fodder for Pakistan in justifying its intervention in the State and yet, Delhi did not find merit in the argument. The consequence of this unabated propaganda was that Sheikh Abdullah became bolder as time passed. Partisans have focused on Prime Minister and accused him of being solely responsible for the mess that was ultimately made of the State. But there is no evidence to suggest that any other leaders in the Government, including, Sardar Patel opposed this treatment of the Maharaja. It was their collective silence and meek acquiescence that made Sheikh Abdullah what he became. Encouraged, and considering this as approval of his confrontational and revolutionary attitude towards the Maharaja, he ignored his existence because 'where they felt necessary they got the consent of the Government of India to do what they [Sheikh Abdullah and leaders of the National Conference] liked in the State disregarding the Maharaja and his wishes. This gradually led to deterioration and to the outside world, State and Sheikh Abdullah became convertible terms. The people of Kashmir were utterly ignored and everything that Sheikh Abdullah desired to do was done in the name of the State with the express or tacit consent of the Government of India.'[359] Even if this grievance is attributed to differences in perceptions there were other examples where not only the egos clashed but also unacceptable and provocative interference in religious and personal subjects of the Maharaja happened.

In his letter to the Maharaja dated 1st March 1948, Ayyangar had written, among other things, that the Maharaja give up his reserve and reticence and go out among the people so as to rally them around the concept of union with India. Accordingly, he began to go out among the people even though he was never comfortable among the refugees living in desperate conditions. Their defeated faces, dusty and tear marked, showed all the signs of the traumatic experiences that had made them destitute in mind and spirit. He was uncomfortable among them because he could not give them back their homes, lands and lost ones, not to speak of the honour that they had lost to lusty men and marauding armed gangs. Worst of all, they were baffled as to why their king was unable to help them and what future awaited them under the new Government. They were also baffled by the fact that all of a sudden they were to be ruled by Kashmiris whom they had always considered inferior. He had no answers to these questions and was therefore embarrassed by them.

On the other hand, it appeared that his wife, Maharani Tara Devi had discovered the calling of her life in the relief work that she undertook in the relief camps. She got deeply involved with it and did not hesitate to donate the clothes of the young Yuvraj and collect many more from those who could make such a donation. With thousands of refugees pouring in, she displayed organizing capacity that none had ever credited her with. Her days would be spent moving from one camp to another, distributing rations and clothes. Often she would be so late in reaching the palace that the Sandhya (evening worship) had to be skipped. These camps were overflowing as a number of Jammu towns like Mirpur, Bhimber, Rajouri and border settlements had fallen one by one. Among those to have fallen were also the twin villages of Deva and Batala, the home of the Bhau and Chib Rajput clans. These proud and warrior people had been rendered homeless and destitute and the carnage they had fled had left orphans and aged widows, who now needed all the care with the approach of the winter. This news had shaken the Maharaja because the twin villages had done enormous service to the State and formed an important ingredient of its army. The compassion and generosity of the Maharani was now being manifested in her work, which also included financing the marriages of those girls who had attained the marriageable age. She, indeed, brought comfort to the lives shattered by the cataclysmic events. Simultaneously, she organized women volunteer forces under the banner of Maharani Seva Dal. It was given paramilitary training to meet any eventuality since the enemy was knocking at the gates of Jammu repeatedly.[360]

The Maharaja, however, found the trips embarrassing as the vexed people in the countryside thronged, wondering why they should be ruled by the Kashmiris. The crowds would be huge and they did not hesitate to express their resentment at the change that was taking place. The news of the reception that the Maharaja was given by the people, and the fact that he enjoyed enormous popularity and loyalty even in those difficult times, must have reached Sheikh Abdullah and he was perturbed because on his visits to Delhi, he apparently poisoned the ears of Nehru even more than they already were. He had come to recognize that Nehru was very sensitive to the wellbeing and safety of the Muslims, particularly in the wake of the country-wide violence that had taken place in the wake of partition. It was he who repeatedly carried the tales of violence against Muslims in the State and pinning the blame on the Maharaja, the Maharani, the State Forces and the RSS. The Maharaja's Prime Minister had in a detailed letter to Mahatma Gandhi even rebutted the allegations and had also clarified that the one incident of firing by the Forces while being escorted to the border of Pakistan, had indeed, happened but the Force belonged to the Indian Army. But the tool of propaganda had been used by Sheikh Abdullah so effectively that it would have made Goebbels envy him. In the end, Delhi, still wallowing in the guilt of its inability to contain violence in areas under its command, was a willing listener to his accusations and complaints against the Maharaja, and finally told the Maharaja to stop his public relations exercise.

As 1948 came to end, India agreed to a Security Council brokered cease fire with Pakistan though at that time of the total area of the State—2,22,236 square kilometres—only 1,53, 224 kilometres had remain with the State, the rest being under Pakistan occupation. Most of this area had been occupied after the Indian Army had landed in the State and taken over the operational charge of all forces. It certainly appeared that the political class was not really too deeply concerned about the fate of the State as it existed before the crisis engulfed it and was content to having the Valley of Kashmir where Sheikh Abdullah had following and which was the home of the ancestors of Pandit Jawaharlal Nehru.

If militarily India had not succeeded in evicting the enemy from the State, politically it had done even worse. It needs to be underlined that the Proclamation of 5th March 1948, appointing Sheikh Abdullah as the Prime Minister of the State under the powers vested in the ruler by the Constitution of 1939, and was based on the Mysore model that entitled the Maharaja to a Dewan of his choice, who would also sit in the Cabinet meetings. Soon after the appointment, Sheikh Abdullah in connivance with Delhi began to bring arbitrary changes in the Constitution of the State. The modus operandi of both was simple, the Maharaja pointed out in his Memorandum: 'The mischief began with Sheikh Abdullah going direct to the Government of India on certain points over my head and the Government of India countenancing him and giving the desired directions and then informing me of what they had done at the instance of Sheikh Abdullah. The correspondence on the subject and the events following on each change bear testimony to what Sheikh Abdullah was trying to achieve in breach of the solemn promises and assurances given by him and also by the Government of India on his behalf.'[361] In view of these facts, not all the blame can be laid at the door of Sheikh Abdullah for whatever was happening but it was because of the active consent and connivance of the Government of India. It is difficult to imagine what good it was doing to the State or the cause of the country in the Security Council. In the end, Pakistan had succeeded in converting the issue of its invasion of the State into a dispute regarding the accession of the State to India. It had also demonstrated the timidity of Indian leaders and the lack of confidence regarding its own moral stand over Kashmir.

Sheikh Abdullah did not stop in illegally usurping the powers that the State Constitution did not give him. Growing in confidence at having the Government of India toeing his arbitrary decisions, he then encroached upon the subjects reserved for the Maharaja. It has been noticed how he had made a pitch for the control of the armed forces of the State, and failing, he had retaliated with venomous fury and stopped their salaries and allowances. This also happened to be the time when Yuvraj Karan Singh had left for the States for the treatment of his hip joint. The Maharaja remained in constant touch with him through letters, and though young, he was updated regularly about the developments in the State, the progress of the war and the general affairs of life. In one of his letters it was very clear that he was deeply agitated by the attempts of Sheikh Abdullah to wrest control over State Forces. He informed the Yuvraj of the failure of his efforts.

Another department, which was close to the heart of the Maharaja was the *Tawaza* (hospitality) department. From the budget of this department pension was paid to the various members of the Royal family. Sheikh Abdullah wanted complete control over this department too because it did not fit in the much-touted Naya Kashmir vision. His focus on such subjects and the priority that he was giving to all those subjects that affected the Dogras was obviously because he had already embarked upon the policy of victimization. If there was any doubt regarding this, he had dispelled that too by pressing for radical land reforms.

He also made a sinister move for taking control over the Dharmarth Trust that had been established by the founder of the

Dogra ruler, Maharaja Gulab Singh, and which received liberal contributions from the succeeding rulers. It was a family Trust and had nothing to do with the State and no ruler donated from the State treasury. Its income was used for the administration, upkeep and the performance of ceremonies of all the hundreds of Hindu temples and shrines in the State. During that critical period when refugees swarmed Jammu, not only from within the State but also West Punjab, several lakhs of rupees were spent by the Trust for feeding them. Probably, the communalist in Sheikh Abdullah did not appreciate that and he and his henchmen launched a despicable attack on the Maharaja by propagating that the Trust money had been used for fanning Hindu communalism and political purpose to help establish a new Jammu based political party, *Praja Parishad.* The Trust account was operated either by the Maharaja or the President of the Trust, who was responsible for its day to day work. In an extremely mean act, Sheikh Abdullah tried to take control of the private family Trust, but failing that he prevented the income of Trust from coming into the Maharaja or the President's hands. This obstructed the Puja ceremonies of the *Devasthans* as they were starved of the flow of funds for daily expenses. Later, the Maharaja wrote in his Memorandum to the President of India, that the 'Jammu branch of the Imperial Bank of India[362] refused to pay even to me the amounts of the fixed deposits of the Trust and also refused to transfer such deposits to the Bombay Office of the Imperial Bank of India with the result that I had to renew the deposits to avoid loss of interest to the Trust.'[363] The moot point was that under whose orders did the Jammu Branch of the said Bank stop the transactions by the authorized signatories and under which law? It could possibly not have been done without the intervention of a more powerful entity than the account holder, but it raised many questions regarding the impartiality and secularism of the Abdullah Government.

The situation at that point in time was that with the Muslim League leaders having crossed over to Pakistan, he had become the undisputed leader of the Kashmir valley and the Muslims of Jammu region had no one left but him to follow. Thus, by default, Sheikh Abdullah had found a little constituency in the region that did not recognize him as a leader. A fair number of Kashmiri Pandits had already aligned themselves with him and the rest also recognized that they would be better off if they too became his supporters. But to his chagrin, he found Jammu obstinate in its opposition to him. The people of Jammu could never forgive, Jawaharlal Nehru and Sheikh Abdullah for the humiliation that the duo heaped upon them and their symbol of history and legacy. How intense that feeling has been can be judged by the fact that this resentment and animus has become an abiding characteristic of their worldview. Often this resentment has been attributed to the loss of privileges, which of course is one aspect, but if Delhi had been less intransigent and more pragmatic on the issue of accession then Jammu would have been spared the misery that befell it. The issue of transfer of power to the people would have been in any case dealt with at an appropriate time, just as it had been done in the other princely states. The Maharaja was acutely aware of this and had already begun to prepare his son, the Yuvraj for the changes that were ahead of the princes. As noted earlier, he was in regular correspondence with his son and would keep him informed of all the developments in the State and the country. During the absence of Yuvraj, the Constituent Assembly of India had been busy in framing the various Articles of the new Constitution of India. In one of his letters, the Maharaja prophetically wrote, 'I have no idea of how the new Constitution for India is going to affect us beyond the fact that before very long the Rulers will disappear even in name.'[364]

There is little doubt about his being an *absolute monarch* by virtue of his birth and training, but he had also received modern education and believed in pragmatism. His whole life had been oriented towards the welfare of his people and the creation of a modern State. He had been instrumental in spreading education in the State and had particularly given incentives to the Muslims for modern education. His record as a ruler is embellished by radical land, economic and constitutional reforms and it is futile to judge them by the present day standards because then even the British India as well as the India that framed a modern and progressive constitution would fall short since those sitting in the Constituent Assembly were elected by a limited franchise. It is true that sometimes he ushered in reforms because of the pressing demands of the people or the urgings of the British but he did respond to both, need for change, demands and pressure. This compares favourably with some of the other princely states that constituted a Legislative Assembly only when they had been forced to do so on the eve of the British departure. But, unfortunately, the State's affairs after the British exit had been dictated by personal egos, biases and prejudices. The stubborn refusal of Delhi to accept accession without transfer of power to Sheikh Abdullah has been the mother of all problems for the State, with its immediate consequence being suffered by the Jammu region where it resulted in the annihilation of hundreds of villages. It also led to events that gave Sheikh Abdullah a larger than life image even while he remained a small, short-sighted and vindictive man. Nehru's role during that important phase of history is borne out by his speech that was broadcast by the All India Radio on 2nd November 1947 when he gave a brief account of the events that had taken place:

> ...About this time we were asked by the Kashmir State to provide them with arms. We took no urgent steps about it and although sanction was given by our States and Defence Ministries, actually no arms were sent.
>
> It was on the night of the 24th that for the first time a request was made to us on behalf of the Kashmir State for accession and military help. On the morning of the 25th we considered this in the Defence Committee but no decision was taken about sending troops in view of the obvious difficulties of the undertaking. On the morning of the 26th we again considered this matter. The situation was even more critical then. The raiders had sacked several towns and had destroyed the great power house at Mahoba which supplies electricity to the whole of Kashmir. They were on the point of entering the Valley. The fate of Srinagar and the whole of Kashmir hung in the balance.
>
> We received urgent messages for aid not only from the Maharaja's Government but from representatives of the people, notably that great leader of Kashmir, Sheikh Mohammed Abdullah, [*sic*] the President of the National Conference. Both the Kashmir Government and the National Conference pressed us to accept the accession of Kashmir to the Indian Union. We decided

> to accept this accession and to send troops by air, but we made a condition that the accession would have to be considered by the people of Kashmir later when peace and order were established. We were anxious not to finalize anything in a moment of crisis and without the fullest opportunity being given to the people of Kashmir to have their say. It was for them ultimately to decide.
>
> And here let me make clear that it has been our policy all along that where there is a dispute about the accession of a State to either Dominion, the decision must be made by the people of that State. It was in accordance with this policy that we added a proviso to the Instrument of Accession of Kashmir…
>
> Srinagar was in peril and the invader was almost on its doorstep. There was no administration left there, no troops, no police. Light and power had failed and there were a vast number of refugees there and yet Srinagar functioned without obvious panic and the shops were opened and people went about the streets. To what was this miracle due? Sheikh Abdullah and his colleagues of the National Conference and their unarmed volunteers, Muslim and Hindu and Sikh, took charge of the situation, kept order and prevented panic. It was a wonderful piece of work that they did at a moment when the nerves of most people might have failed them. They did so because of the strength of their organization, but even more so, because they were determined to protect their country from the ruthless invader who was destroying their country and trying to compel them by terrorism to join Pakistan. Whatever the future may hold, the people of the Valley of Kashmir have exhibited during these past few days remarkable courage, capacity for organization and unity.
>
> It would be well if this lesson were understood by the whole of India which has been poisoned by communal strife. Under the inspiration of a great leader, Sheikh Abdullah, the people of the Valley, Muslim and Hindu and Sikh, were brought together for the defence of their common country against the invader. Our troops could have done little without this popular support and co-operation.[365]

Prime Minister Nehru had admitted that arms and ammunition was deliberately withheld by the Government of India and the situation was allowed to deteriorate into a human tragedy. But he stuck to his role in leading the State into a quagmire. He emphasized the role of the Government of India in giving a false narrative about the role and importance of the National Conference. If it is to be believed then one must question what role it played in Baramulla and why the massacre and rapes happened there and in Muzaffarabad. In view of all this, the people of Jammu saw no reason to admire either Nehru or Abdullah. But both in turn saw no reason for the Maharaja to continue to pretend that he was still the Maharaja not only in name but deed also. He, in fact, had nothing in his hands after he had signed that proclamation on 5th March 1948. Sheikh Abdullah, on the other hand, had all the aces, with Nehru as the trump card. But soon enough, Nehru had landed himself in a bind after having referred the Kashmir invasion to the Security Council and the self-created trap of plebiscite. Thus a situation had been created where Delhi willy-nilly did what the State's Prime Minister asked. It was an opportune time for Abdullah to strike. Nehru had easily come to terms with Princes who were downright autocratic, who obstructed integration of their princely states, and who—at least in one case—even lent money to Pakistan to tide over its financial difficulties (at a time when the war was still going on and that money could have been used for the war effort against India)! Yet, the same Nehru could not strike a cordial relationship with Maharaja Hari Singh—which he should have done, if for no other reason, for the fact that this Prince was the ruler of the most important Princely State from the geostrategic point of view. And the reason for this is clearly the fact that he had allowed himself to be manipulated by Sheikh Abdullah. If the hatchet with the British, who had unleashed Jallianwala Bagh on India, could be buried, then what stopped Nehru and others from forgetting Domel and influencing both the Maharaja and Sheikh Abdullah to build a new State with a new dawn? Gandhi, Nehru and other great leaders of India had often shown maturity and forgiveness towards their opponents and enemies. There is the remarkable example of Nehru's civility towards the arch enemy of India, Winston Churchill. Visiting London as Prime Minister of free India in 1953 for the coronation of Queen Elizabeth, Nehru emerged from 'Buckingham Palace, with Indira in tow, and saw Churchil [*sic*] waiting for his car, and went to greet him. Afterwards, Churchill said to Indira, "I didn't expect it. This man whom I have jailed so many times has conquered hate. He acts without a trace of rancor." Indira noticed that there were tears in Churchill's eyes as he spoke.'[366] It is both sad that such a person could not make up with someone like Maharaja Hari Singh.

That Nehru and India felt they needed Sheikh Abdullah more during that time goes without saying, but subjecting Maharaja Hari Singh to humiliation was uncalled for. Perhaps it was thought that Jammu, with its predominant Hindu population, had no choice but to vote for India in a plebiscite and therefore whether the Maharaja was there or not, did not matter. Another reason why Jammu could not afford not to vote for India, was that if Pakistan got Kashmir, they would lose their homes and hearths if not lives. With Mirpur, Muzaffarabad and the Gilgit Agency already lost, the battle of the ballot was to be fought in Kashmir and there, at the moment, Sheikh Abdullah alone was capable of swaying the votes. He knew of the fears of Delhi and had already begun to use them to settle scores and pave the way towards unbridled power to rule the State and, most importantly, rule the Dogras.

19

The Invitation

The New Year of 1949 had begun with the cease fire between India and Pakistan. Pakistan had been thwarted in its design of capturing the State of Jammu and Kashmir, but it had succeeded in taking complete control of the strategic region of Gilgit and Baltistan. In addition, it had occupied more than one lakh square kilometres of State territory. In the process it had also discovered, though used it only crudely, a weapon that it would go on honing in succeeding years, when it used the tribal warriors from the north-west region as raiders to establish some kind of parity with the Indian Armed Forces. In February Yuvraj Karan Singh also arrived after his treatment in the United States and to his dismay found the environment tense and stifling. He had been aware of the changes that had taken place in his absence but in his youthful exuberance, particularly after having watched the Presidential election in USA, he had been looking forward to his return. But he had no idea about the impact of the changes on the Dogras in general and his family in particular.

As soon as his flight landed in Bombay (now Mumbai) he noticed ominous signs. Instead of the expected warm welcome, he was hurriedly whisked away from the airport by a friend of the Maharaja, as there were reports of some possible attempt to assassinate him. It was only after settling down that he realized how badly his family had been affected by the changes that had been thrust upon them. He knew that his father had really no problem in becoming only a constitutional head of his State, but he 'deeply resented the manner in which Jawaharlal had made his handing over power to Sheikh Abdullah a virtual condition for extending military aid to save the State from Pakistani occupation.'[367] After that blackmail, with the help of Jawaharlal Nehru, Sheikh Abdullah had not only headed the administration but also enjoyed arbitrary and enormous executive powers. It was not realized that this complete role reversal had aggravated the bitterness between the Dogras and the Kashmiris, was bound to, sooner or later, create serious trouble.

In contrast to the hush-hush welcome at the Bombay (Mumbai) airport, the Yuvraj's reception in Jammu was tumultuous. 'The whole town was out to greet us on my return from America after a prolonged absence, and the people of Jammu took the opportunity to reiterate their loyalty and affection for the Dogra ruling family... it took us the better of three hours to get from the airport to the palace via Raghunath Temple.'[368] After settling down, he realized the enormity of tragedy that had befallen Jammu region with many having lost all the members of their families in the massacres of Muzaffarabad, Mirpur, Rajouri, Bhimber and other towns. He also visited the various refugee camps and saw for himself the plight of the people. In fact, during the absence of nearly fourteen months, the world had changed beyond recognition with even the visitors to the palace being different. Earlier it had not been easy for everyone to visit the palace and meet the Maharaja. Only a select band of friends and visitors were allowed, but the situation had now drastically changed and the Maharaja needed to meet all kind of people representing different sections. The army officers had always been welcome in the company but now, the senior officers of the Indian Army, often visited the palace in the evenings and, of course, the hot topic of discussion in the palace was the proposal of plebiscite and the merits of the conditional acceptance of the Instrument of Accession by the Dominion Government of India. This had virtually made Prime Minister Nehru a prisoner of self-created problems. More than seventy-five years on Kashmir has become, like Jerusalem, the most complex and debated subjects among historians who remain divided on fixing responsibility, with some blaming the Maharaja for failing to accede in time and Nehru for having referred the matter to the Security Council. However, blaming the Maharaja is rather misplaced as the issue would have remained contested because on the face of it, it was no different from Junagarh. But notwithstanding the blame game, there is little doubt that the country has paid, and continues to pay, a very heavy price for the missteps of the times.

Sheikh Abdullah had recognized that in plebiscite and his perceived ability to swing votes in favour of India, he had a trump card in his hands and that he could demand any price from India. It is ironic that though everyone routinely writes that Sheikh Abdullah was a friend of Nehru, examining their relationship at the ground level makes it clear that it was a very complex friendship where one friend was continuously making demands to the other, in return, conceding each and every demand. Except for the fact that when the first Article of the State's Constitution was being debated, Sheikh Abdullah piloted it to assert that the State was an integral part of India, there is no other example where he might have thought or behaved like an Indian. Thus Sheikh Abdullah was allowed to treat the constitutional provisions with contempt, repeatedly encroaching upon the reserved subjects and losing no opportunity of defying the Maharaja and encouraging his followers to launch vicious propaganda against him. What was needed in those circumstances was the presence of an honest broker between the two, but the person who should have been doing this had himself become a partisan.

By March 1949, the relationship between the Maharaja and Sheikh Abdullah had grown bitter and had literally broken down. The latter used every opportunity to belittle the former, and the former, unable to speak out publicly, seethed with anger. The definition and administration of Reserved Subjects had become a bone of contention with the State Forces, among others, being at the core of it. The Maharaja was determined to guard the independence of that Force as long as it was possible for him. For Nehru it was just another rag-tag of an army, created and fed by Princes who pretended to be independent rulers; for the Maharaja it was a symbol of the ingenuity, gallantry and creativity of a people who, alone in the history of the subcontinent, had fought and defeated opposing forces at those forbidding heights and passes in the trans-Himalayan and Karakoram region. It was not a ceremonial force to feed the fancy of Dogra rulers, nor was it a tool to repress the aspirations of any people. The refusal of the Imperial Bank of India branch of Jammu to follow the instructions of the sole trustee of the Dharmarth Trust had also galled the Maharaja and the atmosphere had been generally vitiated by the slanderous attack unleashed on his honour. It did not help that the people of Jammu refused to even acknowledge the supremacy of Sheikh Abdullah and his National Conference, particularly with the talk of the impending land reforms, which were going to hit the owners of mostly arid lands of Jammu region. On the other hand, small men stuttering with new found power, many among them with no qualification but the membership of National Conference, made mockery of the original grievance of the Kashmiris led by Sheikh Abdullah that jobs given on the basis of merit rather than any other consideration, and this antagonized the Dogras further.

Nehru, on the other hand, equally consumed by his dislike for the Maharaja and the desire to prove to the Pakistan population that Muslims were equal partners in the making of new India, could not see the fatal flaw in his friend. Balraj Puri, one of Sheikh Abdullah's associates commented:

> He was the supreme leader of National Conference and an unrivalled master of the political scene. As life president of the Auqaf[369] trust he controlled most of the mosques and *ziarats* in Kashmir. The sacred shrine of Hazratbal in Srinagar from where he launched his offensive...became the political, religious and emotional centre of Kashmiri life. One-leader [Abdullah], one party [National Conference] and one programme [party manifesto called Naya Kashmir] were the basic slogans of the freedom movement in Kashmir and permitted little dissent.
>
> Kashmir thus became monolithic society led by an authoritarian leader who did not tolerate the slightest dissent. When Abdullah took over as Head of the Emergency Administration on 27 October 1947...his party filled the administrative vacuum. The National Conference workers not only manned the 23-member Emergency Council but were also appointed government officials.

> Many government officials also held positions in the party. The State was still governed by the J&K Constitution Act of 1935 which had no provision for an emergency administration. The Abdullah administration functioned arbitrarily and without any defined powers—party workers assumed the de facto authority to arrest and punish whoever they held guilty. With unchecked political power and a tightly controlled administration, Abdullah was able to further regiment all aspects of Kashmiri life.
>
> ...Being under the influence of the communists in those days, some of whom held positions in the National Conference, he preferred the Soviet model in which the party controlled every branch of the administration.[370]

Balraj Puri was among the first to protest against these tendencies and approached Nehru to warn of the impending dangers to democracy that the kind of regimentation towards which the state was being led, would create. 'As a glaring illustration, [Puri] showed him [Nehru] a copy of a letter of the *Wazir Wazarat* [as the Deputy Commissioner was then called] of Doda district, who was also the president of the district unit of the National Conference. He had after visiting Kishtwar, ordered the expulsion of the officer-bearers of the local National Conference, [vide his order No. HC 989, dated 24th November 1948] allegedly "for their anti-government and anti-national activities" and appointed new office-bearers in their place. Copies of the order were sent to the prime minister of the state and the general secretary of the party.' Puri had further warned in a letter that 'identification of the government with the National Conference would lead to the setting up of a totalitarian regime.'[371] But not only did nothing moved Nehru, he also appeared to be even more determined to champion the cause of Sheikh Abdullah for reasons not difficult to fathom. He had repeatedly asserted that it was on the basis of common policies and programmes that the State had willingly acceded to India. It was reported on 19th June 1948 that one of his addresses was quoted in a newspaper: 'We, the people of Jammu and Kashmir have thrown our lot with the Indian people, not in heat of passion or a moment of despair, but by deliberate choice.'[372] The address continued, 'Our decision to accede to India is based on the fact that our programme and policy are akin to those followed by India.'[373] Nehru believed that with Sheikh Abdullah's support, the popular acceptance of a Muslim majority state acceding to secular India would not only prove Jinnah and his philosophy wrong but also absolve him and Indian leaders of some of the guilt of widespread bloodshed, tears and devastation that followed partition. He ignored the backlash in Jammu where there were few supporters of the Kashmiri and the more Nehru supported him the more it antagonized the Dogras. This, in turn, was attributed to the communalism of Dogras. It did not help that the Maharaja was not willing to accept that Sheikh Abdullah was a true representative of the State or even capable of running it. Between the two, Nehru chose Sheikh Abdullah.

It was during this period when the Maharaja was at a low that Sheikh Abdullah insisted upon his removal from office. In the first flush of power-wielding, he and his leftist friends found an opportunity to bring in a bloodless revolution, something that had not been achieved in none of the other states. His confidence grew so high that his Cabinet submitted a resolution to the Government of India that demanded the removal of the Maharaja. But the Government of India knew that it could be done only by raising a furore in the country and outrage in the world. However, fortuitously for it, 9th March fell the birthday of Yuvraj Karan Singh who turned eighteen and legally, an adult. In these circumstances an invitation arrived from New Delhi. Sardar Patel had invited Maharaja Hari Singh, his wife Maharani Tara Devi, and the young Yuvraj Karan Singh, to Delhi for consultations. They chartered the DC-3 flight to Delhi in April.

According to Karan Singh's narrative, the three checked into Maidens in Old Delhi but soon shifted to the Imperial Hotel. They were invited to lunch at Teen Murti House by Prime Minister Nehru. It was obvious that, though, the Prime Minister and the Maharaja were uncomfortable in each other's company, they made sure that high standard of civility was maintained and there was no sign of hostility. One played the hospitable host, the other the graceful guest. A few days later, on 29th April, Sardar Patel invited the three of them for dinner. Also present during the dinner was his daughter Maniben and his Private Secretary V. Shankar. With the dinner over, the Sardar asked the Maharaja and his wife to join him in his library. The rest got busy in making small conversation to keep the Yuvraj occupied.

The conversation between Sardar Patel and Maharaja Hari Singh was no ordinary after-dinner talk. It soon turned into a monologue as the Sardar spoke as gently as he could and the Maharaja listened to him in utter disbelief and shock. He was stunned by the enormity of what he was being told. What he was being told could certainly not have been delivered by Sardar Patel in whom the Maharaja had placed his utmost trust. Ever since Sardar Patel had come into the handling of the matter he had been guided by him and he had followed his advice. In fact, he had also followed the advice of Prime Minister Nehru, even when it was made clear to him that the price for saving Kashmir from the hordes from Pakistan was handing over power to Sheikh Abdullah. What good had all that trust been? He had thought that his interests were safe as long as Patel was in Delhi and that he would see that his role and sacrifice was duly acknowledged. Alas! He had been betrayed.

Sardar Patel had begun the conversation in the library, ironically, by recounting the contribution of Maharaja Hari Singh in the accession of the State to India but dwelt at length on India's difficulties in the UNO over the plebiscite issue. Of course, he did not acknowledge the negative role played by Prime Minister Jawaharlal Nehru in not accepting the offer for accession without the pre-condition of the transfer of power to his friend Sheikh Abdullah. Patel did not even dwell on the deliberate delay in sending the Indian Army or the failure of the Indian Army to free the State from Pakistani occupation. The memory of the events of the past two years whirred past the Maharaja as he sat there frozen by the words of the formidable man who had mastered the art of dealing with the most difficult of men. But the Maharaja knew there was little that he could do now. The time for that had passed. He remembered that more than a year ago he had been ready to put the spanner in the schemes of India. He was prepared to give a new dimension to a dispute that had been unnecessarily internationalized by referring the Jammu and Kashmir invasion to the United Nations. The ground for this had been prepared by Delhi when it accepted the Accession on the condition of it being subject to the will of the people. But for that the State had to be freed from the forcible occupation of raiders and Pakistan. In this, India had miserably failed, thereby making a mockery of the accession. He had then wanted to withdraw the Instrument of Accession, which in any case, had lost its sanctity by its conditional acceptance. His withdrawal would have meant that the reference before the Security Council would have automatically lapsed. That would have left him free to either strike a deal with Pakistan or approach other countries for help. It was Sardar who had counselled and dissuaded him from taking such a drastic step. In fact, he had repeatedly assured him that the interests of his dynasty would be taken care of. He had trusted him. It was a grave mistake. He should have known that people like him who are independent and uncompromising rarely have genuine friends.

It was later, much later that he started wondering if the invitation to Delhi, the lunch with Nehru and then the dinner with Sardar Patel was not a well-planned strategy between Nehru and Sardar. And, people never tired of claiming the differences between the two and that both were poles apart in policies and their implementation! Nehru had not spoken a word of what was happening in the State or about the need for the ruler of Jammu and Kashmir and his Prime Minister to work for the wellbeing of their people. Now he knew that Nehru had left everything to Patel.

Opening the conversation about the State, Patel had told the Maharaja how difficult Sheikh Abdullah had become and that he was insisting that the Maharaja abdicate in favour of his young son. However, he said, he was, as was the Government of India, of the opinion that it was not necessary for the Maharaja to abdicate. They all felt that if the Maharaja and Maharani stayed out of the State it would serve the purpose of fighting India's plebiscite battle in the UNO by Sheikh Abdullah and National Conference. This was the need of the time and as a loyal son of India the Maharaja will not hesitate in making this sacrifice in the national interest, added Patel. He suggested that since now Yuvraj Karan Singh had arrived from America, after undergoing a successful operation, he could be appointed as Regent to carry out his duties and responsibilities in his absence. So this was it. The knife had finally been put in his heart and twisted. And, of all the people it was Sardar Patel whose hands wielded it! There had been rumours about it for a long time now. Of course, Sheikh Abdullah and his National Conference had spread the word that very soon they will finish the dynasty for all times to come. Kashmir would then be free, he had boasted! He had always thought that they were just part of the rhetoric meant to belittle him by bringing out his helplessness and the power of the National Conference leaders of Kashmir. But not in his wildest dreams had he thought that Sardar Patel would be the man to render him speechless by the cruel suggestion. In fact, it was not even a suggestion for it was a decision that had been conveyed to him. It had been made by the Government of India to appease Abdullah because it was not confident that it could win the plebiscite vote, not because of Sheikh Abdullah's indifference but because the Muslims of Kashmir had already suffered at the hands of Pakistani raiders. But now the Maharaja had no option but to comply.

He had come out of the library bewildered at the turn of events; the Maharani was clearly distressed to the point where any question from her son would have triggered a burst of tears. It was in that state that they rode back to the hotel where the Maharaja went into a huddle with Bakshi Tek Chand and Mehr Chand Mahajan without exchanging any words with his wife or his son.[374] The Maharani tearfully told Yuvraj Karan Singh that she along with the Maharaja was being banished from the State! It was unbelievable. The plebiscite net had entangled the wise men of Delhi and now they needed to sacrifice the Maharaja to extricate themselves out of it! The person under whose signature India was laying claim on Jammu and Kashmir had served the purpose of India, and was, therefore, being discarded? The Maharani was a plain and simple being who was happy and contented in Jammu among her own people and the Maharaja, who loved to travel yet he loved his city beyond words though he would not admit it openly. Could there be happiness again in life if you knew that you can never visit your home?

The Maharaja had another meeting with Sardar Patel the next day on 1st May. Once again Patel went over what he had spoken the night before. Nothing had changed between the night and then.

In fact once again much of the talking was done by Sardar Patel as the Maharaja still could not find words. In fact, hurt as he was, he just did not know how to express it. This was one of those occasions when inside he was full of resentment and seething in anger, yet he pretended to be cool, collected and philosophical about the tragedy that was engulfing his world. Sardar Patel suggested, as if offering a palliative, that he should make the excuse of leaving the State for a few months on grounds of health. Maharaja Hari Singh returned to his hotel, convinced that what had happened was no nightmare but the unfolding of the most treacherous of events. The new rulers of India had sacrificed patriotism, trust and loyalty at the altar of their political exigencies and follies. It was not before 6th May, that he could bring himself to respond to what Sardar Patel had told him.

Now that he was away from the presence of the person who had hurt him by betraying his trust, he could express his bewilderment, disappointment and a feeling of betrayal.

> I would not, however, be human if I did not express my sense of keen disappointment and bewilderment at having been called upon to make such a sacrifice of personal prestige, honour and position when all along I have been content to follow, sometimes even against my own judgment and conscience, the advice in regard to the constitutional position in the State which I have been receiving from the Prime Minister of India or yourself, sometimes even against arrangements which were agreed to only a few months before. Now would it be fair on my part to conceal from you my feeling that while Sheikh Abdullah has been allowed to depart from time to time as suited his inclination from the pledged and the written word, to act consistently in breach of the loyalty which he professed to me prior to his release from jail and the oath of allegiance which he took when he assumed office, and to indulge openly along with his colleagues in a campaign of vilifications and foul calumny against me, both inside the State and outside, I should have had to be driven from position to position each of which I thought I held on the advice of the States ministry.[375]

He could not understand why he was being asked to make such a huge sacrifice of personal prestige, honour and position. He had, against his better judgment, acted on the advice that he received from Prime Minister Nehru and Sardar Patel on the constitutional reforms in the State. Often the advice he got was to alter the terms and agreements that had been agreed upon only a few months earlier and yet he had followed without demurring. He lamented that, on the other, hand Sheikh Abdullah was allowed time and again to depart from the earlier arrangements on the pretext of getting his hands strengthened in order to win the plebiscite for India. Here was a man who had professed his loyalty to the Maharaja prior to his release from jail but breached the oath of allegiance, which he took on assuming office again and again. He had repeatedly gone back on the spoken and the written word and had, in addition, along with his colleagues orchestrated a vilification campaign by launching slanderous propaganda against him. And, the Government of India had continuously driven the Maharaja from one position to another, positions that he had taken on the explicit advice of the States Ministry of the Government of India! In the light of the bitter experience with the Government of India going back on its assurances to him, he owed it to himself, his family and his dynasty a clear declaration in respect of certain matters:

> He should like to be assured that this step is not a prelude to any idea of abdication. I should like to make it clear now that I cannot entertain the latter idea even for a moment and am fully prepared to take the consequences. I regard such a demand from my Prime Minister and his colleagues as a clear breach of the many understandings on which constitutional arrangements have been based from time to time and a positive act of his disloyalty, treachery and deception.
>
> Sheikh Abdullah should be clearly told to stop the campaign of vilification against me and to abandon all activities, both on his part and that of his followers, aimed at securing my abdication. I feel that the sacrifice that I am being called upon to make would be in vain if I continue to be the target of their public or private attacks.
>
> There should be clear assurance of protection of myself and my adherents against any victimization. In this connection, I should like, especially to draw your attention to the facts that

> have been reported to me about persons having been detained in jail for their failure to sign for my abdication.[376]

After making it clear that the idea of abdication was abhorrent to him and that he was willing to face all consequences that might follow his refusal, he addressed the other issues that were part of the proposal of Sardar Patel. Even while he gradually resigned to the fate that had been presented to him, he expressed his concern for the wellbeing of his adherents in the State, who had refused to succumb to the bullying and victimization unleashed by Sheikh Abdullah, and wanted an assurance about them. He also addressed in the same letter the excuse that he was supposed to make for his absence from the State. He wrote:

> The question that I should remain out of the State for three or four months for reasons of health, will, I am afraid, not be believed by anybody and is likely to give rise to many misgivings and speculations within and outside the State as:-
>
> (i) Everybody knows that I am not in such a state of health as would necessitate a long rest outside the State. I have on your advice been recently touring parts of Jammu province in the heat of April;
> (ii) For everybody in bad health Kashmir is considered to be the best health resort and it will certainly look strange if I went outside the State giving out that I am doing so for reasons of health;
> (iii) Wherever I take my temporary residence I cannot confine myself to the four walls of the house. I am bound to meet people, who, when they meet me, will never believe I am staying there for reasons of health;
> (iv) Some other reasons which may be plausible and also at the same time may not compromise my dignity and position, should be given out. The best thing would be that the Government of India should find suitable position for me in Delhi where my services may be utilized in a fitting manner during the above period of three or four months.[377]

But of all the demands made upon him by Sardar Patel, he found the demand of making the Maharani too leave the State very inconsiderate and inhuman. What political purpose would her absence serve the Indian cause or the wellbeing of Kashmiris, unless they had been seriously accusing her of being complicit in the killings of the Muslims? But that lie had been rebutted many times over. Therefore, he protested against such a demand and added in the same letter:

> It is matter of paramount necessity that Her Highness should remain with the Yuvraj in the State during the period of my absence. He is young and impressionable and requires paternal guidance and personal supervision of at least one of his parents. I can see no reason either of political expediency or justice in insisting in the separation of a mother from her only child whom she is seeing after thirteen months of absence abroad. Consideration of humanity alone should suffice to rule out this altogether.[378]

He also wanted an assurance that while he was away from the State, his private estates, houses and other properties were protected from the aggressive intent of Sheikh Abdullah and his party. He suspected that just to spite and humiliate him further, they would make an attempt to grab possession of his gardens and lands. He had information that during the few days that he had been away from Jammu, a few encroachments had been made on his lands in Srinagar. He was even more concerned about the status of the State Forces. He wished to be assured that in his absence no change in it would be mooted and that the constitutional position and prerogatives of the Ruler would remain what they were presently. As far as the Yuvraj was concerned, the Maharaja wanted his protection to be undertaken by India and the Indian Military. Moreover, he preferred, the issues of the State Forces, Civil Lists and *Hazur* Departments be settled immediately, before he took a final decision on abstaining from the State.

Even as Sardar Patel dealt with the Maharaja, Nehru had got busy planning for the future. He invited the Yuvraj for breakfast at his residence. This was the first occasion that the Yuvraj had been invited in his individual capacity. It was obvious that the dinner at Sardar Patel's residence and its purpose was in the knowledge of Nehru. The breakfast lasted more than an hour and was dominated by a monologue by the Prime Minister. Nehru was charming, full of ideas and a man who wanted to frog-leap decades to lead India into the modern era and much of what he spoke focused on the need for the feudal order to change. He emphasized the need for the young generation to divorce itself from the past and be a republican in letter and spirit. Only then could a new India be forged. Probably the purpose of his conversation was to tell the young Yuvraj about the need for him to get disconnected with the value system that was the mainstay of his father. He did that very convincingly. Yuvraj Karan Singh in turn, with his youthful idealism, and the recent exposure to the democracy of America, understood that the world of his father had collapsed and could not be resurrected, and that it was desirable for youngsters like him to accept and adjust to the change. There was so much more to the world than palaces, *shikar* and privileges! It was a matter of national interest that harmony be established in the State but since the Maharaja was disinclined and incapable of accepting the inevitability of change, Pandit Nehru and Sheikh Abdullah had concluded that it would be better for the State if the young Yuvraj be appointed the Regent and a new beginning between the Kashmiri leader and the representative of the Dogra dynasty be made.[379]

After a few days, while the Maharaja awaited a response, it was the turn of Sardar Patel to invite Yuvraj Karan Singh one evening. Patel discussed in detail the events that had taken place. As a matter of fact, he admitted that it was unfortunate that grave injustice was being done to the Maharaja, but the circumstances had so developed because of the reference of Kashmir to the UNO that he had to agree to the insistent demand of Sheikh Abdullah. Thus having disarmed the young Prince, he exhorted him to go ahead and meet the challenges with fortitude and confidence. He talked of the responsibilities that the Yuvraj would have to undertake and the importance of discharging them faithfully and efficiently.

There were some in the entourage of the Maharaja who were aghast at the suggestion that after virtually banishing the Maharaja, the Yuvraj was being asked to act as a ruler. This in their opinion was a cunning move of the Congress-National Conference combine to drive a wedge in the family and neutralize the anticipated furore in the State. They, in fact, wanted the Yuvraj to decline the offer but the Karan Singh told them as politely as he could that in such an eventuality the whole family would be completely out of touch with the State.[380] Those who were unable to reconcile to the reality of the situation ignored the fact that if the Yuvraj would refuse to be the Regent then who else? In the circumstances, the only way of keeping the dynasty relevant was to appoint him since he was the heir apparent! The Yuvraj was obviously still very young but difficult circumstances had suddenly put a wise head on the young shoulders of an eighteen year old and he was ready to unhesitatingly hold his own in discussions about not only the impending disaster but generally about life and the world around.

Sardar Patel could not immediately respond to the letter as he was taken ill and had to move from the heat of Delhi to Dehradun. He was, however, deeply concerned about the unfinished agenda and was fully aware of the pressure that Sheikh Abdullah was exerting on Nehru. Importantly, he had no qualms about what he had done. A nation is much bigger than individuals and especially for a nation like India, which was in the difficult process of rebuilding and rediscovering itself, it was important that personal feelings of generosity and animosity be set aside. He had high regard for Maharaja Hari Singh and also had deep sympathy for him. It was not easy for him, he understood. It is not easy for anyone to give up a life of privileges. He had dealt with many Maharajas during the past two years and there was none who was called upon to make a greater sacrifice. It is also possible that he would not have displayed the patience that he was exercising if the accession had not been mired in controversy. The situation would have been different if Jawaharlal Nehru had not allowed himself to be influenced by Lord Mountbatten, or had been motivated by the desire to demonstrate his lofty ideals of international brotherhood to the world community when it was known that Jinnah and his Pakistan would have no compunction in trying to grab Kashmir by force.

Sardar Patel had dealt with the likes of the Nizam of Hyderabad and the Maharaja of Jodhpur and exposed their fragility. But he could not use those tactics with Maharaja Hari Singh. He also had a healthy regard for him and his family. Unlike many other Princes they were not tainted in their personal lives, and Maharaja Hari Singh, indeed, had a difficult choice to make. Who would have faulted him, except the affected Hindus, if he had followed the dictates of the communal numbers, geography and logistics, and acceded to Pakistan? In fact, if the Gurdaspur district had not been given to India, the Maharaja would have had to accede to Pakistan. With no link to Pathankot, Pakistan would have just got hold of the State by capturing Jammu from its southern borders. But after he realized that Pakistan was not going to give him a chance to make up his mind after the passions had cooled, he knew that the wellbeing and physical safety of his Hindu and Sikh subjects rested upon his decision to accede to India. He had saved their lives even though he loathed giving up his independence.

Therefore, when Sardar Patel replied to him on 23rd May, he tried to assuage his hurt feelings and made a subtle appeal to his sense of duty to his country:

> No one can be more cognizant than myself of the attitude which Your Highness has adopted ever since you signed the Instrument of Accession. I am grateful to Your Highness for the spirit of cooperation and understanding which you have always extended to me and also for the kind sentiments which you have expressed. I can assure Your Highness that, before putting forward my proposal, I had, after careful consideration, come to the conclusion that the interests alike of Your Highness, the dynasty and the country demanded the step which you have now agreed to take. I know full well the interest involved in it, but, I am sure, along with so many other changes to which Your Highness has accustomed yourself, you will undertake this step also with a sense of duty to your country and in a spirit of calm resignation to the superior dictates of events.[381]

He also informed him that it had been made clear to Sheikh Abdullah that the Maharaja's abdication was out of question and that all slanderous attack on his person and family from public platforms in the State would be brought to an immediate end. But he also signalled that an era was coming to an end and changes were inevitable in the future and prepared the Maharaja for them by stating, 'Your Highness will of course, appreciate that the future constitution of the State would be determined by the duly elected Constituent Assembly.'[382] This meant that it was for the Constituent Assembly to decide the course that the future would take since the new constitution would be what the Assembly decides. He also assured that if any specific instance of harassment of his close people or encroachment upon his properties was brought to his notice then he would ensure that prompt action is taken to get justice done.

The Maharaja's suggestion of giving a respectable reason for his absence was declined without assigning any reason and, instead, told to simply put out that because of the strain of the past few months he would stay out of the State and that, the period of his absence need not be mentioned. Polite and suave when needed, Sardar Patel also refused to entertain the request based on 'consideration of humanity' that the Maharani be allowed to stay with her only child by saying, 'We have carefully considered the question of Her Highness staying with the Yuvraj during your absence, but for a variety of reasons, we feel that it would be best, for the present, for her also to stay away for a while. Later, she can certainly visit the Yuvraj from time to time, and the Yuvraj can also visit Your Highness and Her Highness occasionally.'[383]

This ruthless refusal to allow a mother stay with her only child was clearly a sign that the decision had been influenced by the effectiveness of the propaganda of Sheikh Abdullah and his colleagues about the alleged Muslim massacres. The fact that Mahatma Gandhi and Nehru had believed in that propaganda is understandable but the same could not be said about the pragmatic Sardar Patel almost two years later. Therefore, it must be concluded that in the Maharaja's case he was doing what Nehru could not have done without creating more friction with the Maharaja. That, however, does not absolve him of the culpability and it must be said that there was really not much difference between Nehru and Patel, except for the style and idiom of language. They were a very effective team, complementing and covering each other's shortcoming. This is borne out by the fact that when Sardar Patel responded to Maharaja on 23rd May 1949, he sent a copy of the letter to Nehru with the following covering note:

> As regards the Yuvraj, we have had a very detailed talk with him and I have impressed upon him the significance and importance of the agreements reached and the consequences which flow therefrom. He is a sensible lad and I think he appreciated the situation fairly well and realizes his responsibilities. He is, of course, still in his teens and would require some guidance. I am looking for a suitable adviser for him on whose advice he can lean. We shall have to be very careful in the choice of a suitable person.[384]

It was also clear that having secured the exit of the Maharaja from the scene, Sheikh Abdullah too was content for the time being with that victory and was, therefore, more amenable to assuring the safety of the properties of the Maharaja. Probably with the Maharaja out of the scene he was confident of manipulating the young Regent to impose his will. On the suggestion of Sardar Patel, the Maharaja and Maharani along with Yuvraj shifted to Dehradun where the former's ill-health had brought him. While the Maharaja and his party stayed at a hotel, the Yuvraj was invited by Sardar Patel to stay as his guest for three weeks in the Doon Court. During those few days the Yuvraj learnt a lot about life and was deeply impressed by the fact that though not happy with Nehru's handling of Kashmir, Patel never once criticized him in his presence. About Sheikh Abdullah, he was more forthcoming and rarely held himself back from expressing his distrust and dislike.[385]

20

The End and a Beginning

June is a hot and oppressive month in Delhi. If the dust storms do not force one to stay indoors the stillness of the high noon sun discourages movement. Delhi is no place to live for the Ruler of the Dogra dynasty during this time of the year. This is the time when the Durbar[386] of Jammu and Kashmir is settled in the cooler climate of Srinagar. But in June 1949 the Valley already seemed to be in some distant past. Here he was, sacrificed for the supposed interests of the State and country, and now preparing to close a chapter in Indian history while wondering what was in store for him, his family and his people in the future.

The business in Delhi was almost over. The die had been cast, as they say, and he had no option but to accept the dictates of the Government of India. No other Prince had been treated so shabbily, pushed from one position to another, and now, even forced out of his State. In his hour of dire need he had been friendless. The time to argue and appeal to the outside world had passed. He decided to return to Delhi and move on with life. He had done his best to secure the interests of his family and ensure the protection of the Yuvraj. In any case, Dehradun was no substitute for Kashmir.

In the meantime, the Yuvraj appeared to be excited at the prospect of being part of the emerging world. To his father's discomfort, he had always admired Nehru but now he seemed to be eager to work with him. In a different way, even Sardar Patel had cast a spell on him and he had been asked to stay back in Dehradun while the Maharaja and the Maharani returned to Delhi. By the time Yuvraj too returned to Delhi, his mother had also reconciled to the proposal. But since she was extremely sensitive to the heat of Bombay, she had decided to live in Kasauli, perhaps in the hope of seeing her son more often and also visit her parental home in Kangra more easily.

However, there was one matter the parents wanted to settle before embarking upon their new lives. The *Yagyopaveet*[387] ceremony of the Yuvraj had to be performed and Mehr Chand Mahajan, who even after relinquishing the office of Prime Minister had continued to be the adviser of the Maharaja stepped forward to make the necessary arrangements at his residence in Delhi. Pandits from Jammu were sent for along with two young Rajput boys to undergo the ceremony with the Yuvraj, who loathed the thought of going through the compulsory ritual of having his head tonsured. He argued hard and finally managed to convince his parents that a ceremonial cut of a tuft of hair should serve the purpose.

It was not only in the matter of that ceremony that the Maharaja noticed that his son had created a distance between their world and his. While the Maharaja's world still consisted of the unique grandeur created by both his ancestors and the thousands of Dogra soldiers who had marched long distances in the mountains to achieve what no other people in the country had, he rued with some trace of bitterness the fact that the young Yuvraj's world now consisted of Nehru, Patel and Sheikh Abdullah. In this he would not be allowed to play an active role but, in his opinion, be reduced to being a puppet in the hands of that arch enemy of the Dogras. He loathed the thought of his son being ordered about by Sheikh Abdullah and was bitter about the fact that not for a moment had the Yuvraj demonstrated his inclination to stand by his father and family even though he was aware that there was no other option for the family. In fact he had appeared eager for the change, perhaps a little too eager, to step into the role of Regent.

The night of 19th June, was extremely hot. Outside, not a leaf fluttered. Inside the hotel the calmness barely managed to suppress the emotional turmoil the three in the family were undergoing. The frailest among them frequently broke down and did little to hide her tears. The Maharaja was seething not only at the perfidy of the Government of India but also at Yuvraj who was apparently excited at the prospect of a new and independent life. He had a right to be so, after all, he was well past eighteen now. Grown up enough to understand what was good or bad. But somehow his eagerness appeared like betrayal to the family. The Maharaja, even after becoming so accustomed to setbacks and betrayals by now, was uncomfortable.

As he sat drinking his favourite scotch he looked back at the number of times he had been let down by those he had trusted. Foremost among them was Malka Pukhraj. He wondered if she had set the ball rolling or if was she the symptom of the storm that had been about to strike his world. Even now he was convinced Sheikh Abdullah was not such an intractable problem that he became later. It was the formidable force that stood behind him that had finally forced him to buckle. First, the British and then Nehru and the Government of India had beaten him. He was sure that even now if there was to be a straight contest between him and Sheikh Abdullah, he would win in the battle of the ballot. Even in the Valley!

It was a long night, much longer than the one when he had driven from Srinagar to Jammu. With dawn, he knew, he would be bringing an end to a journey that had begun in the first decade of nineteenth century. He was not sure if there was any life after death or a world after. But if there was then he would have to do a lot of explaining to his great-grandfather. Eighteenth century had been chaotic with the Dogras unable to maintain unity and the Sikhs too unruly to aspire for an organized kingdom. It was in that chaos that Gulab Singh had taken his first steps in the battlefield and the politics of the time as a sixteen-year-old soldier. Jammu had been once again attacked by Ranjit Singh's army under Hukam Singh. Among those defending the city was Gulab Singh, whose fighting skills were noticed by all. However, it was in 1809, soon after the Jammu's capitulation to the Sikhs that the big opportunity knocked at his door. He had been serving under the Sikh Dewan Kushwaqt Rai, the manager of Sardar Nihal Singh Attari's estate, when a rebellion broke out. It was put down by Gulab Singh. This time the news of his courage and skill spread and reached Maharaja Ranjit Singh who sent for him. He had joined the Sikh Army as a common trooper under Jemadar Khushal Singh's command. The rise, thereafter, from commanding a small force of his own to becoming a general was swift and unobstructed.

In 1814, the campaign of Ranjit Singh to capture Kashmir had met with failure. His forces had been forced to retreat because his army's rear had been attacked by the Raja of Rajouri who had turned against the Lahore forces. The leadership qualities of Gulab Singh had then come to the fore, with him rallying the forces and then organizing an orderly retreat. The defeat had taught Maharaja Ranjit Singh a lesson that without securing his flanks, consisting of the twenty-two Dogra hill states, he could not conquer Kashmir. Young Gulab Singh's daring during that retreat, however, came to be noticed and his reputation was further enhanced, in the spring of 1818 during the Sikh Army's siege of Multan. In that battle, one of the favourite Sardars of Maharaja Ranjit Singh had fallen to the swords of the Afghans. Maharaja Ranjit Singh expressed deep anguish at the prospect of his body being defiled by the enemy. Gulab Singh had then recklessly forayed into enemy territory to recover the dead body. Impressed by the loyalty and bravery, soon thereafter Gulab Singh was made the commander of Ranjit Singh's army in Jammu. He was also given Jammu as *jagir*. It was on the pretext of efficient collection of revenue that he was allowed to raise his own small army. The next opportunity came when he undertook the task of punishing the King of Rajouri who had, during the campaign of Kashmir, deserted the Sikh army to side with the Afghans when the army was moving towards Pir Panjal. This had thwarted Maharaja Ranjit Singh's ambition of conquering Kashmir. Gulab Singh was quick to defeat the recalcitrant king and bring him as prisoner to Maharaja Ranjit Singh. However, the crowning glory came when in 1822 he was anointed the King of Jammu on the banks of Chenab in Akhnur. With it, Jammu had once again been brought back to the hands of Dogras. He had become the king but he still needed to subdue the smaller States that were mostly proud of their independence. Though the Sikhs had defeated the Dogras and conquered Jammu, these independent States had not submitted to the authority of Lahore. Thus the next few years were devoted to consolidating them under Gulab Singh's banner, by force, negotiations or, sometimes by forging marital ties.

Maharaja Hari Singh proudly recalled the progress of Raja Gulab Singh and his two brothers. His great-grandfather had been wise enough not to covet the plains. These were the territories directly under the control of his benefactor, Maharaja Ranjit Singh. Therefore he had chosen the harder option of consolidating his sphere of influence to the mountains. Like his benefactor Maharaja Ranjit Singh, he had the knack of sighting talented people and the best among them was General Zorawar Singh. Consequently the expansion thereafter had been relentless. The more he succeeded, the more people from the Dogra hills flocked to his camp. Much before he became Maharaja of Jammu and Kashmir, and was recognized as an independent entity by the British Empire, he had expanded his kingdom, even without Kashmir, to Central Asia. Not since the times of Chandragupta Maurya had any one from the subcontinent reached those icy cold, untamed frontiers. Conquering Ladakh was a monumental achievement as were the other campaigns. Skardu was the next to fall, it being the first of the Baltistani States to accept the suzerainty of Jammu. Later, Gilgit and Hunza were added by Maharaja Gulab Singh's successors.

Holding these provinces was not easy but he had not only held on to them but been forced to conquer more as the neighbouring Dard and Chilasi warriors challenged his suzerainty over the region. This had lasted more than a century till the Northern Areas were lost with the fall of Skardu in 1948. History will judge if he, Shriman Indar Mahindar Rajrajeshwar Maharajadhiraj Shri Hari Singhji, Jammu and Kashmir Naresh Tatha Tibbet adi Deshadhipati, Ruler of Jammu and Kashmir State, lost those areas or were they lost because of the myopic world view of Jawaharlal Nehru? Why could the Government of India not ask the Indian Army to launch an attack on Skardu with the same urgency that it had demonstrated in defending the valley of Kashmir? Why could it not land its troops in Gilgit to pre-empt the nefarious designs of Major Brown of the Ladakh Scouts? It could be argued that he was the Maharaja and it was his responsibility to ensure the sanctity of the borders of his kingdom. But then he was already hamstrung by the British, as also by the fact that the Treaty of 1846 between Maharaja Gulab

Singh and the British stipulated that in case of external threat, it would be the responsibility of British Empire to defend the State. Now with India as the successor-State of the British, was not the Government of India bound to defend its borders, the lapse of paramountcy notwithstanding? India had, in fact, appropriated the advantages of making all treaties and agreements with British that came with their lapse but did not accept any of the responsibilities that came with that.

He had no doubt that history would hold India guilty of dismantling the State that had been so assiduously built by the Dogras. The Northern Areas had been deliberately allowed to remain in the hands of Pakistan. Perhaps Delhi did not think that those snow-bound regions that barely grew grass were worth holding. In the process, it had become guilty of letting hundreds of fine soldiers, men, women and children be killed and raped in Skardu. Or, perhaps India's secularism was fake. Indian leaders also displayed apathy to the geostrategic importance of that region and had absolutely no clue to the machinations of the British bureaucracy, civil and military.

In fact, now that he looks back at the way the war in Kashmir had been conducted, he was convinced that the Government of India had hoped that the Muslim-dominated Poonch and Rajouri in Jammu too would fall to Pakistan. Fortunately, the 8 JAK had held on to Poonch, which was ultimately rescued by the Indian Army for fear of endangering the security of Kashmir. The Indian Army had been asked to recapture Kargil and Dras. Why? Was it not because India had realized that unless that was done the Buddhist Ladakh was in danger of falling in Pakistani hands? Pakistan could also breathe down the valley of Kashmir from the forbidding heights of Zoji La. But the Government of India did not think it right to display the same urgency in recapturing Skardu and Gilgit, where the most gallant defence was put up by the State Forces. The political behemoth that Maharaja Gulab Singh had created would be effectively dismantled the next morning, he told himself as he rose to go to a sleepless bed.

The next morning, 20th June 1949, Maharaja Hari Singh signed a Proclamation that read:

> Whereas I have decided for reasons of health to leave the State for temporary period and to entrust to Yuvraj Shri Karansinghji Bahadur for that period all my powers and functions in regard to the Government of the State.
>
> Now, therefore, I hereby direct and declare that all powers and functions, whether legislative, executive, or judicial which are exercisable by me in relation to the State and its Government, including in particular my right and prerogative of making laws, of issuing Proclamations, Orders and of pardoning offenders, shall during the period of my absence from the State be exercisable by the Yuvraj Shri Karansinghji Bahadur.
>
> HARI SINGH
> MAHARAJADHIRAJ

By the time he had finished with this, the entourage of his personal staff and servants was ready to go to the New Delhi Railway Station to board the early train to Bombay.

Soon after, Maharani Tara Devi, still tearful and bleary eyed, her brother and servants left by road for the cool air of Kasauli.

The Regent, Yuvraj Shri Karansinghji Bahadur was left alone in the hotel with the burden of a past that had been stripped of its original geographical contours and grandeur and a future that held forth so much potential but also contained the seeds of unending strife.

Appendix 1

Extracts from the British Mission's Statement of 16th May 1946

Paragraph 14: Before putting forward our recommendation we turn to deal with the relationship of the Indian States to British India. It is quite clear that with the attainment of independence by British India, whether inside or outside the British Commonwealth, the relationship which has hitherto existed between the Rulers of the States and the British Crown will no longer be possible. Paramountcy can neither be retained not transferred to the new Government. This fact has been fully recognized by those whom we interviewed from the States. They have at the same time assured us that the States are ready and willing to cooperate in the new development of India. The precise form which their cooperation will take must be a matter for negotiation during the building up of the new constitutional structure, and it by no means follows that it will be identical for all States. We have not therefore dealt with the States in the same detail as the Provinces of British India.

Appendix 2

Extracts of The Cabinet Mission's Memorandum on India States, Treaties and Paramountcy

Prior to the recent statement of the British Prime Minister in the House of Commons an assurance was given to the Princes that there was no intention on the part of the Crown to initiate any change in their relationship with the Crown or the rights guaranteed by their treaties and engagements without their consent. It was at the same time stated that the Princes' consent to changes which might emerge as a result of negotiations would not unreasonably be withheld. The Chamber of Princes has since confirmed that Indian States fully share the general desire in the country for the immediate attainment by India of her full stature. His Majesty's Government have now declared that if the Succession Government or Governments in British India desire independence no obstacle should be placed in their way. The effect of these announcements is that all those concerned with the future of India wish to attain position of independence within or without the British Commonwealth. The Delegation has come here to assist in resolving the difficulties which stand in the way of India fulfilling this wish.

During the interim period, which must elapse before the coming into operation of a new constitutional structure under which India will be independent or fully self-governing, Paramountcy will remain in operation. But the British Government could not and will not in any circumstances transfer paramountcy to an Indian Government.

In the meanwhile, the Indian States are in a position to play an important part in the formulation of the new constitutional structure for India, and His Majesty's Government have been informed by the Indian States that they desire, in their own interests and in the interests of India as a whole, both to make their contribution to the framing of the structure, and to take their due place in it when it is completed. In order to facilitate this they will doubtless strengthen their position by doing everything possible to ensure that their administrations conform to the highest standard. Where adequate standards cannot be achieved within the existing resources of the State they will no doubt arrange in suitable cases to form or join administrative units large enough to enable them to be fitted into the constitutional structure. It will also strengthen the position of the States during this formulative period if the various Governments, which have not already done to take active steps to place themselves in close and constant touch with public opinion in their State by means of representative institutions.

During the interim period it will be necessary for the States to conduct negotiations with British India in regard to future regulation of matters of common concern, especially in the economic and financial field. Such negotiations, which will be necessary whether the States desire to participate in the new Indian constitutional structure or not, will occupy a considerable period of time, and since some of these negotiations may well be incomplete when the new structure comes into being, it will, in order to avoid administrative difficulties, be necessary to arrive at an understanding between the States and those likely to control the succession Government or Governments that for a period of time the then existing arrangements as to those matters of common concern should continue until the new agreements are completed. In this matter, the British Government and the Crown Representative will lend such assistance as they can should it be so desired.

When a new fully self-governing or independent Government or Governments come into being in British India, His Majesty's Government's influence with these Governments will not be such as to enable them to carry out the obligations of paramountcy. Moreover they cannot contemplate that British troops will be retained in India for this purpose. Thus as a logical sequence and in view of the desires expressed to them on behalf of the Indian States, His Majesty's Government will cease to exercise the powers of paramountcy. This means that the rights of the States which flow from their relationship to the Crown will no longer exist and that all the rights surrendered by the States to the paramount Power will return to the States. Political arrangements between the States on the one side and the British Crown and British India on the other will thus be brought to an end. The void will have to be filled either by the States entering into a federal relationship with the successor Government or Governments in British India, or failing this, entering into particular political arrangements with it or them.

The following explanatory note was issued by the Cabinet Mission in New Delhi on the date of publication (22nd May 1946):

> The Cabinet Delegation desire to make it clear that the document issued today entitled 'Memorandum on States' Treaties and Paramountcy presented by the Cabinet Delegation to His Highness the Chancellor of the Chamber of Princes' was drawn up before the Mission began its discussions with the party leaders and represented the substance of what they communicated to the representatives of the States at their first interviews with the Mission. This is the explanation of the use of the words 'succession Government or Governments of British India', an expression which would not of course have been used after the issue of the Delegation's recent statement.

Appendix 3

Extracts from The Indian Independence Act, 1947

Be it enacted by the King's most Excellent Majesty, by and with the advice and consent of the Lords Spiritual and Temporal, and Commons, in the present Parliament assembled, and by the authority of the same as follows:-

1. *The new Dominions*:- (1) as from the fifteenth day of August, nineteen hundred and forty-seven, two independent Dominions shall be set up in India, to be known respectively as India and Pakistan.

2. The said Dominions are hereafter in this Act referred to as 'the new Dominions', and the said fifteenth day of August is hereafter in this Act referred to as 'the appointed day'.

3. *Territories of the new Dominions*:- (1) Subject to the provisions of sub-sections (3) and (4) of this section, the territories of India shall be territories under the sovereignty of His Majesty which, immediately before the appointed day, were included in British India except the territories which under sub-section (2) of this section, are to be the territories of Pakistan.

(2) Subject to the provisions of sub-sections (3) and (4) of this section, the territories of Pakistan shall be:-

(a) the territories which, on the appointed day, are included in the Provinces of East Bengal and West Punjab, as constituted under the two following sections;

(b) the territories which, at the date of the passing of this Act, are included in the Province of Sind and the Chief Commissioner's Province of British Baluchistan; and

(c) if, whether before or after the passing of this Act but before the appointed day, the Governor-General declares that the majority of the valid votes cast in the referendum which, at the date of passing of this Act, is being or has recently been held in that behalf under the authority in the North-West Frontier Province are in favour of representatives of that Province taking part in the Constituent Assembly of Pakistan, the territories which, at the date of the passing of this Act, are included in that Province.

(3) Nothing in this section shall prevent any area being at any time included in or excluded from either of the new Dominions, so, however, that:-

(a) no area not forming part of the territories specified in sub-section (1) or, as the case be, sub-section (2) of this section shall be included in either Dominion without the consent of that Dominion; and

(b) no area which forms part of the territories specified in the said sub-section (1) or, as the case may be, the said sub-section (2), or which has after the appointed day been included in either Dominions, shall be excluded from that Dominion without the consent of that Dominion…

(7) *Consequences of the setting up of the new Dominions*:-

(1) As from the appointed day:-

(a) His Majesty's Government in the United Kingdom have no responsibility as respects the governments of the any of the territories which immediately before that day, were included in British India;

(b) the suzerainty of His Majesty over the Indian States lapses, and with it, all treaties and agreements in force at the date of the passing of this Act between His Majesty and the rulers of Indian States, all functions exercisable by His Majesty at that date with respect to Indian States, all obligations of His Majesty existing at that date towards the Indian States or the rulers thereof, and all powers, rights, authority or jurisdiction exercisable by His Majesty at that date in or in relation to Indian States by treaty, grant, usage, sufferance or otherwise; and

(c) there lapse also any treaties or agreements in force at the date of the passing of this Act between His Majesty and any persons having authority in the tribal areas, any obligations of His Majesty existing at that date to any such persons or with respect to the tribal areas, and all powers, rights, authority or jurisdiction exercisable at that date of His Majesty in or in relation to the tribal areas by treaty, grant, usage, sufferance or otherwise:

Provided that, notwithstanding anything in paragraph (b) or paragraph (c) of this sub-section, effect shall, as nearly as may be continued to be given to the provisions of any such agreement as is therein referred to which relate to customs, transit and communications, posts and telegraphs, or other like matters, until the provisions in question are denounced by the ruler of the Indian State or persons having authority in the tribal areas on the one hand, or by the Dominion or Province or other part thereof concerned on the other hand, or are superseded by subsequent agreements...

8. *Temporary provision as to government of each of the new Dominions*:- (1) In the case of each of the new Dominions, the powers of the Legislature of the Dominion shall, for the purpose of making provisions as to the constitution of the Dominion, be exercisable in the first instance by the Constituent Assembly of that Dominion, and references in this Act to the Legislature of the Dominion shall be construed accordingly...

Appendix 4

The Maharaja's Emergency Administration Order on 30th October 1947 Appointing Sheikh Mohammad Abdullah as the Head of the Administration

We are hereby pleased to command that pending the formation of the Interim Government as agreed upon and in view of the emergency that has arisen I charge Sheikh Mohammad Abdullah to function as the Head of Administration with power to deal with the emergency.

Sheikh Mohammad Abdullah be sworn in by the Chief Justice or any other Judge of the High Court at Srinagar.

Hari Singh
Maharaja

Emergency Council

1. The Hon'ble Sheikh Mohammad Abdullah, Head of Emergency Administration.
2. The Hon'ble Bakshi Ghulam Mohammad, Deputy Head of Administration.
3. The Hon'ble Mirza Mohammad Afzal Beg, Emergency Officer, Anantnag District.
4. The Hon'ble G.M. Sadiq, Emergency Internal Security Home Guards, Cultural Front.
5. The Hon'ble Sham Lal Saraf, Emergency Officer, Trade and Supplies.

6. The Hon'ble Girdhari Lal Dogra, Emergency Officer, Kathua.
7. The Hon'ble Sardar Budh Singh, Emergency Officer (Goodwill Mission to Jammu)
8. The Hon'ble Pandit Jia Lal Kilam, Emergency Officer Food.
9. Maulana Mohammad Syed, Emergency Officer, Publicity.
10. Khwaja Ghulam Moni-ud-din, Emergency Officer, Communications.
11. Khwaja Abdul Ahad, Emergency Officer (Firewood, Fuel)
12. Soofi Mohammad Akbar, Emergency Officer, Baramulla.
13. Peer Mohammad Maqbool, Emergency Officer, Muzaffarabad.
14. Pandit Kashpa Bandhu, Emergency Officer, Refugees & Rehabilitation.
15. Mr. Mohi-ud-din Hamdani, Emergency Officer Peace Brigade.
16. Mr. D.P. Dhar, Secretary, Internal Security & Law and Order.
17. Mr. J.N. Zutshi, Private Secretary to the Head of Administration and Secretary to the Emergency Council.
18. Khwaja Ahsan Ullah, Emergency Officer, Transport.
19. Mr. Mohammad Amin, Emergency Officer, Banihal.
20. Colonel Ram Lal, Emergency Officer, Home Guards.
21. Ccolonel Baldev Singh Pathania, Chief Emergency Officer, Jammu.
22. Colonel Akbar Khan, Chief Administrative Officer, Bhadarwah.
23. Colonel Baldev Singh Samyal, Emergency Officer, Border Scouts, Jammu.

Appendix 5

Memorandum to the President of India

August 1952
Poona

Dr Rajendra Prasad
President of India
New Delhi

Sir,

I am making a direct approach to you in the matter of the affairs of the State of Jammu and Kashmir and its Ruler as the situation has become acute owing to the rapid developments that are taking place and the further steps which are being taken in the next few days as these will vitally affect me personally apart from the repercussions they will have on the subjects of the State.

2. It is necessary to set out very briefly the events that have happened so far as the State of Jammu and Kashmir is concerned since my accession to the Gaddi.

3. I became the Ruler of the State in 1925. I then found that the British had strengthened their hold on the State by taking advantage of certain circumstances because, it being a border State of great strategic and political importance, they wanted it to be completely in their grip. The British created the myth of paramountcy without any historical or political sanctions and exploited the State as a set off against the fast approaching political awakening and urge for freedom in what was then known as British India.

4. Realizing what was coming, I took it upon myself to shake

off the British yoke by insisting that the relations of the State with the British should be governed by the Treaty and all other strings which had been attached to such relationship with a view to gain domination over the State should be removed. I succeeded in my efforts to a large extent but incurred the wrath of the British who thenceforth became openly hostile to me.

5. Simultaneously with this, I started taking measures to ameliorate the condition of my people and to organize my Government on progressively democratic lines. I enacted laws to relieve rural indebtedness and to improve generally the lot of the agriculturist and the economic and social condition of my people. Some of these enactments were resented by my Hindu subjects who thought that their interests were being sacrificed in the cause of Muslim uplift. I established industries and made provisions for education and medical relief far in advance of any other State. Special provision was made for educational advancement of Muslims who were then considered backward. I was even more enthusiastic as regards the better organization of my Government. In this, I had the assistance of men of unquestionable integrity and ability from British India as my Prime Ministers and other Ministers and head of various Departments. It will not be out of place to name a few of them, such as, Raja Harikishen Kaul, Mirza Sir Zaffar Ali, Mr V.N. Mehta, Mr Vijahat Husein, Sir Burjor Dalal, Sir Abdus Samad Khan, Sir Lal Gopal Mukerji, Sir K.N. Haksar, Sir N. Gopalaswami Ayyangar, Sir B.N. Rau. As a result, the administration of the State in the matter of efficiency and organization was better than even in some of the Provinces of British India. One further fact to which I wish to draw your attention in this connection is that I invariably acted on the advice of such Ministers and did not interfere or overrule their directions. It therefore, follows that if any fault is now to be found with the administration of the State and/or the policies then pursued, the blame cannot be laid at my door alone. It is significant that for six years (1938-1943) Shri N. Gopalaswami Ayyangar was the Prime Minister of the State and he will bear me out that I never interfered with his policies and decisions adopted and taken from time to time. Consequently with my desire to give to the people of the

State complete self government, I discussed in 1945 with my Prime Minister, Sir B.N. Rau, in the presence of Sir Tej Bahadur Sapru and Sir Kailash N. Haksar, the inauguration in the State of Full Responsible Government with Provincial Autonomy and a Central Government comprised of Representatives of the Provinces and a Board of Judicial Advisers with myself as the Constitutional Head. I was prepared to do this even with the knowledge that it would not be relished by the British. Sir B.N. Rau wanted this to be put into execution within the next fortnight. I was of opinion that it should be done in about six months so as to enable us to complete the scheme. The news leaked out, there were intrigues, position became very difficult and Sir B.N. Rau left shortly thereafter.

6. The finances of the State were governed on modern principles. My expenditure was strictly limited and kept separate and distinct from the State finances and proper and well defined limits were laid down as between my personal and private matters and matters of the State. Thus, I had well organized and efficient executive, a democratically elected Legislature, an independent judiciary, definite policies for expansion of education medical relief and all other essential features of a progressive state. The eminent administrators and judges who worked for the State from time to time will bear testimony to this.

7. All that I did aggravated the hostility of the British towards me as they were not sincerely inclined towards ameliorating the conditions of the people or for the freedom of the country.

8. In those days, the Rulers of the Indian States were judged by the condition and feelings of their subjects and I can say, without fear of contradiction, that the people of my State were content and had no cause for grievance against me or the administration of the State.

9. It is not unknown that trouble started in the State in 1931 and what has on occasions been described by so called 'national leaders' of the State as 'the Freedom Movement' was engineered by elements outside the State under the instigation of the British. The movement in the beginning was a religious movement with slogans like 'Down with Hindu Raj' and 'Islam in danger'. The leaders of the movement were the men who now figure as Ministers and Administrators in

Azad Kashmir under Pakistan such as, Chaudhary Ghulam Abbas and Maulvi Yusuf Shah and some others. To gain sympathy and cooperation from those fighting for freedom from the British yoke in British India, the Muslims who were running this movement gave it the name of 'National Conference'. The name was adopted also to fall into line with the movement carried on in other States in the name of the 'States People Conference' and to take advantage of the declining prestige of the British. The movement thus gained the sympathy of the Indian National Congress. It became known in British India as the National Movement in the Jammu and Kashmir State.

10. These facts clearly showed that my people had no grievance against me, that the movement was started by disgruntled people with the British behind them and that those in charge of the movement gained the confidence and sympathy of the Indian National Congress by adopting the name of the 'National Conference'.

11. I have been accused by the Prime Minister of not listening to the advice of the Congress leaders during the fateful period 1946-47. I deny that charge. In 1946 when the leaders of the Indian National Congress formed the Viceroy's Cabinet for the Interim Government, I had occasion to meet Mahatma Gandhi and Shri J.B. Kripalani, the then President of the Indian National Congress, when they both visited the State. Mahatma Gandhi suggested that I should have the backing of the people in whatever I did, Shri J.B. Kripalani suggested the immediate release of Sheikh Abdullah because the nominees of the National Conference who were in the Government had resigned. I pointed out to them that I had already set up a Constitutional government which included two nominees of the National Conference and that it was not then possible to entrust the Government entirely in the hands of one group, *viz*, the National Conference. I said to them that I was willing to make such further changes as might be suggested towards making it a completely popular Government in consonance with the safety of the State and to keep the balance between the divergent views of different parts of the State. The matter rested there for the time being.

12. Then came the development of 1947 and the question of

accession. The position of my State was very different, situated as it was in contiguity to India and Pakistan as also to Afghanistan, Tibet and Russia. The situation therefore required to be dealt with more tact and foresight than in the case of other states. Mahatma Gandhi and the Prime Minister were anxious that I should not make a declaration of Independence and the Prime Minister was anxious to secure the release from prison of Sheikh Abdullah. Having regard to what my Government had done when the Prime Minister visited the State in 1946, Lord Mountbatten chose to visit the State in June 1947 and we had several talks. Lord Mountbatten then urged me and my Prime Minister, Kak, not to make any declaration of Independence but to find out in one way or another, the will of the people of Kashmir as soon as possible and to announce our intention by the 14 August to send representatives accordingly to one Constituent assembly or the other. Lord Mountbatten further told us that the newly created States Department was prepared to give an assurance that if Kashmir went to Pakistan, it would not be regarded as an unfriendly act by the Government of India. Lord Mountbatten stressed the dangerous situation in which Kashmir would find itself if it lacked the support of one of the two Dominions by the date of the transfer of power. The impression which I gathered from my talks with Lord Mountbatten who explained the situation with plans and maps was that, in his opinion, it was advisable for me to accede to Pakistan. I thought that in the circumstances it was advisable to have Standstill Agreements with India and Pakistan and get breathing time to decide which accession would be in the interests of the State. Pakistan very quickly and willingly agreed to a Standstill arrangement, perhaps with mental reservations, as appears from their subsequent conduct. On the other hand, the Government of India did not make up their mind and, if I may be permitted to say so, dealt with the situation in a half-hearted and desultory manner; thus giving an opportunity to Pakistan to do mischief, as they did. This gave rise to misunderstandings on both the sides resulting in dissatisfaction and delay in coming to an understanding. The results have been detrimental to both the State and India. Pakistan became impatient and, having failed to force accession, started with blockading the supplies to the State and ended by invading the State. Lord Mountbatten realizing the uncertain and dangerously unstable position of the State, asked Lord Ismay to approach me and get me to decide on accession without further delay to whichever Dominion I and my people desired. This was at the end of August 1947.

My difficulties were as follows:-

(1) The People of the State were divided in several groups, each group having its own idea about accession;

(2) The Border Feudatory Territories such as Hunza, Nagar and Chitral and the District of Gilgit, where British influence was supreme were definitely for accession to Pakistan and pressing me to accede to Pakistan without delay and threat-ening me with dire consequences if I did not act according to their suggestion;

(3) The Muslim population of the State was also divided into groups with divergent views. Muslims from parts of Jammu such as, Mirpur, Poonch, Muzaffarabad were for accession to Pakistan because of Pakistan propaganda inside the State. Muslims of Kashmir and some Muslims of Jammu who were led by Sheikh Abdullah and the leaders of the National Conference did not want the question of accession to be decided at that stage but wanted me to part with power in their favour so that they could decide the question independently of me. They made no secret of their views and obstructed me in deciding the question of accession instead of helping me to accede to India;

(4) Hindus of Jammu and all the people of Ladakh were for affiliation with or accession to India;

(5) A portion of the population of Kashmir was also for accession to Pakistan.

Thus, there was a sharp division of opinion. The partition aggravated the situation and unhinged and unbalanced the minds of the people with the result that the people of the State were not in a position to give any considered opinion if I chose to consult them.

13. In September 1947, it was suggested to me that it would be a wise move on my part to appoint Shri Meher Chand Mahajan [*sic*] as my Prime Minister as he would be able to handle the affairs of the State in the then critical period firmly and in a statemanlike manner. Before Shri Meher Chand Mahajan [*sic*] took up his appointment

he discussed with Sardar Patel about immediate requirements of the State and Sardar Patel promised him full support and cooperation on behalf of the Government of India. Sardar Patel also wrote to me stating this and adding, that the Government of India fully realized how difficult the situation in the State was and assured me that the Government of India would do their best to help the State in the critical period...I then wrote to Sardar Patel that a little further elucidation of the points of view regarding the essential requirements of the movement would result in a satisfactory solution. Sardar Patel replied on 2 October 1947 that he had a further talk with Shri Mahajan and understood that Shri Mahajan was joining my service very shortly. As by that time I had proclaimed a general amnesty, Sardar Patel expressed his pleasure at the step I had taken and stated that thiswould rally round me the men who might otherwise have been thorn in my side. He also stated that he was expediting as much as possible the linking up of the State with the Indian Dominion. Shri Mahajan then received Sardar Patel's letter of 21 October 1947 in which he said that he had further discussion with Sheikh Abdullah, that Sheikh Abdullah seemed to him genuinely anxious to cooperate and sincerely desirous of assisting the State in dealing with external dangers and the internal troubles with which the State was threatened. He further said that at the same time Sheikh Abdullah, as was natural, felt that unless something was done and done immediately, to strengthen his hands, both in popular eyes and in dealing with the dangers, it would be impossible for him to do anything substantial. He said he felt the position which Sheikh Abdullah took up was understandable and reasonable, that in the mounting demands for the introduction of a Responsible Government in the State, such as was witnessed in Travancore and Mysore, it was impossible for me to isolate myself, that the upsurge was bound to affect me sooner or later, that the Government of India on their part had pledged to give me the maximum support and would do so, but without some measure of popular backing, particularly from amongst the community which represented such an overwhelming majority in Kashmir, it would be difficult to make such support go to the farthest limit that was necessary if the disruptive forces which were being raised and organized, were to be crushed. He advised me in the circumstances to make a substantial gesture to win Sheikh Abdullah's support. He said he had no desire to suggest that I should do so in a manner which would be completely revolutionary in character, that such a step might undermine the loyal and willing support which the Sate had commanded from strong elements of the body politic.

14. Shri Mahajan also received the Prime Minister's letter dated 20 October 1947 in which he referred to the friendliest feelings the Government of India had towards Kashmir and its people and their desire to help to the best of their ability in providing Kashmir with the commodities it needed. He said the Government of India would like to do so for humanitarian reasons as well as because of their deep interest in the future of the people of Jammu and Kashmir State. That the self interest of India also demanded that and that Government of India were strongly of the opinion that no coercion should be exercised on Kashmir and its people and that they should be allowed to function in their own way and to make such decision as they thought fit and proper and that in the furtherance of this policy the Government of India would direct their efforts. The Prime Minister in his letter dated 21 October 1947 to Shri Mahajan said that the future of Kashmir was of the most urgent importance to the Government of India and for him, it was both a personal and a public matter, that it would be a tragedy so far as he was concerned, if Kashmir went to Pakistan. The Prime Minister referred to the urgent need of Pakistan to get Kashmir's accession to Pakistan and that they were threatening every now and then to that end and that everything else that they did was an accessory to the same, that the top ranking leaders of Pakistan were continually approaching the Kashmir National Conference leaders, that they assured to them for their best behaviour and promised them something approaching independence if only they would agree to Kashmir acceding to Pakistan. They were even prepared to give the right of secession. The Prime Minister then suggested the urgency of taking some step like the formation of a Provincial Government and that Sheikh Abdullah, who was obviously the most popular person in Kashmir, might be asked to form such a Government. The Prime Minister further added that in view of all

the circumstances he felt that it would probably be undesirable to make any declaration of adhesion to the Indian Union at that stage, that this should come later when a popular Interim Government was functioning.

15. After the amnesty proclaimed by me, Sheikh Abdullah wrote to me on the 26 September 1947 in which, after referring to his incarceration for about a year and a half, he said as follows:-

In spite of what has happened in the past I assure Your Highness that myself and my Party have never harbored any sentiment of disloyalty towards Your Highness; person, throne or dynasty. The development of this beautiful country and the betterment of its people is our common aim and interest and I assure Your Highness the fullest and loyal support of myself and my organization.

He added:-

In order to achieve the common aim set forth above, mutual trust and confidence must be the main step. Without this it would not be possible to face successfully the great difficulties that upset our State on all sides at present.

He concluded:-

Before I close this letter, I beg to assure Your Highness once again of my steadfast loyalty and pray that God grant me opportunity enough to make this country attain under Your Highness' aegis such an era of peace, prosperity and good Government that it may be second to none and be an ideal for others to copy.

16. I wrote to Lord Mountbatten on the 26th October 1947 informing him of the situation in the State. I received his letter dated 27th October 1947 stating as follows:-

In the special circumstances mentioned by Your Highness my Government have decided to accept the accession of Kashmir State to the Dominion of India x x x

It is my Government's wish that as soon as law and order has been restored in Kashmir and her soil cleared of the invaders the question of the State's accession should be settled by a reference to the people.

My Government and I note with satisfaction that Your Highness has decided to invite Sheikh Abdullah to form an interim Government to work as your Prime Minister.

The Prime Minister also wrote to me on the 26th October 1947 stating as follows:-

Shri V.P. Menon returned from Jammu this morning and informed me of his talks there. He gave me the Instrument of Accession and the Standstill Agreement which you had signed and I saw also your letter to the Governor-General of India. Allow me to congratulate you on the wise decision that you have taken. I earnestly hope that they will lead not only to the effective protection of Kashmir State in the present but also to the freedom and well-being of Kashmir and India as a whole.

I then acceded to India.

17. The Prime Minister in his letter dated 13th November 1947 pointed out to me that the only person who could deliver the goods in Kashmir was Sheikh Abdullah, that he was obviously the leading and popular personality in Kashmir, that the way he had risen to grapple with the crisis had shown the nature of the man, that the Prime Minister had a high opinion of his integrity and general balance of mind and that he was likely to be right in regard to major decisions.

18. Shri Gopallaswami, who was then a Minister without Portfolio, wrote to me on the 9th December 1947 indicating for my consideration his views on the changes which in the critical situation of the State, were immediately called for in the then existing constitutional and administrative set up in the State.

19. A draft of the Proclamation which I was intended to issue, was sent to me by the Government of India. It was seen by Sheikh Abdullah. Sheikh Abdullah also saw the correspondence which had passed between Sardar Patel and myself.

Shri Gopalaswami wrote to me on 1st March 1948 as follows:-

1st March 1948

My Dear Maharaja Sahib,

Messrs V.P. Menon and Mahajan are going to Jammu this afternoon to discuss and finalize with you the draft of the Proclamation which Your Highness has to issue for appointing Abdullah as Prime Minister and others on his advice. The draft has been very carefully considered by myself, Panditji and Sardarji, and we are of the opinion that the whole of it should be accepted by you. Anything less would not satisfy the requirements of the present situation.

2. As a friend of yours, I consider it most important that Your Highness must make a very big gesture in order to rally the maximum percentage of the population of the State behind you with the help of Abdullah. Things are moving very fast and we are yet to fight a great battle at Lake Success. I have already stated during the discussion at Lake Success that Your Highness had only been waiting for Sheikh Abdullah to return from America to convert the Emergency Administration into an Interim Council of Ministers with Abdullah as Prime Minister. I am leaving Delhi for Lake Success the day after tomorrow, and it would be a great strength to the cause I have to plead there on behalf of Kashmir if this Proclamation is issued before I leave. I have not the slightest doubt that the issue of this Proclamation at this juncture, is, in the circumstances that confront us at present, in the best interests of yourself and your people.

3. It is further very important that everything that has happened in the past should be forgotten and forgiven and that Your Highness should take Sheikh Abdullah into your fullest confidence. In fact, I was almost going to suggest that you should give up your usual reserve, come out in the open and put yourself at the head of your people, both Muslims and non-Muslims, for the purpose of consolidating and strengthening the large volume of support for preserving the integrity of the State and maintaining its accession to India, which thanks to Sheikh Abdullah and the Indian Army, you have already behind you.

With kind regards,

Yours sincerely

N. Gopalaswami

Sheikh Abdullah in his letter dated 24th March 1948 stated as follows:-

The situation in the Jammu and Kashmir State is, as you are well aware, a difficult one and requires the utmost careful handling. The emergency continues and has to be dealt with as such till normal conditions are restored. The burden of a Prime Minister in these circumstances will be a heavy one. He cannot function effectively without the fullest cooperation of his colleagues and the people as well as, of course, Your Highness. I have consulted some of my colleagues, who were available and have come to the conclusion that it is my duty in these circumstances to undertake this burden. I trust that in the heavy work ahead I shall have Your Highness' full help and cooperation. I appreciate the spirit in which you have made the offer of the Prime Minister to me and on my part I assure Your Highness that I shall fully reciprocate it.

20. Then came the Proclamation dated 5 March 1948 which was drafted by Shri Gopalaswami and approved by the Government of India and Sheikh Abdullah. It has been referred to in Article 370 of the Constitution of India and the State of Jammu and Kashmir has so far been governed under the constitutional set up for the Proclamation.

21. It is necessary to set out briefly what happened in the State and between Government of India and Sheikh Abdullah in relation to the State after the Proclamation of 5 March 1948 and my leaving the State at the end of April 1949. Sheikh Abdullah and the men of his party took all powers to themselves, ignored my existence and where they felt necessary, they got the consent of the Government of India to do what they liked in the State disregarding me and my wishes. This gradually led to a deterioration and to the outside world, the State and Sheikh Abdullah became convertible terms. The people of Kashmir were utterly ignored and everything that Sheikh Abdullah desired to do was done in the name of the State with the express or tacit consent of the Government of India. At this juncture on a suggestion from Sardar Patel, I and my wife began a tour of the State. This did not suit the books of Sheikh Abdullah. He approached the Government of India with the result that I was asked to stay out of the State for a few months. I accepted the advice of Sardar Patel and agreed to stay out. The Yuvraj was appointed Regent. It need hardly be pointed out that the Yuvraj became a figurehead and had to take orders from Sheikh Abdullah. In this connection it may also be pointed out that although my Proclamation of 5th March 1948 was based on the Mysore Constitution, which

stipulated the appointment of a Dewan and reserved subjects yet gradually Sheikh Abdullah succeeded in getting the approval of the Government of India to making changes in the Constitution of the State, so as to make it very different from what it was expressly intended to be. The mischief began with Sheikh Abdullah going direct to the Government of India on certain points over my head and the Government of India countenancing him and giving the desired directions and then informing me of what they had done at the instance of Sheikh Abdullah. The correspondence on the subject and the events following on each change bear testimony to what Sheikh Abdullah was trying to achieve in breach of the solemn promises and assurances given by him and also by the Government of India on his behalf. After my leaving the State things went from bad to worse. Sheikh Abdullah was not satisfied with what he had achieved and aspired to absolute control of the State. He became openly inimical and hostile to me. He even interfered with my private properties and personal belongings, issued orders to humiliate me and even interfered with the administration of the Dharmartha Trust, a Trust created by my forefathers of which I am the Trustee and which is being administered from day to day by the President of the Dharamarth Council appointed by me. The charities and institutions maintained from the revenues of the Trust are starved. Even the routine expenses of the Trust, such as, for Puja in temples and Devasthans cannot be met because it pleases Sheikh Abdullah to prevent the income of the Trust coming to my hands or to the hands of President of the Dharamarth Council. The Jammu branch of the Imperial Bank of India refused to pay even to me the amounts of the fixed deposits of the Trust and also refused to transfer such deposits to the Bombay Office of the Imperial Bank of India with the result that I had to renew the deposits to avoid loss of interest to the Trust. It would be interesting to know under whose order the Jammu branch of the Bank acted in the manner it did. As will be apparent from my correspondence with the States Ministry my complaints as regards both my personal properties and the Dharamarth Trust have been galore and none of them has been remedied either by Sheikh Abdullah or by the States Ministry. Leaving aside for the moment my grievance as regards what is being done with reference to my personal properties in Jammu and Kashmir, how can Sheikh Abdullah's attitude towards the administration of the Dharamarth Trust be reconciled with secularism and impartiality?

22. I may now refer to Mr V.P. Menon's letter to Shri Mahajan dated 30 January 1948 in which he stated as follows:-

As I told you, I have already contradicted the news that the Maharaja fled from Srinagar to Jammu. I propose to take up this question with Ministry of Information and have asked Sharma, our Publicity Co-ordination Officer, to get into touch with foreign correspondents and give them the correct picture. I hope, this canard will stop once for all.

This gives a direct lie to the report set afloat both inside and outside the State by Sheikh Abdullah and his party that I had run away from my State in October 1947 leaving the State in chaos and people at the tender mercies of the invaders. It appears that the Prime Minister was deliberately misinformed as to what I then did and he was also misinformed that my officers had deserted their posts and runaway. In third week of October 1947 Lord Mountbatten was of opinion that it would be dangerous to send any Indian troops to the help of the State unless the State first offered to accede particularly as such accession would be temporary being prior to a plebiscite. No final decision was, however, taken on these vital questions by 25th October 1947 but Mr V.P. Menon was asked to fly to Srinagar to find out the true position there. He met me at Srinagar and I made him realize the urgency of the situation and that unless India helped immediately, all would be lost. It was then that on the strong advice of Mr V.P. Menon who said it would be foolhardy for me to stay in Srinagar when raiders were as near as Baramulla then, I left Srinagar with my wife and son. I also ignored the Letter of Accession which Mr V.P. Menon took back with him.

None of my officers fled. The families of some of the officers left for Jammu as the Government used to move to Jammu at the end of October and open at Jammu on the first Monday in November.

On the other hand, it was Sheikh Abdullah who fled from Srinagar and did not return till the Indian troops had started coming into Srinagar.

23. Regarding my leaving the State, I may refer to my letter dated the May 1949 to Sardar Patel and Sardar Patel's letter to me dated 23rd May 1949. I may also refer to my letter dated 1st June 1949 to Sardar Patel and Sardar Patel's letter dated 9th June 1949 to me. I attach herewith copies of the letters. In June, 1949 I issued a Proclamation appointing the Yuvraj as my Regent during my stay outside the State.

24. This was in compliance with the wishes of the Government of India.

25. In November 1950 I received from Mr Vishnu Sahay his letter dated 30th November 1950 wherein he drew my attention to the resolution passed by the Council of the National Conference asking that a Constituent Assembly be set for the State and to my Proclamation of 5th March 1948 wherein the setting up of such an Assembly was foreshadowed and stated that it appeared to the States Ministry that the time had come to reduce the uncertainty in Kashmir by going ahead with this proposal. He sent a draft Proclamation to set up the Constituent Assembly, for my comments. I took exception to the proposed manner and method of setting up the Constituent Assembly. I summarized my objection to it as follows:-

(1) That the Proclamation with the object and spirit of which I wholeheartedly agree be issued by me as Ruler who is the properly constituted authority in law to promulgate it and not by my Regent;

(2) The powers and functions of the body intended to be constituted should be express, well defined and accurately worded and should exclude from the purview of their enquiry and consideration matters not expressly entrusted to them;

(3) They should report to the authority that constitutes it, i.e., the Ruler who shall seek the advice of the Parliament of India in the matter. I refer to the correspondence that took place, the interview which Mr Menon had with me in Bombay in February 1951 under the instructions of the Prime Minister and the subsequent negotiations which ended with my giving consent to the Yuvraj for setting up the Constituent Assembly. I also refer to the assurance given to me by the Minister of States (Shri N. Gopalaswami Ayyangar) in the course of the negotiations

as to the position of myself and my dynasty and other important matters. I am constrained to refer to the relevant portions of his letter which, I quote below.

5 April 1951

x x x

Developments have, however, since taken place both in the State and Lake Success which make it imperative that the issue of this proclamation is not delayed any longer. The Government of India are committed to the convening of a Constituent Assembly, the preparations for which are in active progress in the State. That Assembly will be held whether the formal Proclamation issues or not. In the view of the Government of India it must be convened, if both their commitments to the people of Kashmir and their stand at Lake Success are to be implemented in spirit and in the letter. From the beginning they have held that this Constituent Assembly should be called under the provisions of the Constitution of India and that this should be done from both a tactical and constitutional point of view, on the authority of Proclamation issued by the Head of the State. The draft of the Proclamation has been agreed between the Government of India and the Government of Jammu and Kashmir. No purpose will, therefore, be served by any act of Your Highness which holds up the signing and issue of this Proclamation by Shri Yuvraj.

On neither of the two matters about which I can understand your entertaining apprehensions, namely, the continuance of the accession of the Jammu and Kashmir State or of part thereof to India and the connection of the Headship of the State with your dynasty, no final decision could be taken by the Constituent Assembly to be convened. They are essentially matters which could be decided only as a matter of agreement between the Government of India and the Parliament on the one side and the Government of Jammu and Kashmir and the State Constituent Assembly or Legislature on the other. The Government of India will, no doubt at the proper time take the decision on these matters, which, I need hardly assure you, will be essentially just from the standpoint both of your dynasty and the people of the State. You have obviously to put your trust in the people of the State and the Government of India in respect of this matter. I hope, therefore, you will immediately lift the ban which you have placed on Shri Yuvraj affixing his signature to the agreed Proclamation and which naturally placed him in great embarrassment.

26. Apprehending what was coming and in order not to embarrass the Government of India and the Yuvraj, I have been prepared to abdicate provided that a satisfactory arrangement was to come with me by the States Ministry and provided also that the Yuvraj's position as the Head of the State was assured. The negotiations in this behalf which were carried on with Shri Gopalaswami as the States Minister was left in an indecisive state because of Shri Gopalaswami having been succeeded as the States Minister by Dr K.N. Katju.

Having regard to the trend of events I wrote to Dr Katju on the 29th June 1952. I waited for Dr Katju's reply as foreshadowed in the Prime Minister's letter. I then received Dr Katju's reply dated 30th July 1952. I replied to Dr Katju by my letter dated 8th August 1952. In enclose copies of these letters as they have an important bearing on the situation.

27. These letters speak for themselves. Dr Katju's reply is not a reply at all. The legal position, it appears to me, has not been considered and it further appears that it is being taken for granted by the Prime Minister and Dr Katju that the relevant Articles, particularly Article 370, of the Constitution of India can be altered and/or amended to suit the present attitude of Sheikh Abdullah. It would not be out of place to point out that Article 370 refers specifically to my Proclamation of 5th March 1948. That is the law which governs the State of Jammu and Kashmir until a new Constitution is framed, approved and adopted not only by the Constituent Assembly of the State but also approved by me and then by you and yet, I learn that the Prime Minister has asked the Yuvraj (who is acting only as my Regent and represents me) to agree to be the elected Head of the State forthwith, that is to say, even before the Constitution of the State is framed much less approved and adopted thus throwing over not only me but also the dynasty. I do not know what reply Dr Katju proposes to make to me but it

appears that the Prime Minister is dealing with the matter. (vide his letter dated 5th July 1952). I have, therefore to specifically deal with the charges made in the Prime Minister's letter.

28. The Prime Minister in para 4 of his letter refers to the Constitution of India as having been based on and derived from the people of India and says with regard to the Jammu and Kashmir State that the Government of India felt that the people would prefer accession to India but the matter was delicate and not beyond dispute and therefore, the Government of India did not press for the accession of Jammu and Kashmir State but suggested that the matter should be considered at a later stage when the people's wishes could be ascertained in some form or the other and the suggestion was that some kind of a Constituent Assembly might be set up in the State to decide the question of accession as well as other questions. I grant all this but how can the Government of India take all these steps over my head on whose authority they entered the State and are continuing there and who was the Chief Author of the Proclamation on which is based the future construction of political set up in the country? In para 5, the Prime Minister says that on the invasion of the State by tribal raiders and others in late October 1947 the crisis arose and at that time I left Srinagar at the dead of night for Jammu and many of my officers followed me and the State was left without leadership or means of defence in so far as official authority was concerned. This is in fact, untrue as pointed out above. I left Srinagar for Jammu on the advice of the Government of India conveyed to me through Mr. Menon. The Prime Minister says further that in basic picture of the crisis of Kashmir I do not come in at all. The statement amounts to *suppresio veri* and *suggestio falsi*. I have acted all throughout from September 1947 under the advice of the Government of India, Lord Mountbatten, the Prime Minister, Sardar Vallabhbhai Patel and Shri Gopalaswami and, as pointed out herein above, Sheikh Abdullah himself made promises and gave assurances, which he is now backing out of. Even in the book called, New Kashmir published by the Kashmir Information Bureau, New Delhi, in 1950 and which is the political Bible of Sheikh Abdullah, Sheikh Abdullah has based his case for a Responsible Government in the State under the aegis

of the Maharaja and even gone on to the length of setting out what functions the Maharaja was to perform. The Prime Minister in his letter says that the people of Kashmir must decide their own future. I may well ask whether Sheikh Abdullah is a synonymous term with the people of Kashmir. The people of Kashmir have not been consulted. According to Sheikh Abdullah, the people of Kashmir have changed their mind to such an extent that they are determined to get rid of the idea of a hereditary ruler of the State. The Constituent Assembly has been packed with Sheikh Abdullah's men and even that Assembly has not yet come to a decision nor has it framed and constitution providing for the functions of the Head of the State either hereditary or elected and what one would like to know is where is the reason for this frightful hurry to elect the Head of the State thus doing away with me and my dynasty before the Constitution is framed and before the fate of the State is determined in the fight that is raging before the UNO between India and Pakistan. Are myself and my dynasty to be pawns in the game which Sheikh Abdullah is playing with the Government of India on the representation that he is actively helping India in the case before the U.N. Security Council. The Prime Minister says that he has seen no evidence of any sympathy on my part for the people of Kashmir who have gone through fire and suffering during the past four and a half years. May I ask who is responsible for this state of affairs? Have the Government of India given any choice of action to me during the last four and a half years? Have they at any time pulled up Sheikh Abdullah knowing as they did, on what promises and assurances Sheikh Abdullah became the Prime Minister? May I again point out that even before I left the State under the advice of Sardar Patel, I and my wife had started on a tour of the State as Sardar Patel had told me that I should see more of my people and that they should see more of me. Sheikh Abdullah did not like this tour and approached the Government of India with the result that I was called at Delhi and asked to desist from returning to the State and finally to leave it. The Prime Minister says at the end of this letter that the only assurance he can give to me is that the first place will be given always to the right of the people and to the wishes of the people and that if I fall in with those rights and wishes, the Government of India will endeavour to help me to the best of their ability. I am prepared to take up the challenge. Let the people of Jammu and Kashmir freely decide between me and Sheikh Abdullah without interference from the Government of India. Let me point out what has been happening. The world has been given to understand that the march of events, the changed political values have brought about rapid and inevitable changes and we must accept them no matter what the obligation of the Government of India, Government of Jammu and Kashmir, the assurance of both the Governments to me and their duties under certain legal and constitutional arrangements may be. With all due deference to this opinion, I must say that I emphatically challenge the contention that whatever has happened is in accordance with the will of the people and that the sovereignty has effectively and really passed to the people as it should and that they are consciously exercising their will and ask for changes which are being brought about by an oligarchy backed by Government of India. I cannot conscientiously recognize the changes in the Proclamation of 5th March 1948 which governs the relations of the State with India. But if the Government of India and you, Sir, feel that in the present stage of negotiations with Dr Graham it would be inconvenient for the Government of India to allow this matter to be raked up, then at least, the Government of India should not succumb entirely to the wishes of Sheikh Abdullah but hold the balance equally between him and me and at least preserve the status quo as regards the headship of the State until the field is clear for the necessary steps to be taken to determine the will of the people of Kashmir...

29. Copies of the following documents are attached for your ready reference:-

(1) Note given to the Prime Minister of Kashmir by Prime Minister of India on 26th October 1947;

(2) Letter dated 26th October 1947 from the Prime Minister of India to the Prime Minister of Kashmir;

(3) Letter dated 27th October 1947 from the Prime Minister of India to the Prime Minister of Kashmir;

(4) Letter dated 27th October 1947 from the Prime Minister of India to me;

(5) Letter dated 26th October 1947 from me to Lord Mountbatten;

(6) Letter dated 27th October 1947 from Lord Mountbatten to me;

(7) Letter dated 24th December 1947 from Shri N. Gopalaswami to me.

30. Secure in the knowledge that I was out of the picture and could not reply I was, be a series of false statements and speeches intended to humiliate and malign me, painted black and unpatriotic. The Government of India who had assured me that I would be protected against such onslaughts remained an unconcerned spectator. Not only that, it is most distressing to know and feel that whenever Sheikh Abdullah and his party talked of me in disparaging and spiteful terms, the highest authority in the Government of India immediately endorsed it. If Sheikh Abdullah said I could not return to the State, the Prime Minister with all the authority, prestige and might at his back, endorsed it. If Sheikh Abdullah said I had lost the confidence of the people the Prime Minister referred to my alleged wrong-headed and mistaken policies, without saying exactly what they were and said the people had suffered on account of these. This no doubt had the effect of suppressing what is said to be the will of the people. Being placed as I was, I was absolutely unable to answer any of these accusations. I feel grievously wronged in that the Government of India whom I looked up to as the ultimate authority I could go to for redress, instead of stopping such malicious and false propaganda, not only went on countenancing it but endorsing it disregarding their solemn assurances.

Having eliminated me in a manner which had neither the sanction of law nor political morality, it was the duty of the Government of India to protect me. But that was not done and the matter did not end there. My properties and privileges etc., were attempted to be interfered with, I protested and asked for redress but never got it.

As I have said above, I was eliminated by a process which was neither fair nor honourable. It was not and it has never been due to the will of the people. It was entirely to the machinations of Sheikh Abdullah and his party. They got themselves appointed on the definite assurances and later, with the connivance of the Government of India, systematically ignored all their legal and moral obligations and ultimately without rhyme and reason but to suit the books of Sheikh Abdullah successfully got me out of the State. Taking advantage of my absence and helplessness, started a campaign of vilification and harassment and thus created conditions wherein they could tell an unknowing world that they were doing what the people desired. I have taken the responsibility of making these statements and I earnestly request you, Sir, to ascertain the views of your Government about them and then come to an independent opinion as to whether I have not been seriously wronged and to redress the wrong.

31. I may be permitted to summarize the position:-

(1) The Government of the State of Jammu and Kashmir was more advanced and enlightened than that of any other India State in the pre-Partition days;

(2) I employed men of undoubted ability and standing to be my Ministers from time to time;

(3) In August 1947 Lord Mountbatten gave me the impression that I should accede to Pakistan, Government of India was undecided about the matter, wanted every step by me endorsed by Sheikh Abdullah, the people of Jammu and Kashmir were divided in their opinion and I decided to enter into Standstill Agreement with both India and Pakistan in order to have time for things to settle down;

(4) Pakistan did not act up to the Standstill Agreements, blocked supplies to the State and aided and abetted the raiders;

(5) I released Sheikh Abdullah as advised by Sardar Patel and relied on the assurance given by Sheikh Abdullah backed by the assurances given by the Government of India;

(6) I took Sheikh Abdullah in my Government;

(7) I issued the Proclamation on 5 March 1948;

(8) Sheikh Abdullah with the connivance of the Government of India started tinkering with the Constitution of 5 March 1948;

(9) Sheikh Abdullah persuaded the Government of India to drive me out of the State;

(10) I left the State and appointed the Yuvraj, my Regent;

(11) My rights of personal property and the affairs of Dharmarth Trust were interfered with by Sheikh Abdullah;

(12) Sheikh Abdullah by maligning me created an impression that the people of Kashmir were against me;

(13) The Constituent Assembly was set up;

(14) The will of the people of Jammu and Kashmir is now judged by the whims and caprices of Sheikh Abdullah;

(15) Sheikh Abdullah having made up his mind to get rid of the Ruler and his dynasty, persuaded the Government of India to see eye to eye with him and to lay down that this could be done even before the new Constitution was framed much less approved by you on behalf of India;

(16) I get no redress and am told that I am in the wrong, the will of the people is all that counts and I must abide by such will;

(17) The Press carries reports from day to day creating feelings against me. False reports are not contradicted;

(18) The Prime Minister got angry as evidenced by his letter dated 5th July 1952 because I stated facts;

(19) The States Minister avoids giving a proper reply to me and yet the Press says I have been asked and have not replied;

(20) The Yuvraj is being coerced by the Prime Minister and Sheikh Abdullah to accede to their suggestions.

32. Finally, I have to say that I had my range of controversy with Sheikh Abdullah and Prime Minister and I am bitter about the fact that the Government of India have been unable to afford me protection and safeguard m rights in spite of the fact that throughout these four and a half years, I have given full cooperation and the fact that my pre-1947 conduct did not compare unfavourably with that of the other Rulers who at present enjoy Government of India's protection and favour. During the last three years of my enforced absence from the State I have given them no cause for grievance and at the most, I have been charged with delay in permitting the Yuvraj to take action which having regard to the consideration involved and my better experience, was natural and understandable. Even in this matter ultimately I did fall in line with the Government of India. If the result of all this in the final stage has again to be a betrayal by the Government of India of their assurances and

promises etc. and is to result not only in my final removal from the State but also of the sacrifice of the Yuvraj whom I had entrusted to the Government of India's protection. I can only say that it would be an ill return for the faith which I and the Yuvraj placed in the Government and the help and cooperation to the extent of self effacement that we rendered to it. Only history and posterity will be able to do justice to our respective points of view.

33. In these circumstances, I appeal to you to consider the matter impartially in all its aspects with all your sagacity and wisdom and guide me as to what would be in the best interests of the State.

I remain,
Yours faithfully,
Hari Singh

Appendix 6

From, *Hari Singh, The Maharaja, The Man, The Times: A Biography of Maharaja Hari Singh of Jammu and Kashmir State* by Somnath Wakhlu

Proclamation of Maharaja Hari Singh, July 9, 1931

To My Beloved People

From time immemorial, all communities within the State have been living on terms of closest harmony and friendship with each other and I used to take the greatest pride in the fact that we were happily free from all communal strife. I am, therefore, greatly pained to see that quite recently, owing to external influences, a changed and regrettable attitude is observable in certain sections in cities of Jammu and Srinagar. This is greatly to be deplored. Two unfortunate incidents occurred recently in Jammu city, which could not, by any stretch of imagination, be associated with any action or policy of my Government and for which the responsibility widely misrepresented inside and outside the State so as to convey to those who were not in a position to know the true facts that the policy of my Government is such that Islam is in danger. It is not my intention to deal with the details of these incidents in the message as they are being dealt with separately. So far I have preferred that my Government be judged by its actions alone. But, numerous representation from my loyal subjects of all sects and creeds have reached me within the last few days to the effect that even though at present it finds no response, it is calculated to promote communal strife and might lead to the breach of the public peace in some cases. It has accordingly been deemed necessary to make this formal announcement of policy and intention of myself and my Government in regard to such propaganda and communal relations within the State generally.

At the beginning of my rule, I announced to you my people, that my religion is justice. That announcement has guided all my public acts and policies and I shall always adhere to it. I have made up my mind and will not permit any discrimination against any class of my people on grounds of religion. The humblest of my subjects have free and direct access to me and any grievances my people may have can be submitted by them to me personally. Subject to two fundamental conditions, *viz*

(i) that political activities are confined within the law of the land, and

(ii) that no outside intervention is sought in any shape and form.

I have no desire whatsoever to suppress the legitimate requests and voice of my people whether expressed in writing or in speech. It is my intention to give effect to these views, but I am unable to do, so long as communal tension exists, for fear of aggravating it. Consequently, the first essential thing is that the leaders of various communities should take immediate action to put a stop to all political activities tending to prevent the re-establishment of friendly relations between them. As soon as it is reported to me that any community has faithfully responded to my desire, I shall be prepared to receive and consider most sympathetically any representation that community may desire to submit to me.

Every person with the State is, and shall always be, free to practice his own religion, subject to the paramount necessity of maintaining public peace and public order. I, particularly wish to refer in this connection to a malicious rumour now being spread that cow killing is shortly going to be permitted. And, it has given me great pleasure to receive from my Muslim subjects' spontaneous condemnation of such an insinuation or any other insinuation likely to injure the religious susceptibilities of any other community. There is no question of making any change in the matter.

In regard to the recruitment to the State services, prior consideration is and shall be given to the public interest and the obligation of maintaining the efficiency of the administration at the highest possible level can never be overlooked. There is also no desire to follow the blind rule of parentage for various communities irrespective of qualification and merit. Subject to these conditions, the policy governing recruitment will be such that no class or community should gain undue predominance in any branch of the public service and that adequate responsibility is secured to duly qualified [*sic*] hereditary State Subjects from all classes and communities of my people. Instructions to this effect have recently been issued and I shall watch closely their practical execution by my officers.

I have dealt in a brief manner with what I conceive to be points of major importance with regard to which some misunderstanding prevails in certain quarters. I trust such misunderstanding will be dispelled by the authorities, enunciation of my beliefs and intentions in consonance with these views in your best interests. Whenever I have found that any of you have been led into wrong action, I have always tried to make you see the error of your ways and to win you over the right path by reasoning and conciliation. I am not a believer in false ideas or prestige, for I hold just action a sign of strength and not of weakness. But should, God forbid, all appeal to reason fail, I must discharge in effective manner the supreme responsibility which rests on me for the maintenance of law and order. I cannot allow my Government to be coerced by threat into unjust action and it is my duty to protect the law abiding sections of my people from encroachment on their lawful rights. The immediate burden of maintaining law and order necessarily falls on the Magistracy and the Police whose duty it will be to see that law is upheld at all costs, and where the law is defied, its authority will be restored. It is the duty of the Police to act impartially and with calm judgement in such emergencies and I wish to assure them that they will be supported by myself and my Government in the due discharge of their duty and will not be sacrificed to unjust clamour or intrigue.

In conclusion, I trust that the old policy of 'live and let live', which characterized your relations with each other in the past, will be restored. It is easy to excite public feeling by misrepresentation, but it is difficult to restore harmony and friendship. Do not attribute false motives to those placed in authority over you or to one another. As regards people outside the State, whether Hindus or Mohammedans, I ask them not to interfere in any way in matters concerning my State and my people, as I do not interfere in matters concerning British India and British Indians. The whole basis of political action is impaired if one political unit interferes in the domestic concern of another. I do not wish to claim immunity from legitimate criticism of the acts and policies of my Government, which I have no hesitation in saying, have always been designed to promote the moral and material progress of my people. It is my duty and my one aim in life to maintain the progressive character of my administration. But this end is defeated by unjustifiable outside intervention which has, within the last weeks, done nothing but immense harm to the true interests of you all. I pray to God that you will receive the light of truth and wisdom and that you will live peacefully and happily with one another as before.

Sd/- Hari Singh, G.C.I.E.,
K.C.V.O., A.D.C.
Maharaja of Jammu and Kashmir

Appendix 7

The Round Table Conference

India's Demand For Dominion Status

Speeches by the King, the Premier, the British Party Leaders and the Representatives of the Princes and the People of India

G.A. Ganesan & Co.
Madras

The Maharaja Of Kashmir

The Maharaja of Kashmir expressed deep gratitude for His Majesty's cordial welcome and prayed Providence to grant them the vision and will to realize the hopes expressed in the inspiring words of their beloved King Emperor. He drew attention to the unprecedented nature of the gathering and continued:- 'Allied by treaty with the British Crown, and within our territories independent rulers, we have come with a full sense of the responsibility to our states and all India. As allies of Britain we stand solidly by the British connection. As Indians and loyal to the land of our birth, we stand as solidly as the rest of our countrymen for our lands the enjoyment of a position of honour and equality in the British Commonwealth. Our desire to cooperate to the best of our ability with all sections of the Conference is genuine as also is our determination to base our cooperation upon the realities of the present situation. Neither England nor India can afford to see this Conference end in failure. We must resolve to succeed. The difficulties shall not be insuperable. We must exercise patience, tact and forbearance and be inspired by mutual understanding and goodwill. We must give and take. If we succeed, England no less than India gains. If we fail India no less than England loses. The task is gigantic. In the case of no people would such aim as ours be easy to accomplish. In the case of India, the complexity of the factors is unique, but, by the grace of God, with goodwill and sympathy on both sides the difficulties shall be surmounted and with the words of the King-Emperor still ringing in our ears we Princes affirm that the Conference shall not fail through any fault of ours.

Notes

Introduction

1 *Kashmir: A Disputed Legacy 1846-1990*, Oxford University Press, 1991, pp. 8.

2 Cited in *The Jammu Fox: A Biography of Maharaja Gulab Singh of Kashmir, 1792-1857*. From 'Tibet in Anglo-Chinese Relations: 1767-1842', *Journal of the Royal Asiatic Society of Great Britain and Ireland*, Cambridge University Press, 1957. pp. 38-40.

3 Article 1 of the Treaty of Amritsar read: 'The British Government transfers and makes over, for ever, in independent possession, to Maharaja Gulab Singh, and the male heirs of his body, all the hilly or mountainous country, with its dependencies situated to the east ward of the river Indus, and westward of river Ravi, including Chamba and excluding Lahul, being part of the territory ceded to the British Government by the Lahore State, according to the provisions of Article 4 of the Treaty of Lahore, Dated 9th March, 1846.

4 Article 4 of the Lahore Treaty of 9th March 1846read: 'The British Government having demanded from the Lahore State, as indemnification for the expenses of the war, in addition to the cession of the territory described in Article 3, payment of one and a half crores of rupees, and the Lahore Government being unable to pay the whole of this sum at that time, or to give security satisfactory to the British Government for its eventual payment; the Maharaja cedes to the Honourable Company, in perpetual sovereignty, as equivalent for one crore rupees, all his forts, territories, rights and interests, in the hill countries which are situated between the rivers Beas and Indus, including the provinces of Kashmir and Hazara.' In addition to this Article, the Article 12 of the said Treaty mentioned: 'In consideration of the services rendered by Raja Golab Singh [*sic*] of Jammu to Lahore State, towards procuring the restoration of relations of amity between

the Lahore and British Governments, the Maharaja [of Lahore] hereby agrees to recognize the independent sovereignty of Raja Golab Singh [*sic*], in such territories and districts in the hills as may be made over to the said Raja Golab Singh [*sic*] by separate agreement between himself and the British Government, with the dependencies thereof, which may have been in the Raja's possession since the times of Maharaja Kharak Singh; and the British Government, in consideration of the good conduct of Raja Golab Singh [*sic*], also agrees to recognize his independence in such territories, and admit him to the privileges of a separate treaty with the British Government.' The Treaty of Amritsar of 16th March 1846 was thus born out of the Article 12 of the Lahore Treaty of 9th March of 1846.

5 *The Jammu Fox,* Southern Illinois University Press, 1974, pp. 24-25.

6 *History of Jammu and Kashmir Rifles, 1820-1956,* Lancer International, 1990, pp. 286-289.

7 *Ladakh and Western Himalayan Politics, 1819-1848,* Munshiram Manoharlal Publishers, 1973, pp. 81.

8 Ibid. pp. 94.

1. Seeds of Flowers and Weeds

9 *The Valley of Kashmir*, Henry Frowde, Oxford University Press, 1895.

10 Ibid, pp. 4.

11 It is a day's unpaid labour owed by a vassal to his feudal lord or in lieu of unpaid taxes.

12 In the era gone by, it was the right of the sovereign to buy provisions and use horses and vehicles for a fixed price lower than the market value.

13 Op cit, *The Valley of Kashmir*, pp. 4.

14 Ibid, pp. 4.

15 *Political Conspiracies of Kashmir,* Light & Life Publishers, 1973, pp. 20.

16 *Indian Summer: The Secret History of the End of an Empire,* Simon & Schuster, 2007, pp. 215. From *The Lost Dominion*, William Blackwood and Sons, 1924, pp. 27.

17 Op cit, *Indian Summer*, pp. 215.

18 Ibid, pp. 16.

19 Ibid, pp. 17.

20 Ibid, pp. 17.

21 *The Round Table Conference*, G.A. Natesan and Company, 1931.

2. The British Web

22 *Song Sung True*, Kali for Women, 2003.

23 *Political Conspiracies of Kashmir*, Light & Life Publishers, 1973, p. 20.

24 Ostensibly formed by the newly educated Muslims to inculcate reading habits among young Muslims. However, it soon became the hotbed of communal forces.

25 It is ironical that the National Conference, the political party that gathered a rich harvest from the fallout of the incident went on to observe the day, on which twenty-one Kashmiris lost their lives in firing by security forces, as Martyrs Day, yet it did little to perpetuate the memory of Abdul Qadir, the person who was at the heart of that momentous event. He had disappeared as mysteriously as he had appeared on the scene.

26 *Kashmir: A Disputed Legacy 1846-1990*, Oxford University Press, 1991, pp. 86. The Ahamadiya movement was founded in about 1879 by Mirza Ghulam Ahmad, who lived in Qadian in the Punjab, and died in 1908. Its doctrines were, in Islamic terms, extremely unorthodox; and, in that the Ahamadiyas have been deemed to have cast doubts on the uniqueness of the Prophethood of Mohammad. Many Muslims consider the followers of the sect to be either heretical or, indeed, not Muslims at all.

27 The Jammu and Kashmir Muslim Conference was co-founded by Sheikh Mohammad Abdullah from Kashmir and Chaudhary Ghulam Abbas from Jammu in 1932. However, as Sheikh Abdullah desired to broaden the base of the party by opening it up to other communities, differences arose between the two and in 1939 Sheikh Abdullah parted ways to found All Jammu and Kashmir National Conference.

28 Op cit, *Kashmir: A Disputed Legacy*, pp. 86. In 1924 Mirza Kamal-ud-Din head of the Ahamadiyas visited Kashmir. While Mirwaiz Ahmed Ullah Shah, the religious leader of the day, dismissed him as an unbeliever, the second-most-important Muslim divine in Srinagar, the Mirwaiz Hamadani of Khanqah-i-Mualla (the shrine sacred to the memory of Mir Syed Ali Hamadani, the saint who had arrived from Persia and had done so much to establish Islam in the valley of Kashmir in fourteenth century) gave the Ahmadiya leader permission to hold a public meeting in the building of which he had charge.

29 These killings have remained a contentious issue between the National Conference, under whose leadership, it came to be observed as the Martyrs Day. The Dogras of Jammu have always contended that the

unfortunate incident was a result of a conspiracy. In 2020, after the State was downgraded and bifurcated as the two Union Territories of Jammu and Kashmir and Ladakh, the commemoration of the day as Martyrs Day was stopped. It is too early to say if this has ironed out the fault line between Kashmir and Jammu.

30 The famine and the circumstances leading to it have been described in detail by Walter Lawrence in *The Valley of Kashmir*. Walter Lawrence had been entrusted with the task of preparing a report on the lines of the Punjab Gazetteers for Revenue Settlement that led to large scale reforms and modernization of administration.

31 Op cit, *Song Sung True*, pp. 93; *Jammu*, Manas Publications, 2004.

32 Ibid.

33 Justice T.S. Thakur's speech during a function, *Discource on Maharaja Hari Singh Aur Kashmir*, YouTube, 2017. (youtube.com/watch?v=yWAJgHuKXac&t=37s, last accessed 16 March 2023).

34 Many modern historians, like Ramachandra Guha, have based their understanding on the information provided by anti-Indian historian Alastair Lamb's *Kashmir: A Disputed Legacy, 1846-1990* and commentator Ajit Bhattacharjea's work *Kashmir: The Wounded Valley,* which have distorted the events of 1931 and its aftermath. Guha sums up the events in the following words: 'In the summer of 1931 Abdullah was chosen as part of a delegation of Muslims that hoped to place their case before the Maharaja. Before they could meet with him, an activist named Abdul Qadir was arrested and put on trial. This led to a clash between protesters and the police in which 21 people died. This was followed by a wave of communal violence in the Valley, in which many Hindu shops were looted and burnt.'—*India After Gandhi* by Ramachandra Guha, pp. 61. None of these assertions were found to have any basis by the Glancy Commission Report 1932.

35 The legendary poet, Mohammad Iqbal was of Kashmiri descent whose family had migrated to Sialkot in Western Punjab. His cultural and political views and commitment to the wellbeing of Muslims was to become the impulse for the demand for Pakistan. He is considered to be the spiritual father of Pakistani nation.

36 Mirza Bashir Ahmad was the son of Mirza Ghulam Ahmad, the founder of the Ahamadiya sect, declared as un-Islamic by Pakistan.

37 Mirwaiz Mohammad Yusuf Shah was one of the two Mirwaiz's of Kashmir, who traditionally held great influence among the people. He, along with Sheikh Abdullah and Chaudhary Ghulam Abbas, had founded the All-Jammu and Kashmir Muslim Conference. But after

breaking away from Sheikh Abdullah, he forged an alliance with the Muslim League and soon became one of the founders of modern Islamic politics in Kashmir. He supported the accession of Kashmir to Pakistan and opted to flee from Srinagar to PoJK. Later, he became 'President' of that part PoJK in 1952 and 1956.

38 *Political Conspiracies of Kashmir,* Light & Life Publishers, 1973, pp. 33. The part played by Mr Wakefield in encouraging the agitation was also highlighted by many other witnesses before the Glancy Enquiry Commission.

39 Ibid, pp. 20. *Begar,* a Persian word, was a system of forced labour practiced in pre-independence India. In this members of populace were compelled to perform unpaid work for the government. In the Maratha Confederacy, *Veth*—the Sanskrit origin word for *begar*—was practised on a wide scale during the Peshwa's rule. Certain groups of high caste people were exempted. The system continued to be practiced in the princely states during the British Raj.

40 *Kashmir: The Wounded Valley,* USB Publishers' Distributors, 1994, pp. 67

3. The Dream of Naya Kashmir

41 'Commission appointed under the Orders of His Highness the Maharaja Bahadur, dated 12th November, 1931, to enquire into GRIEVANCES AND COMPLAINTS (Unpublished Report)', quoted from *Constitution of Jammu & Kashmir,* Universal Book Traders, 1994, pp. 35.

42 *Ibid,* pp. 37.

43 *Political Conspiracies of Kashmir,* Light & Life Publishers, 1973, pp. 150.

44 *Census of India, 1941: Volume XXII,* Office of the Commissioner of Census, 1943, pp. 5.

45 Op cit, *Constitution of Jammu & Kashmir,* pp. 38. From *Keesing's Contemporary Archives (1931),* Keesing Limited, 1931, pp. 127.

46 Op cit, *Constitution of Jammu & Kashmir,* pp. 39.

47 *Understanding Kashmir and Kashmiris,* C. Hurst & Co. (Publishers) Ltd, 2015 and *Kashmir: The Unwritten History,* HarperCollins Publishers India, 2013, pp. 242.

48 *Kashmir: A Disputed Legacy, 1846-1990,* Oxford University Press, 1991, pp. 87. Lamb noted that though the Kashmiri-Muslim community was introduced to the name of Mahatma Gandhi because of the

Khilafat movement, it made no significant impact on the local Pandit community, despite the role played in it in British India by Kashmiris like Sir Tej Bahadur Sapru and Motilal Nehru.

49 *The Lives of Freda,* Speaking Tiger Books, 2019, pp. 162.

50 *The Blazing Chinar*, trans. Mohammad Amin, Gulshan Books, 2013, pp. 217.

51 Born in Ajnala, Amritsar, Mohammad Din Taseer was the father of the former Governor of Pakistani Punjab Salman Taseer, who was assassinated by a Muslim fanatic for having espoused the cause of those suffering because of the blasphemy laws in Pakistan. Senior Taseer was one of the founding members of the Progressive Writers Movement along with Faiz Ahmed Faiz and Sajjad Zaheer. For some time, he was also the Principal of Sri Pratap College, Srinagar.

52 'Naya Kashmir', *Wikipedia* (en.wikipedia.org/wiki/Naya_Kashmir, last accessed 16 March 2023).

53 Ibid.

54 Ibid.

55 Ibid.

56 Ibid.

57 Ibid.

58 Ibid.

59 Ibid.

4. The Politics of Quit Kashmir Movement

60 B.P.L. Bedi's interview manuscript, Nehru Memorial Museum and Library (NMML), quoted in *The Lives of Freda,* Speaking Tiger Books, 2019, pp. 158-159.

61 *Autobiography*, Oxford University Press India, 1994, pp. 40–44.

62 *Political Conspiracies of Kashmir*, Light & Life Publishers, 1973, pp. 40.

63 Quoted from a letter written by Freda Bedi to her son Kabir Bedi when he had grown up. Op cit, *The Lives of Freda*, p 166.

64 Ibid, pp. 167.

65 Ibid, pp. 169.

66 Op cit, *Political Conspiracies of Kashmir*, pp. 150.

67 Doctor Arthur Neve was an Englishman who heard the call for missionary work quite early in his career and came to Kashmir as a young man of twenty-three years and stayed there for the next thirty-seven years to work at the Kashmir Mission Hospital. He wrote a

number of books, including, *Picturesque Kashmir* (Sands & Company, 1900) from where the quote has been taken. His other significant books were *Kashmir, Ladakh and Tibet* (1899) and *Thirty Years in Kashmir* (1913). He died in Kashmir in 1919.

5. Under the Shadows of Partition

68 *Jinnah*, Penguin Random House India, 2020 pp. 413.

69 *History of Partition of India*, vol. 1, Atlantic Publishers and Distributors, 1995, pp. 40-41.

70 Mir Taqi 'Mir' was a proponent of Urdu ghazal and lived much of his life in Delhi in the eighteenth century and the first decade of nineteenth century in Lucknow. He had moved to Lucknow after Delhi was repeatedly sacked by Ahmad Shah Abdali after 1848 and is arguably considered the greatest Urdu poet.

71 Mirza Asadullah Baig Khan 'Ghalib' lived during the dying days of Mughal Empire and suffered the pain of its replacement by East India Company, and, also the beginning of the direct British rule. His eternal fame and popularity rests on his Urdu poetry though his Persian poetry is more voluminous.

72 Op cit, *Jinnah*, pp. 122 and *A New History of India*, Oxford University Press, 1982, pp 317-318.

73 Ibid, *Jinnah*, pp. 123.

74 Theodore Beck was a Quaker by faith and an educationist who worked in India. From 1883 to 1899 he worked as the Principal of Muhammadan Anglo-Oriental College, Aligarh till it became Aligarh Muslim University.

75 Theodore Morison was a British educationalist who served as a Member of the Council of India and Director of the University of London Institute in Paris. He is best known as an interpreter of Muslim life in India. He was also the principal of Muhammadan Anglo-Oriental College from 1899-1905 and member of the Council of India from 1906.

76 *The Shadow of the Great Game: The Untold Story of India's Partition*, HarperCollins Publishers India with India Today Group, 2005, pp. 21-22.

77 *Indian Summer: The Secret History of the End of an Empire*, Simon & Schuster, 2007, p. 146.

78 Ibid. pp. 147-148.

79 *Wavell: The Viceroy's Journal*, Oxford University Press, 1973, p. 120.

80 *Viceroy's Journal* by Lord Wavell, 5 July 1944, pp. 78.
81 Mohammad Ali Jinnah gave a call to Muslims for a General Strike on 16th August, 1946 all over the country and termed it Direct Action Day. In effect it was show of strength by the Muslim League and turned into an orgy of violence in Calcutta.
82 *The Punjab Bloodied, Partitioned and Cleansed*, Oxford University Press, 2012, pp. 210 and Op cit, *Jinnah* pp. 415-416.
83 *History of Jammu and Kashmir Rifles, 1820-1956*, Lancer International, 1990, p. 206.
84 Ibid, pp. 207.
85 Ibid, pp. 209.
86 From the notes of Brigadier Krishna Singh as cited in *History of Jammu and Kashmir Rifles, 1820-1956*, pp. 214.
87 Ibid, pp. 214-215.
88 Ibid. pp. 215.
89 *Constitutional Relations Between Britain and India: The Transfer of Power, 1942-47*, vol 10, Her Majesty's Stationery Office, 1981, pp. 774-775.
90 Op cit, *Indian Summer*, pp. 138.
91 Ibid, pp. 135.
92 Ibid, pp. 154.

6. The Maharaja Vacillates?

93 *Jammu and Kashmir 1949-64: Select Correspondence Between Jawaharlal Nehru and Karan Singh*, ed. Jawaid Alam, Penguin/Viking, 2006, pp. 309-330. It was only in 2008 that the document was made public when it was included in the compilation of this select correspondence though a few people close to the Maharaja had an idea of such a memorandum but no one really knew its contents in detail.
94 The Cabinet Mission Plan proposed a federal India, with a ten-year constitutional review which would have allowed Muslim Provinces to leave the Indian Union if they wished.
95 *Divide and Quit*, University of California Press, 1962, pp. 52-55.
96 *Time Only to Look Forward: Speeches as Viceroy of India and Governor-General of the Dominion of India, 1947-48*, Nicholas Kaye, 1949, pp. 3.
97 *Indian Summer: The Secret History of the End of an Empire*, Simon & Schuster, 2007, pp. 166.
98 Ibid, pp. 182.

99 *Constitutional Relations Between Britain and India: The Transfer of Power, 1942-47*, vol 10, Her Majesty's Stationery Office, 1981, pp. 543.
100 Ibid, pp. 160.
101 Ibid, pp. 540.
102 *My Days With Gandhi*, Orient Longman Limited, 1974, p. 187.
103 Op cit, *Indian Summer*, pp. 191.
104 *Mountbatten:* The Official Biography, Knopf, 1985, pp. 383-384.
105 Op cit, *Indian Summer*, pp. 215.
106 Ibid, pp. 217.
107 'Chapter 30', *Indian Independence Act, 1947*, (legislation.gov.uk/ukpga/1947/30/pdfs/ukpga_19470030_en.pdf, last accessed 16 March 2023).
108 Prime Minister Clement Attlee's letter to Lord Mountbatten, Op cit, *Indian Summer*, pp. 218.
109 *Kashmir: A Disputed Legacy, 1846-1990*, Oxford University Press, 1991, pp. 127.
110 Ibid, pp. 127.
111 *The Shadow of the Great Game: The Untold Story of India's Partition*, HarperCollins Publishers India with India Today Group, 2005, pp. 311.
112 Ibid. pp. 322.
113 Op cit, *Jammu and Kashmir 1949-64*, pp. 312.
114 Ibid, pp. 312.
115 Ibid, pp. 312.
116 Op cit, *Kashmir: A Disputed Legacy*, pp. 109-10.
117 Op cit, *Indian Summer*, pp. 218: 'Mountbatten was supposed to "aid and assist the States in coming to fair and just arrangements with the leaders of British India as to their future relationship." But there was also the command that "you will do your best to persuade the rulers of any Indian States in which political progress has been slow to progress rapidly towards some form of more democratic government." Mountbatten interpreted this to mean that he should exert pressure upon each prince to go with the majority of his people in deciding whether to join India or Pakistan.'
118 Op cit, *Jammu and Kashmir 1949-64*, pp. 313-314.
119 *Mission With Mountbatten*, R. Hale, 1951, pp. 289.
120 *Eminent Churchillians*, Simon & Schuster, 1995, pp. 91.
121 Cited from *Transfer of Power* in *Kashmir: A Disputed Legacy 1846-1990*, pp. 109-110.

7. Before Accession

122 *Jammu and Kashmir Arms: History of the J&K Rifles*, Palit & Dutt Publishers, 1972, pp. 148.
123 Ibid, pp. 149.
124 *Looking Back: The Autobiography of Mehr Chand Mahajan, Former Chief Justice of India*, Asia Publishing House, 1963, pp. 124.
125 *Gilgit Rebellion: The Major Who Mutinied Over Partition of India*, Pen & Sword Books, 2014, pp. ix-x.
126 Op cit, *Jammu and Kashmir Arms*, pp. 156.
127 *Political Conspiracies of Kashmir*, Light & Life Publishers, 1973, pp. 53.
128 *Kashmir: A Disputed Legacy, 1846-1990*, Oxford University Press, 1991, pp. 111-116.
129 Ibid, pp. 116.
130 *Indian Summer: The Secret History of the End of an Empire*, Simon & Schuster, 2007, pp. 330.
131 *Kashmir: The Unwritten History*, HarperCollins Publishers India, 2013, pp. 26.
132 Ibid, pp. 31-32.
133 Ibid, pp. 41. Cited from *Kashmir Saga* by Sardar Mohammad Ibrahim Khan who is also the President of Pakistan-Occupied-Kashmir.
134 UNCIP document, *Report of the Sub-committee on Western Kashmir*, 1949, pp. 87. This allegation is said to have been made by a *Zaildar* (a revenue official) from Bhimber but curiously has not been named. Another instance of cooked up allegation by partisan west influence report.
135 Ibid, pp. 32.
136 Op cit, *Kashmir: The Unwritten History*, pp. 26.
137 *Jammu and Kashmir 1949-64: Select Correspondence Between Jawaharlal Nehru and Karan Singh*, ed. Jawaid Alam, Penguin/Viking, 2006, pp. 310.
138 Op cit, *Jammu and Kashmir Arms*, pp. 179.
139 Op cit, *Indian Summer*, pp. 318.
140 Op cit, *Kashmir: The Unwritten History*, pp. 53.
141 Ibid, pp. 254.

8. Strategic and Feudatory States

142 Kalhana in his Rajatarangini credits King Emperor Lalitaditya Muktpada (724–760 A.D.) with leading an aggressive military campaigns in

Northern India and Central Asia. He conquered most of Aryavarta, while defeating Yasovarman of Kanyakubja and conquering Bengal, Kalinga, Karnataka, the Kaveri Valley, Mount Malaya, the Konkan, Dvaraka, Avanti and Gauda. He then broke into the Uttarapatha and defeated the rebellious tribes of the Kambojas, Tukharas (Turks in Turkmenistan and Tocharians in Badakhshan), Bhautas (Tibetans in Baltistan and Tibet) and Daradas (Dards). His campaign then led him to subjugate the kingdoms of Pragjyotisha, Strirajya and the Uttarakurus.

143 *Guilty Men of India's Partition*, Kitabstan, 1960.

144 *Heights of Madness: One Woman's Journey in Pursuit of a Secret War*, Rupa and Company, 2007, pp. 102.

145 William Moorcraft widely travelled in the north-western region of the Indian subcontinent, ostensibly looking for good horses for the East India Company. But he was surrounded by mystery as his activities did not confine to only the purchase of horses and subtly indulged in the politics and trade of the region for the benefit of the Company. See *Kashmir: A Disputed Legacy, 1846-1990*, Oxford University Press, 1991, pp. 19.

146 *Pashm* is the wool extracted from the undercoat of a special breed of goat and sheep from eastern Ladakh and Tibet. It is the raw material for weaving expensive *pashmina* shawls from Kashmir.

147 Op cit, *Heights of Madness*, pp. 101. William Moorcraft saw Leh as a staging post for 'a great thoroughfare for an active commercial intercourse between Tibet, Turkistan, China and even Russia on the one hand and Kashmir, the Punjab and the plains of Hindustan on the other.' Op cit, *Kashmir: A Disputed Legacy 1846-1990*, pp. 19.

148 Disraeli, the Conservative Prime Minister, was the champion of the 'forward policy' that advocated moving as far as possible in the north-western frontier of Indian subcontinent to contain any march by the Russians towards India in opposition to the views of Gladstone, the leader of the Liberal Party.

149 In fact, the British remained obsessed with the fear of Russians marching towards India right through the nineteenth century. This fear had its roots in the Treaty of Tilsit 1807 between Napoleon of France and King Ferdinand of Prussia, in which there was a proposal for France and Russia to attack India by land route and destroy the British strength by annexing India.

150 In Article 4 of the Treaty, the Maharaja agreed that he would not alter the limits of his territories without the concurrence of the British. In

Article 5, it was implied that the Maharaja would permit the British to supervise his foreign policy. But this Article was vague and was directed towards Jammu and Kashmir's disputes with other States within the Sphere of British influence.

151 Op cit, *Kashmir: A Disputed Legacy 1846-1990*, pp. 22–23. The prejudiced interpretation of the author notwithstanding, it is crystal clear that the Dogra Ruler had launched successful military campaigns beyond the traditional borders. For obvious reasons this achievement has been underplayed by historians belonging to the British school.

152 *Autobiography*, Oxford University Press India, 1994, pp. 2. The conspiracy of the Political Department was exposed by the *Amrita Bazar Patrika* causing a furore in the House of Commons and the abandoning of the plan to depose the Ruler.

153 Ibid, pp. 57–59.

9. The Gathering Clouds

154 *Jinnah*, Penguin Random House India, 2020, pp. 500.

155 *India and Pakistan: Continued Conflict or Cooperation?*, University of California Press, 2010.

156 *Indian Summer: The Secret History of the End of an Empire*, Simon & Schuster, 2007.

157 *Kashmir: A Disputed Legacy, 1846-1990*, Oxford University Press, 1991, pp. 122; The Memorandum submitted by Maharaja Hari Singh wherein he writes about the Standstill Agreement being agreed to by Pakistan, and, 'on the other hand, the Government of India did not make up their mind and, if I may be permitted to say so, dealt with the situation in a half-hearted and desultory manner; thus, giving an opportunity to Pakistan to do mischief, as they did.' Cited in *Jammu and Kashmir 1949-64: Select Correspondence Between Jawaharlal Nehru and Karan Singh*, ed. Jawaid Alam, Penguin/Viking, 2006, pp. 313.

158 *Political Conspiracies of Kashmir*, Light & Life Publishers, 1973, pp. 49 'His declared views on accession were 'freedom first [meaning removal of Maharaja] and accession to India Pakistan afterwards.'

159 *Autobiography*, Oxford University Press India, 1994, pp. 55.

160 Op cit, *Jammu and Kashmir 1949-64*, pp. 314.

161 *Looking Back: The Autobiography of Mehr Chand Mahajan, Former Chief Justice of India*, Asia Publishing House, 1963, pp. 124.

162 Ibid, pp. 126.

163 Ibid, pp. 128.

164 Op cit, *Autobiography*, pp. 81-82. Later, in response to a barely polite correspondence by Sheikh Abdullah, Sardar Patel had taunted him by responding, 'I am also surprised that you, who had a different attitude towards H.H. when you were in jail, as typified in your letter to him a copy of which is with me, should speak in such terms of him'. (*Patel volume I, text of letters exchanged.*)

165 Ibid, pp. 130.

166 Ibid, pp. 131.

167 Ibid, pp. 131.

168 Ibid, pp. 53.

169 Ibid, pp. 54.

170 Op cit, *Looking Back*, pp. 142 and Op cit, *Kashmir: A Disputed Legacy, 1846-1990*, pp. 126.

171 Op cit, *Looking Back*, pp. 269.

172 Op cit, *Kashmir: A Disputed Legacy, 1846-1900*, pp. 126.

173 Ibid, pp. 127.

174 Op cit, *Jammu and Kashmir 1949-64*, pp. 314-315.

175 V.P. Menon writes in *Story of the Integration of the Indian States*: 'Pakistan signed a Standstill Agreement. But we wanted time to examine its implications. We left the state alone. We did not ask the Maharajah to accede...Moreover, our hands were already full and, if truth be told, I for one had simply no time to think of Kashmir'. H.V. Hodson too writes in *The Great Divide: Britain-India-Pakistan*: 'The States Ministry of the Government of India meanwhile was strictly passive. Kashmir was deliberately omitted from a committee of States' representatives called by the pre-independence States Department to discuss terms of accession, though Hyderabad was included'.

176 'Memorandum to the President of India, Dr Rajender Prasad', Op cit, *Jammu and Kashmir 1949–64*, pp. 315–316, 384.

177 Op cit, *Looking Back*, pp. 143.

178 Ibid, pp. 145.

179 Ibid, pp. 146.

180 *Jammu and Kashmir Arms: History of the J&K Rifles*, Palit & Dutt Publishers, 1972, pp. 179.

181 Op cit, *Looking Back*, pp. 139-140; from *The Tribune*, 23 October 1947.

10. The Invasion

182 *India's Wars: A Military History 1947-1971*, HarperCollins Publishers India, 2016, pp. 113-114.

183 *Operations in Jammu and Kashmir (1947-48)*, Ministry of Defence, Government of India, 1987, pp. 16.
184 *History of Jammu and Kashmir Rifles, 1820-1956: The State Force Background,* Lancer International, 1990, pp. 223; from the notes of Major General H.L. Scott.
185 Ibid, pp. 17.
186 Ibid, pp. 17-18.
187 *Jammu and Kashmir Arms: History of the J&K Rifles,* Palit & Dutt Publishers, 1972, pp. 142.
188 *The Battles of Zojila, 1948*, Har Anand Publications, 1997; Op cit, *History of Jammu and Kashmir Rifles, 1820-1956*, pp. 222–223 from the *Draft Regimental History Jammu and Kashmir Rifles* produced by the Regimental Centre, 1965, pp. 182-183.
189 Op cit, *Jammu and Kashmir Arms*, pp. 149.
190 The rebellion theory suited both Pakistan, the National Conference and the anti-Dogra forces. Pakistan used it to justify the support it lent to those forces and National Conference and anti-Dogra forces to discredit the rule of the Maharaja. Op cit, *The Battles of Zojila, 1948,* pp. 39: 'On August 29, the Maharaja received a telegram from Raja Yakub Khan, on behalf of the public of Hazara, alleging attacks on Muslims in Punch [*sic*] and informing him that the Hazara Muslims were much perturbed. Through this telegram he also threatened to enter the State fully equipped with arms to fight the State forces'.
191 Op cit, *Jammu and Kashmir Arms*, pp. 159.
192 Op cit, *History of Jammu and Kashmir Rifles, 1820-1956*, pp. 228.
193 Ibid, pp. 229.
194 Ibid, pp. 229, and Op cit, *Jammu and Kashmir Arms*, pp. 142.
195 *Looking Back: The Autobiography of Mehr Chand Mahajan, Former Chief Justice of India*, Asia Publishing House, 1963, pp. 150.
196 Ibid, pp. 149.
197 Op cit, *Jammu and Kashmir Arms*, pp. 179, and Op cit, *History of Jammu and Kashmir Rifles*, pp. 331.
198 Op cit, *History of Jammu and Kashmir Rifles*, pp. 331.
199 Some historians and many Indian commentators have blurred the distinction between treachery and rebellion. While historians like Alastair Lamb have used the term rebellion to obfuscate the Pakistani invasion, the many of the Indian commentators use it to malign the Maharaja and his Forces.
200 Op cit, *Jammu and Kashmir Arms*, pp. 179.
201 Ibid, pp. 180.
202 Ibid, pp. 180-181.

11. Heroic Retreat

203 *Jammu and Kashmir Arms: History of the J&K Rifles,* Palit & Dutt Publishers, 1972, pp. 182.
204 Ibid, pp 182-183.
205 Ibid, pp. 184, and *History of Jammu and Kashmir Rifles, 1820-1956: The State Force Background,* Lancer International, 1990, pp. 237-238.
206 Country-made rifle, freely available in the frontier region.
207 Op cit, *Jammu and Kashmir Arms,* pp. 185.
208 Op cit, *History of Jammu and Kashmir Rifles,* pp. 238-239.
209 Op cit, *Jammu and Kashmir Arms,* pp. 185-186.
210 Ibid, pp. 186.
211 Op cit, *History of Jammu and Kashmir Rifles,* p. 239.
212 Op cit, *Jammu and Kashmir Arms,* p. 188.
213 Ibid, pp. 188, and Op cit, *History of Jammu and Kashmir Rifles,* pp. 239.

12. The Saviour of Kashmir

214 *Autobiography,* Oxford University Press India, 1994, pp. 56.
215 *History of Jammu and Kashmir Rifles, 1820-1956: The State Force Background,* Lancer International, 1990, pp. 233.
216 *Jammu and Kashmir Arms: History of the J&K Rifles,* Palit & Dutt Publishers, 1972, pp. 190, and Op cit, *Autobiography,* pp. 56.
217 Op cit, *Jammu and Kashmir Arms,* p. 190.
218 Op cit, *History of Jammu and Kashmir Rifles,* pp. 234.
219 Op cit, *Jammu and Kashmir Arms,* pp. 192.
220 Ibid. p. 192 and *History of Jammu and Kashmir Rifles (1820-1956)* by Major K. Brahma Singh, p. 234.
221 Op cit, *History of Jammu and Kashmir Rifles,* pp. 234-235.
222 Ibid, pp. 235.
223 Ibid, pp. 235 and Op cit, *Jammu and Kashmir Arms,* pp. 193.
224 Op cit, *History of Jammu and Kashmir Rifles,* pp. 235.
225 Ibid, pp. 235.
226 *Looking Back: The Autobiography of Mehr Chand Mahajan, Former Chief Justice of India,* Asia Publishing House, 1963, pp. 148-149.
227 Ibid, pp. 151.
228 Op cit, *Jammu and Kashmir Arms,* pp. 195.
229 *Operations in Jammu and Kashmir (1947-48),* Ministry of Defence, Government of India, 1987, pp. 22-23.
230 *Political Conspiracies of Kashmir,* Light & Life Publishers, 1973, pp. 54

231 *The Shadow of the Great Game: The Untold Story of India's Partition*, HarperCollins Publishers India with India Today Group, 2005, pp. 360, and *Field Marshal KM Cariappa: His Life and Times*, Lancer, 1995, pp. 165-66.

232 *Jammu and Kashmir 1949-64: Select Correspondence Between Jawaharlal Nehru and Karan Singh*, ed. Jawaid Alam, Penguin/Viking, 2006.

233 *Tracts For The Times: Kashmir Towards Insurgency*, Orient Longman, 1993, pp. 12.

13. The Politics of Accession

234 *Looking Back: The Autobiography of Mehr Chand Mahajan, Former Chief Justice of India*, Asia Publishing House, 1963, pp. 150.

235 Ibid, pp. 151.

236 *Jammu and Kashmir 1949-64: Select Correspondence Between Jawaharlal Nehru and Karan Singh*, ed. Jawaid Alam, Penguin/Viking, 2006, pp. 321.

237 *Autobiography*, Oxford University Press India, 1994, pp. 86.

238 *Slender was the Thread: Kashmir Confrontation, 1947-48*, Orient Longman, 1969.

239 *Operations in Jammu and Kashmir (1947-48)*, Ministry of Defence, Government of India, 1987, and Op cit, *Slender was the Thread*, pp. 84-85.

240 Op cit, *Looking Back*, pp. 151.

241 Ibid, pp. 151-152.

242 Op cit, *Autobiography*, pp. 58.

243 Ibid, pp. 59.

244 *Article 370: A Constitutional History of Jammu and Kashmir*, Oxford University Press India, 2011, pp. 41-43. From *White Paper on Jammu & Kashmir, Government of India*, 1948.

245 Ibid, pp. 43.

246 Ibid, pp. 44.

247 *Political Conspiracies of Kashmir*, Light & Life Publishers, 1973, pp. 89.

14. The Defence of Poonch

248 *Jammu and Kashmir Arms: History of the J&K Rifles*, Palit & Dutt Publishers, 1972, pp. 148-149.

249 *Indian Summer: The Secret History of the End of an Empire,* Simon & Schuster, 2007, pp. 146-148.
250 *The Shadow of the Great Game: The Untold Story of India's Partition,* HarperCollins Publishers India with India Today Group, 2005, pp. 340-341.
251 *History of Jammu and Kashmir Rifles, 1820-1956: The State Force Background,* Lancer International, 1990, pp. 222-223.
252 *Kashmir: A Disputed Legacy, 1846-1990,* Oxford University Press, 1991, pp. 123-125 and *Kashmir: The Unwritten History,* HarperCollins Publishers India, 2013, pp. 41. Both have tried to de-link the killings, rape, plunder and arson there from the hostilities in Kashmir. They have argued that because of the local circumstances the 'people' there 'rebelled' against the Dogra rule. They have even gone on to equate the treachery of the Muslim soldiers of the State Forces with rebellion. However, the fact remains that all of them agree that the State Forces had been fighting a war much before the 'acknowledged' hostilities broke. Had the designs of Pakistan succeeded, Kashmir would have been in its vice like grip from its launch-pad, Jammu.
253 Op cit, *Jammu and Kashmir Arms,* pp 202.
254 Op cit, *History of Jammu and Kashmir Rifles,* pp. 226.
255 Op cit, *Jammu and Kashmir Arms,* pp. 202–203.
256 Ibid, pp. 204.
257 Ibid, pp. 206.
258 Ibid, pp. 207.
259 Ibid, pp. 208.
260 Ibid, pp. 200-223.
261 Ibid, pp.208-209.
262 *The Battles of Zojila, 1948,* Har Anand Publications, 1997, pp. 46–57.
263 Op cit, *The Shadow of the Great Game,* pp. 360.
264 *Slender was the Thread: Kashmir Confrontation, 1947-48,* Orient Longman, 1969, pp. 52-53.
265 Op cit, *History of Jammu and Kashmir Rifles,* pp. 249.
266 Op cit, *Jammu and Kashmir Arms,* pp. 209–210.
267 Op cit, *History of Jammu and Kashmir Rifles,* pp. 249.
268 Ibid, pp. 210.
269 Op cit, *Jammu and Kashmir Arms,* pp. 214.

15. Gilgit–The British Conspiracy

270 *Gilgit Rebellion: The Major Who Mutinied Over Partition of India,* Pen & Sword Books, 2014, pp. x.

271 Ibid, pp. 2.

272 'Colonialism to Postcolonial Colonialism: Changing Modes of Domination in the Northern Areas of Pakistan', *The Journal of Asian Studies*, vol 64, no 4, 2005.

273 Ibid, pp. 959.

274 Ibid, pp. 965-966.

275 Ibid, pp. 969.

276 Op cit, *Gilgit Rebellion*, pp. 71-72.

277 Ibid, pp. 81.

278 Ibid, pp. 96-97.

279 Ibid, 108-109.

280 *Gilgit Before 1947*, n.p., 1983, pp. 28.

281 Ibid, pp. 88.

282 Ibid, pp. 31.

283 Ibid, pp. 32.

284 *Jammu and Kashmir Arms: History of the J&K Rifles*, Palit & Dutt Publishers, 1972, pp. 227.

285 Ibid, pp. 228. The author noted, 'Lieut, Haider Ali, presumably in a gesture of gallant bravado, was thrice moved to volunteer to shoot Brigadier Ghansara Singh himself. Fortunately he was deterred by public opinion.'

286 Op cit, *Gilgit Before 1947*, pp. 35.

287 *The Battles of Zojila, 1948*, Har Anand Publications, 1997, pp. 59.

288 Op cit, *Jammu and Kashmir Arms*, pp. 228.

289 Op cit, *Gilgit Before 1947*, pp. 36.

290 Ibid, pp. 40.

291 Op cit, *Jammu and Kashmir Arms*, pp. 229 and Op cit, *Gilgit Before 1947*, pp. 36.

292 Op cit, *Gilgit Rebellion*, pp. 145.

293 Ibid, pp. 145.

294 Ibid, pp. x.

16. The Saga of Skardu

295 *Gilgit Rebellion: The Major Who Mutinied Over Partition of India*, Pen & Sword Books, 2014, pp. 213.

296 Ibid, pp. 179.

297 Ibid, pp. 179.

298 Ibid, pp. 179.

299 *Jammu and Kashmir Arms: History of the J&K Rifles*, Palit & Dutt Publishers, 1972, pp. 231; *History of Jammu and Kashmir Rifles*,

1820-1956: The State Force Background, Lancer International, 1990, pp. 259; and *Operations in Jammu and Kashmir (1947-48),* Ministry of Defence, Government of India, 1987, pp. 285.

300 Op cit, *Operations in Jammu and Kashmir (1947-48)*, pp. 285.
301 Op cit, *Jammu and Kashmir Arms*, pp. 232.
302 Ibid, pp. 232.
303 Op cit, *History of Jammu and Kashmir Rifles*, pp. 261.
304 Op cit, *Jammu and Kashmir Arms*, pp. 233.
305 Ibid, p. 233.
306 Op cit, *History of Jammu and Kashmir Rifles*, pp. 261-262.
307 Op cit, *Operations in Jammu and Kashmir (1947-48)*, pp. 325-326.
308 Ibid, pp. 327.
309 Lieutenant General Baljit Singh (Retired), *The Tribune*, Chandigarh, 17 February 2019.
310 Op cit, *Operations in Jammu and Kashmir (1947-48)*, pp. 290.
311 Ibid, p. 290.
312 Ibid, p. 291.
313 *History of Jammu and Kashmir Rifles (1820-1956)* by Major Brahma Singh, p. 263.
314 Ibid. p. 263.
315 Op cit, *Jammu and Kashmir Arms*, pp. 235.
316 Ibid, pp. 235-236.
317 Ibid, pp. 236.
318 Ibid, pp. 236.
319 Ibid, pp. 236-237.
320 Op cit, *History of Jammu and Kashmir Rifles*, pp. 261-262.
321 Op cit, *Jammu and Kashmir Arms*, pp. 239.
322 Ibid, pp. 239-240.
323 Lieutenant General H.S. Panag, 'Brigadier Sher Jung Thapa, MVC—The Hero of Skardu Part 2', *Newslaundry*, 16 August 2017 (newslaundry.com/2017/08/16/sher-jung-thapa-skardu-gilgit-kargil-pakistan, last accessed 17 March 2023).
324 Ibid.

17. The Political Battleground

325 *Autobiography*, Oxford University Press India, 1994, pp. 83 and *Jammu and Kashmir 1949-64: Select Correspondence Between Jawaharlal Nehru and Karan Singh*, ed. Jawaid Alam, Penguin/Viking, 2006, pp. 317.

326 Op cit, *Autobiography*, pp. 81-82.

327 *Looking Back: The Autobiography of Mehr Chand Mahajan, Former Chief Justice of India*, Asia Publishing House, 1963, pp. 126-127.

328 Op cit, *Autobiography*, pp. 88.

329 Ibid, p. 89.

330 Op cit, *Looking Back*, pp. 158.

331 Ibid, pp. 159-160.

332 Ibid, pp. 161.

333 Raj Kumari Amrit Kaur was a princess of the Kapurthala (Punjab) family who became active in the independence movement. She was also member of the Constituent Assembly and appointed Health Minister in India's first Government in 1947.

334 Op cit, *Looking Back*, pp. 161-162.

335 Op cit, *Autobiography*, p. 86.

336 *The Punjab Bloodied, Partitioned and Cleansed: Unravelling the 1947 Tragedy Through Secret British Reports and First-Person Accounts*, Oxford University Press, 2012, pp. 515-603.

337 Op cit, *Looking Back*, pp. 162.

338 Ibid, pp. 162-163.

339 After migrating to Pakistan, Chaudhary Ghulam Abbas held a Government position for a while but quit all association with it as Pakistan began to take complete control of that area.

340 Op cit, *Looking Back*, pp. 165.

341 Ibid, pp. 164-165.

342 Mirza Afzal Beg, senior most lieutenant of Sheikh Abdullah and a member of the State Assembly had been appointed a Minister by the Maharaja as a part of the constitutional reforms before the Quit Kashmir movement, had this to say in the Assembly: 'When we see that in spite of being able to put off any progress till sometime in the future [in wartime], His Highness has come forward and conferred reforms on the people of the State, we feel sure of the intention that underlies the Command and of the unerring instinct for constitutional government that His Highness the Maharaja Bahadur possesses.' Cited in *Sheikh Mohammad Abdullah: Tragic Hero of Kashmir*, Roli Books, 2008.

343 Lake Success is a village on the North Shore of Long Island, New York, United States. The Village of Lake Success was the temporary home of the United Nations from 1946 to 1951.

344 *Jammu and Kashmir 1949-64: Select Correspondence Between Jawaharlal Nehru and Karan Singh*, ed. Jawaid Alam, Penguin/Viking, 2006, pp. 318.

345 *Kashmir: A Disputed Legacy, 1846-1990,* Oxford University Press, 1991, pp. 166.
346 Ibid, pp. 167.
347 Op cit, *Jammu and Kashmir 1949-64*, pp. 319.
348 Op cit, *Looking Back*, pp. 174.
349 Ibid, pp. 175.

18. Despair of a Maharaja

350 *Autobiography*, Oxford University Press India, 1994, pp. 83.
351 *Constitution of Jammu & Kashmir: Its Development & Comments,* Universal Book Traders, 1994, pp. 46.
352 Op cit, *Autobiography*, pp. 84.
353 Ibid, pp. 84.
354 Ibid, pp. 89.
355 Ibid, pp. 90-91.
356 Op cit, *Constitution of Jammu & Kashmir*, p. 47.
357 Ibid, pp.67. The State of Cochin had a Legislative Assembly and separate Judiciary and Executive in 1925; Mysore had an elected Legislative Council in 1907 but the Praja Sabha of Jammu and Kashmir, with limited powers, had circumscribed many princely prerogatives and passed many landmark Bills that became law. These were related to widow remarriage, inheritance among Hindus, suppression of immoral traffic in women, village panchayats, the defence of the State, income tax, sale of goods, land alienation, arms and census.
358 Op cit, *Autobiography*, pp. 86-87.
359 *Jammu and Kashmir 1949-64: Select Correspondence Between Jawaharlal Nehru and Karan Singh*, ed. Jawaid Alam, Penguin/Viking, 2006, pp. 319.
360 Op cit, *Autobiography*, pp. 60. While we only have the letter written by Gopalaswami Ayyangar, suggesting the Maharaja to move out among the people, in his Memorandum to the President of India, the Maharaja wrote that he had also been advised by Sardar Patel to move among the people, probably to give the impression that whatever changes were taking place were with his consent and that there was no reason for him to sulk.
361 Op cit, *Jammu and Kashmir 1949-64*, pp. 320.
362 Before the formation of the Reserve Bank of India in 1935, The Imperial Bank of India was the chartered Bank of British India. Later, in 1955 it was transformed into the present day State Bank of India.

363 Ibid, pp. 320.
364 Op cit, *Autobiography*, pp. 67.
365 Nehru's address to the nation on 2nd November 1947: *Jawaharlal Nehru Speeches: September 1946—May 1949*, vol 1, Ministry of Information and Broadcast, Government of India, 1958.
366 *Indian Summer: The Secret History of the End of an Empire*, Simon & Schuster, 2007, pp. 346.

19. The Invitation

367 *Autobiography*, Oxford University Press India, 1994, pp. 77-78.
368 Ibid, pp. 79.
369 Google definition: Auuqaf/Awqaf (also spelled awkaf, singular waqf/ wakf) is an Arabic word meaning assets that are donated, bequeathed, or purchased for being held in perpetual trust for general or specific charitable causes that are socially beneficial. In many ways, the concept of waqf is similar to the Western concept of endowment.
370 *Tracts For The Times: Kashmir Towards Insurgency*, Orient Longman, 1993, pp. 47.
371 Ibid, pp. 48.
372 *Constitution of Jammu & Kashmir: Its Development & Comments*, Universal Book Traders, 1994, pp. 108; cited from *National Herald*, Lucknow, 19 June 1948.
373 Op cit, *Constitution of Jammu & Kashmir*, pp. 108; cited from *Hindustan Times*, New Delhi, 16 October 1948.
374 Op cit, *Autobiography*, pp. 92.
375 *Jammu and Kashmir 1949-64: Select Correspondence Between Jawaharlal Nehru and Karan Singh*, ed. Jawaid Alam, Penguin/Viking, 2006, pp. 331.
376 Ibid, pp. 332.
377 Ibid, pp. 332.
378 Ibid, pp. 333.
379 Op cit, *Autobiography*, pp. 93.
380 Ibid, pp. 94.
381 Op cit, *Jammu and Kashmir 1949-64*, pp. 334.
382 Ibid, pp. 334.
383 Ibid, pp. 335.
384 Op cit, *Autobiography*, pp. 99-100.
385 Ibid, pp. 100.

20. The End and a Beginning

386 *Durbar*, essentially meaning the Court and by extension, the capital, as a gesture of equal importance given to the two main regions of the State of Jammu and Kashmir, moved in winter to Jammu and in summer to Srinagar. This customary movement has now been brought to an end by the Bharatiya Janata Party (BJP) after the de-operationalization of Article 370 on 5th August 2019.

387 It is a religious ceremony among the Hindus that marks the entrance of a person in one of the philosophies practiced by the Hindus. It also signifies the acceptance of a disciple by a religious Guru among the Hindus. It is called under various names, notably, *Upnayana* and more commonly as the *Janeu* ceremony.

Bibliography

Abdullah, Sheikh Mohammad. *The Blazing Chinar: Autobiography*, trans. Mohammad Amin, Gulshan Books, 2013

Ahmed, Ishtiaq. *The Punjab Bloodied, Partitioned and Cleansed: Unravelling the 1947 Tragedy Through Secret British Reports and First-Person Accounts*, Oxford University Press, 2012

———. *Jinnah: His Successes, Failures and Role in History*, Penguin Random House India, 2020

Anand, Justice Adarsh Sein. *Constitution of Jammu & Kashmir: Its Development & Comments*, Universal Book Traders, 1994

Aziz, K.K. *History of Partition of India*, vol. 1, Atlantic Publishers and Distributors, 1995

Bhattacharjea, Ajit. *Kashmir: The Wounded Valley*, USB Publishers' Distributors, 1994

———. *Sheikh Mohammad Abdullah: Tragic Hero of Kashmir*, Roli Books, 2008

Bloeria, Sudhir S. *The Battles of Zojila, 1948*, Har Anand Publications, 1997

Bose, Nirmal Kumar. *My Days With Gandhi*, Orient Longman Limited, 1974

Brown, William. *Gilgit Rebellion: The Major Who Mutinied Over Partition of India*, Pen & Sword Books, 2014

Campbell-Johnson, Alan. *Mission With Mountbatten*, R. Hale, 1951

Carthill, Al. *The Lost Dominion: The Story of England's Abdication in India*, William Blackwood and Sons, 1924

Datta, C.L. *Ladakh and Western Himalayan Politics, 1819-1848: The Dogra Conquest of Ladakh, Baltistan, and West Tibet, and Reactions of the Other Powers*, Munshiram Manoharlal Publishers, 1973

Guha, Ramachandra. *India After Gandhi: The History of the World's Largest Democracy*, Macmillan, 2007

Hodson, H.V. *The Great Divide: Britain-India-Pakistan*, Hutchinson & Co (Publishers) Ltd, 1969

Jawaharlal Nehru Speeches: September 1946—May 1949, vol 1, Ministry of Information and Broadcast, Government of India, 1958

Keesing's Contemporary Archives (1931), Keesing Limited, 1931

Khanduri, C.B. *Field Marshal KM Cariappa: His Life and Times*, Lancer, 1995

Lamb, Alastair. *Kashmir: A Disputed Legacy, 1846-1990*, Oxford University Press, 1991

_______. 'Tibet in Anglo-Chinese Relations: 1767-1842', *The Journal of the Royal Asiatic Society of Great Britain and Ireland*, Cambridge University Press, 1957

Lawrence, Sir Walter Roper. *The Valley of Kashmir*, Henry Frowde, Oxford University Press, 1895

Lohia, Rammanohar, *Guilty Men of India's Partition*, Kitabstan, 1960

MacDonald, Myra. *Heights of Madness: One Woman's Journey in Pursuit of a Secret War*, Rupa and Company, 2007

Mahajan, Mehr Chand. *Looking Back: The Autobiography of Mehr Chand Mahajan, Former Chief Justice of India*, Asia Publishing House, 1963

Mansergh, Nicholas and Penderel Moon (ed). *Constitutional Relations Between Britain and India: The Transfer of Power, 1942-47*, vol 10, Her Majesty's Stationery Office, 1981

Moon, Penderel. *Divide and Quit*, University of California Press, 1962

Mountbatten, Earl Louis. *Time Only to Look Forward: Speeches as Viceroy of India and Governor-General of the Dominion of India, 1947-48*, Nicholas Kaye, 1949

Neve, Arthur. *Picturesque Kashmir*, Sands & Company, 1900

Noorani. A.G. *Article 370: A Constitutional History of Jammu and Kashmir*, Oxford University Press India, 2011

Palit, Major-General D.K. *Jammu and Kashmir Arms: History of the J&K Rifles*, Palit & Dutt Publishers, 1972

Parvez, Dewan. *Jammu-Kashmir-Ladakh: Jammu*, Manas Publications, 2004

Phukraj, Malka. *Song Sung True: A Memoir*, Kali for Women, 2003

Prasad, D.N. and Dharam Pal. *Operations in Jammu and Kashmir (1947-48)*, Ministry of Defence, Government of India, 1987

Puri, Balraj. *Tracts For The Times: Kashmir Towards Insurgency*, Orient Longman, 1993

Roberts, Andrew. *Eminent Churchillians*, Simon & Schuster, 1995

Sarila, Narendra Singh. *The Shadow of the Great Game: The Untold Story of India's Partition*, HarperCollins Publishers India with India Today Group, 2005

Sen, L.P. *Slender was the Thread: Kashmir Confrontation, 1947-48*, Orient Longman, 1969

Singh, Bawa Satinder. *The Jammu Fox: A Biography of Maharaja Gulab Singh of Kashmir, 1792-1857*, Southern Illinois University Press, 1974

Singh, Ghansara. *Gilgit Before 1947*, n.p., 1983

Singh, Karan. *Autobiography*, Oxford University Press India, 1994

———. *Jammu and Kashmir 1949-64: Select Correspondence Between Jawaharlal Nehru and Karan Singh*, ed. Jawaid Alam, Penguin/ Viking, 2006

Singh, K. Brahma. *History of Jammu and Kashmir Rifles, 1820-1956: The State Force Background*, Lancer International, 1990

Singh, Lieutenant Colonel Bhagwan. *Political Conspiracies of Kashmir*, Light & Life Publishers, 1973

Sökefeld, Martin. 'From Colonialism to Postcolonial Colonialism: Changing Modes of Domination in the Northern Areas of Pakistan', *The Journal of Asian Studies*, vol 64, no 4, 2005, pp. 939-973 (boris.unibe.ch/115111/1/S0021911805002287.pdf, last accessed 17 March 2023)

Snedden, Christopher. *Kashmir: The Unwritten History*, HarperCollins Publishers India, 2013

———. *Understanding Kashmir and Kashmiris*, C. Hurst & Co. (Publishers) Ltd, 2015

Subramaniam, Arjun. *India's Wars: A Military History 1947-1971*, HarperCollins Publishers India, 2016

The Round Table Conference: India's Demand for Dominion Status. Speeches by the King, the Premier, the British Party Leaders and the Representatives of the Princes and People of India, G.A. Natesan and Company, 1931

Tunzelmann, Alex von. *Indian Summer: The Secret History of the End of an Empire*, Simon & Schuster, 2007

Wavell, Archibald Percival. *Wavell: The Viceroy's Journal*, Oxford University Press, 1973

Whitehead, Andrew. *The Lives of Freda: The Political, Spiritual and Personal Journeys of Freda Bedi*, Speaking Tiger Books, 2019

Wolpert, Stanley, *A New History of India*, Oxford University Press, 1982

———. *India and Pakistan: Continued Conflict or Cooperation?*, University of California Press, 2010

Wreford, R.G. *Census of India, 1941: Volume XXII: Jammu and Kashmir: Parts I & II, Essays and Tables*, Office of the Commissioner of Census, 1943

Zeigler, Philip. *Mountbatten: The Official Biography*, Knopf, 1985

Index

C

G

H

I